*The Collector's Encyclopedia of*

# Hatpins and Hatpin Holders

by
**Lillian Baker**

**COLLECTOR BOOKS**
*A Division of Schroeder Publishing Co., Inc.*

Additional copies of this book may be ordered from:

COLLECTOR BOOKS
P.O. Box 3009
Paducah, Kentucky 42001

or

Lillian Baker
15237 Chanera Avenue
Alondra Park, Gardena, Ca. 90249
@ $ 19.95 postpaid

Dealers and clubs should write for quantity discounts.

Copyright:  Lillian Baker, Bill Schroeder, 1976
ISBN: 0-89145-016-5

*This book or any part thereof may not be reproduced without the written consent of the author and publisher.*

*Printed by Taylor Publishing Company, Dallas, Texas*

# DEDICATION

For my Husband
Loving Family
Faithful Friends
and
For the *FAITH* that makes all things possible.

# PREFACE
## by
### Dr. Fairfax Proudfit Walkup, B.A., M.A., Ph.D.
### ( Former Dean of the Pasadena Playhouse)

Why write a book on hatpins? Why laboriously scale a mountain of probabilities for the pin-peak of information? Because, like the mountain, it is there. The evidence is there, waiting to be withdrawn from the obscurity of the out-moded into the high light of contemporary appreciation.

Only a woman could have utilized an *object de toilette* as a defensive weapon, as the Victorian lady employed her hatpin. Only a woman could enjoy transfixing butterflies on a sharp pin to anchor her hat from the wings of the wind, as the Edwardian damsels did. Only a woman, such as Lillian Baker, could patiently have gathered these slim slivers of metal, tipped with magic, into a sheaf of compelling interest, into this book that reveals one more aspect of the romantic and artistic urge of our seemingly staid ancestors.

Lillian Baker, after years of careful study, of dedicated collecting and exchanging of notes with other collectors far and near, has finally arrayed and assayed, for our enjoyment, a record of the hatpin of the Victorian, Edwardian, and *Art Nouveau* periods. Her rich informative source material is illustrated with delightful examples of the various types. An amazing and varied array of gold, silver, inlay, mosaic, crystal, porcelain, and other media, cunningly wrought into cherubs, birds, petite figurines, and other designs, tip the ends of these long and slender accessories which once held hats — themselves of variously frivolous trends — upon the towered tresses of our grandmothers and great-grandmothers.

Not only is this the only book, I believe, on this intriguing subject, but also it presents, in scholarly form, the original, world-wide research of one who has carried on a long and varied affair with that slim, attractively-headed subject, HATPINS.

As one of the authorities on costume, I regret that Mrs. Baker's material was not available to me when I was working on my costume book, for she has added a wealth of definitive, documented information on this charming accessory. Certainly no library on costume can be complete without her book.

> Fairfax Proudfit Walkup, author
> "Dressing the Part" and "Modern Theatre
> Practice," both Appleton-Century-Crofts
> and
> State of Utah Centennial Source Book,
> (Division of Costume)

Fullerton, California
1975

*Footnote to the reader: Dr. F. P. Walkup was honored at a reception Nov. 5, 1972, by Patrons of the Library, California State University, Fullerton, for her gift of a large collection of books, manuscripts, dolls and costumes principally relating to the theatre. Subsequently, three rooms in the University library building were named for Dr. Walkup and contain the rich addition of materials for students, writers, and researchers.*

*Dr. Walkup, although technically retired and now residing in Fullerton after a forty-year residency in Pasadena, still lectures on the topic, "Modes and Manners."*

*Despite her eighty-odd years, she is still as full of the same enthusiasm which she possessed and instilled in others during her many years with the venerable, much-beloved Pasadena institution which gained international recognition as the "Pasadena Playhouse."*

*An honorary Phi Beta since 1965, Dr. Walkup's biography appears in AMERICAN WOMEN: DICTIONARY OF INTERNATIONAL BIOGRAPHY; WHO'S WHO IN THE WEST; CALIFORNIA BLUE BOOK, etc.*

*This venerable teacher has taught the subject of costume, manners and customs, and the history of theatre at several universities including, U. of Arizona, U. of Utah, Stanford, U.C.L.A., and U. of Iowa.*

*Dr. Walkup is considered by many as the authority for costume in the theatre.*

*The use of Dr. Walkup's private library at her residence in Pasadena, California, was the springboard from which most of the research for this book began and received impetus. I owe this warm and gracious person much and it's not only my duty but my welcome privilege to acknowledge same. In addition, I am grateful for the Preface to my book which Dr. Walkup willingly contributed in such kind fashion.*

L.B.

# TABLE OF CONTENTS

PREFACE . . . . . Dr. Fairfax Proudfit Walkup, former Dean, *Pasadena Playhouse* . . . . . . . . . . . . . . . . . . . . . . . . Page iv

*SECTION ONE*

Chapter I . . . . . . INTRODUCTION TO THE COMPREHENSIVE STUDY OF . . . . . . . . . . . . . . . . . . . . . . . . Page 1
               HATPINS and related items. (Part 1.)

               THE HANDMADE PIN AND THE INVENTION OF THE . . . . . . . . . . . . . . . . . . . . . . . . Page 5
               PIN-MAKING MACHINE — Its effect upon Hatpins. (Part 2.)

Chapter II . . . . . HATS, HAIR STYLES, and HATPINS . . . . . . . . . . . . . . . . . . . . . . . . . . . . . . . . . . . . . . . . . . Page 9

Chapter III . . . . . HATPINS AS WEAPONS and other points of interest . . . . . . . . . . . . . . . . . . . . . . . . . Page 27
               to the collector. (Including an addendum)

Chapter IV . . . . . THE PERIOD HATPIN. (Including an addendum) . . . . . . . . . . . . . . . . . . . . . . . . . . . . . Page 54

Chapter V . . . . . HOW TO RECOGNIZE AND AVOID FAKE HATPINS . . . . . . . . . . . . . . . . . . . . . . . . Page 95

Chapter VI . . . . . HATPIN HOLDERS, including Look-Alikes and Reproductions . . . . . . . . . . . . . . . . . . Page 101
               Dresser Sets, Toilet Sets, Pincushions, and other related articles
               to the Hatpin.

Chapter VII . . . . MEMOIRS OF A COLLECTOR . . . . . . . . . . . . . . . . . . . . . . . . . . . . . . . . . . . . . . . . . . . . . . Page 144

Chapter VIII . . . . CONCLUSION: WITH REMARKS TO COLLECTORS OF HATPINS . . . . . . . . . . . . . . . . Page 155

*SECTION II*

   GLOSSARY . . . . . . . . . . . . . . . . . . . . . . . . . . . . . . . . . . . . . . . . . . . . . . . . . . . . . . . . . . . . . . . . Page 159

   SUPPLEMENT . . . . . . . . . . . . . . . . . . . . . . . . . . . . . . . . . . . . . . . . . . . . . . . . . . . . . . . . . . . . . . Page 165

       *Gems, Gemstones and Natural Elements* Popular During the Hatpin Era
       Hatpin Heads of *Man-Made* Materials
       Popular Designs and Motifs Used for Hatpin Heads (1850-1920)
       Exhibitions and Expositions where Hatpins and Hatpin Holders were Exhibited or Sold as Commemorative
         Souvenirs

   CROSS-INDEX BY SUBJECT FOR PLATES . . . . . . . . . . . . . . . . . . . . . . . . . . . . . . . . . . . . . Page 168

   BIBLIOGRAPHY . . . . . . . . . . . . . . . . . . . . . . . . . . . . . . . . . . . . . . . . . . . . . . . . . . . . . . . . . . . . Page 177

   SOURCES AND ACKNOWLEDGEMENTS . . . . . . . . . . . . . . . . . . . . . . . . . . . . . . . . . . . . . . Page 180

   REFERENCE NOTES AND APPENDIX . . . . . . . . . . . . . . . . . . . . . . . . . . . . . . . . . . . . . . . . . Page 184

   TEXT FOR PLATES . . . . . . . . . . . . . . . . . . . . . . . . . . . . . . . . . . . . . . . . . . . . . . . . . . . . . . . . . . Page 186

   NUMERICAL INDEX FOR PLATES WITH PAGE NUMBERS . . . . . . . . . . . . . . . . . . . . . . . Page 214
     (Credit and/or Source)

*The Collectors Encyclopedia of*

# Hatpins and Hatpin Holders

**Plate 145:** Courtesy Milly Orcutt Archives

# INTRODUCTION TO THE COMPREHENSIVE STUDY OF HATPINS AND RELATED ITEMS.

There's a need to record for future generations, in word and picture, the art and implements of the past. Why the Victorian, Edwardian, and *Art Nouveau* hatpins have been overlooked, I can scarcely imagine. Perhaps it is because the period of the hatpin in its greatest glory lasted for so short a time, and the pin — from the early thorn to later thrusts — has been taken all too much for granted.

In any event, the subject is badly documented; strange, since the first principle of the best art should be both usefulness and ornamental and what other item can better qualify than the hatpin! The fact is, however, that until the recent 15th edition of *Britannica*, the subject had even been neglected by that encyclopedia. Not a single reference to hatpins! The pinpointing of that respected work is not meant as criticism but rather as the ultimate example of the common neglect of a decorative, functional, and historic item. I can only trust that the brief article which will appear in the new edition of this celebrated publishing event, will include enough factual reporting to overcome speculation and rumor regarding hatpins as weapons as well as informing the reader on the influence on costume design which was regulated by the functional hatpin.

The writer has been informed by the editorial department of the *Encyclopaedia Britannica* that "hatpin" will be spelled as one word. This will be helpful as it should then separate "hat pin" (two words) in describing an actual pin which was worn by men as badges or pins in their illustrious headgear. Women's jewelry, in the form of hatpins, is correctly one word and I, for one, am very glad it will appear as such so that once and for all the distinction will be made for those researching articles, etc.

In addition to encyclopaedic neglect, fashion plates of the period woefully disregarded the hatpin by whose virtue the precarious balance of the lady's chapeau was maintained. With hundreds of books published for both connoisseur and novice on the subject of antiques and collectibles, there are but fragmentary reports and little if any manufacturing information, history, or pictorial reference pertaining to the unique hatpin of the 1850-1920 period.

There are many clubs whose antique buffs represent collectors of hatpins and associated Victoriana; however, the periodicals published contain only scattered bits of orientation material incorporated in various magazines. To date very little illuminating data regarding the hatpin has been published. The fascinating history and legal ramifications involved in this unique accessory have been hinted at but never fully detailed. I emphasize this lack of vital information as justification for this publication. I also suggest that because of its common usage, the hatpin has simply been disregarded or overlooked. I liken this to some instructions I read just the other day in a "do-it-yourself" guide.

In this manual, the reader is instructed to "place two pieces of redwood lumber together and hammer." Now, because of the "common usage" of the household nail, it's assumed the reader knows what to hammer! Thus, when other writers describe the sumptuous hats of a bygone era, they erroneously assume that the reader knows how the hat is secured to the hair and head!

When this quaint "instrument" was exhibited by the writer at various showplaces, it was met with curiosity and amazement. Most people had a preconceived notion that a hatpin resembled a corsage pin and thought them likely to be worn interchangeably.*

For those whose faint recollections glimmered with the memory of the Victorian era, the use of long, fancy hatpins on the fantastic hats of the "Gay Nineties" were but fragments of nostalgia lying dormant until pricked by the sight of my exhibit.

For the child growing up in our 20th Century, there's hardly a reference; only a touch or two of description in texts wherein hatpins are merely referred to usually as long with fancy knobs at the ends.

Too much of the past has been lost to our heritage simply because there were few historians who lent importance to the simple items in common usage; yet how they rejoice upon discovery of these everyday "tools" in excavations, and how they bemoan the non-existence of manuals.

In my documentation, I've tried to provide the handbook to hatpins. However, to be an inclusive story, I had to include some history of the ordinary — yet extraordinary — pin, the ancestor to the "period" hatpin which performed as the most functional and decorative in the pin family, and which certainly showed it at its greatest length!

But to be all inclusive regarding the pin would necessitate volume after volume. Instead, I've tried to present a significant picture of the subject, never attempting to be more than informative and entertaining. If it's at all scholarly, it's the result of factual reporting through intensive research, valuable interview, and willing assistance.

My line-by-line material was gathered from many varied sources; the more I delved into the subject the more I realized that the hatpin was not only worthy of documentation because of its interesting and fascinating history, but also because it would prove invaluable to the many other hatpin collectors throughout the world.

---

* *Kate Millet in "MS" Magazine, Sept. 1972, writes about Angela Davis: "One almost sees the mark of the hatpin in her lapel where they pinned the corsage."*
*Here's the perfect example of the preconceived notion that a corsage pin and a hatpin are one and the same thing.*

There's a fascinating and absorbing history about the hatpin involving much myth and legend; since much of it involves the "rise and fall" of the feminine hat and headdress, I've covered a bit of this subject, too. Primarily, however, this book deals with the hatpins of the Victorian, Edwardian, and *Art Nouveau* periods, and in my thesis I avoid the use of the word "antique" — substituting for it *period hatpin*. This is because the hatpins of that era do not fall within the definition of an antique as stated in the United States Tariff Act of 1930:

> *"Antiques are works of art — (except rugs and carpets made after the year 1700), collections in illustration of the progress of the arts, works in bronze, marble, terra cotta, parian, pottery or porcelain, artistic antiquities and objects of ornamental character or educational value which shall have been produced prior to the year 1830."*

PERIOD HATPINS shall refer primarily to hatpins whose ornaments set astride the MANUFACTURED-BY-MACHINE shank (or pin) which is dated from the invention of a successful pin-making machine in 1832. This will immediately separate those hatpins referred to by costume authorities as being utilized in the 18th and early 19th centuries. Pins at that time were expensive and had not yet earned the reputation or notoriety of its later ancestors which were soon to be mass-produced. (Pins from antiquity have had a history all their own; but that's another story!)

Refer to Plate No. 63 for a photograph of an actual pair of brass wire handmade hatpins (circa 1825) which makes them genuinely antique. They are thin wire, easily bent, and extremely sharp at the point. Plate No. 135 shows the process required in making these pins, fully described in Part 2 of this Chapter.

But the hatpins mainly represented in this book follow that period of antiquity (1830) by little more than a decade; therefore they can only be considered for now as "collectibles." Yet, just as our modern costume jewelry bears little resemblance to the antique *parure* or *Art Nouveau* baubles (except in reproduction), so the common hatpin in use today bears little or no resemblance to the "period" hatpin.

However, to keep within the letter of the law, and for the sake of clarity in differentiating between the hatpins of the 1850-1920 era and the *aigrettes* and numerous hat ornaments and hair pins of earlier dates, I shall refer to my hatpins as "period" and not "antique."

Since only by photographs and advertisements could I faithfully record that era in illustrating my text, in addition to using my own large and unique collection of hatpins, hatpin holders and related accessories, I've been fortunate in procuring either pictures or drawings from other collections of equal importance and oftentimes of greater monetary value. Most of the drawings used in this book for illustration purposes were accomplished by my friend and talented artist, Joyce Fairchild.

I'm hopeful a book such as mine will do much to fill a void and will be a valuable aid to collectors and all those interested in period costume, jewelry, and memorabilia. My research introduced me, through hundreds of letters, to many great collectors, experts, and curators in their own fields of endeavor; each encouraged me with great enthusiasm and added some

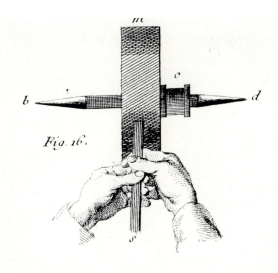

*Fig. 16.*

*The picture above shows a method of holding wire against the grinding stone and rotating it to achieve an even point.*

**Plate 135**

(From "The Pindustry"; courtesy of THE STAR PIN COMPANY, Shelton, Conn.

useful information or helpful reference.

However, in the end, the results of research are inconsistent. Some items in this book have detailed accounts; others appear to be treated more trivially or upon hearsay on the subject. If the latter be true, it was joined by logic or deduction and thus the subject was appraised by the author in her best manner possible.

This writer never maintains nor claims to be an assayist of metals nor an appraiser of jewels; rather let me say I am an essayist, writing words from printed words in old journals and from more recently published works.

This writer is a collector — an advanced hobbyist — who is anxious to share the crumbs of data and specks of illuminations on the subject of HATPINS, much of which has been gained from worldwide correspondence, personal interview, and inquisitive research in public and private libraries.

Combining all this allows me to expose, unmask, clarify, and perhaps separate rumor from fact or fancy, and even familiarize the reader with newsy, informative, enlightening, and hopefully the most correct account of a truly fascinating period in fashion history whose era might well join with Margaret Mitchell's Civil War period as "gone with the wind."

It's been my experience that antique book buyers do not limit themselves to any one subject, nor do historians. For the historian "purist," here's an interesting note: the assortment of pins used for fastening or ornamentation or both, includes the common straight pin, pushpin, T-pin, safety pin, brooch, bobby pin, cotter pin, stickpin, veil pin, corsage pin . . . and finally, a hatpin. Nothing has been done with the common shaft of wire since the "invention" or advent of the hatpin of the 1890-1920 period. The pin had then reached the "end of the wire," so to speak, at its greatest length . . . and glory!

Because, as I say, antique buffs and historians do not confine their search to one corner of the book-shelf, my book should prove of interest to many besides hatpin collectors. But for the collector of hatpins, I hope this volume will serve as an entreaty to continue; for the collector of antiques and memorabilia it may serve to open new horizons. It is certainly meant to serve the costumer and to augment the many reference books depicting fashions of a bygone era.

I am beholden to so many who have helped me in this project which has taken well over a decade to complete . . . but even now, forthcoming information has necessitated some addenda and footnotes to this manuscript. I realize that even when the final work is at the bindery, I'm bound to receive vital information I'll wish was included!

Because my thanks should not and cannot be brief, I have devoted that portion of my "introduction" to a separate section under the heading: "SOURCES AND ACKNOWLEDGEMENTS."

Lillian Baker

Alondra Park,
Gardena, California
1975

**Plate 147:** Fashionable Promenade from "Leslie's Weekly", April 1897. F. P. Walkup Archives; Photo by George Castro.

# THE HANDMADE PIN AND THE INVENTION OF THE PIN-MAKING MACHINE — ITS EFFECT UPON HATPINS

Although the 1885 *Encyclopaedia Britannica* was published during the popularity of the period hatpin, there's no reference to this fashionable accessory in the splendid summation on the PIN.

Scribner's *Ninth Edition* is from Dr. F. P. Walkup's personal library and contains information pertinent to pin manufacture:

"*A pin is a small spike, usually of metal, with a bulbed head or some other arrangement for preventing the spike passing entirely through the cloth or other material it is used for fastening together. In one form or another pins are of the highest antiquity, and it may be assumed that their use is connected with human dress of any kind, the earliest form doubtless being a natural thorn, such as is still often seen fastening the dresses of peasant women in upper Egypt. Pins of bronze, and bronze brooches and pins on which considerable artistic ingenuity was lavished were universally used among the civilized nations of antiquity.*

"*The ordinary domestic pin had become in the 15th century an article of sufficient importance in England to warrant legislative notice, as in 1483 the importation of pins was prohibited by statute. In 1540 Queen Catherine received pins from France, and again in 1543 an Act was passed providing that 'no person shall put to sale any pinnes but only such as shall be double headed, and have the heads soldered fast to the shank of the pinnes, well smoothed, the shank well shapen, the points well round, filed, canted, and sharpened.' At that time pins of good quality were made of brass; but a large proportion of those against which the legislative enactment was directed were made of iron wire blanched and passed as brass pins. To a large extent the supply of pins in England was received from France till about 1626, in which year the manufacture was introduced into Gloucestershire by John Tilsby. His business flourished so well that he soon gave employment to 1500 persons, and Stroud pins attained a high reputation.*

"*In 1636 the pinmakers of London formed a corporation, and the manufacture was subsequently established at Bristol and Birmingham, the latter town ultimately becoming the principal center of the industry. So early as 1775 the attention of the enterprising colonists in Carolina was drawn to the manufacture by the offer of prizes for the first native-made pins and needles. At a later date several pin-making machines were invented in the United States. During the war of 1812, when the price of pins rose enor-*

*mously the manufacture was actually started, but the industry was not fairly successful till about the year 1836. Previous to this an American, Mr. Lemuel W. Wright of Massachusetts, had in 1824 secured in England a patent for a pin-making machine, which established the industry on its present basis.*

*The old form of pin, which has become obsolete only within the memory of middle-aged persons, consisted of a shank with a separate head of wire twisted round and secured to it. The formation and attachment of this head were the principal points to which inventive ingenuity was directed. The old method of heading involved numerous operations, which had to be expeditiously accomplished, and, notwithstanding the expertness of the workers, the result was frequently unsatisfactory. Fine wire for heads was first wound on a lathe round a spit the exact circumference of the pin shanks to be headed. In this way a long elastic spiral was produced which had next to be cut into heads, each consisting of two complete turns of the spiral. These heads were softened by annealing and made into a heap for the heading boy, whose duty was to thrust a number of shanks into the heap and let as many as might be fit themselves with heads. Such shanks as came out thus headed were passed to the header, who with a falling block and die arrangement compressed together shank and head of such a number as his die-block was fitted for. All the other operations of straightening the wire, cutting, pointing, etc., were separately performed, and these numerous details connected with the production of a common pin were seized on by Adam Smith as one of the most remarkable illustrations of the advantages of the division of labour.*

"*The beautiful automatic machinery by which pins are now made of single pieces of wire is an invention of the present century. In 1817 a communication was made at the Patent Office by Seth Hunt, describing a machine for making pins with 'head, shaft, and point in one entire piece'. By this machine a suitable length of wire was cut off and held in a die till a globular head was formed at one end by compression, and the other end was pointed by the revolution around it of a roughened steel wheel. This machine does not appear to have come into use; in 1824 Wright patented the pin-making apparatus above referred to as the parent form of the machinery now employed. An extension for five years, from 1838, of Wright's patent, with certain additions and improvements, was secured by Henry*

*Shuttleworth and Daniel Foote Tayler, and in the hands of Tayler's firm in Birmingham the development of the machine has principally taken place. In a pin-making machine as now used, wire of suitable gauge running off a reel in drawn in and straightened by passing between straightening pins or studs set in a table.*

*"When a pin length has entered it is caught by lateral jaws, beyond which enough of the end projects to form a pin-head. Against this end a steel punch advances and compresses the metal by a die arrangement into the form of a head. The pin length is immediately cut off and the headed piece drops into a slit sufficiently wide to pass the wire through but retain the head. The pins are consequently suspended by the head while their projecting points are held against a revolving file-cut steel roller, along the face of which they are carried by gravitation till they fall out at the extremity well-pointed pins. The pins are next purified by boiling in weak beer; and so cleaned, they are arranged in a copper pan in layers alternating with layers of grained tin. The contents of the pan are covered with water over which a quantity of argol (bitartrate of potash) is sprinkled, and after boiling for several hours the brass pins are coated with a thin deposit of tin, which gives them their silvery appearance. They are then washed in clean water and dried by revolving in a barrel, mixed with dry bran or fine sawdust, from which they are winnowed finished pins.*

*"A large proportion of the pins sold are stuck into paper by an automatic machine no less ingenious than the pin-making machine itself. Mourning pins are made of iron wire, finished by immersing in black japan and drying in a stove. A considerable variety of pins, including the ingeniously coiled, bent, and twisted nursery safety pin, ladies' hair pins, etc., are also made by automatic machinery. The sizes of ordinary pins range from the 3½″ stout blanket pin down to the finest slender gilt pins used by entomologists, 4500 of which weigh about an ounce. A few years ago it was estimated that in the United Kingdom there were made daily 50,000,000 pins, of which 37,000,000 were produced in Birmingham, and the weight of brass and iron wire then annually consumed was stated at 1275 tons, of which one-eighth part was iron wire. The annual value of the whole British trade was stated at 222,000 pounds. United States was estimated to be from 350 to 500 tons per annum, the value of the trade being 112,000 pounds."\*\**

(*Note to reader:* When the author of the above *Britannica* article refers to manufacturing, particularly up to 1832, he refers to the handmade industry of pin manufacture.)

Elizabeth Barrett Browning put it poetically in *"Aurora Leigh, Book VIII"*:

*". . . Let us be content, in work,*
*To do the thing we can, and not presume*
*To fret because it's little. 'Twill employ*
*Seven men, they say, to make a perfect pin:*
*Who makes the head, content to miss the point;*
*Who makes the point, agreed to leave the join;*
*And if a man should cry, 'I want a pin,*
*And I must make it straightway, head and point,'*
*His wisdom is not worth the pin he wants.*
*Seven men to a pin — and not a man too much!"*

The excellent encyclopaedic writer in the 1885 thesis on the pin, also refers to legislative action taken regarding this all-important "point." What might he have written were he to document the "laws and wars" against the period hatpin of my thesis? (But then my history and handbook as set forth would have been pre-empted by such documentation!)

As it is, no subsequent *Britannica* nor other relied-upon reference work has outlined the hatpin which had become the subject of court action, legislative measures, the brunt of many a joke, the instrument of dramatic incident in books and theatre, and — finally — among other things, a common household word which when used covered a multitude of meanings.

This glaring oversight on the part of the modern chronicler or scribe in reference books of world import, now seems to be compounded in the 1975, *15th Edition of Britannica.* Although the word "hatpin" finally makes its premier, the sheer simplicity and briefness of its inclusion simply "scratches the surface" of its deserved definition.

> (*Vol. IV, 15th Edition, 1975 Encyclopaedia Britannica*) **"hatpin**, a long, ornamental pin used for fastening a woman's hat to her hair. In the late Victorian era and the beginning of the 20th century, the hatpin became a popular and important accessory. They were usually about 8 inches (20 centimetres) long and often worn in pairs. They frequently had ornamented heads."

The 1975 edition devotes exactly seven lines to this item so rich in historical and legal ramifications — no less "modes and manners!" I have had to edit down to better than 50,000 words on the subject which I doubt has more than scratched the surface regarding actual legal cases, anecdotes and folklore, notwithstanding the commercial aspects of the hatpin industry itself which eventually evolved and expanded to encompass other products and production clear into our space age! The most important by-product for collectors of hatpins was the hatpin holder, of course. This enlarged milady's dressing table assemblage of vanity "somethings" which still puzzles today.

Hopefully, this history and handbook of hatpins will provide the absent reference book on the subject, and perhaps some future historian will add his findings and point out my own omissions.

Of course the story of hatpins is full of contradictions. There's no sharp cut-off date, either at the beginning of the fad or fashion, nor at fashion's fading. As with all attempts at pinpointing a specific "point in time" in fashions and accessories, there is always the definite and gradual overlapping. The eventual renaissance, repetition or resurrection of fashion and faddism comes back as sure as the sun rises and sets; so the rage or craze of the prevailing taste of yesteryear or long bygone days is bound to be marked once again on a future calendar year.

Perhaps the one great exception is the period hatpin of the late Victorian, Edwardian, and early *Art Nouveau* epoch!

In undertaking the gigantic job of researching and compiling information on the hatpin and its accessories, I specifically aimed for the following goal: that my book be all things on the subject of hatpins for the benefit of costumers, historians, antique buffs, and especially that it serve as a suitable guide for hatpin collectors. It should supply the missing reference work, complete in one volume.

Other books on antiques and collectibles usually provide manufacturing, pricing, and technical information mainly because the subject matter has little else to offer as dramatic and historically fascinating as the functional and decorative hatpin.

Although the quotes used in my manuscript may seem ludicrous in today's light, they were of a serious and factual nature during the time of the unique history of the hatpin.

I can recall no other collector's piece that has initiated laws, caused international furor, been a tool of authors and playwrights, nor has been so misused in literature, dress, and weaponry. All this is part of the hatpin story; but the ingredients causing the rise and fall in fashion plates is also part of the legend.

All collectors hunger for every tidbit of information they can get on their subject regardless of the nature of the report. This volume should satisfy or at least placate the long-time famine of hatpin hunters.

\* \* \*

The pin, itself, in many of its forms, is gradually becoming obsolete, made so by the arrival of zippers, elastic, inexpensive buttons, hook fastening, snaps, and miracle adhesives. But it's interesting to note that the original straight-pin for which the term "pin money" was derived, is still as effective as ever and just as useful in the garment industry.

The author of an article which appeared in one of the numerous "collector's" magazines, wrongly stated that the origin of the term *pin money* came from "the early use of hat pins." The author continues to compound his error: "When first introduced, jeweled hatpins were costlier than the average housewife could afford. So these eager ladies saved their spare pennies and in so doing coined a new phrase, 'pin money'."

Although no doubt there were women who did put away a few coins for such trifles, it's more likely that the appropriate phrase would have been "butter and egg money." This term was common during the period of the hatpin.

The term *pin money* actually reverts back centuries ago to the handmade, expensive pins, the cost of which represented a considerable expense until the advent of the pin-making machine in 1832.

During the War of 1812, the importation of pins was so expensive they began to be manufactured in America, but this industry was not truly successful until about 1836. Prior to this, pins had to be cut from a length of wire, then sharpened and headed, one by one, by hand. The cost was from fourpence to sevenpence EACH, which made them so expensive it was not uncommon for pins to be presented as gifts to the ladies on birthdays or other occasions of note. When no pins were available, it was perfectly proper to give "pin money" which was put aside for the time they were available.

In the 13th and 14th centuries, a tax was actually levied on the common people to pay for the queen's pins. When pins became a commodity for all to use, women of all classes saved their "pin money" to buy the necessary article on the first and second days of January — the two days set apart by Parliamentary decree which permitted pin-makers only that 48 hours in which to sell their coveted wares. This took place in the late 14th century.

The extravagantly executed hatpins of the Victorian, Edwardian, and *Art Nouveau* periods are a far cry from the original pin consisting of "a shank of wire with wire round one end, forming a head."

There's an interesting summary regarding "pin money" in the publication, *The Pindustry*, the history of The Star Pin Company, Shelton, Connecticut, founded Sept. 25th, 1866. The brochure was published in 1966, in celebration of its Centennial:

> *"It was during the late 1820's that Dr. John Ireland Howe developed a machine for making and heading pins, which proved both practical and efficient. It was patented in the United States in 1832 and in England and France in the two years following.*
>
> *". . . it took a team of ten men all day to make 12 pounds — about 48,000 — of pins. This was considered a great advance over the 20 pins that a skilled pinner could make by hand, working alone, as indeed it was.*
>
> *". . . There are many versions of the origin of the term PIN MONEY. Probably the most authentic is that it was the amount which a husband allowed his wife for spending money. Another possible explanation is that it referred to the custom of giving a lady a gift of money for the purchase of pins.*
>
> *"As late as the early 19th century in England, PIN MONEY sometimes had an entirely different meaning. It was the name for certain gifts, (no doubt the forerunner of our trading stamps), which were used to enhance or clinch a bargain. This gift was supposed to be given to provide pins for the wife or children of the person with whom the bargain was made."*

Whatever the origin of PIN MONEY, it's obvious that the term was in use long before the coming of the HATPIN. In fact, of all the pins in the "pin family," the hatpin has been the least coveted and the one most taken for granted. It was also the very last innovation of the pin whose family tree now appears to be rootbound.

To the collector of hatpins, PIN MONEY is merely an abbreviation for hatpin expenditures!

these hats worn by women until the late 16th century except for traveling, and these flat caps were only a kind of foundation for billows of veiling.

Nineteenth century hats were primarily designed to attract male attention, therefore they were considered not only poor manners "in polite society" but improper wear on Sundays or in church. This was the socially accepted rule as late as 1875.

In *Godey's Ladies' Book*, (Feb. 1853), there's a bit of gossip and information concerning headdress which addresses itself to the topic covered in this chapter:

*"We have seen that Jenny Lind could introduce a new fashion of wearing the hair, and a new form of hat or bonnet. The eccentricities of fashion are so great that they would appear incredible if we had not ocular evidence of their prevelance (sic) in the portraits which still exist. At one period we read of horned headdresses, which were so large and high that it is said the doors of the Palace of Vincennes were obliged to be altered to admit Isabel of Bavaria (Queen of Charles VI of France) and the ladies of her suite.*

*"In the reign of Edward IV, the ladies' caps were three quarters of an ell\* in height, and were covered by pieces of lawn hanging down to the ground, or stretched over a frame till they resembled the wings of a butterfly. At another time, the ladies' heads were covered with gold nets like those worn at the present day. Then, again, the hair stiffened with powder and pomatum, and surmounted by flowers, feathers, and ribbons, was raised on the top of the head like a tower. Such headdresses were emphatically called 'tetes.'*

*"It was not until the reign of Elizabeth (1558-1603) that we begin to perceive the elaborate head-gears which a century later became so ridiculous in their size and height. We find this queen delighting in marvelous structures of curls, frizz, gems, and gold; in some portraits her hair appears to be folded over a cushion — we say 'her hair', but history strangely belies her if the false portion did not far exceed that supplied by Nature; and indeed, if she had not several entire wigs.*

*"So much hair was worn about that period that the price of false hair became very high; indeed, it was scarcely possible to obtain the requisite quantity by any fair means, and it is said that poor women were bribed with large gifts to part with their tresses, children were enticed into lonely places and robbed of theirs, and even the dead in their graves were despoiled.*

*"In the 18th Century the hair suffered to grow very long and either curled and allowed to float over the neck in multitude of wavey ringlets interspersed with ribbons and jewelry, or built up into edifices of curls and frizz, and surmounted with feathers, or gauze or flowers, or ribbons.*

*"Some fifty years later the absurd fashion of put-*

*ting a cushion on the head and combing the hair smoothly over it came in; some of these cushions were of a ridiculous height. Various stiff and unnatural-looking curls also came in vogue, as the French, or sausage-shaped curl, and the German or roll-shaped curl, which had to be well frizzed underneath, to give it amplitude and roundness."*

Regarding the use of "rats" and "coils," Emily Post remarked in a letter to her father: *"It was the first time I had ever seen her face without its hideous roll bolster overhang and bun-like coil of hair pinned where her forehead ought to be."*

Author Pearl Binder, referring to the use of artificial hair and padding, put it down rather pat: *". . . even those with abundant natural locks were obliged to resort to hair-pads to puff out what they had. And the insertion of the long, spiked hatpins, used to skewer the immense hats to the pagoda of hair, resembled a dangerous surgical operation."*

And from *The Ladies Friend*, (Sept. 1872): *". . . when the hair is insufficient in quantity, there is added, here and there, a puff or two, a few floating curls, a bow of ribbon, one or two pins of precious stones, metal, or simply shell, or when the dress permits the ornament, two or three flexible stems with a few flowers . . ."*

References to Jenny Lind were numerous in fashion's heyday of the 1850's. Jenny was born in Sweden in 1820 and in her twentieth year she was proclaimed "Court Singer." When she toured America, she was dubbed by 19th century "PR men" as "The Swedish Nightingale," and from all international reports it was a well deserved plaudit. Commemorative items dedicated to preserving the memory of this legendary songstress included the hatpin. (See Plate No. 160.)

It's almost ironic that not even a decade was allowed to pass since the *Godey's* 1853 article, when women once more accepted the fashion of enormous hairdos aided by the introduction of a padded contraption known as a "rat." A 7-pack of "rats" were known to be worn at one time. And of course we well know that today the "well frizzed" method is called "teasing" or "back-combing" the hair. And wigs are in, and in plentiful use! However, there's no longer the need to resort to devious methods of obtaining hair; modern technology has helped fashionable women with the introduction of synthetics that challenge not only the beauty but the manageability of real silky, shining, locks. Wigs have become so inexpensive, they are no more the province of royalty nor the elite; women go to the hairdresser as commonly as to market.

We must remember that in the 1890s the hats that challenged the "three quarters ell" in size were plopped on top of a seemingly ridiculous height of hair, but that was the fashion of the time. And the hatpin became the mainstay of every woman's coiffure and chapeau. These hats were so burdened with buckles, beads, flowers, and even "fully-stuffed birds and ostrich plumes," that three to six hatpins were required to balance them. Without these hatpins, the millinery creation could miscarry and capsize the complex and intricate coiffures of the era.

These enormous hats were a far cry from the middle-of-the-century and from the 17th century head-covering when the

\*Equal to 45 inches of measure on the old British scale.

term "bonnet" was first applied to feminine headgear. Called *"chapeau-bonnette,"* it was simply an enlarged cap to which tiny silk flowers and fancy lace-edge lappets had been affixed.

The fantastic hats of the period required more than veiling or "brides" to secure it firmly to the head. ("Brides" was the name given to a broad ribbon-string attached inside the brim of an open bonnet or the broad-brimmed hat.) But nothing secured as well as the functionary hatpin(s). One may well ponder the question as to whether the invention of the pin-making machine revolutionized the hair and headdress indus-try as well, for without these pins to skewer the hat on safely and attractively, the bonnet and not the hat might have pre-vailed. But it was not enough that the hatpin be functional; it must add beauty to the overall picture, just as jewelry set off a gown or a stickpin enhanced the cravat.

It's interesting to note that all headgear was tied with strings, thongs, or ribbons, and not until 1794 was the word "bonnet" designated specifically as "a woman's hat tied under the chin."

As for the "traveling hat," the first was of straw, called a *tholia*, which tied under the chin with ribbons. A special man-tle worn to shield the head from the sun was called the *palla*. Those worn as protection against the elements or to signify sta-tion in life, or modesty, were of varied designs. Greek and Roman women wore wimples or veils, mantles and hoods. These were not considered "hats" but part of women's habit. Most prevalent were ornaments for the hair which varied from crown to simple garlands or wreaths of myrtle, symposia, lau-rel or olive, each worn in favor of a favorite god.

Art Nouveau design incorporated many of the leaf motifs so highly apparent in its two-dimensional decorations, and may be seen in the hatpins of that period. (Plates 34 and 108) Several cameos in the color plates show the influence of Roman and Greek design, even to the favored wreaths worn in the hair. (Plates 4 and 94)

Greek and Roman coiffures included strings of pearls or beads entwined in the hair; sometimes these were threaded on a hairpin, the forerunner of our period hatpin. Many of the ancient jewels were worn as talismans, just as they were to be worn centuries later and up to the present time.

During the Dark Ages, women did not wear either hats or bonnets but wore their hair long. Unmarried girls had to wear theirs loose and flowing, without ornamentation, as a sign of virginity. Married women were allowed to braid their locks and adorn them conservatively with tiny ribbons or garlands. The young maidens often covered their flowing hair with a veil or mantle while the married women sometimes buried theirs completely under a cloth best described as a turban.

The Middle Ages introduced the snood, a band of silk or velvet ribbon that was tied around the head similar to the head-bands worn by the American Indian and by our genera-tion of "hippies." (From 1900-1942, off and on, nets made of chenille or protruding pile were worn to carry the heavy coil of hair at the back of the neck. These were incorrectly called "snoods" in fashionable circles.)

The 12th and 13th centuries showed the more elaborate veil with crown or chaplet so familiar to us in the costuming of Juliet, one of the pair of star-crossed lovers in Shakespeare's immortal play. This role was made famous in the 1939 movie adaptation starring Norma Shearer, who then popularized the "Juliet Cap" which has since been adopted for use in bridal salons. The elaborate veils used with the caps in the olden days, were often secured by delicate hand-made, wire-thin, brass or gold veil pins.

During the 14th century, the fantastic crespin and caul were added along with the wimple and gorget, the type of head-covering usually associated with an order of nuns, such as The Sisters of Notre Dame. In that religious Order, the crimped or pleated crespin was worn sewn on a French hood. Women of the court wore a caul, which was nothing more than a cagelike cylinder of fine wire mesh used to encase long braids or rolls of hair; it received its name from the inner fetal membrane which covers the head of newborn babies.

Also familiar to these times was the wimple, a long piece of white linen or silk draped over the front of the neck and swathed round the chin, the ends being pinned to the hair above the ears. Juliet's nurse in *"Romeo and Juliet"* is cos-tumed in such headgear; it can also be recognized as the head-dress of nuns and of the Virgin in early paintings. All this elaboration of headgear was the beginning of an era for wom-en's fashions, and when the wimple and hood were discarded, the refinement called "hats" came into their own as a comple-ment to the coiffure.

Turbans were still in use, but it was not until the 15th cen-tury that exaggerated headdresses were introduced with the addition of hennins from six inches to three feet high. The report in *Godey's Ladies' Book* elaborated on this subject.

By the 16th century, the hair was drawn off the forehead in pompadour fashion and dressed over a wire frame. The bod-kin, known in the 16th, 17th, and 18th centuries, was intro-duced as a long pin used for dressing ladies' hair and might well have been the barb which is the forerunner of the long, ornamental hairpin of the 19th and 20th centuries and the ear-liest ancestor of the period hatpin.

The bodkin was made of steel, bone, or ivory, with a sharp point which was not only used for hair-dressing, but for mak-ing holes and eyelets in cloth.

It was during the 16th century, too, that the introduction of caps of cloth and velvet appeared, decorated with one or more feathers. Although these were considered men's wear, some women of "carriage" wore a modified version as a velvet bon-net or beaver hat. "French Hoods" which were nothing more than a throw-back to the wimple, and a wired cowl called "Mary Queen of Scots cap" drifted in and out of fashions, but most favored were veils and scarves and small "Juliet caps" which were worn under hoods and hats.

It was during the reign of Louis XIV, (1643-1715), that the greatest development of headdress and hair ornaments began. The flamboyant Marie Antoinette introduced luxuriant hair-styles — hair rolled over puffs and pads of horsehair, brushed high in fantastic coiffures over wire frames — and "orna-ments, ornaments, ornaments!"

One might well call the advent of the 18th century the cen-tury of "woman's emancipation," for women were in rule ever-ywhere. There was Queen Anne in England, Empress Cather-ine in Russia, and Bohemia's monarch, Maria Theresa of Aust-ria, whose daughter, Marie Antoinette, became the power behind the throne of Louis XVI (whom she married at the age of 15).

Emancipation was everywhere with the establishment of the

free press in 1735, the Declaration of Independence in 1776, and the first President of a free country, George Washington, who saw the first American patriots through their "revolution against tyranny."

With these revolutionary ideals came the great ideas for change in women's fashion — a complete turnabout in which women's vogue began to challenge men's fashionable dress. The vogue introduced the enormous hats of silk, lace, velvet, beaver, felt, horsehair and straw — the latter materials previously reserved for the male of the species.

By 1850, Leghorn hats made of the finest Tuscan straw from Italy were considered proper traveling headgear. The hats were wide, with drooping brims called "flats," and were worn as a protection against the sun. Many of these "flats" were of a less expensive straw from Switzerland and Belgium. For the common trade there was a cheaper substitute imported from China called "English sewn straw." By 1860, this competitive product gained that Asian nation a monopoly on the straw market, for Occidental workers could not compete with the terribly cheap labor of the Orientals. Both expensive and imitative straws were not secured by ribbon ties, but with the long hatpins especially bought for the purpose of anchoring the large-brimmed hats to the head.

The ornamentation of both the large brim and crown ran the gamut from the daring to the devilish in the use of combined fabrics and embellishment. Taffeta, organdy, and silk might be used with feathers or kidskin, laden heavily with beads of steel, bronze and jet.*

Although the "revolution" in hats came slowly but surely, (if in erratic fashion), women's headgear was the most important fashionable accessory from the late 17th century until World War II.

Before World War I, the hat or bonnet was a matter of unrestrained excesses; even the ordinary bonnet ties remained a surplus when they were no longer functional. Instead of discarding the useless strings, they, too, were garnished with pleated lace, tiny garlands of flowers, puckered satin ribbons, bits of savage fur, and even straw.

With the death of Queen Victoria in 1901, came a completely new and unrestrained era of women's dress, modes and manners. The Edwardian period (Edward VII, 1901-1910) witnessed a relaxation of Victorian conservatism, and introduced probably the most opulent and elegant era save that of the French Court. During this decade of Edward's brief reign, women's role in society changed drastically, egged on by such writers as George Bernard Shaw and Arnold Bennett who wrote so sympathetically about women.

But lest it be said that women of the Victorian era were completely stifled or unaware of social needs and change, Charlotte Bronte was busy at work with Dickens and Disraeli, pleading for change. And it was in 1859, during Victoria's reign, that the daring Charles Darwin's "Origin of Species" was published. Probably no one but a Queen Victoria could have allowed such freedom of criticism of the *status quo*. In her 64-year reign, this mighty monarch actually gave free rein to her subjects on every level. While foreign courts kept their "class status," England witnessed and was first to approve the advancement and industrialization so beneficial to the masses.

Whereas before only the elite had subservient help; there were now established *couturiers* or dressmakers, *modistes* or milliners, and jewelers for a more "common" trade.

During the Victorian Days there were goldsmiths and silversmiths along with locksmiths and laundresses. And there was no end to the variety of fabrication in English factories, made expressly to order for the department stores which were springing up in San Francisco, Chicago, or New York. These were the ports for English goods.

New Orleans had a fine carriage trade with direct imports from France, including work of the finest artisans and jewelers. It's here, in New Orleans, that many of the valuable hatpins and ornaments are found, some of fantastic designs copied from baroque antique jewelry and heirloom pieces belonging to royalty.

It was Queen Victoria who favored the *frisette*, (Plate 144, Fig. f) which remained popular from 1850-1900. It was a tightly curled affair of either fringe or curls worn under a cap or as a help for thin forelocks. Mohair pads were also used to puff out the hair at the sides, and false hair was worn in all shapes and in incredible quantities. Puffs, switches, braids, curls, hairnets and chignons were fastened with a comb or kept secure by ornamental hairpins.* And all of this weight under the weight of an elegant chapeau affixed with hatpins!

In *Arthurs' Magazine*, (Feb. 1866), we read a testimonial to the times of "abundant hair" and other fashion "offenses":

> "Whether more false jewelry or more false hair is worn at the present day would be a curious question to solve.
>
> "A new gold cord for the hair has been introduced in Paris, and has already been adopted by the Empress. It is about as thick as a moderate sized finger, and is so pliable that it is arranged in loops, which alternate with the small false curls now so fashionable around the top of the forehead, and which are continued along each side to the top of the chignon. This arrangement of head-dress is represented to be very becoming to oval-formed heads.
>
> "Fancy earrings are likewise worn, some represent dog's heads, others a horse or a whip and I have seen even an owl crowned with a wreath of laurel. I would advise all those who have a taste of such eccentric ornaments to purchase imitation ones, for the fashion once passed away, to what use can they be turned?"

The question of false jewelry and false hair *today* can easily and quite frankly be solved without a blush, for both items are in plentiful use in endless variety, a fact easily proven by scouting any major shopping area. As for "eccentric ornaments," many of these have been preserved in hatpin collections. (See Plates 81, 113, and 123.)

With such emphasis on the nostalgia of yesteryear, (real or imagined), the "fashion once passed away" is being copied and imitated in an almost frenzied effort to recapture lost values, or to revive and preserve what seems to some the dwindling American heritage.

To seek change, to discard the old, is nothing new. Those

*Plates 140 and 142

*Plate 139

12

**PARIS SPRING WRAPS** *(4.4.1896, p. 305).* **Fig. a:** a smart little cape is of taffeta silk made with an empièce-ment of embroidered tulle, and finished with a ruffle of mousseline de soie. The collar is faced with a frill of white lace and has white lace tabs. A hat to wear with this cape is of fine straw trimmed with five ostrich plumes and bunches of yellow primroses. **Fig. b:** another fashionable cape is of stiff silk covered completely with embroidered tulle and trimmed with soft rosettes and a ruffle of mousse-line de soie. The hat is indescribably light and dainty; it is of straw, but covered over with tulle, in which are placed ostrich tips and bunches of roses.

*a*

*b*

**Fig. c:** a wrap equally suitable for a young or middleaged woman has a perfect-fitting empiècement of black net heavily embroidered in jet. From the empiècement starts a very full flounce of mousseline de soie edged with rows of narrow satin ribbon. The entire wrap is lined with stiff taffeta silk. The high collar is trimmed on the outside with bunches of mousseline de soie and inside with a white lace frill. The hat shown with this wrap is of fancy straw, with bows of black and white lace, through which show glimpses of bright flowers. **Fig. d:** a cloth jacket fitted tight is quite distinctive with its revers faced with velvet and the sleeves buttoned to the elbow. The hat is in sailor shape, trimmed with accordion-pleated changeable taffeta. At the back are bunches of violets and roses with an aigrette formed of violets.

*c*

*d*

**Plate 142**

**Plate 144**

**COIFFURES** *(10.8.1881, p.653).*

**Fig. f:** frisette.
**Fig. g:** looped braid.
**Fig. h:** braid with curls.
**Fig. i:** braid with curls.
**Fig. j:** chignon with comb.
**Fig. k:** coiled chignon.

who turned away from Victoriana in seeking "new" values and found it in the *Art Nouveau* movement, considered Victorian jewelry "eccentric." These ornaments of precious stones and metals, "the fashion once passed away," were melted down and the stones reset. (Thus we have the scarcity of these heirloom pieces for collectors and in museums.) We can always be thankful that among the "revolutionaries" — or at least alongside — there were sentimental persons unwilling to change original concepts in jewelry, and we are able to see some of the most fabulous examples of the jewelers' trade thanks to them. This was essentially true of hair ornaments and hatpins, for there are still many exquisite creations remaining in solid gold set with rubies, diamonds, and emeralds. (Plate 206.) I have seen examples of these in an antique shop on Royal Street in New Orleans.

An appraiser of fine art reported to me that at a recent auction in Switzerland, a small heirloom collection of hatpins brought a starting bid of $10,000! Unfortunately, the stones were what interested the bidder and not the relics of a bygone era. "The fashion once passed . . ."

But who originates fashions? We know the fashion center of the hatpin period was Paris, the "city of taste." *"To create a new style,"* wrote a fashion expert of the late nineties, *"is of as great import to the Parisian dressmaker as the building of an empire, and as much thought is given to it as to the adjustment of some international question."*

Can one imagine a crisis in fashion today competing, let us say, with the "international oil crisis?" Yet, had it not been for World War I, the "hatpin crisis" of 1913-14 might truly have caused a "cold war" epidemic both here and on the Continent!

We are aware that to keep a style too long in vogue is bad for business. It does not make "the wheels go round." Change is necessary from the dollar-and-cents point of view. Yet change is never "new", regardless of today's popular coinage of that phrase. After all, there's little that's purely original; instead, it's merely fashion history repeating itself either from the pages of *La Mode* publications or from the galleries of historic paintings from which so many designers seek fresh inspiration for stale styles that have gone to trunk or attic.

We know that painters have had much to do with the popularity of a mode. Rubens loved to depict women in the small picturesque velvet toques, while the famed English artist, Gainsborough, preferred the large wide-brimmed hats with their flourish of plumes, ribbons, and bows.

The inimitable Sarah Bernhardt, Lillian Russell, and Lily Langtry, (who, incidently, introduced the curling iron and peroxide), had a great effect upon fashion. What was seen in front of the footlights was soon adopted by fashionable society and then eagerly copied by small town dressmakers and milliners. With Russell and Langtry known rivals — both being "peroxide blondes" — the competition between them as style-setters must have been keen but exasperating to fashion's followers. Which one to follow? No doubt loyalties provided the answer: Langtry was English; Russell was American. But an all-around adoption on stage and in fashion circles was the "Merry

Illustration: Victorian Fashions and costumes from HARPER'S BAZAAR, 1867-1898. Editor, Stella Blum. Use by permission of Dover Publications, Inc.

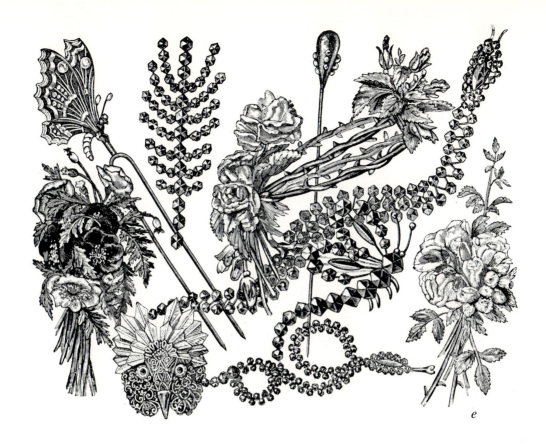

**HAT ORNAMENTS** *(5.9.1891, p. 360).*
**Fig. e.**

**TORTOISE-SHELL COMB AND HAIR-PINS**
*(5.14.1887, p. 353).* **Figs. f and g.**

**Plate 139**

Widow" hat — a real cartwheel confection for the head which was introduced in 1903. It required incredibly long hatpins to hold the hat securely to the head.

The "Merry Widow" was so large that the same theatre personalities who heralded its wear were to rue the day it was first introduced on the stage! How many admirers bought tickets to see their sultry sirens only to view the back of the stylish headgear? High, wide, and handsome, these hats were gala with ornamentation of which the bejeweled hatpins were not the least in elegance.

The suffering male finally succeeded in pushing through a theatre ruling which compelled a woman to remove her extravagant headgear during a performance. Such a ruling in polite society was not an easy accomplishment!

For the man dining at Maxim's, what were his thoughts as he sat opposite his female partner adorned in a hat whose crown and brim boasted argus breasts, quills, plumes, entire birds, insects and other fetishes! Even the protruding hatpins suggested flying or crawling "bees in her bonnet." *Bon appetité!* (See Plate No. 7.)

"Diamond" Jim Brady's lavish gifts of jewelry to Lillian Russell and her public display of same, popularized the slogan, "those who has 'em, wears 'em" . . . and those who did not have the genuine, sought out paste imitations. But her fondness for diamonds was a revival of fashion a quarter century earlier, as shown by an ad in *The Lady's Magazine*, July 1866. Diamond dealer and jeweler Lewis Ladomus of Philadelphia, wanted readers to know:

*"ON HAND A LARGE AND SPLENDID ASSORTMENT OF DIAMOND JEWELRY OF ALL KINDS — Such as Rings, Pins, Studs, Diamond Sets, etc. My assortment of Jewelry is COMPLETE IN ALL RESPECTS, EMBRACING ARTICLES OF THE HIGHEST COST, AND ALSO ARTICLES OF COMPARATIVELY SMALL VALUE."*

Since hatpins had been on the fashion scene for over a decade, the "Pins" referred to in Mr. Ladomus' ad surely included hatpins of "the highest cost" as well as hatpins of "comparatively small value."

In examining catalogues, magazines, and brochures, I have found that hatpins of precious stones and metals were priced out of reach for all but the affluent society. There were, however, imitations selling for as little as 29¢. There was also a "middle price" for good French paste articles, a substance used and accepted as a substitute rather than as an imitation of the real stone.

A letter from Mrs. Vera Maternova, curator for The Museum of Glass and Jewelry, Jablonec, Czechoslovakia, was helpful in describing several hatpins in my collection which was similar to some on exhibit at the Museum. (See Plates 25, 26, 27.)

*"The pins are made from so called coal or burel-glass. Its production name is **hyalith** and is the invention of glassmakers in South Bohemia in the glass-works of Count Buquoy in the beginning of the 19th century, (1825). The ornament on these pins represents the period after the Second Rococo and the shapes like pears or globules with engrav-*

ings were made about 1880 and later and belong to the period known as 'Black Jewelry'."

It's entirely possible that *burel-glass* was first used as hairpin ornaments; the glass is extremely fragile and would have to have been worn where the risk of breakage was least likely to occur . . . on the head!

In an attempt to gather further manufacturing and historical information regarding American importers of Bohemian hatpins, Mrs. Maternova informed me that *"after the compulsory emigration of Germans in 1945 who took (up to this date) the whole jewelry trade in their hands, we are without these historical documents. So we have no catalogue of hatpins (as they are too specialized a department of costume jewelry) and then the continuation with the old production was destroyed."*

Several American companies wrote that their records too were destroyed, while several had no archives whatsoever.

One interesting letter is from Otto C. Hanisch, President, Geo. H. Fuller & Son Co., manufacturers of jewelers findings:

*"Dear Mrs. Baker:*

*Answering your letter of January 8 on the subject of hatpins, we never made the complete item, we sold the pins only and the small ornament which held the pin onto the ball ornament. The small ornament was a tubular item about ¼" long which the manufacturing jewelers soldered onto the fancy ball or a similar item and in that way they completed the hatpin.*

*These hatpins were made in length from six inches to nine inches, the popular size was 7½". They were also made up into novelties so that an ordinary brooch pin could be used as a hat pin ornament. In that way a lady could wear her brooch either on her dress or if she wished on a hat pin.*

*We are enclosing herewith two samples so that you will get the idea; perhaps you have never seen the one used as a novelty as a combination hat pin or brooch pin, so that should be of interest to you.*

*Hat pins were out of style along about 1920 — but they were a big item along about 1900.*

*We hope that we have been of some assistance to you."*

Needless to say I was most happy to receive the two samples, particularly the novelty hat/brooch pin which was an entirely new type and style pin for my collection. It is illustrated within the pages of this book. (See Plate 161.)

I would like to point out that although the above letter does mention the use of solder in the manufacture of hatpins, this adhesive is not visible on authentic hatpins because it was used between the special "jewelers finding" and the mounting of the hatpin. This would be similar to the use of "french seams" in sewing in that the rough seam-edges became invisible in the process.

Also, there is a vast difference in the *mass* produced hatpin and the hatpin conceived by custom jewelers. These jewelers copied the masterful designs of the ancient artists who worked in precious stones and metals, duplicating their feats in both precious materials and gilded base-metals. And the mountings were constructed as part of the overall creative work, not as an after-thought.

Another letter which was most helpful with regard to source

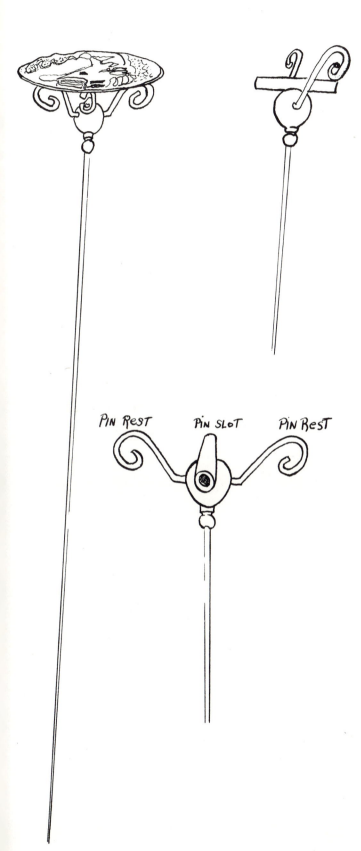

PIN REST     PIN SLOT     PIN REST

material, is that from Dorothy K. Allen, President, F. H. Noble & Company:

> ". . . Although my grandfather started the business on Jewelry Findings in 1876, the advent of Costume Jewelry and Japanese imports forced us to discontinue this particular division.
>
> However, I have located some old catalogs of past years and Xeroxed the pages on hatpins and dated them as near as possible.
>
> I hope this is of some help to you, as I am most sympathetic with your problem, having background and association with design and its history myself."

The pages that were enclosed appear illustrated in this book and are certainly most helpful in completing a study and history of hatpins.

Returning to the resumé of hats, hair, and hatpins, we read in *Arthur's Magazine*, (Dec. 1866):

> "We have no bonnets now-a-days,* and the apologies for the same are continually growing beautifully less. The last innovation is a square piece of straw, silk, or lace tied over the top of the head, relieved with a bit of trimming, bugles, lace or velvet around the edge, and a flower or two in front. This is like a saucer upon the head, and is sort of a compromise between a bonnet and a hat. It will be curious to see what steps will be next taken in this matter.
>
> Coiffures are worn much higher than usual, and plaits, which are rapidly advancing in favor, are arranged very high at the back of the head, and take the place of the chignon. Straw nets for the hair and nets with artificial mohair curls covering the back are fashionable."

* Katharine Hepburn's line in "Love Among the Ruins": ". . . Nobody under seventy wears a bonnet . . ." (Year: 1911)

**Plate 161**

Most neglected in this report are the necessary hairpins and hatpins needed to secure both coif and hat! The inevitable "steps" aforementioned, were that bonnets were almost discontinued entirely and those that lasted were almost as large as hats.

Toward 1880, bonnets and hats grew larger and larger, some with upturned brims sewn back with festoons of feathers or flowers. (Plate 134.) The headgear was often placed back on the head, making the hatpin an absolute necessity!

A few years later, with the advent of cycling and sporting events, the familiar sailor hat came into use. It had the usual low crown and wide brim and was held straight on the head by a pair of hatpins. (See Plate 141.)

By 1900 the hair was piled high on the head in a pompadour which, as the first decade of the new century ended, had been puffed out in a continuous circle around the head, almost like a wreath. To keep the hair in place, a padded roll was worn underneath with additional rolls wherever fullness was required. (See Plate 143). With this type of hairstyling, hats were designed much larger with wide brims tilted forward or sideways. In either fashion, the sumptuous hat was pinned on — back or front and sometimes both — with very long hatpins.

The aforementioned "Merry Widow Hat" — so called after the Franz Lehár musical of that name — measured fifteen to twenty inches in diameter with the crown often measuring ten inches across. These "monsters" required extremely long hatpins thrust through the crown from either side. Most of these hatpins had fanciful ornaments which were intended to make them decorative as well as functional.

The "Merry Widow" chapeaux* were befeathered concoctions which were worn high on the pompadour hair-style. Because of the craze for this hat, ostrich plumes of the variety known as "willows" which drooped over the brim, were so much in demand that actual ostrich-farms became a profitable enterprise in Pasadena, California.

An ad in *Woman's Home Companion*, (May 1906), offers feathers, boas, plumes, tips and fans from the . . . "Original Home of the Ostrich in America," established 1886 in South Pasadena. Also offered were Bird of Paradise plumes and ornaments of cut steel and jet. Most hats, including "The Merry Widow," were decorated with additional ornaments of rhinestones and gold, but cut steel and jet were most desired.

The ornate hatpins worn with these hats provided additional targets for the comics and cartoons because of their great length. The hat with its feathered counterparts also provided food for serious thought to conservationists.

*"Some twenty to thirty million dead birds are imported to this country annually to supply the demands of murderous millinery . . .",* (Cunnington); thus was formed the National Audubon Society whose chief aim was to prevent the wholesale slaughter of native birds and the importation of such exotic specimens as the osprey, egret, paradise, ostrich, and other exquisitely feathered birds which continued, (despite protests from "the American colonies"), to be the rage in Paris.

Because of the Society's efforts, American women seemed content, if not sympathetic to the cause, to use substitute goose and chicken feathers, "beautifully dyed and fashioned

*(Plates 149, 151, 152, and 153)*

into wings and cockades". These glycerined quills were gathered and sewn as a decoration resembling a feather duster which was fastened in place with a fancy buckle or pin.

One can truly say that *1850-1950* were the 100 years of hats and hatpins. In the last of the 1960's and again in 1972, small hatpins began to re-appear on women's hats. Whether this was due to publicity which urged women to wear "hatpins as weapons," is only speculation. Having visited some millinery salons in several department stores, I can only report that the design of hats were such as *not* to require hatpins for the security of the hat on the head. Today's millinery and hairstyles preclude the necessity of long hatpins, and any short hatpins must be considered purely decorative or "defensive." A recent advertising brochure, seeking to profit on the current nostalgia binge, offered the following:

> *"hat tickler" (peacock feather hatpin with rhinestones)*
> *and an "Aunt Hattie's Hat Pin" (pear-shaped pretend pearl hatpin with rhinestone base. We found it in the attic.)*

But back in 1850 and right on up through 1910, the millinery trade was booming with all kinds of chapeaux requiring "spearing and settling": pillboxes, leghorn hats with streamers down the back, the scotch bonnet, riding hats, sailor hats, caps of all description, all these in a true free-for-all frenzy in millinery magnificence! (Plates 154 and 155)

A popular way of wearing the above chapeaux was perched on top of the psyche knot which was brought from the back of the neck (where it was worn in ancient times), to the top of the head; and to keep the hat from spinning off, a pair or more of decorative hatpins were put to good use. The bun or psyche knot, itself, was often held secure by a comb made of ivory, tortoise shell, amber, or celluloid. The hatpin's function was not to secure the hair but to transfix the hat and all the underpinnings of pads so as to remain "motionless on the head." No small feat!

Extremely large hats reached their prime from 1907 until 1928. American Heritage Publishing Co.'s 1975 edition, *"Hometown U.S.A.,"* is a study of what life was like seventy-five years ago. In the book is a reproduction of a glass-plate photo taken in 1907 by Solomon D. Butcher, on carnival day in Kearney, Nebraska.

The advertising blurb for the book describes the picture: "Everybody wore a hat in Kearney . . ." Surely this is one of the finest photographic and historic records of the sumptuous hats of the period. It shows the use of the period hatpin as the instruments they were, with literally inches of steel protruding from crown and brim. Fashion plates, to the contrary, rarely show the required hatpins. (Exceptions are seen on Plates 134

Plate 141 (Opposite)

SPORTING COSTUMES (5.30.1896, p. 464).
Fig. a: gown with bolero jacket.
Fig. b: tailor costume for driving.
Fig. c: gymnasium suit.
Fig. d: shirt-waist and tweed skirt.
Fig. e: outing gown.
Fig. f: bathing suit.
Fig. g: mountain costume.

**Where are the Hatpins?**

a

b

c

d

e

f

g

Plate 141

19

**Plate 143**

and 140 Fig. C.)

The smaller hat received emphasis during the war years (1914-1919), and finally reached full acclaim even to the present day. And with the smaller hat came the smaller hatpin, sometimes worn merely by force of habit rather than necessity. Later on, hatpins became nothing more than frivolous ornaments that were trivial and sometimes comic in design. (Plate 113.)

The 1907 hat, as shown on "carnival day" and in fashion plates, had grown to such improbable dimensions — with brims spanning the shoulders — there was no other fashion alternative but that the hat must shrink in size. And so, the umbrella-sized chapeau began to close — very slowly at first — until by the second decade of the 20th century, it hugged the head like the helmet just recently discarded by fighting men.

Aesthetically speaking, there is much to be applauded in the big hat which was immortalized in English portraiture. It was most becoming to ladies because it framed the hair and face and could be brimmed in such manner as to flatter the individual wearer. The large brim could be pinned to the crown or left to "droop" naturally; or it could be enhanced with flowers or the ever-flattering veiling. Decorations and ornaments were pinned on and could thus be arranged to suit

**Plate 152**
Photographs *opposite* from "Hello, Dolly", Courtesy of 20th Century-Fox.

**Plate 151**

**Plate 149**

**Plate 153**

21

Plate 140

**Plate 154**

**Plate 155**

**Plate 140** (Opposite)

**DEMI-SAISON GOWNS FROM PARIS**
*(8.20.1898, cover).* **Fig. a:** checked tan gown. Every thorough summer outfit contains one or two thin woollen gowns that are worn early in the spring, on cool days in summer and then reappear in the autumn. A particularly smart one from Félix is of wood-color with a small check in the front and in the back, and is effectively trimmed with a yoke of fancy silk on which are lines of gold embroidery. Around the yoke and on the side of the waist that crosses over is a band of black velvet embroidered to match the yoke. Around the wrists are bands of velvet embroidery, and just below the yoke in front the embroidery is put on to give the effect of a bow. Worn with this gown is a hat from

Virot, of yellow straw, and trimmed with ostrich plumes and a large rosette of black mousseline de soie. The brim has a narrow fold of black velvet inside, and is turned up at the left, showing a rosette of yellow mousseline de soie. **Fig. b:** blue serge gown. One of the newest models for a blue serge gown comes from Félix. In effect it looks somewhat like a redingote, but in reality is made with waist and skirt. The skirt, quite different from anything that has been introduced, is fastened at the side, and is elaborately trimmed with bands of black braid of different size, the lowest braid outlined with a fancy gold and red velvet on a bias band of white silk. The waist, fastened at one side, has

a most effective yoke of the fancy white silk embroidered in gold thread both in the front and back of the waist, and with a straight band collar with pointed pieces of the same silk. The sleeves are of medium size, with a puff at the top partly covered with a pointed epaulette, and are trimmed from shoulder to wrist with graduated bands of black braid; at the wrist is a line of the fancy gold braid. The hat worn with this gown is one of Virot's designs, and is of dark blue straw trimmed with black feathers and a large rosette of black mousseline de soie, with several deep red roses inside the brim at the left side. **Fig. c:** checked gown, back. **Fig. d:** blue serge gown, back.

The Ladies' Home Journal (1910)

## The New Velvet Hat "The Shirley"

*With Pond Lilies for Daytime Wear*

*Gardenias for Church or Dress Occasions*

Especially Designed for The Ladies' Home Journal by N. F. Morrill

### Drawings by Jessie Barrick

THIS is a modification, and in a sense a new shape, of the beautiful black velvet picture hat, which is one of the most becoming hats ever designed for the American girl. It combines also the advantage of being in good style at all times.

On this page ten variations of trimming are shown. In each case only one ornament or flower is used, demonstrating the beauty of simplicity not only in a single hat but also in ten variations of one hat.

*One Large Plume for Special Occasions*

*A Red Velvet Poppy for the Matinée*

**Plate 134**

the mood and mode of the day. Need I stress at this point the importance of pins? And hatpins not the least of these!

The entrance of the exciting automobile as a new mode of travel caused the eventual exit of the big hat. Because the first cars were open touring vehicles, women began to substitute hats for yards and yards of veiling to keep wind and dust from their hair. It was not uncommon for a chiffon veil, two or three yards in length, to be worn tied under the chin. It was such a veil which tragically took the life of Isadora Duncan when the gossamer material blew, then tangled, in the spokes of the rear wheel of a classic car.

Ironically, after centuries devoted to discarding under-the-chin ties, came many styles of "automobile bonnets" designed especially for riding in open cars.* These vehicles, especially the open roadsters, changed fashions in millinery. Crowns of hats necessarily fitted the head, secured by hatpins, though

much smaller in pin-size. Eventually came the *cloche*, plain in design with little or no ornamentation except for a simple bauble at the end of a pin. Often these pins were old "stock" hairpins or hatpins used as purely decorative items, or as mentioned previously — out of habit.

By 1923 hats took on a definite mushroom shape and with short hair the rage, came the introduction of the bobbypin (1922) — a handy "cotter pin" for the hair which often replaced the hatpin in later years.

During World War II, with women taking over men's jobs in defense factories, the hat became a sometime thing. The uncovered female head became accepted even outside the factory, in social gatherings and on city streets. After the war there was a revival of interest — mostly stirred by stylists such as Christian Dior — of a half-hat, half-hairdo that was a modern version of the velvet cap which young men of the Renaissance wore over one ear. Once more hatpins were employed as functional accessories, but these small hatpins were unobtrusive and lacked the artistic design of their predecessors.

* *The automobile bonnet (c. 1908) has a long chiffon veil attached to protect the face and neck of the wearer when riding in an open motorcar of the period." (Clarence T. Hubbard) See Plate 183.*

With a Bow to Match the Suit

A Tailored Bow With a Buckle for General Use

Almost a Sailor With a Silk Scarf

**Plate 134**

It is the rare fashion plate that shows the much-needed hatpin, without which the "New Velvet Hat — The Shirley" could hardly nestle safely nor securely on the hair and head. Courtesy Woman's News Editor: Milly Orcutt, ANTIQUE MOTOR NEWS. Plate 134 appeared in the October, 1974, article, "After a Fashion", by Milly Orcutt.

To date, hats vary in shape and overall size, and fashion no longer dictates time nor place. But along with the feathers, flowers, ribbons, velvets, tulle, jewels, buckles, felts and straws, is worn the occasional handy hatpin. But oh how far these hatpins are removed from the period pins of the Victorian, Edwardian, and *Art Nouveau* eras to which this book is primarily devoted.

The hatpin is still making the news, if only in the obituary column! The following is from *The Shenandoah Herald-Ashland News*, Ashland, Pennsylvania, (Jan. 22, 1969):

*"DEATH CLAIMS LOCAL DOCTOR*
*. . . Dr. Spencer was trained in the operation of the bronchoscope and for years was the only physician to undertake bronchoscopy in this section of the state. Among his mementoes is a collection of objects which he removed from patients' lungs by inserting the bronchoscope after he had X-rayed the lungs and located the objects.*

*One of the most startling of these operations was his removal, from the lung of a child, a hatpin four inches long with a large black knob which the child had swallowed."*

I believe a welcome conclusion to this chapter would be a few important remarks from the pen of Lawrence Langner on the *Importance of Wearing Clothes:*

*"It may be interesting to note that all of the thousands of different hats and head coverings invented throughout the ancient and modern worlds are variations of seven basic shapes, which are (1) the flat hat, like the mandarin's, held onto the head by cords attached under the chin or back of the head (2) the bonnet, a variation of the above, with the brim flattened against the ears (3) the crown or bell which is held on the head by encompassing the cranium (4) the crown with a rim of many sizes and functions (5) the turban consisting of layers of fabric wound on the head (6) the beret or cap (7) and finally the cloth or scarf tied around the head.*

*And of course not forgetting the little feminine hat which breaks all the rules including the law of gravity, and stays on the head by animal magnetism, or by the piercing of the hair with vicious-looking hatpins which on occasion can serve as concealed weapons."*

\* \* \*

**Plate 162**

# CHAPTER III

# HATPINS AS WEAPONS AND OTHER POINTS OF INTEREST TO THE COLLECTOR — Including an Addendum

*". . . Men are notoriously old fashioned. It takes them ages to rid themselves of preconceived ideas. They associate hatpins and hairpins with the female sex, and call them 'women's weapons.' They may have been in the past, but they're both rather out of date now. Why, I haven't had a hatpin or hairpin for the last four years."*

**Dame Agatha Christie's PARTNERS IN CRIME, (1929)**

\* \* \*

The most immediate and frequent reply to my question about the hatpin as a weapon is, "Well, I don't remember ever sticking any one with one!"

Yet in a letter from the respected authority on costume, Doris Langley Moore of the *Museum of Costume*, Bath, England, came this illuminating bit of information:

*"I am old enough to remember, faintly, that a law was passed prohibiting the use of hatpins without a guard on the end as they had caused serious accidents, and my mother told me that the women of the slums in her day would attack each other with hatpins when physically fighting, (a common sight at that time)."*

The mystery of the hatpin as a weapon persists as recently as August 28, 1970, when a letter appeared in "Answer Line," printed as a service to *Los Angeles Herald-Examiner* newspaper readers:

*Question:*

*What is a hatpin? I am serious. In a national magazine and in your paper, law enforcement officials advise the use of hatpins for women to use as protection from attackers. I have been to several stores and asked for them and the clerks look at me like I am crazy. Will you please describe one?*

*Answer:*

*Hatpins are no longer used for their original purpose which was to hold ladies' hats on their heads. Originally designed to transfix a knob of hair on top of the head and secure a hat, the hatpin has been obsolete for that purpose for well over 40 years. The pin is approximately six to seven inches long and usually has an ornamental knob on one end and a very sharp point on the other. You might possibly obtain one from a shop which deals in antique jewelry.*

Antique dealers have told me there has, indeed, been a sudden burst of business for hatpins — coinciding with the above publicity — however, when potential customers see the *period* hatpin for the first time, they generally gasp and exclaim, "Where in heaven's name would I ever hide one?" (Plate 164.)

*The Wall Street Journal* (1969) carried an item about the scarcity of hatpins because the demand for them had increased due to women buying them for protection. It's hoped that the purchaser was cautioned about concealed weapons, for although our Constitution allows all persons to "bear arms" for self-protection, the weapons cannot be concealed on one's person.

Thus, a woman can wear a hatpin on the *outside* of her coat or on the *outside* brim of her hat, but it cannot be concealed in the coat's lining or under the hat-band. She may not carry the hatpin concealed inside her purse, but she may wear it pinned on the outside as an "ornament."

Even as a person may lawfully own a registered firearm but may not carry it concealed on his person, so a hatpin may be owned but worn *only if it can be seen*. Both guns and hatpins, under the law, are subject to the same codes. A small revolver cannot be hidden inside a pocket, garter, or covered by outer clothing; neither can a hatpin! A gun or hatpin may be stored inside a glove compartment or in one's nightstand — but not under one's dressing gown.

In the 1934 movie, "Belle of the Nineties," Mae West threatens a suitor with a "stick of the hatpin." The enormous hatpin is hardly concealed in the enormous hat which was part of her trademark.

Sometimes a potential buyer of a "hatpin protector" becomes so enchanted with a display of ornate hatpins that she starts a collection and, what perhaps *began* as a more serious introduction to the hatpin, ends as a fun thing or even an obsession!

A merchant friend told me that the reputation of hatpins being used as weapons must have originated with the "women of ill-repute," for she assured me that no decent lady of refined breeding would ever be caught alone after dark. *"There was no need for a lady to worry about an assailant,"* she insisted, *"for a lady of breeding — in my day — never went unchaperoned during the day, and never went unescorted after twilight. It just wasn't done!"*

These words were followed with a further condemnation of our younger generation and how much more crime there is on the streets today. *"If young girls would stay home or not stray out alone,"* she admonished, *"they'd be a lot better off!"*

If you believe that our young ladies today have caught "the dickens" from her, you'll be even more amused by the famous Charles Dickens who, in his notes about New York in 1842, scribbled this testimony of his times when women did venture out — if not alone, in pairs and troops:

# THE AUTOMOBILE BONNET

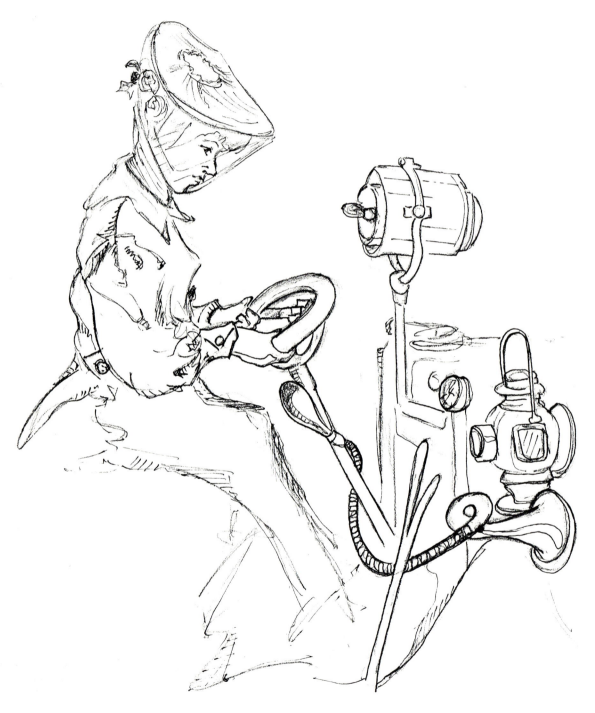

**Plate 183**

*"Heaven save the ladies, how they dress! We have seen more colours in these ten minutes, than we should have seen elsewhere in as many days . . . What rainbow silks and satins! What pinking of thin stockings, and pinching of thin shoes, and fluttering of ribbons and silk tassels, and display of rich cloaks with gaudy hoods and linings! The young gentlemen are fond, you see, of turning down their shirt-collars and cultivating their whiskers, especially under the chin; but they cannot approach the ladies in their dress or bearing, being, to say the truth, humanity of quite another sort."*

In an article of advice aimed at "the lady who travels alone," comes this tidbit of information on hotel life for the "unprotected female": (*Godey's Lady's Book*, Feb. 1853) — (Also, see Plate 184)

*". . . it's the chambermaid's place only to arrange your room, or pay you any personal attention necessary. Through her, you can make any inquiries you desire; but we need not repeat the caution against gossiping with this important functionary as to your past, present, or future intentions."*

The lady who travels alone has often been cast in a murder mystery of the twenties, such as Mary Roberts Rinehart's 1909 saga of *The Man in Tower Ten*. Events take place in that "hatpin year" of 1909, with murder on a train and a witness describing the sensation of the train wreck which is part of the scheme: *"I . . . I heard a woman near me sobbing that she had lost her hatpin, and she couldn't keep her hat on . . ."*

Authoress Dame Agatha Christie's *"Partners in Crime"* a series of twenty-three chilling murder-mystery episodes, (Dodd, Mead & Co.), involves one murder in which the hatpin is unveiled as the death-weapon. From *"The Sunningdale Mystery"* of this series: *". . . examination by a doctor revealed the sinister fact that he had been murdered, stabbed to the heart with*

**Plate 164**

29

*a significant object, a woman's hatpin . . ."*

The woman suspect denies that *"she ever struck at him with a hatpin in self defense — a natural enough thing to do under the circumstances"*, being threatened by a man who *"seemed to go completely mad."*

The wife-half of *"Partners in Crime"* sees a picture of the woman-suspect in a newspaper clipping and immediately surmises: *"She didn't murder him . . . not with a hat pin."* She explains to her much befuddled mate, *". . . She's got bobbed hair. Only one woman in twenty uses hatpins nowadays, anyway — long hair or short. Hats fit tight and pull on — there's no need for such a thing."*

When her partner suggests that the "murderess" might have had a hatpin regardless of fashion, there's an exasperated reply: *"My dear boy, we don't keep them as heirlooms!"* (Regrettably so, may I add!).

There's quite a continuing hoopla about the hatpin, including the suggestion that another woman might be open to suspicion, especially a wife who is "away at the time" and returns to find her husband in love with another woman. *". . . it would be quite natural for her to go for him with a hatpin,"* declares our lady-detective.

Since I do not wish to give away the entire "point" of the story, may I heartily suggest that the still-curious read *"The Sunningdale Mystery"* by that great baffler-writer, Dame Agatha Christie.

One more stubborn source which perpetuates the hatpin as a weapon is fictional dialogue such as appeared in a story by Edwin L. Sabin, titled, *"By Aid of the Stenographer,"* Ladies Home Companion, (Oct. 1901).

In this fetchingly romantic turn-of-the-century frolic, the timid female clerk advises her boss — whom she worships from afar, regarding a love-match:

> *". . . but if she does not find out pretty soon that he loves her she may fall in love with another — and then he'll be too late. Besides, it makes me mad to read page after page of a story where the man wants to tell her, and is afraid, or else won't. I feel like sticking a pin in him."*

Surely our distraught heroine alludes to the hatpin, for in 1901 a lady would never mention the use of any other kind of pin on her person — modesty forbid!

And in Perceval Reniers', *"Roses From the South,"* his heroine *". . . mounted her train without Mr. Talboys but not without one last militant and unladylike gesture. Whisking her hatpin from her hat, she threatened to use it. 'Don't you dare come uptown with me or I'll stick you with this . . .'"*

Of course removing her hatpin resulted in the inevitable description by the author: *". . . her hair was tumbled and her hat askew."*

Fact or fiction? Or is it poetic license?

As recently as January 1974, Ann Landers replied once more regarding the mysterious hatpin; this time regarding archaic laws that are a part of many city ordinances.

The famed columnist stated that nobody bothered, (until recently), to look into old codes which perpetuate injustices or are outmoded. *"I am told,"* she wrote, *"it is still unlawful in Chicago to wear a hatpin whose point sticks out more than half an inch."*

Because of this *Los Angeles Herald-Examiner* column by Ann Landers, (Jan. 26, 1974), I wrote to Bernard Carey, State's Attorney of Cook County, Illinois, and received this gracious and informative reply:

> *Dear Mrs. Baker:*
> *Pursuant to your request concerning information about a 'hatpin ordinance' in Chicago, we have researched the problem and discovered that in the Chicago Municipal Code, Section 193-11, there is in fact such a statute.*
> *A copy of this statute is enclosed. If you desire any further information, do not hesitate to write again.*

\* \* \*

Here is that ordinance:

*PUBLIC PEACE AND WELFARE, Section 193-11 (1911)*
*"193-11. Hatpin with point exposed.*
> *No person while on the public ways of the city, nor while riding upon any street or elevated railroad car running from place to place within the city, nor in any elevator operated in any building in the city to which the public is admitted, shall so wear any hatpin that the exposed point thereof shall protrude more than one-half inch beyond the crown of the hat in, upon, or through which such pin is worn.*
> *Any person violating any of the provisions of this section shall be fined not exceeding fifty dollars for each offense."*

\* \* \*

If, as a writer of fiction, I wished to fabricate stories about the hatpin, I doubt if my vivid imagination could produce the epic which was reality! Therefore, I feel that only by reprinting the actual records and reports of the happenings during the momentous months, prior to World War I, involving the hostilities on all shores against the most fashionable hatpin, can a true picture project itself in the reader's mind.

Let us begin with the more recent newspaper coverage, that of Reporter Barbara Flanagan of *The Minneapolis Star*, and her remarkable story, headlined: "WOMEN USE HATPINS TO FIGHT CRIME," (Mar. 21, 1967).

This staff writer's story is an appropriate commentary on our troubled times of "the sixties," and what one U.S. city attempted to do about its problems.

Reporter Flanagan's story:

> *Minneapolis women will fight crime with 10,000 hatpins — each four inches long. Mashers shouldn't take long to get the point even if they are thick-skinned.*
> *'The best thing a woman has going for her is a loud scream and a long hatpin,' said Inspector Donald R. Dwyer of the Minneapolis Police Department.*
> *It was Dwyer who suggested hatpins as weapons to the women's division of the Minneapolis Chamber*

of Commerce. Their current project is a Citizen Alert campaign to help police adequate law enforcement.

"I'm always amazed at the capabilities of women," said Dwyer. "When they get hot they stay hot. They really went for the idea."

On March 28 the hatpins will be sold for 50 cents each at a public luncheon in the Curtis Hotel. Mrs. Virgille Peeke, division chairwoman for the Chamber, said the hatpins are being made by the Williamson Stamp Co., of Minneapolis. The four-inch pin will have a maroon-and-gold head bearing the Chamber of Commerce emblem. *1.

The head of the hatpin is sturdy enough to give any woman a good grip on it. *2. Dwyer, who will speak at the luncheon, said a hatpin is a familiar object to a woman and a better weapon than a tear gas gun, for example.

"She should carry it in her hand getting off a bus, walking alone at night or just going out to the garbage can, Dwyer said.

"As for the likeliest penetration point," Dwyer said, "Just pick your spot, ladies. Choose your target and jab."

Thanks to Editor Robert C. King, *The Minneapolis Star*, the reader is able to follow through with two marvelous and diverse reactions to this "Citizens Alert" campaign of using hatpins as weapons:

March 29, 1967, headline:
HATPINS LIBERATE WOMEN
                                        Phone 'Out' As Defense
by Jim Klobuchar, (Staff Writer): *Minneapolis Star*

Until Police Inspector Donald Dwyer began pushing hatpins, the most natural and dangerous weapon of the Minneapolis woman — and even the St. Paul woman — had been the simple dial telephone.

It consumed her interests and time, functioned as her courtroom and her punching bag, and supported the automatic oven industry.

This was especially true of Barbara Flanagan Sanford, for whom the telephone is not so much an instrument as a way of life.

Miss Flanagan walked into the office Tuesday, however, brushed her telephone aside, reached into her crocodile-skin handbag and withdrew a four-inch hatpin.

With this she flung herself into a melodramatic swordsman's pose and hissed something that sounded like "en garde".

"I feel a new, liberated woman," she said fingering an imaginary cape.

"You look," I said, "ridiculous. Where did you get that dippy little spear?"

"Those who follow civic affairs would know that the Women's Division of the Chamber of Commerce is distributing 10,000 self-protecting hatpins to Min-

neapolis women as part of a citizens' anti-crime campaign," Miss Flanagan explained.

"What is-it," I asked, "you are seeking to protect so zealously"

"Please," Miss Flanagan replied regally, "Try not to be crude. With this four-inch hatpin, embossed with the Chamber seal in attractive maroon and gold, I can protect my fortune, my life, and my sacred honor."

"But not necessarily in that order," I observed.

"I'm going to ignore that and give you a demonstration," Miss Flanagan continued. "As you know, this is the season of cutpurses and mashers. Thousands of women will now be able to battle on terms of equality and may even have the edge."

"Miss Flanagan," I said, "all you're going to give me is a wide berth. I don't distrust your intentions, merely your aim. Go hunt yourself a masher for the demonstration. In short, I think you people are going to hurt yourselves more than the cutpurses with those little spears."

Miss Flanagan now performed her usual eloquent rebuttal to logical argument by stomping her foot. She summoned Roy Justus, the resident Picasso in the plant, a man of great and gentle wisdom.

"Pretend," she told Justus, "that you are the masher."

Justus was extremely agreeable but also was, in the fashion of most cartoonists, baffled. Miss Flanagan now launched into a series of intricate maneuvers, first concealing the pin and then displaying it in a striking exhibition of bullring virtuosity.

Justus stood around like a bored matador.

He left, leaving Miss Flanagan holding an ear — mine.

"Pretend you have sneaked up behind me and are trying to wring my neck, the better to take advantage of me," she said.

"All right," I agreed, "put some moves on me and see whether I'll take the fake."

I seized Miss Flanagan about the neck and, for this faint glimmer in time, had an opportunity which never again will recur, a moment in which I might avenge all of Miss Flanagan's numberless hours of telephonic monologues at the desk next door.

"Act," she said, "like you meant it."

Thus, on command, I began to wring her neck.

Miss Flanagan came at me with an overhand thrust, the hatpin describing a low trajectory intended to plant the point in my wrist.

The pin flew past my right ear.

"Dwyer's theory is ok," I said, "but in the heat of combat you are going to cut your own jugular vein instead of the masher's watch band. Why not do a low, forearm reverse and come up with the pin somewhere between the masher's knees and his chest? It's a simple flip, technically sound and a good deal more artistic than the overhand thrust."

Miss Flanagan obliged.

I am in the 11th Ward of the hospital, and can

*1. Plate No. 10
*2. Readers will please refer to the opening lines of this Chapter. And now, in the 1970s, Inspector Dwyer perpetuates the myth that a hatpin ". . . is a familiar object to a woman and a better weapon . . ."

**A FRENCH AUTUMN CLOAK** *(9.29.1894, cover).*
The travelling cloak illustrated is of a lustrous cloth called drap de soie, which is rendered impermeable by a process that does not detract from its beauty. The carrick capes of the same and a large ruche of Tosca net around the neck make it rather ornamental. It is worn with a hat of dark rough straw or of stiff-brimmed felt trimmed with many loops of ribbon that form a large bow, and some clusters of flowers.

**Plate 184**

accept letters but perform nothing strenuous for five days.

March 30, 1967, *THE MINNEAPOLIS STAR,*
*Don Morrison's 2 Cents' Worth*
*Flanagan and Klobuchar, that mettlesom pair, have been*
*doing another buck-and-wing — this time about her hatpin.*
### Hatpin Project May Be a Stab in Hubby's Back

*Miss F. is worried about rapists, mashers, foot-pads and suchlike lurkers and liers-in-wait who might menace her purse, person or pudicity. Master K. is worried that this amateur Amazon not only might fail to pink any would-be assailant but most likely would end up perforating some hapless bystander.*

*Now, I stand foursquare against any molesting of our womenfolk and am not exactly protesting the project of the Women's Division of the Chamber of Commerce to distribute 10,000 handsomely engraved, four-inch hatpins with which they can defend themselves. In like manner, I appreciate James' anxiety that some amok maiden might skewer him instead of a more deserving malefactor.*

*However, I have an entirely different worry about the whole proposition. I am worried about getting into trouble with my wife. Any married man of mature judgment tends to look at every new thing, whether it be an electric shoe-horn or admitting China to the U.N. in terms of whether it will get him in trouble with his wife.*

*Consider the situation of 10,000 women roaming Minneapolis armed with their tiny poniards and prepared to jab mashers. Now, doesn't it stand to reason that if I come home with a small hole anywhere in my epidermis, my wife will assume that I have been mashing? As a matter of fact, she probably would assume even worse.*

*But, I am continually sustaining injuries of exactly this nature and in the most innocent manner possible.*

*I frequently stab myself when I forget to take the toothpick out of my martini olive. Considering the state of my wardrobe, it is hard to fasten my jacket without pricking either my thumb or abdomen with the safety pin. Sometimes, when I reach incautiously into a desk drawer, I jab myself on my collection of Alf Landon buttons.*

*Phonograph needles, splinters from pool cues, ballpoint pens, thumb tacks, scissor points, upholstery pins, fine shards of broken glass, parakeet talons, all have a special affinity for my integument, and I usually go around with more holes in various portions of my anatomy than if I had wandered onto a skeet range.*

*Now, thanks to the ladies of the Chamber, each of these honorable wounds could be construed as prima facie evidence that I am a slavering sex maniac.*

*I suppose I could mollify my wife by bringing home a medical certificate as to cause of injury each time I acquired some punctate lesion but this could be embarrassing also.*

*Suppose I am holed in some extremely bizarre fashion — such as running afoul of an enraged unicorn on S. 7th St., or maybe blundering into a patch of cactus in Loring Park. The doctor would probably reject my lame explanation and notify the cops, just as they do with gunshot wounds. Worse, he might even notify my wife.*

*I rather envy one chap who is well out of the whole mess. He is a retired colleague, a former slot-man on the Minneapolis Tribune copydesk. It used to be awesome to watch him reach backwards without looking and impale copy on a vicious-looking spike behind him. From time to time, a waggish copyboy would surreptitiously move the spike an inch-and-a-half closer, so that the next time Lou lunged, he would harpoon his hand. I'd like to see him explain those wounds to the girls down at the Chamber.*

*I warn you, fellow, there is more to this hatpin business than meets the eye, if you will forgive an unfortunate figure of speech.*

\* \* \*

The above newspaper reporters have been writing with tongue-in-cheek, but a truly harrowing story of hatpin-in-cheek appears later in this chapter. Meanwhile, hatpins in the *hands* of male attackers made factual headlines in Los Angeles about 30 years ago with reports about "Hatpin Harry" and "Jim the Jabber."

"Hatpin Harry" victimized women as they boarded downtown trams and trolleys, but he was considered nothing more than a general nuisance.

However, hatpin in the other hand, "Jim the Jabber" was actually involved in several murders in which a hatpin was determined to be the murder weapon.

Now it's a matter of conjecture whether in 1901, Jeanne Chauvin, the first woman lawyer of France, ("determined to plead in court"), was actually involved in the ruckus caused by the "innumerable jewelled conceits" that were beginning to be reported as dangerous. Certainly the hatpins with gold mountings set with rhinestones or turquoise matrix, or the engraved silver hatpins with their elaborate *repousse* chasing, were not considered weapons by the fashion-conscious Parisian nor by her counterparts elsewhere in the fashion world.

It is a fact, however, that Los Angeles Municipal Court Judge Noel Cannon, holding a six-inch jewel-encrusted hatpin, advised with somber regard her concern for the increasing number of attacks on women:

". . . such a weapon worn on a hat or sleeve, probably would not be construed as a concealed weapon in court."

Pointing to the hatpin, the female jurist added, "A quick jab to the midsection of an attacker with this should be very effective. It has a triple advantage. It doubles him up, leaves an iden-

*tifying mark and requires him to seek medical attention."*

Allow me to point out that it would be virtually impossible to "conceal" a *period* hatpin, six inches or longer, and would be an actual hazard for any person to handle the pin uncorked. Hatpins often measure ten inches and sometimes a foot long! (Plate 16)

The publication of Judge Noel Cannon's advice in *The Los Angeles Times*, Thursday morning, May 18th, 1967, caused no hysteria and little excitement or agitation. Contrast this reaction with the international furor reported in newspapers a little more than half-century ago, such as when London's *Daily Mail*, (Nov. 1908), printed the story about the jailed "suffragettes." These daring women were ordered to appear before the bench in rather unusual fashion:

Headline: *SUFFRAGETTES DISAPPOINTED*

The article then describes the occasion when there was some fear in the courtroom of a *"dangerous attack of pin-pricks"* by the accused; and thus came the order that *". . . women prisoners of Clerkenwell Sessions . . . were allowed to appear in hats, but without hatpins."*

It seems that a great dramatic plum was overlooked in the filming of the wonderful award-winning BBC television show of the past season, "Upstairs, Downstairs."

One exciting episode featured the efforts of upper middle-class English women and their "lesser sisters" of servitude in campaigning for suffrage. The enormous-hatted females, wearing two, three, and more hatpins protruding in dangerous fashion, were hauled before the magistrate, hatpins intact! Perhaps because of their class-status, the society matrons would not have been ordered to remove their potential weapons. But what an exciting true-to-life scene that would have made on the old "telly"!

While the English women were occupied in such protests, (which included acts of violence), their American counterpart in the "women's rights movement," had already considered the hat almost symbolic of emancipation, and the styles were worn to be seen! Simply monstrous in size!

Incidently, this 1973 television special, "Upstairs, Downstairs," was re-broadcast in America over KCET, (Los Angeles Public Broadcasting), through the sponsorship of Mobil Oil Company. The series featured more varied examples of the sumptuous hats and glorious hatpins of the 1890-1910 period than ever seen by this author in any other staged production of that era.

Perhaps the edict regarding the ordered removal of hatpins in the courtroom by "prisoners of Clerkenwell Sessions," came about because of the past performance of the Athenian women who were deprived of their stiletto pins owing to the deadly use they made of them.

Greek legend tells us that following the disastrous episode at ancient Thermopylae (480 B.C.), when three hundred brave Spartans fought for three successive days against the Persians, only one Spartan returned alive to Athens. The wives of those soldiers who had fallen in battle were so infuriated that this sole warrior had escaped when their own husbands had "been cut to pieces," they attacked the survivor *en masse*, stabbing the poor wretch with the brooches and bodkins with which the ladies' tunics were fastened. This unprecedented behavior on the part of these females led to a different style of dress being imposed upon them which did not require large pins; instead,

the tunics were then *sewn* at the shoulder.

In Harrison's *History of the Hat*, the author might have been referring to the above incident when he wrote: *". . . had the modern hatpin been invented — or, even, had the Roman matron's hair-skewer remained in use . . ."* mediaeval female head-fashions might have been very different.

Poet James Jeffrey Roche also makes reference to the episode:

*Thermopylae left one alive —*
*The Alamo left none.*

The wider, more alarming and shocking use of public transportation by "emancipated women," caused many new problems — including the "hatpin danger." Interestingly enough, closed-vestibule railroad passenger cars had not been in general use until 1900. The "street railway" in American began in 1888, and the New York "elevated" in 1883. Male and female, "perfect strangers" were "touching and brushing" each other. By World War I, less than a quarter century later, the *machine age* set the die, and no longer was man, (or woman), an "island unto himself." No more would the social, political, economic, or private world of the individual or family be as it once was — male dominated and male orientated.

(The last statement is fact, and the writer excuses herself from further comment, pro or con!)

But of the hatpin, I have much to say! Never has an article of fashion been so slandered; never in modern European or American societies had so many laws been passed governing a fashion-ornament — an ornament soon to pass into oblivion!

Author Bill Severn in his 1963 edition, *Here's Your Hat*, states:

*". . . another worldwide cry of protest arose against hat ornaments. This one was over the long hatpins that women wore to keep the big hats of the early 1900s in place. Men, who traditionally poked fun at the things that women put on their heads, declared hatpins were no laughing matter. The outraged males complained they were in danger of being stabbed, scratched, scarred and blinded."*

That marvel of a woman writer, Taylor Caldwell, in her book, *A Prologue to Love*, stated it more forcefully: *". . . nothing stirred, except on the surface, in peaceful, jocular and buoyant America of 1910."* And she continues regarding the threat to world peace and the oncoming horrors of World War I: *". . . Americans were more concerned with the danger of women's hatpins, long and sharp, in streetcars and in crowded places, than with faint murmurs in the press of some horror gathering."*

Once a thing of beauty and utility, the hatpin's reputation has outlived its usefulness. What has remained is a monstrous myth of highly exaggerated and only partially deserved misdemeanors. Of the thousands upon thousands of hatpins manufactured, how many were "the real culprits"?

Laws were enacted, it seems, out of the sheer boredom of the times. Certainly the hatpin was not the perpetually murderous weapon fiction-writers delight in using, although it does lend itself to such *novel* approach.

For instance, in *Strike Terror*, Hy Steirman's novel of breathtaking suspense, there appears a truly terrorizing sequence:

*"He moved like a panther now, his left arm around the girl's waist, his right fist gripping an eight-inch needle with a baroque top on it . . ."* — (The weapon involved is a hatpin with curare on the tip.)

*"I've got a hatpin in my hand. It has a poison tip. I'll kill her if you come closer . . ."*

Steirman continues the dramatic event with machine-gun versus a *"skinny young man holding a hatpin like a switchblade."*

Completely caged in by the advancing Federal agents, the Communist enemy spy finally jabs the hatpin into his own arm ending his life in final dedication "to the cause."

The use of hatpins as a *fashion* accessory has never been outlawed, but many laws remain on the books concerning the safety factor. Some of these laws have been rescinded as recently as 1962! Others still remain unaltered and archaic.

The "accursed" hatpins were not only used to secure hats upon the heads of the elite, but may have also doubled as a vanity pin. Some hatpin heads actually held such necessary items as small straight brass dress pins, or a velvet perfumed cushion hidden under a secret lid. Another large ornament atop a pin, opened to reveal a compact, complete with lamb's wool miniature powder-puff equipped with a tiny ivory-loop handle. Even a mirror was encased in the cover! (See Plate No. 64.)

Rumor has it that specially designed hatpins opened and concealed poison which was dropped into a drink by the *femmes fatales*, those seductive women who lured men with their aura of charm and mystery only to "do them in." But this bit of buzz has proven to be nothing more than an additional slur against the reputation of the much-maligned hatpin.

Despite the dashing and daring pictures of damsels with hatpins clenched between their teeth,* actual close inspection of period hatpins reveal they are true works of the jewelers' art and a necessary accessory for comfortable and correct head-attire. (It may not be entirely correct to use the term "comfortable" considering the outlandish weight of cotton "rats," batting, puffs and artificial hair pinned into place under those millinery concoctions.)

Some hatpin ornaments were made to match fashion accessory pieces such as belt buckles, shirt-studs, brooches, veil pins, scarf pins, corsage pins, earrings, or finger rings; many were in the newfangled designs craved for by the *Nouveau* cult.

One of the finest tributes to the period hatpin, both in correctness of utilization and beauty, was seen in Luchino Visconti's film, *"Death in Venice."* Particular praise is due costume designer, Piero Tosi and art director, Ferdinando Scarfiotti. The beauty of the hatpins used in conjunction with the gorgeous chapeaux is perfectly breathtaking. But, may I smugly note, the exquisite millinery creations in the movie film could not have existed without the aid of the period hatpin! Useful and ornamental — the first principle of the best in artistic endeavor — makes the period hatpin a true work of art.

---

* *Julie Andrews danced with a hatpin between her teeth in the film, "Darling Lili." The hatpin was especially made for this production by W. Reyhill, designer of jewels for Hollywood.*

But with so little reference material available, it's no wonder that fine caliber authors like Irving Wallace uses description merely for effect rather than for technical perfection.

In his book, *"The Twenty-Seventh Wife,"* (Brigham Young's 27th!), his descriptive use of the hatpin is incorrect.

Wallace's text reads: *". . . that first night Ann Eliza primly reclined in her berth armed with muslin blouse, balmoral skirt — and hatpin."*

Being "armed with hatpin" is the phrase which perpetuates the myth of hatpins as "weapons"; it is also an example of how the lack of encyclopaedic reference on the subject of the hatpin can be the downfall of fictional and factual reporting. The severe hair-styles of the Mormon women — which includes the 27th wife of Brigham Young — and their close-fitting bonnets, dismisses the need for a hatpin. Besides, the shunning of most ornamentation by strict Mormons would have prohibited the use of fancy hatpins. For these reasons, the credibility of Ann Eliza being "armed" with a hatpin, may logically be questioned and challenged.

A more factual bit of reporting comes in John Springer's *"Innocent in Alaska"*. Here is an author who conjures up quite another and truer picture for us:

*"My feet had only touched the floor when the details of the contest returned to my mind. After wounding myself four times with a hatpin, neglecting to nest one of my hair rats . . . I finally got downtown."*

Speaking of conjured pictures, there's an interesting story in William Seabrook's, *"Witchcraft: Its Power in the World Today."* It's called, *"W. E. Woodward With a Hatpin Driven Through His Jaws."*

In this chapter the author tells of a Polish gentleman who had studied in India among the fakirs and had the self-made reputation of having extraordinary powers "peculiarly conducive to miracles." Among his so-called supernatural gifts was one of feeling no pain, a claim which did not go unchallenged. Seeking to vindicate himself before some parlor-guests, he insisted he would drive *"something long and sharp and pointed through his jowls."*

*"It was in the days when ladies still wore hats,"* wrote the author, *"and one of them delightedly proffered an extra-long and murderous hatpin, adorned with a gold-plated Prussian eagle. It was a war souvenir — had been part of an officer's insignia — and had been welded to the hatpin, for a head."*

The Polish gentleman accepted the hatpin while relishing the frightful squeals of the ladies present; he was preparing to accomplish his feat with all the necessary gestures for suspense when the host, Mr. Woodward, decided to call a halt to the proceedings.

There was a debate, then a challenge from one of the male guests with a bit more bravado than the others, until the upshot was that a young challenger named Bill decided he was going to become the hero of the evening — *trying the stunt of thrusting a hatpin through his jowls.*

Author Seabrook gives a vivid description of Bill's performance:

*. . . He took the hatpin, puffed his cheeks, opened his mouth like a dying fish, and began pushing the hatpin slowly into the flesh. After about five inches*

*of it had disappeared laterally, traversing the buccal cavity, the cheek on the other side began to bulge slightly outward. The hatpin point came through. He kept pushing until it was sticking out several inches on both sides of his head. He smiled, or tried to, and began talking baby talk.*

Mr. Seabrook insists in his book that this hatpin stunt is theatrically impressive, but involves no more concentration strain and discomfort, than does the self-induced hypnotic state of psychic anesthesia used by the fakir on a bed of nails in Turkestan.

Author Seabrook ends this tale of truth by reprinting a letter received from "Bill" Woodward of the willing jowls:

*. . . I had never thrust a hatpin through my cheeks before, and I did it then just to see if I could . . . Since then, I have thrust hatpins through my cheeks numbers of times. There's nothing to it; anybody can do it. Just get a clean hatpin, which must be very sharp. There's a slight pricking pain as it goes in through the skin of the right cheek, and when it comes out through the skin of the left cheek, but the slight pain stops immediately. While the pin is in place, you can't move your tongue, or talk, and that is a nuisance . . .*

Although Mr. Woodward could feel little pain in his jowls, there have been reports to the contrary regarding the thrust of the hatpin into another part of the male anatomy. The popular columnist, Ann Landers, printed such a report via a letter from one of her avid readers. I know it's bound to provide a chuckle or two.

*"Dear Ann: Regarding those 'snore cures' sent to you by that El Paso Doctor, I thought you might like to know how one of his suggested 'cures' turned out. My husband had been a heavy snorer for some time. I studied the doctor's list and decided to try his 'hatpin cure.' You did not state in your column if the doctor had tried any of these 'cures' himself or if his approach was purely academic. Now that I have tried one I'd like to warn others to stand at a safe distance when using the 'hatpin' technique. The doctor said the snorer would wake up suddenly and ask, 'What happened?' Well, it didn't quite work that way with my husband. He woke up mad as hell and swinging . . . Please get this word to your readers as fast as possible."*

The letter was signed, "Sadder But Wiser,". Ann Landers thanked the writer for sharing her "research" but reminded all her readers that she had not endorsed or recommended the doctor's cures but had, in fact, cautioned against using them.

I'd like to thank *Sadder But Wiser* and that wonderful writer of wisdom and wit, Ann Landers, for adding another tidbit of folklore to the hatpin legend. (I suppose if one wanted to use that "hatpin cure", one should use a 12″ pin-length for "safe distance".)

It's amazing to learn some of the uses for the "defunct" period hatpin. For instance, over the ocean and settled in the green hills of Ireland, are the ancestors of a lass who recently visited America. This young woman tells me that in her community of frugal housewives in Ireland, the old-fashioned hatpin is utilized up to the present day in a rare manner. The hatpins nestle in a container in the center of a kitchen or dining table, much like the spoon-holder of old. These pins are used as prongs to dig out the clam-like *escargot* or snail, which is a delicacy on most European tables.

Spearing and stabbing and other such vices were attributed to the hatpins, especially as the hatpin became more absurdly longer and worn in closer quarters.

Although not meant nor manufactured as weapons, hatpins did become somewhat dangerous instruments, as witness the tidings in the *London Daily Mail*, (Dec. 17, 1908):

*DEADLY HATPIN — HEAVY CASUALTY LIST IN BERLIN*
*A campaign against the murderous hatpin has been instituted by the newspapers of Berlin, in view of a series of accidents which have already occured (sic) during the busy period of Christmas shopping.*
*Numbers of more or less serious injuries have been caused by these dangerous implements protruding from the huge hats of fashionable ladies. Last Sunday a lady was permanently blinded in one eye when taking part in a rush at a 'bargain sale.' Two days later a lift attendant at a neighboring shop had his face so badly injured that it was necessary to take him to a hospital. Many cases of scratched faces are reported from many quarters.*

Now, dear reader, even as I type this portion of my text, I can feel a grin spreading across my face; I'm sure you have chuckled, too. But don't we all find ourselves laughing at the poor victim who slips on a banana peel, or at the shenanigans of the Keystone Kops whose pranks involve bruised and broken bones? Well, we can smother our guilt with Mark Twain's words:

"The secret source of Humor itself is not joy but sorrow . . ."

I say, we pity the victim but smile at the vice — and victims there were many, and the vice of wearing "dangerous weapons" continued on and on.

The *London Observer* reported on Sunday, Sept. 12, 1909, that there would actually be a competition among exhibitors to display new inventions to make the ladies' hatpins safer while still satisfying the fashion decrees of the day:

*"M. Lepine, head of the Paris police, has been much moved by the number of accidents caused through the use of ladies hatpins. Dagger-like points gleam from out the mass of furs and feathers, to the infinite danger of other people's eyes.*
*The paternal Prefect let his wish to curtail this dangerous practice be known among his proteges, as a stimulus to their inventiveness. As a consequence, a large part of this pleasant exhibition (the Lepine exhibition, held in the garden of the Tuileries every year for the encouragement of the modest inventors and toymakers of Paris), of 'camelot' genius, is devoted to women's hatpins of the safety order."*

\* \* \*

In my own collection are various "safety" tips used for period hatpins — cork tips, screw-type ornamental knobs, clasp-type tips, endless "ends" of hatpin safeties including small chains to prevent their loss and finally a truly remarkable spring-loaded affair with a beautifully wrought design to enhance its use.* (See Plate No. 11.)

However, across the seas on the "new" continent of America, there was no such invitation to artistic endeavor nor appeasement.

*The Paris Mail* (1909) reported:
BACHELORS, BABIES, HATPINS, AND BATHS
*"According to a New York telegram a bill has been introduced into the Arkansas Legislature. It introduces some most curious laws now under consideration in different states.*

*From Illinois: 'To limit the length of women's hatpins to nine inches, and make them take out permits for longer ones, just like all deadly weapons'."*

\* \* \*

Five years later, Dec. 3, 1913, *The London Times* headlined, *DANGEROUS HATPINS*, and went on to report:

*Mr. I. D. Gelpert asked the chairman of the Highways Committee whether in view of the new by-laws allowing passengers to stand in the tram-cars, the committee had considered the advisability of issuing notices similar to those on use in Manchester asking ladies to have all hatpins protected. Mr. Hume replied that he had seen the notices issued by Manchester Corporation and the committee would certainly consider the matter.*

\* \* \*

Another bit of news followed in the same publication, (Dec. 10, 1913), with the appearance in bold print of the following message:

*WARNING POSTED IN LONDON TRAMCARS*
**The attention of Lady passengers is drawn to danger to other passengers and the Council's servants through the practice of wearing hatpins with unprotected points.**
*"The above notice signed by the chief officer of tramways (an A.L.C. Fell) was posted on all the London County Council tram-cars yesterday, owing to the complaints that had been received of injury caused to passengers and others by the dangerous hatpins which are used by ladies. It will be observed that the notice on London tram-cars is only a warning, but on the continent more drastic measures have*

*been taken; the Prefect of Police in Paris having prohibited the use of unprotected hatpins in public places within that city. For a long time past sheaths have been sold in milliner's shops whereby the points of pins can be protected after they have been thrust through the hat, but hitherto these have not been generally used. The danger to fellow passengers sitting by the side of, or walking past a wearer of a long unprotected hatpin, especially when the car suddenly stops or starts, is considerable.*

*"The Metropolitan Police of course have not the extensive power with which the police of continental capitals are armed. They can only issue warnings to the public but in the case of licensed vehicles they could probably insist on the warning being made an effective prohibition by means of a by-law of the company concerned. Any other action would belong to the province of the local authorities or the Legislature.*

*"Should serious cases of injury caused by unprotected hatpins come to the notice of the Police commissioner, representations would no doubt be made to the Home office, but it is believed that hitherto the Metropolitan Police have found no occasion to consider the matter seriously."*

\* \* \*

Once again I wish to remind the reader that I have purposely used the factual, specific, newspaper reports of events during the "hatpin crisis" of 1908-14, in order to accurately acquaint the stranger to the situation as it existed at that time.

Only three short days after the appearance of the aforementioned warning, *The London Times*, (Dec. 16, 1913), reported an unusual reprimand in the court room:

*Headline: JUDGE AND A DANGEROUS HATPIN\**
*"Judge Mackariness at the Worthing County Court, yesterday addressing a lady who was wearing a cap fastened to her hair with a long pin, remarked as she was leaving the court:*
*". . . If you walk about like that you will be up for murder some day. Take my advice and take it (hatpin) out."*
*The lady replied: "Well, I must keep my cap on somehow."*

Contrary to this rebuff is the advice in *"No Star Is Lost"*, a novel by James T. Farrell, in which the heroine is urged, *". . . ah, Peg, you should have spit in his face and stuck your hatpin into the eyes of that chippy."*
Oftentimes in fiction, a hatpin is the implement used to further the action or plot. But in *most* cases it's the murder weapon, a homicidal instrument in the hands of the wicked or a protective implement for the winsome woman out to save her virtue.
When Steirman described the weapon in his book as *"an*

\*   From "Hatpinology" by Tom J. Lawson, ("Antique Collecting," Dec. 1974, Vol. 9, No. 8): "The earliest patent I have been able to trace on hatpins is no. 4412 of 1897 *dealing with hatpin point protection. Several other patents were issued dealing with the protection of hatpin points, manufacture of heads, hatpins which do not injure heads or hats, point shapes (for penetrating materials more easily with less damage to the hat), methods of preventing withdrawal of the pin, hinge between head and pin, and probably many other aspects of hatpins.)*"
   Patent No. 17653, *". . . allowed the user to clip fasten the head onto the pin point and so acted as a point protector." (See Plate 11)*
   (Mr. Lawson's article and examples represent the English trade.)

*\*Plate 163*

*eight-inch needle with a baroque top on it"*, his descriptive notes could have fit any number of hatpins from my own inventory of pins with baroque tops. There are those from crown to culet in brilliant stones; or crystal, cloisonne, and gemstones in filigree framed in illusion settings.

Now had the Steirman weapon been a *gun*, it no doubt would have been carefully described as to size, make, caliber, and other vital statistics!

Hatpins have been used in numerous productions in the theatre, the movies, and in television programs. They often play a major role in the plot but receive minor spotlight as to size and description, and oftentimes are improperly used.

For instance, in one television story, a heroine of Spanish descent, wears a flat-brimmed hat on a smooth hairdo. The heroine enters the scene (and television screen) pulling a twelve-inch hatpin out from across the back brim of her Spanish head-gear. Now a hatpin would not have been worn, neither by style nor necessity, on such a "sombrero"! Yet, with weapon in hand, the senorita stabs the wicked jailor in the heart, makes off with the keys to the cell, and frees her innocent brother.

Oh the handy hatpin!

Angela Lansbury, in the first act of "*Gypsy*," uses a hatpin in a typical "stage-mother" gesture during an "all's fair" competiton between her talented youngster and a competing act. She simply eliminates the competition by pricking the props which are balloons. How? With a deft stroke of a hatpin which is conveniently stored in a tight-fitting cloche hat which in reality would never had required such an "instrument."

The Academy-Award winning actress, Maggie Smith, made her initial appearance on stage in "*Three Sisters*," by walking to a mirror, then with flourish enough to ingratiate her forever in the heart of a hatpin lover, Miss Smith withdrew the "skewer" from her hat! (The actress advised in a letter regarding her hatpin, that she had personally selected it in an antique shop in Arundel "some time ago.")

"*The Day After the Fair*," is a play which covers a three-month period during the summer of 1900. Miss Deborah Kerr's stellar role as "Edith," remains a memorable one for me; moreover because of the authentic use of period costume, including hats and hatpins!

Once more, as with Miss Maggie Smith, the leading lady gracefully removes the hatpin and gently places it into the crown of her small hat. Miss Kerr's lovely "summer of 1900" costume is shown on Plate 148. It is modelled by the beautiful actress in a typical Victorian parlor of the day, designed especially for the stage setting of "*The Day After the Fair.*"

In the T.V. series, "The Streets of San Francisco," an episode titled, "The Mask of Death," by Robert Malcolm Young, provides a bravura performance by female impersonator, John Davidson. His portrayal as a murderess of middle-aged jet-setters was extraordinary. So was the use of the hatpin as the weapon which is deftly placed in the various victims' anatomy. Once again, the hatpin became the "murderous weapon!"

Those who recall the movie, "The Hallelujah Trail," will remember that a short hatpin withdrawn from the hat of a female prohibitionist is used to prick the hide of a horse and start a stampede.

A woman of my generation mentioned to me that she keeps

**Plate 148:** Miss Deborah Kerr as "Edith" in THE DAY AFTER THE FAIR. Play covers period of three months in summer of 1900 — the height of hatpin era. Photograph courtesy: THE SHUBERT ORGANIZATION and Publicity Director, Edward Parkinson, Shubert Theatre.

a hatpin handy to prick out particles of imperfection caught in the small screen or aerolater used inside her kitchen faucet. (The hatpin as an anti-polluter? What next!)

Well, another informant told me that her grandmother's hatpin has served two generations as a cake-tester!

38

In Frank Yerby's "*Gillian*," the hatpin played an unusual part:

"*. . . I wasted two full hours opening drawers, drawers which clearly showed the signs of prior search, sticking hatpins into cushions, mattresses . . .*"

The hatpin mentioned above was used for search; more often than not it was the subject of seizure. Note *The London Times* story of Jan. 27th, 1914:

> *Berlin, Jan. 26, 1914, 'Campaign Against Hatpins'*
> *The campaign against protecting hatpins which has been carried on for some time by the German police authorities is now being taken up by the railways. In the Breslau district the authorities have posted notices to the effect that the wearing of hatpins with unprotected points is forbidden in railways stations and in trains and the offenders can be refused railway tickets and are liable to fines up to the amount of 5 pounds.*

In David L. Cohn's, "*The Good Old Days*," the author covers what he calls "the hatpin war" in a most intriguing fashion. He suggests that in April 1914, "*. . . the hatpin war reached England*," but that it was a mere skirmish. The ruffle was nothing more, reports Mr. Cohn, than a *suggestion* that by-laws be passed to cope with hatpins.

My further research contradicts the notion that England never adopted by-laws effecting the hatpin. The hatpin controversy had, indeed, reached England BEFORE April 1914, and some by-laws *were* adopted and passed.

According to *The London Times*, (Feb. 10th, 1914), the City Council of Cardiff, England, adopted a by-law "*requiring any female person wearing a hatpin in any street or public meeting place to cause the point to be properly protected by a blunt guard of metallic or other material.*"

England's attack on the hatpin is further substantiated by a letter to the editor, *The London Times*, (February 18th, 1914):

> "*Sir: How long is London to be left exposed to the daily peril from the protruding hatpin? One is in constant danger in the crowded traffic in the street, entering omnibuses, trams, tubes or lifts of being stabbed or perhaps blinded for life.*
> *In Germany the authorities have forbidden the use of hatpins unless protected, at any rate as far as tram and trains are concerned and in Paris a similar regulation is in force.*
> **In our own country, Cardiff has recently set the example of enforcing the use of protectors and why should London lag behind?**
> *It is of little use to warn people in individual cases, it is a matter for the community to take up, and I earnestly hope that this letter may be read by someone who is in a position to put a stop to this intolerable danger.*
> *I remain yours faithfully, (signed) A. Chaplin (Mrs.)*
> *13, Addison Garden, Kensington*

* * *

This was only the beginning of the barrage, the volley of animus attitudes against the hatpin which had become part and parcel of fashionable attire. The hatpin was an adornment in a flamboyant society, an accessory-aesthetic culture known as *Art Nouveau*. Why, to ask a lady to forego her hatpin was akin to asking a soldier to surrender his sword!

However, even then there were the appeasers or peacemakers — take your choice — who wrote charming notes made public:

> *The London Times*, (Feb. 20, 1914)
> THE HATPIN DANGER — *To the Editor of the Times:*
> Sir,
>     *To avoid all appearance of advertisement I do not give my name or address.*
>     *Why are hatpins essential? My wife has invented a little metal fastening, with no point, to keep a hat on the head, and some are being made for her own use. Having ascertained the names of several firms in the city who make or supply things of this sort, I have offered it to them, but they all say it is impossible to induce ladies to buy anything but hatpins. As a private individual cannot manufacture metal articles, it seems probably that my wife's benevolent invention to supersede the dangerous hatpin will never go beyond her own head. I enclose my card, and I am, Sir,*
> *Your obedient servant*
> *H.B.D.*

* * *

> *The London Times*, (Feb. 25, 1914)
> HATPINS — *Mr. Cowan (Aberdeenshire, E. Min.) asked the House Secretary whether his attention had been called to regulations recently enforced in France and Germany forbidding the use in public places of unprotected hatpins, and whether having regard to the number of serious accidents which had resulted in this country from the use of unprotected hatpins, he would take such steps, by legislation or otherwise as might be necessary to protect the public from a serious and growing danger.*
>     *Mr. McKenna (Monmouth, N.): The answer to the first part of the question is in the affirmative. With regard to the second part, I have no power to make any regulations in the matter, and I am afraid that I cannot undertake to introduce legislation, but if the practice can be shown to be a public danger the local authorities might deal with it under their power of making by-laws for good rule and government. In the case of tramcars, by-laws might be made under the Tramways Act, 1870.*
>     **Mr. Watt ( Glasgow, College, Min.): Will the right Honorable gentleman see that women do not get the vote till they voluntarily adopt this? ( Laughter)**

However, it was no laughing matter for women who were struggling to gain "women's rights." Witness Miss Harriet Stanton Blatch's letter to *The New York Times*, (1914):

39

*"In your telegraphic news from Paris recently we are informed that Prefect Hennion . . . has twice issued edicts against unprotected hat pins, but that the Pariesenne merely smiles and goes her way."*

Miss Blatch referred to the Chief of Paris police as one who was held "in terror by the Apache", but could not hold the fort in his own gay city where pointed "arrows" darted out from women's fashionable feathered head-gear!

*"This is,"* Miss Blatch's letter continues, *"but another argument for VOTES FOR WOMEN and another painful illustration of the fact that men cannot discipline women . . . Give women political power and the best among them will gradually train the uncivilized, just as the best among men have trained their sex . . ."*

A longer lament arrived at the Editor's desk, *The London Times*, (March 31, 1914). The missive was captioned:

### THAT HATPIN DANGER — A CONSTANT MENACE TO THE UNDERGROUND

*Sir, it is almost a daily occurrence that some accident of one kind or another has to be reported through the negligent way in which ladies wear hatpins.*

*Last night about 6 o'clock, I entered the tube lift at the Post Office Station, just at the time when the crush of the people homewards bound is at its height, when I saw two young girls entering the lift just in front of me, both wearing two or three hatpins protruding about three or four inches. While I was still contemplating on the very evident danger and trying in a pure sense of self-preservation not to come into touch with these uninviting necessities of the otherwise attractive toilette of the woman of today, one of the young ladies moved, in conversation with her friend, her head to one side, and one of her hatpins went right into the eye of a gentleman standing next to me. It was quite a miracle that he was not seriously hurt or blinded in one eye, perhaps for a lifetime. He only complained of a momentary pain, and evidently no harm being done, very little further notice was taken of this incident.*

*But what would have happened if the man had lost his eyesight, which after all was only saved by a fraction of an inch? Would he have been able to get adequate compensation? As it was, the girl seemed to belong to the poorer class, and she could have hardly been expected to pay any damages, as in a case in the Law Courts a few weeks ago when a lady was fined 3 pounds for having inadvertently scratched the face of another lady with her hatpin. Besides any monetary compensation would have been only a very poor consolation and both parties can be jolly glad that nothing serious had come of it.*

*But this is only one case, one case out of many. As a daily user of the tube and the congested lifts in the morning and evening I can invariably see people dodging protruding hatpins. There you stand in the lift, cramped in from all sides, no room to move even your arm and there in front of you, only inches away, a well-pointed hatpin is blinking at you, only*

*waiting for the fair owner, standing with her back to you and quite unaware of it, to move her head in order to give you a little souvenir. Who has not experienced the same feeling? And who has not asked himself the question how this nuisance can be done way with?*

*We must look to other countries to find a solution. In France, in Germany, and many other parts of the world, specially not forgetting our own colonies, it has long been made compulsory that ladies should wear protected hatpins, and it is also seen to that the law is properly enforced. Only here we seem to be in this respect behind our times. Endless correspondence has been written, most of the papers have brought leading articles bearing on that subject, besides giving prominence about accidents in their news columns. Notices have been put up in all the L.C.C. tramcars to urge ladies to wear protected hatpins and still the majority of women go about without even considering to what risks they expose their fellow creatures. Good words or good examples seem to have as little effect as bad ones, but is it not time that something definite should be done and a simple and necessary law which has done any amount of good in other countries introduced also in this country? There would be no need for bothering parliament in these busy times, as according to the Home Secretary, the local authorities have full power to make a by-law which would benefit everyone.*

*Yours faithfully,*
*(signed) ONE FOR ALL*

Before the gallant editor of *The London Times* could muster enough words for the editorial page, a handwritten hand-delivered letter arrived for publication — the very next day, April 1, 1914 — only when it appeared in print it was not meant as an April Fool's joke:

*Sir,*

*In reply to "One for All" I would urge that the hatpin danger is not nearly so prevalent as it was.*

*Now that there is a plentiful supply of short hatpins on sale in all the shops it is the exception to see a projecting hatpin except perhaps in one case of poorer women who hesitate to make new purchases. Does he and other advocates of the "protector" realize the amount of "new-purchasing" he would be requiring of all women?*

*A satisfactory hatpin protector does not yet appear to exist, and at present it is no uncommon thing to come home from a walk to find two out of three of one's protectors missing. Should not any by-law in these circumstances at least give women the option of wearing instead short pins which do not project beyond the brim of the hat? In this case there can be no danger.*

*If, however, these gentlemen insist on the hatpin protector, which is more elusive than any collar stud,*

*will they not give us another by-law as a Quid pro quo?\* Will they not relegate all smokers to the back of the seats of omnibuses? This has long been done quite successfully in some provincial towns.*
*Yours faithfully,*
*(signed) THE OTHER SIDE*

\* \* \*

The validity of the "new-purchasing" slant in the above letter was quite justified inasmuch as the washerwoman's earnings were but a few cents a day and her housewifely counterpart, too, had little more weekly allowance; yet each had the *necessary* purchase of inexpensive hatpins in order to (as the court client rattled to the judge), *"keep my cap on somehow."*

Across the miles of ocean, in the American "colonies," a lady of high fashion could order a *"Gold Filled sword Hat or Hair Pin, very fancy Roman handle, set with eight Pearls and one Amethyst, bright polished Silver Blade, 6½" long. Price $2.15"* — from the newly established *Sears, Roebuck & Co.,* who shipped to even the "most remote parts" for three cents postage. (*Fancy sword pins*, Plates 17, 71, 112.)

Now when one considers that Sears' best "Electric Washer" could be ordered for $3.50, *"guaranteed to do the work and give satisfaction,"* one can readily agree that the jeweled hatpin, priced at $2.15, was certainly a luxury that the ordinary housewife, farmwife, or working girl could ill-afford. "Pin money" or "butter 'n eggs" money was usually set aside for much-needed comforts rather than a sudden splurge on an extravagance for which there were less-expensive substitutes.

In light of the above, inexpensive hatpins were ordered from catalogues by country-folk who resided far from millinery shops, department stores or "general stores" which lacked hatpin counters. Typical of the catalogue offerings were:

*"25270 — Black Pins . . . bright jet heads; why pay the retailer 100 per cent profit on these little things? Each $0.03. Per doz . . . $0.30¢ (Postage 2¢ extra)"*

In the 1897 Sears' catalogue, there appears but two fancy pins for hat or hair; by the Fall 1898 catalogue printing, Sears was able to inform its customers who eagerly awaited the "wish-books":

*". . . owing to increased demand for Ladies' hatpins, we have selected with great care a handsome line of the latest Parisian patterns . . . Designs run from the most simple patterns to the most gorgeous . . . We guarantee our hatpins to be the correct length . . . Nothing is more aggravating than a hatpin that is too short . . ."*

So, in 1898 the "aggravating" short pin was thrust aside along with the then popular sword-shaped hatpins which reached their zenith in 1894-5. These sword-patterns were sheathed in favor of the "dangerously long" seven and eight inch pins which gradually lengthened until they became twelve inch "daggers."

The handy hatpin, often called a "lethal weapon," may be comparable in kin to the small pearl-handled or intricately carved antique firearm, each a thing of beauty, each a lethal weapon when used. For surely the wearing of a hatpin without a nib-protector, with the point protruding inches from the brim of a hat would be as dangerous in a sense as wearing a cocked revolver in ones waistband! Yet the antique weapon in a showcase and the period hatpin in its hatpin holder, can be a simply splendid thing to look upon!

Superstition aside, thirteen was indeed the unlucky number for hatpins, for it was in the year 1913 that this necessary toilette item received its greatest abuse and was literally cut down in size.

(The addendum to this chapter explains this cutting down in more detail.)

In *The New York Times*, (Sunday, May 11, 1913), there appeared this noteworthy disclosure:

> *WORE HATPINS TOO LONG*
> *New Orleans Police Arrest Women for Violating Ordinance*
> *(New Orleans — May 10, 1913) — Six women have appeared as defendants in two courts in this city wearing hatpins that were too long; violating a new ordinance. The police made the arrests in a very polite manner. Large crowds followed them. The policemen endeavored in every way not to give the impression that the matter was a joke, at the same time being careful not to offend any of the women they approached.*
> *"I beg your pardon", the policemen would say, "but I must call your attention to the fact that you are violating the law by permitting the point of your hatpin to project out more than an inch. Kindly give me your name and address."*
> *Invariably the women thus approached would smile, take the matter good-naturedly, and respond by telling where she lived. Some of the women arrested were well-known. One of the policemen who is six feet three inches in height, and weighs 253 pounds, said: "I'd like to have you understand that it's no joke to watch for those shining points and then approach the owner and warn them."*

The Superintendent of Police in New Orleans answered my query of Oct. 14, 1968, relative to "Hatpin Statute and/or Ordinance," advising me as follows:

> *"The delay in responding was caused by the fact that the records had to be researched and was referred to the City Attorney's Office for handling.*
> *"I am now in receipt of report from the Office of the City Attorney in which it is stated that research failed to develop any State Statutes or City Ordinances relative to regulating size and wearing of hatpins by women."*

Obviously, from the previously mentioned news report printed above, such an Ordinance does or did exist; for all we know it is still an obscure by-law on the books and could be

---

\* *Something in exchange; an equivalent.*

41

enforced were hatpins ever to become the danger they were in the past!*

Thus my report from New Orleans. But how about the State of New Jersey? It, too, was vulnerable, for in the same issue of *The New York Times*, (May 11, 1913), there appeared this item:

*NEW JERSEY'S HATPIN LAW*
To the Editor of The New York Times:
*Noticing the letter in the columns of the Times some few days ago on the danger involved in carelessness about hatpins, it occurred to me that it might be of interest to your readers to know the stand taken concerning them through the law in New Jersey, to which law New York women going into New Jersey are also amenable.*
*The New Jersey law provides that all hatpins protruding more than one-half inch without protection of the points are prohibited. In cases of complaint against the offender the fine is fixed at a minimum of $20 and a maximum of $100 for each offense, the complainant receiving one-half of the fine imposed.*
F., New York, May 9, 1913.

The law in New Jersey, as far as I can determine, is still in effect. In 1913, there was an actual BAN on wearing hatpins in Austria. This edict was reported in *The New York Times:*

*Vienna, (May 11, 1913), — MUST REMOVE PINS BEFORE RIDING IN STATE RAILWAYS*
*The Ministry of Railways have (sic) issued an order that women wearing unprotected hatpins shall not be permitted to ride on the Austrian State railways until they have removed the perilous pin. The management of the Vienna municipal tramways have (sic) gone even further in directing tramcar conductors to compel such offenders to leave the car immediately. If they refuse, the conductor will call in the police to remove them by force.*
*Some months ago an order was issued that conductors should request women to remove their hatpins when these threatened to prove dangerous to the other passengers. But the conductors apparently were unwilling to engage in acrimonious dissensions with women passengers over the length of their hatpins and the order produced no effect. And so, to make it easier for the conductors, they are now directed simply to turn out the wearers of long hatpins the moment they step on the car.*
*Whether the conductors will prove equal to their new police duties is another question. Probably the fair Viennese will continue to ride on the muncipal tramways whether their hatpins be long or short, and protected or not.*

* * *

*See addendum to this chapter.

Seemingly the police had little control over the hatpin menace, and irate citizens began to write to the newspapers in earnest.

*To the Editor of the New York Times, (May 12, 1913):*
*HATPINS LAW IN GERMANY — You printed a letter recently signed F.D.K. dealing with the danger of the unprotected point of the hatpin, often protruding from the hat several inches. This is a subject of greater importance than some women care to admit when their attention is drawn to their hatpin by one of their fellow passengers in a crowded car. While abroad two years ago a friend of mine in Hamburg drew my attention to the fact that if I did not put a guard on the end of my hatpin before boarding a street car I would run the risk of being ordered off the car, a law in Germany providing the wearing of a guard. Unnecessary to say that I followed the advice of my friend and purchased several guards in order to have a supply when returning to New York, and now I never go out without placing such a guard on the point of my hatpin.*
*Why not enforce such a law in this city, where the cars are much more crowded than those in European cities? This would avoid serious accidents like the one described by the writer of the above-mentioned letter. (Signed) Meta Von Nuys, New York, May 8, 1913.*

The report above scarcely emphasized the stringency of the German law which had been vigorously enforced just a month previously as reported by *Marcoal Transatlantic Wireless Telegraph* to *The New York Times*. Dateline: Berlin, April 19, 1913.

*EMBARGO ON HATPINS IN FORCE*
*Police President von Jargow's embargo against murderous hatpins came officially into force in Berlin this week. Women who are fond of decorating their millinery with prongs which endanger life and limb hence forth will be subject to a fine of $15 for the first offense and imprisonment upon repetition of the misdemeanor. Police "spotters" are at work in the street cars, underground railways, and motor omnibuses trying to catch offenders. No arrests have been made so far, and the shops report a land office business in the sale of hatpin protectors, which have been nicknamed "jargow-nibs." (Plate 165.)*

* * *

Evidently the jargow-nibs proved unsatisfactory, as explained in a report that came out of London several months later:

The New York Times, Nov. 1913:
*AWARDS HATPIN DAMAGES*
*London Judge Holds Wearer Responsible for Accidental Injuries*
*London, Nov. 15 — "If a lady chooses to carry in*

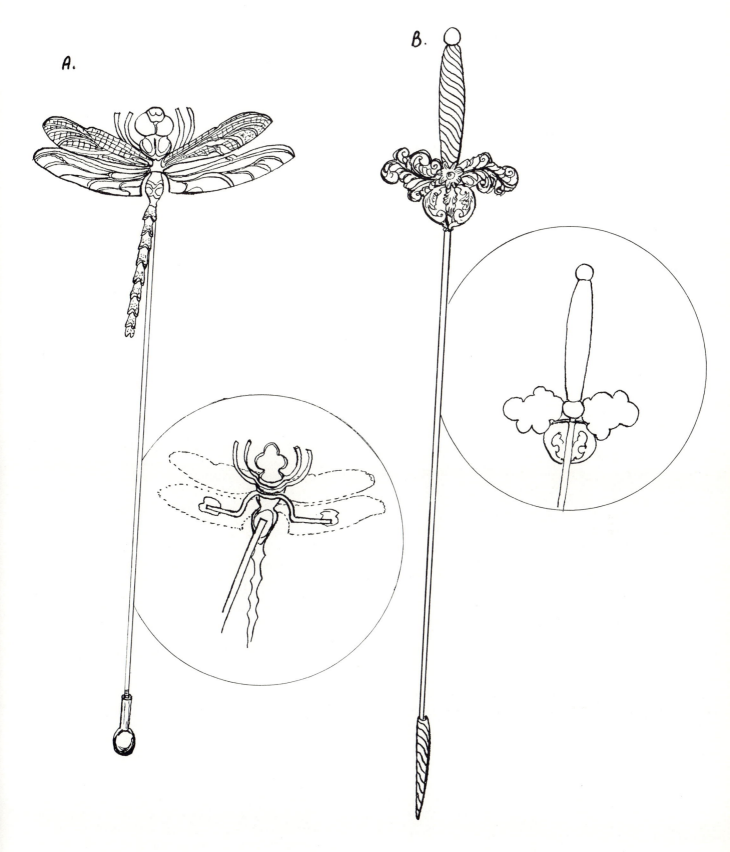

**Plate 165:** Hatpins with safety nibs or protectors.

*her hat a dangerous implement like a hatpin, without a guard, and injures some one with it, she is clearly liable for the injury she causes."*

*Such was Judge Harrington's comment at Wadsworth County Court yesterday, awarding Mrs. Charlotte Osborne of Barnes $15 damages for a wound in the cheek, said to have been caused by a hatpin worn by Miss Olive Smith, an East Sheen typist, while the two women were boarding an omnibus.*

*Answering the Judge, Mrs. Osborne said that the pin projected 2½ inches beyond the hat. Miss Smith denied that the point was sticking out beyond the hat.*

*Judge: — "You agree that a hatpin is dangerous unless it is protected?" "Certainly" (reply)*

*Judge: — "And you are wearing an unprotected hatpin now?" (Reply) "Yes."*

*Judge: — "Why don't you get a guard for it?" (Reply) "I have had dozens but they come off."*

*His Honor said it was unnecessary to prove any other negligence than the wearing of a hatpin without a guard, and awarded the plaintiff $15 damages.*

*By-laws prohibiting the use of unprotected hatpins have been adopted in Berlin, Vienna, Hamburg, Munich, Lyons, Nantes, and in towns in Switzerland and Sweden.*

\* \* \*

It's interesting to note that although there was actually no *ordinance* in London, it was in a London courtroom that the law was enforced in the most meaningful way — where it hurt most — in the pocketbook.

Surely an imposed fine caused more women to wear protectors on the ends of hatpins than had any simple ordinance on the books. The pocketbook, it seems, is more personal than the book of law.

A bit of wry amusement comes in a November 1913 report from the Paris Prefect of Police, M. Hennion, whose edicts regarding the hatpin have already appeared earlier in this book.

Although he was concerned with the danger of hatpins, he was more interested in the personal appearance of his Parisian policeman than with women's fashionable headgear. The reissuance of military-type hats for officers *"made a big hit with the force"* and seemed to give them the necessary *"bearing"* needed to confront women with hatpins protruding from fashion-dictated chapeaux.

The *"return to the dignified and impressive helmet"* for Parisian policemen, could have been partially instigated by the hatpin, for *"ever since the introduction of the kepi the police have complained that they had no protection against heavy missiles, and also that its appearance robbed them of all dignified and military character."*

It could have been quite possible, even highly probable, that they also feared the pointed *missile* of the period hatpin, and like the New Orleans "men in blue", may have felt better about approaching the women of Paris with ample protection against protruding "weapons".

Finally, on Dec. 8, 1913, our Prefect of Police Hennion lost all patience with the women of Paris when he introduced an anti-hatpin ordinance more strict than ever before:

*New York Times*, Tuesday, Dec. 9, 1913:

*An ordinance making it a misdemeanor for women to wear hatpins with unprotected points while in street cars, omnibuses, subway trains, theatres, expositions, or any public place likely to be crowded was issued today by Prefect of Police Hennion.*

*The blinding of several persons and many other serious accidents due to hatpins reported recently caused the Prefect to take this step.*

\* \* \*

It's ironic that in this very same newspaper, indeed on the very same page, should appear the announcement of a "Safety Show Opening;" but no mention of proposals on the hatpin danger by the visiting government and municipal delegates from European and American cities and *"business, scientific and professional men directly interested in railroad and city matters and safety appliances."*

In trying to determine how many states adopted laws regulating the size and use of hatpins, I wrote to the United States Library of Congress, directing my questions to the Law Library. It's most interesting, (and frustrating to the researcher), to note their reply:

*"This is in further reference to your letter of May 28, 1968, which was forwarded to the American-British Law Division to determine whether there have been State laws regulating the size and use of period hatpins.*

*"Our research has failed to reveal the present or past existence of any such laws, either criminal or civil, the latter presumably relating to public safety.*

*"Lawyer's Reports, Annotated, (New Series, Book 21), The Lawyers Co-operative Publishing Company, Rochester, New York, 1909 (consisting of reports of the various state courts for that era, with detailed annotations and encyclopedic treatments of related topics) discusses, at page 497, weapons which may be considered deadly under the law of homicide and assault. There is a comprehensive list of weapons which may be considered deadly per se and of others (such as whips, axe handles, pen knives, etc.) which, owing to their use, become deadly.* **Hat pins are listed in neither category."**

From my own research in the *Jeweler's Circular Weekly* of that same infamous year of the hatpin, 1913, comes this contrary tidbit of information which somehow challenges the above:

*"Massachusetts Legislature Passes Hatpin Law. Attleboro, Mass., March 24. — The much talked of Massachusetts Hatpin Bill, having been passed by both branches of the state legislature and signed by Governor Foss, has become a law and will go into effect on April 12. In view of the wide comment caused by this legislation, a verbatim copy of the bill as enacted, no doubt, will prove interesting:*

*"SECTION 1. It shall be unlawful for any person to wear in public a hatpin which projects more than one-half inch beyond the crown of the hat, unless the point thereof is protected in such a manner as to be incapable of causing injury to others.*

*"SECTION 2. Violation of the provisions of this act shall be punished by a fine of not more than $100 for each offense."*

Continuing the subject quoted from *Jeweler's Circular Weekly* which celebrated its centennial (1869-1969):

*"Attleboro manufacturers have been characteristically prompt to devise guards of various designs which will enable the users to comply with the new law, and already many of them are on sale and widely advertised, especially in Boston. Some of these guards are of designs similar to the heads of hatpins already in stock and others are of contrasting style. The logical effect of the law, if enforced, will be to increase the business of the jewelry concerns munufacturing hatpins.*

*"As to the enforcement of the law, Chief of Police Wilbur, of Attleboro, when asked for a statement, said, 'I, myself, think the law is a good one, as on many occasions I have seen persons injured, accidently, of course, by means of long hatpins protruding from ladies' hats. I will issue orders to have the law strictly enforced in Attleboro. I believe the women of Attleboro are heartily in sympathy with the law and will strive to help the officers to enforce it.' "*

\* \* \*

The advice reaching me via the Citizens' Aid Bureau of the Commonwealth of Massachusetts, Department of the Attorney General, is that it wasn't until 1962 that the above statute was repealed by the Massachusetts legislature!

Perhaps today's women will purchase hatpins in order to "arm themselves," for as our Los Angeles female jurist so aptly stated, *"such a weapon, worn on a hat or sleeve, probably would not be construed as a concealed weapon in court."* And, since "the comprehensive list of weapons which may be considered deadly" EXCLUDES hatpins, it may be safe to assume that although the hatpin has lost its primary function, it has not ceased to be a lethal weapon at woman's disposal.

Of course, to the collector, the hatpin has not ceased to be an ornament of beauty and I suggest that it be preserved as an artifact and discarded as a weapon.

Seems such a suggestion is fruitless in light of the reported activities in Minneapolis and considering that as recently as *Jan. 7, 1953,* C. L. Sulzberger's *A Long Row of Candles* reveals:

*"The women who rioted in Bechuanaland over the Secretse Khama difficulty used hatpins as weapons and it was most effective. Hatpins have gone up in price tremendously and you can't buy one anywhere."*

Perhaps this charming and witty response to my letter of query is an apt and somewhat whimsical ending to this chapter:

*"Dear Mrs. Baker,*

*We received your letter requesting information on the manufacturing background of domestic hatpins.*

*We regret that we can supply no information on hatpins. It may be difficult for a layman to believe, but we have no idea as to what items our firm manufactured in the 1920's. This is due to a change in ownership and management over the years. In addition, we are required to maintain so many varied records of a bookkeeping nature, that we tend to discard our records not required by law.*

*In an industry where there is constant change, and each season and each year a new challenge, artistic records are of little value. Presumably, we would like to forget our mistakes in this regard, and our successes should be reflected in our bank account.*

*Alas, I do not want this reply to be of no value whatever.* **I do seem to recall that hatpins had a secondary function. That is, as an instrument of defense for the poor 'working girl'.** *We regret that we could not be more helpful.*

(signed) Peter Kougasian
Brown & Mill Corporation

---

**"Well, you know the old saying —
walk softly and carry a long hatpin . . ."**
( *THE YEAR OF THE HORSE*, Eric Hatch)

(September 17, 1970)

"There goes their gimcrack six per cent guideline again . . . "

(November 6, 1970)

"I'll certainly be glad when the mayoralty campaign for law and order gets under way officially."

**Plate 201**

(October 23, 1969)

"I'd like half a pound of anything you have that doesn't contain tars, resins, pesticide residues, polysupersaturated fats, artificial sweeteners, softeners, foaming agents or chemical additives . . ."

(November 18, 1970)

"It's no doubt m'stays . . . and for your information, nothing to get excited about."

**Plate 201**

(September 30, 1969)

"Well, now we're students . . . I can feel a wave of revolutionary dissent already."

(January 22, 1974)

"My parents had the power to drive out demons . . . they called it a razor strap."

**Plate 201**

48

# ADDENDUM TO CHAPTER III

On Oct. 14, 1968, I wrote to the District Attorney's office in the City of New Orleans hoping to pinpoint a hatpin ordinance which was reported in the *New York Times*, Sunday, May 11, 1913.

My letter was handled by the Supt. of Police in New Orleans, who in turn requested help from the Office of the City Attorney. The report from the Office of the City Attorney was negative — *"No City Ordinances relative to regulating size and wearing of hatpins by women."*

I believed the case closed and reported as such in my manuscript. That was 1968.

Five years later, while still researching and adding material to my book, a set of circumstances enabled me to reopen the case of the New Orleans' ordinance which I knew had to be on the books, else why the abovementioned report in the reliable *New York Times*? (Or should I not believe everything I read?)

The situation changed to the extent that where a former D.A. and City Attorney had failed, (both men, by the way), a 1974 newly appointed Assistant City Attorney, Parish of Orleans, (Louisiana), namely, Anita Connick, had enough interest in my project to pursue my query with grand success! (I'm sure that the fact she is my sister helped!) In any event, the reader may now be informed as a point of interest, that Article 64 of the Louisiana Criminal Code defines armed robbery as *"theft of anything of value . . . by use of force of intimidation, while armed with a dangerous weapon."* After words and words of *"explanation of charges,"* the judge *"charges the jury"* in such cases, that the term *"dangerous weapon"* includes such articles as a firearm, an iron bolt, an axe, a pocket knife, etc., etc., and **"a hatpin"** as one of many objects which *"might be each a dangerous weapon — depending upon the manner used and whether, as used, the object might be calculated or likely to produce death or great bodily harm."*

The term "manner used" does not necessarily mean that it must have been used to cause either death or great bodily harm. "Manner used," as defined by law, means the manner in which the object might have been used to commit the armed robbery, that is by force or intimidation.

Getting down to specifics, there *is* an ordinance which was approved March 11th, 1913, at New Orleans' City Hall:

*Mayoralty of New Orleans, City Hall, March 12th, 1913:*
*No. 250 Commission Council Series*
*Calendar No. 237.*
*An ORDINANCE prohibiting the wearing of hatpins with points exposed, and providing penalties for violation thereof.*

*Section 1. Be It Ordained by the Commission Council of the City of New Orleans, That no person, while on the public streets or ways of the city, or while riding upon any street car running from place to place within the city, or in any store, or in any theater, or in any elevator operated in any building in the city or in any other place where the public may assemble, shall wear any hatpin the point of which shall extend outside of the hat through which it passes, unless the point of such hatpin is so covered that there will be no danger of its coming in contact with any other person.*

*Section 2. Be It Further Ordained, etc. That any person violating the provisions of section one of this ordinance shall be deemed guilty of a misdemeanor and upon conviction thereof shall be fined not less than one dollar or more than ten dollars or imprisonment for not less than six hours or more than five days, at the discretion of the court having proper jurisdiction.*

*Section 3. Be It Further Ordained, etc., That all ordinances or parts of ordinances in conflict with the provisions of this ordinance be and the same are hereby repealed.*

*Adopted by the Commission Council of the City of New Orleans, March 11th, 1913.*
*George Ferrier, Jr., Clerk of Commission Council.*
*Approved March 11th, 1913.*
*Martin Behrman, Mayor*

\* \* \*

The *New York Times* reported the fracas in New Orleans three months after the Ordinance passed; the *Daily Picayune, New Orleans*, newspaper allowed a full year and three days before it again grappled with the situation. The newspaper story is a rather poetic and "Southern Gentleman" bit of gallantry, appearing in print on March 25, 1914:

*Headline:* **DON'T GO ABOUT**
**WITH HAT PIN OUT**
*A Law's a Law, and Come to Taw\**
**POLICE MUST OBEY**
*Acquiescence the Only Way, and*
*Defiants Suffered Yesterday.*

*\*According to Webster: "prepare for use"*

*After lying dormant for several months the hat-pin ordinance was brought forth and the attention of the Canal Street squad called to violations which it was alleged, had been committed recently.*

*Superintendent Reynolds received a letter the other day from a gentleman who wanted to know what had become of the ordinance, that no violations had been heard of for some time past. Following closely upon this came a complaint from a lady, who said that she had received a reminder that the hatpin ordinance was a thing of the past by having one of the dangerous instruments stuck into her face in a department store.*

*Yesterday the Canal Street squad got busy, and Corporal Casey, who has been keeping quiet since Mardi Gras, loomed up again. One arrest and nine affidavits were made, and this is only the beginning.*

*Mrs. Agnes Bailey, residing at No. 3315 De Soto, was the party arrested, and Judge Fogarty decided not to try her case singly, but to wait for the parties against whom affidavits had been made. The names of those charged with violating the law were:\**

*Up to noon yesterday no affidavits had been made in the Second Recorder's Court, but Judge Gauthreau was holding himself in readiness. The police are conducting the crusade in the same manner in which they commenced, that is, by simply taking the names and addresses of the ladies violating the ordinance and then making affidavits."*

I must again remind the reader that the purpose of using actual stories, without editing, is to provide a true taste of the past regarding the history of hatpins, as well as preserving that inimitable "dated" type of reporting which is so far afield of today's media. It's as important to preserve this form of writing as well as the hatpin, for both are historic and noteworthy. Both are priceless!

Continuing the news:
THE DAILY PICAYUNE (Mar. 25, 1914):
  Sub-headline: HARD TO BE A COP—
    When Tearful Maids You Have to
    Summarily Stop
*. . . the officer gritted his teeth, swallowed his rising heart and said:*
    *"Give me your name, please, Miss."*
*And then he scribbled it in his book. Officer Gordon and Officer Hamilton didn't retreat then. They just took off their chapeaux, and two handsome bachelor officers of Corporal Casey's traffic squad did what any other gentlemen would have done:*
    *"Au revoir, Miss."*
*Last evening when the day's work was done, Offi-*

*cer Hamilton and Officer Gordon said it had been a strenuous day. Besides keeping traffic going through the busiest section of the busiest city in the South, they enforced the Era Club hatpin ordinance. To be exact, they enforced it four times, and four affidavits were filed at the close of the day.*

\* \* \*

When the Ordinance was newborn, *The Daily Picayune* played wet-nurse for the first few months, reporting on April 3, 1913:

*HATPIN LAW CLAIMS FIRST VICTIMS HERE — Half a Dozen Affidavits Against Ladies Who Ought to Know the Law — Campaign Starts Rush for Point Protectors — Police Polite, But Don't Like the Job.*

*Fair feminity was thrown into sorrow and consternation by the initial enforcement of the Newman hatpin ordinance in this city yesterday. Scores of women were intercepted by the police on Canal Street and warned that the hatpins protruding from their hats were in violation of the law. Affidavits were made out against six women, and it is expected that another affidavit will be made out to-day. Those who stand charged with violating the law which prohibits the wearing of long, unprotected hatpins included several who are prominent in social circles. Their cases, it was declared yesterday, will come up for hearing next week, and in the meantime a lookout will be kept for further violators of the ordinance. Corporal Eugene Casey and Patrolman Dominick Claverie were the officers who during the morning warned the women who displayed hatpins of excessive length, and in the afternoon Patrolman Joseph Hadley, the giant of the force, assisted Corporal Casey in warning offenders.*

### *CASEY CHESTERFIELDIAN*

*Excitement prevailed early in the afternoon, while the officers were informing women shoppers, when it became known that the supplies of hatpin shields in various department stores had been depleted by the rush of the morning. Many women, rather than brook a second warning from the officers, removed their hats altogether and returned to their homes bare of head. Several of those accosted were inclined to treat the remarks of the police as a joke, but to some they appeared all too serious. One of those to whom the situation seemed anything but ludicrous was stopped at Carondelet and Canal Street by Corporal Casey, who, by the way, displayed the qualities of a master tactician in carrying out the orders of Superintendent of Police Reynolds.*

---

*\*Ten names and addresses are given, involving affidavits by two policemen.*

*\*If the reader will excuse the pun, seems to be a case of Casey at the hat!*

"Pardon me, madam," said Corporal Casey, in Chesterfieldian* tones, as he raised his hat. "I am sorry to detain you, but I must inform you of the fact that you are violating the law by wearing such long, unprotected hatpins."

The woman smiled, as if to question the corporal's right to denounce the moorings of her hat.

"I am not joking," continued Corporal Casey.

Again did the woman smile the smile that challenges and accentuates man's impotence in verbal battles.

"If I had a protector with me you would not dare to talk to me like that," she remonstrated.

"That's just it," retorted Corporal Casey. "They are selling them for 10 cents apiece in all of the stores around here. Shall I take your name or would you rather buy a hatpin protector?"

Far down the street sounded the raucous clang of the patrol wagon enroute to headquarters with its quota of drunks. The woman mistook the meaning of the sound, and, as the thought of riding through the street in the patrol wagon surged to her mind, picked up her skirts and sought the jewelry counter of the nearest store. A few moments later she emerged smiling, with the points of her hatpins covered with the small, life-preserving protectors.

Will the reader note that the protective ends for the pinpoint have now been called: "nibs", "protectors", "jargownibs", "guards", and "shields", and the introduction of these point-protectors brought artists and inventors to their drawing boards. It's ironic, or so it seems, that the nibs were first shaped like inch-to-the-foot miniature bullets; as if an omen, in 1914 these ominous shapes grew into powderkegs — all hardly a year away from the hatpin headlines!

But now about THE FIRST VICTIM under the hatpin ordinance:

The first lady who was stopped and warned yesterday, (April 3, 1913), was Miss Edna Isichtenstein, of No. 3601 Carondelet Street. Corporal Casey and Patrolman Clayerie approached her at 9:15 o'clock in the morning, at the corner of Carondelet and Canal Streets. She betrayed no resentment because of the warning, and, after her name had been taken, was allowed to proceed upon her way.

Others against whom affidavits were filed during the day were: Miss Mabel Dwyer, of . . . daughter of W. H. Dwyer, president of the Dwyer Piano Company; Mrs. E. M. Miller, . . . president and treasurer of the Liberty Shop on Canal Street; Mrs. Annette Deloech, . . .; Mrs. J. H. Hynson, . . . wife of the deputy United States collector of revenue; Mrs. A. J. Hauser . . .

Corporal Casey said that he expected to make an affidavit to-day against Mrs. A. H. Page, wife of the treasurer and general manager of the Arthur H.

Page Company, steamship agents and ship brokers.

Mrs. Page, according to Corporal Casey, was the only woman who showed any unusual resentment because of receiving the warning. She is alleged to have said that she "would rather take the pin out altogether than be stopped or accosted on the street."

One of Mrs. Page's daughters, in speaking of her mother's experience, said last evening:

"My mother, who is ill to-night, was on her way to the office of a physician yesterday when she was stopped. With her at the time was my 16-year-old sister, who has just recovered from typhoid fever. I was not with them, but I know that the pins in mother's hat did not stick out more than half an inch. There were lots of other women whose pins protruded farther, but it seems that the officers only stopped those whom they noticed were well-dressed and wore a few diamonds."

Mrs. J. B. Parker, president of the Era Club, which was instrumental in bringing about the passage of the ordinance, last evening said:

"I am sorry that any of the ladies were annoyed, but they must have known of the ordinance. Women must be subject to the same laws as are men."*

### ERA CLUB'S COMMENT

Superintendent Reynolds in speaking of the crusade against the hatpin, declared he believed the publication of photographs of violators of the Newman law, would be a good thing.

Evidence of the consternation that ensued from the warning to the first women is the fact that the supply of hatpin protectors in the large department stores was exhausted before noon. Miss Julia Doyle, head of the jewelry department of the D. H. Holmes Company, said that more than a gross of the protectors had been sold. "Our stock of them has been sold out as the result of the first enforcement of the ordinance, but we expect another supply of them tomorrow."

Others also sold out their supplies of protectors, while a great many other stores were taxed to the limit in shortening long hatpins which terror-stricken women brought to them for that purpose.

Corporal Casey said yesterday afternoon that he had experienced but little trouble in performing the duties entrusted to him. "Most of the women I have stopped," said he, "have expressed an ignorance of the ordinance but a desire to comply with it. Nearly all of them promised to procure protectors for their hatpins. I have taken the names of only those who it seems should already be aware of the law. Most of them listened to me good-naturedly, but it certainly requires tact, this work of stopping women and criticizing their hatpins."

---

*18th Century Earl of Chesterfield, "the perfect gentleman."

*All seemingly equal under the law. Shades of ERA already casting its shadow!

*Patrolman Joseph Hadley, who is six feet and three inches tall and who weighs 253 pounds, was strong in declaring that the work of watching for offenders of the Newman law was distasteful to him. Late in the afternoon he assisted Corporal Casey, and scores of people smiled as they looked at the giant whose eyes were focused on the foliage and shrubbery of the "latest creations" as they passed.*

*"I think the women are beginning to realize that the ordinance is no joke," he said. "I'd like to have you understand, though, that it's no joke to watch for those shining points in the middle of a bunch of ribbons and things and then approach the owners and warn them."*

*Referring to the hatpin ordinance, Patrolman Hadley was quoted as saying, "It's a good law, nevertheless . . ."*

However, the final paragraph in the news report is a real clincher! It seems that Officer Hadley would like another law passed against the wearing of "Catch-a-Mike" skirts.

*"I mean,"* explained the bear-of-a-man-in-officer's-clothing, *"these skirts that they're wearing that look like bathrobes and have a little ribbon tied around them. When a girl has one of those things on she looks as though she had just got out of the bathtub. I call 'em 'Catch-a-Mike' skirts 'cause they seem to wear them for the express purpose of catching a Mike."*

Burley Patrolman Hadley enforced his point by *". . . following the excitement on Canal Street,"* and arresting Henrietta Harnes, a washerwoman. The "Catch-a-Mike" skirt-wearer was sent to jail, but was later paroled. *"She will have to answer to court charges,"* said the report.

The arrest of a washerwoman, the police declared, *"refutes the report that the campaign"* (hatpin enforcement), *"is being prosecuted against moneyed people only."* Whether the "Catch-a-Mike" gal was wearing a hat, is unknown.

\* \* \*

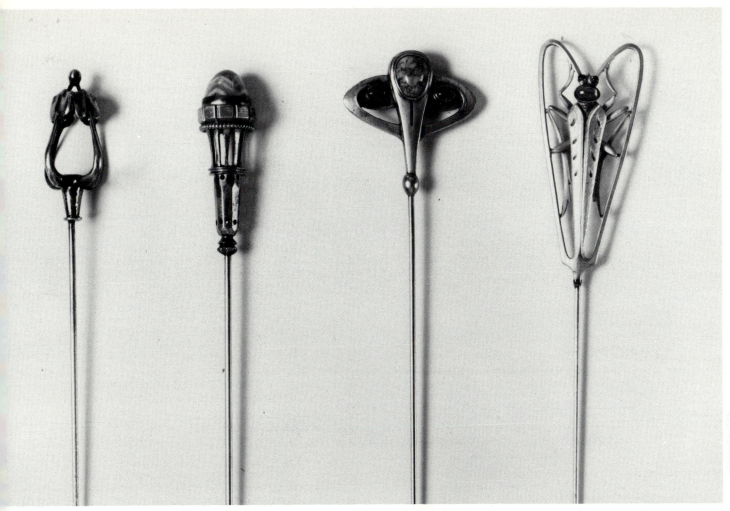

**Plate 204**

which I prefer not to look too carefully detailed but intangible. Then in the execution, the part that I enjoy most, is like a bird building a nest, to discover the materials and devise the ways of putting the pieces together — to realize as near as possible the effect that I have drawn. The affection and enthusiasm shown to me by the whole team of brilliant fitters and laborers at Western Costume Co., however hard the work was, made the time there unforgettable to me. With best wishes and success for your book

(signed) Oliver Messel

"P.S. In another play I dressed Jean Anhouie's 'Le Voyageur sans Bagage,' the hatpin featured as a weapon. The scar of the hatpin scratch on his right shoulder being the clue to the identify of the victim of amnesia."

Martin Shwartz, Press Representative, Los Angeles' Civic Light Opera Co., traveled East with the touring company of "Gigi." As "shepherd" for the show, he was close to many of the featured players. Mr. Shwartz had great admiration for actress Moorehead, not only for her recognized talent but because she was "so professional."

Mr. Shwartz told me:

"Miss Moorehead would be five minutes early for her cue, waiting in the wings," he said to me during

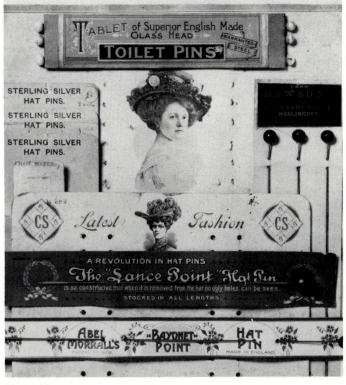

**Plate 166**

57

**Plate 146:** Agnes Moorehead as Aunt Alicia in "Gigi"; Los Angeles Civic Light Opera Production, 1973. Photo taken by Eric Skipsey.

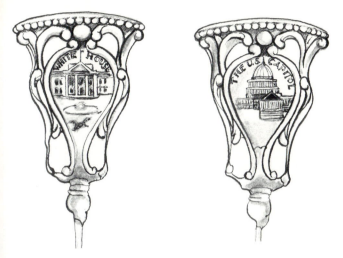

**Plate 190**

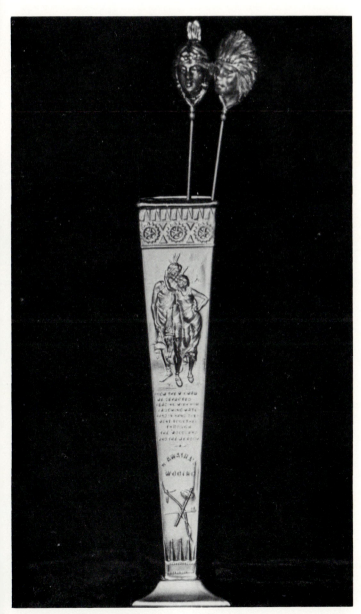

**Plate 28.** Photograph by Charlie Ferrell

a telephone conversation. *"And it was in Detroit, while waiting to go on stage, that a long rope with a pulley — which was supposed to be secure — broke loose from its mooring and like a huge pendulum swung free striking Miss Moorehead with enough force to knock her off her chair. The blow struck the side of her head, but fortunately the huge amount of fabric in the hat, the wig and padding underneath, softened the blow. Although the hat and wig were askew, Agnes made her grand entrance with a stout 'the show must go on' attack at her role. Later, she merely complained of a slight headache."*

The elegant hat designed by Oliver Messel, which provided the buffer against a cracked skull, is shown on Plate 146. Mr. Messel's suggestion about the Los Angeles Civic Light Opera contact for pictures, led me to the head of Press and Public Relations, Mr. Martin Shwartz — who related the aforementioned anecdote — and who also arranged for Eric Skipsey's impressive photograph of Miss Agnes Moorehead. (Plate 146.)

It's also to be noted, that Western Costume Company provided me — as with Mr. Messel — a most happy experience, with their cooperation and eagerness to be of service! Drawings of a partial section of their collection of hatpins and hat ornaments appears on Plate 178.

Meanwhile I scooted to the library for *"Le Voyageur sans Bagage,"* the play translated by Lucienne Hill as *"Traveller Without Luggage."* It appears in *Vol. I., Jean Anouilh — "The Collected Plays,"* (Methuen & Co., Ltd., 1969); but in fairness to my readers, I won't give away the plot which involves the all-important hatpin. Read it for yourself! It's fascinating and thought provoking.

It is misleading when some writers report that the hatpin was invented to "hold the hat onto the high-piled pompadour hair styles," for the pompadour preceded the Victorian and Gibson Girl hair-play.

The true pompadour hair style of its era was decorated with jewels, flowers, fan-fare and elaborate hair decorations including fancy lace-caps. Caps were, indeed, the forerunners of the woman's hat, but the first hat (which was of felt), wasn't introduced in America until 1851. No doubt there were earlier examples of hats on the Continent, since fashion dictates came from European shores to American shores. Prior to the introduction of hats, women were "confined" with their heads in bonnets securely tied under the chin.

As previously pointed out, the early lace or small caps of silk were likely held on the head with wire pins or veil pins. Pins for pinning caps and small hair and head creations were hand-made in Elizabethan times and were merely thin wires, cut, pointed, and headed.

Because the pin-machine had not yet been invented during the ill-fated reign of Louis XVI's Queen of France, Marie Antoinette, her famed caps and bonnets trimmed with yards and yards of pearls and veiling were kept in place with the delicate *hand-made*, short, wire hairpins and double-pronged veil pins. These were worn in such great numbers that the closely pinned hair ornaments looked and sparkled like the heavens on a crisp, clear, Christmas Eve.

The Gainsborough hat which made its debut in England at the same period, was enormous in size, but it had a deep

# fig.1

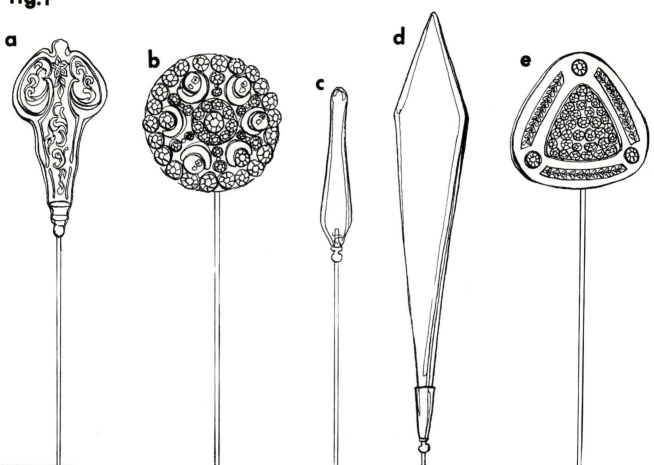

a b c d e

# fig. 2

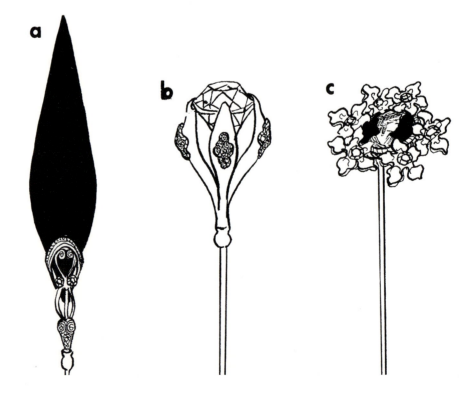

a b c

Plate 178

60

crown which nestled snugly against the closely worn hairstyle of the English lady. Ribbons or elastic helped secure it in place; but especially ribbons, as seen in the famous Gainsborough painting titled "Pinky." It may be correct to call hats of the Gay Nineties "Gainsborough-size," but the actual Gainsborough hat definitely pre-dated the machine-made period hatpin.

MANUFACTURED pins and long hatpins did not invade the fashion scene until after 1832. The pins prior to that time, pins used for pinning wimples, hennens, lace-caps, and other head-coverings for women, resembled today's common straight pins rather than hatpins.

Authorities on costume and headdress often differ as to the dating of the first hatpins. Bill Severn wrote: ". . . *Long hatpins, especially made for the purpose of holding in place large summer straw hats with drooping brims, first came into use in the 1850s. They were soon followed by jeweled-topped hatpins to replace the long ties of ribbon that had been used to hold women's hats on their heads . . . pins often stuck out several inches beyond the hat brim.*"

The "large summer straw hats with drooping brims" may well have been designed after the Gainsborough hat (named for the 18th century painter), but the great difference was that the 19th century "summer hat" was set atop a new hairstyle which required cotton batting, wires, and false hair to make them into "towering tresses." Atop this mass set the chapeau, pinned on with the necessary equipment of 19th century manufactured anchorage which secured all to the head. Many of the horsehair cushions or "rats" were quite heavy, as were the cotton or wool "foundations" on which the hair was built up to be fashionable.

Many hatpins were required to keep these extra additions pinned to the head. Before *manufactured* wire-pins, handmade hair pins were so expensive, ladies kept their hair in place with a sort of gum or mucilage. The bourgeoise used a paste made of dust of rotten oak, and the peasant used flour.

Although bent wire hair pins were known as early as the 16th century, they were hand-wrought and terribly expensive — as were the hatpins before the advent of the pin-making machine. As if fated to be joined, manufactured pins and artificial flowers was perfected at the same time and commercialized in France by the dressmakers and milliners who saw a good thing when they "sewed" it! Thus, as hats came into their own, they were bedecked with a wide range of flowers and brash ornaments. With the advent of commercial enterprise an electrifying progression for the betterment of women emerged on the fashion front.

The period hatpin really challenged man's ingenuity, for women demanded an ever-increasing variety in shapes, sizes and settings. Name the media and it has been used in the making of hatpins!

Who met this challenge? How was it met? Let's touch upon this wide field of endeavor.

In America there was Louis C. Tiffany of New York, William J. Codman of Providence, and the American "clique" comprised of James T. Wooley, (formerly of England), Barton P. Jenks, and George C. Gebelein. These were craftsmen who primarily worked in metals. They yielded the field of *glass-headed* hatpins to the famous New Jersey, Ohio, and Massachusetts, factories producing Victorian glassware and buttons.

In 1878, Louis Comfort Tiffany, son of a well-known jeweler, established C. Tiffany Company which in 1892 expanded Tiffany Glass and Decorating Co. His firm catered to wealthy clientele whose tastes demanded Victorian baroque elegance. There were, no doubt, a few daring society darlings who were intrigued with deviations in the jewelry line, but they were few enough so that Tiffany is not too well represented in the up-and-coming *Art Nouveau* movement — except in his glass-wares. It is here that Tiffany excelled and left his permanent mark in the decorative field.

From 1900 to 1936, Tiffany Studios of New York — which was merely a continuation of the older firm of Tiffany and Co., — produced lovely hatpins which often lacked the traditional signature found on his lovely glassware. Some hatpins are simply marked "Tiffany," but some can be recognized and attributed to *L. C. Tiffany.*

An exhibition at Boston, Mass., (1897), brought about a swift change and rapid public demand for *Art Nouveau* designed hatpins and most of these were in silver.

The American silver companies which were major manufacturers of such hatpins for the masses were Unger Bros., (Newark, N.J.); The Sterling Company and Alvin Manufacturing Co., (Providence, R.I.); and R. Blackinton & Co., of one of the major jewelry center in America, (North Attleboro, Mass.).

Other American companies included, J. E. Caldwell & Co., (Philadelphia); F. M. Whiting & Co., (N. Attleboro, Mass.); William B. Kerr & Co., (Newark, N.J.); R. Wallace & Sons, (Providence, R.I.); Reed & Barton, (Providence, R.I.); and Hyatt Brothers, (Newark). Hyatt Brothers were exponents of the wonderful Art Deco celluloid hatpins. Woodside Sterling and Mauser Manufacturing companies of America's major jewelry metropolis, New York, were also major manufacturers of hatpins.

From F. H. Noble & Co., Chicago, (founded 1876), came the necessary jeweler's findings which were utilized by the manufacturers of hatpins heads, for the individual craftsmen were concerned with the artistic merit of the *ornament* and not with the utilitarian findings which secured the ornaments to the varied lengths of pin-wire. The findings were manufactured as a component part and many pin manufacturing firms in Providence and Attleboro still make these findings today. Their listings in the "yellow pages" reads like some historical document.

Most hatpins by the above manufacturers were of the popular *Art Nouveau* and Art Deco styles of the 1890-1920 era. Many of the hatpins were ordered through jewelers' catalogues or through the popular Montgomery, Ward & Co., and Sears, Roebuck and Co.; these latter catalogues did not feature domestic stock but rather advertised "imported Parisian" merchandise — no doubt because of the "snob-appeal" prevalent *then* as well as today. "American-made" still takes a back-seat to the "imports" — unfortunately!

The major American centers for custom-made jewelry were New York City, Providence, R.I., Philadelphia, Pa., and both North Attleboro and Attleboro, Mass. But archives reveal very little, as do company records, regarding hatpin manufacture.

But we can piece together some half-lucid image of the hatpin era with these conjectures:

The flamboyant hatpin period certainly began by 1890 and it was but five years later (1895) that the *Art Nouveau* influence in design was seen in decoratives which included hair

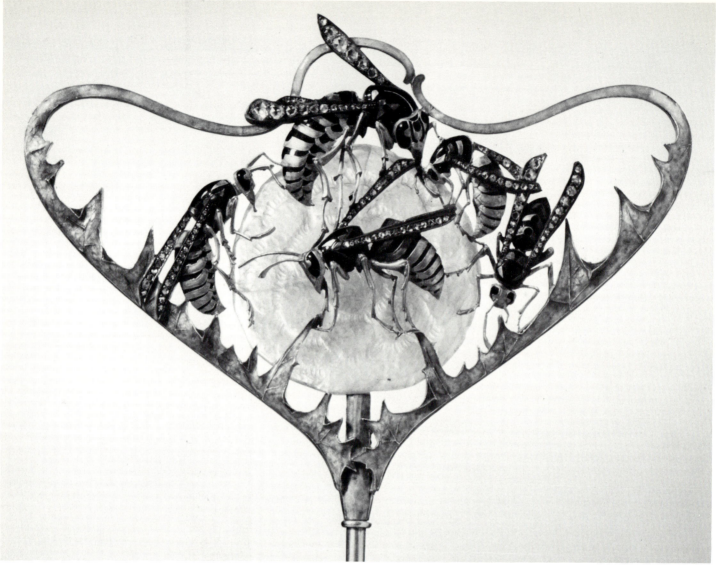

**Plate 167**

ornaments and the hatpin.

*Art Nouveau* reached its height by 1900, being pushed from the scene with the advent of worldwide social and political upheaval. But this brief encounter with such giants as America's Louis Comfort Tiffany, Austria's Gustave Limpt, Belgium's Velde and Horta, England's C. R. Ashbee and William Morris, and the mammoth genius of them all, Reneé Lalique of France, left an impression which is just recently being felt and appreciated by both professional and layman alike.

It was the *Art Nouveau* period which produced the finest examples of hatpin ornaments. Millinery "madness" required multiples of hatpins with the longest stems for sumptuous hats not since matched for millinery perfection.

Who were these intrepid artists and designers who gave hatpin collectors their prized tableau of Art Nouveau hatpins?

They were not the artists who *began* their craft in this famed period, but those who had joined with its founders and innovators: Charles Robert Ashbee of Britain and his countryman, William Morris. The birthplace of *Art Nouveau* was their arts and crafts center — the 1888 School of Handicraft — which in turn bore the influence of Walter Crane (1880), John Ruskin, his contemporary, and the mark of that unpredictable virtuoso of pen-and-ink, Aubrey Beardsley.

"*The Studio*" magazine, London's monthly, (1893 into 20th Century), was greatly responsible for the public acceptance of *Art Nouveau* design, and the influence of the artistic work pictured therein was felt on both sides of the Atlantic.

All the arts are brothers under the media, so to speak, and the natural influence of "blood-relation" cannot be denied. What is rendered on one-dimensional paper can be seen in all-dimensional jeweler's fabric of metal and stone.

Liberty & Company, Ltd., the London Department store, offered mass-produced Art Nouveau jewelry and metallic hatpins whose designs bore the influence of the custom-made craft of rare artisans. The Bohemian, German, and French glassworks produced counterparts in molded and blown creations.

At the Paris Exposition of 1900, the fantastic work of *Art Nouveau* artists from America and the Continent, were copied willy-nilly by the large jewelry houses which mass-produced articles that, I must confess, bear no resemblance to mass-production as we know it today. The mass-produced article of 1890-1920 had the finishing touch of an expert individual craftsman! The human hand and eye were the quality control factors in yesteryear products.

Although America quickly adopted the term *Art Nouveau"*

from the Parisian establishment of Siegfried Bing's "*L'Art Nouveau*" (1895), other countries had other labels:

In Austria: "*Weiner Secession*," for Weiner Werkstatten (Arts & Crafts, 1903), founded by Koloman Moser and Josef Hoffman. In other sections of Bohemia, (Czech.), it was known as "*Recession Period*," or "*Secession*."

In Germany: *Judendstil*," after the art magazine, "*Jugend*," (Youth).

In Belgium: Henri van de Velde and Victor Horta simply worked under the influence of "the movement."

In Italy: "*Stile Liberty*," named for London's Liberty & Co., department store, which as previously mentioned was the market-place for mass-produced *Art Nouveau* jewelry and hatpins.

In Spain: "*Arte Joven*," (Young Art).

It began in Britain — despite the French moniker — with Matthew Boulton's Victorian pieces being challenged by the field of *Art Nouveau* followers of Morris and Ashbee. Glasgow had Charles Rennie MacKintosh, and the Scottish and British clan were copied across the channel by Josef Hoffman of Austria, who was certainly influenced by the designs of Gustave Klimpt. Theodore van Gosen and J. M. Olbrich joined Hoffman in the trend, while Luca von Cranach and Carl Gross in the German manufacturing town of Pforzheim, (with over 1000 jewelry firms), set the standard there. Holland had Jan Toorop; Italy, V. Miranda, who was eagerly copied by manufacturers in the major jewelry center of Valenza Po.

A bit to the North in Spain was Julio Gonzales', (1910-1923), who trailed the *Art Nouveau* movement, yet reflected its effect in his designs; and to the colder North was George Jensen of Denmark, who influenced his compatriots, Johan Rohde and Eric Magnussen right on up into the Art Deco period.

Seemingly, only Russia remained on the seesaw between risque development of *Art Nouveau* and the demand of Russian nobility for the classic ornate, rococo, and baroque in jewels. This is reflected in Russia's most famous jewelry house, Carl Peter Faberge's dynasty of dimensional jewels. These fabulous creations have been pictured and historically recorded in other volumes available to the reader. But we, as hatpin collectors, are interested in the lovely enamel "little things" (hatpins) which, although unmarked, are easily recognized as works of Faberge. (Plate 206.)

Graham Hughes' "*Modern Jewelry*" is an excellent source book of designers, manufacturers, and artisans and is listed in my *Bibliography*.

Unfortunately, to date, no book has treated the greatest master of *Art Nouveau* in depth. He is Reneé Lalique of Paris, the unchallenged innovator of *Art Nouveau* jewelry. Better known for his gorgeous glass-works, Lalique — unlike Tiffany — certainly was a jeweler's idol. A Lalique hatpin is pictured on Plate 167.

Lalique has never been equaled by any other producer of *Art Nouveau* jewelry, although quite nearly matched in the jewelry of George and Jean Fouquent who so beautifully executed in precious ore the designs of Alphonse Mucha. Too, the designs of Delacherche were nobly rendered by Paul and Henri Vever, and L. Gautriant. The little-heralded Dufrene, who came up at the close of the period and on into the Art Deco influence, made superb renderings which lent themselves as prototypes for other manufacturers. The graphic designs of M. P. Verneuil and Georges Auriol were utilized by jewelers as were the designs of lesser-known artists of the period.

The influential exhibitions held in Paris (1900), and in the boutique owned by Louis Sue and Andre Mare *(Compagnie des Arts Francais, 1919),* turned the knob and opened the door to the Art Deco period. The rage in fashion, created by the discovery of King Tutankhamen's tomb in 1920, was clearly influenced by Egyptian design and motifs. *(Geschutzt* is a "trademark" found in a jet-glass mold of the Egyptian scarab — one of many versions of this insect manufactured in various colored glass.)

Thus the vogue of the twenties brought in the deluge of Art Deco, which is mathematical in design (based on the triangle, hexagon, etc.). It can easily be separated and identified from the earlier *Art Nouveau* period which was the first break-away, of the Victorian "stays" of fashion and design.

The Spinx, Pharaoh, and Cleopatra's Royal Asp, were part and parcel of the Art Deco pallette in designing fashions and hatpins. Contrast these stylized, geometric patterns with the *Art Nouveau* ornamentation of Alphonse Marie Mucha (1860-1939), Maurice Pillard Verneuil, (1869-1934), Georges Auriol (1863-1938), and Rene Lalique, (1860-1945).

The above artists, whether in glass or other media, incorporated the sinuous lines of the female figure and nature's curlicues which are found in florals. They grasped in graphics the imaginative, flighty, fanciful, ornate butterflies, birds, and creatures of fantasy-worlds. And these were produced as hatpin ornaments or decorative and functional accessories. For *Art Nouveau* is fantasy personified; Art Deco is geometrically comprised of an abstract design seemingly bizarre in motif.

Art Deco abstract invaded the realm of *Art Nouveau* fantasy about 1910, and finally conquered all interest with the opening of those Egyptian tombs and the beginning of trade-in-earnest with the Orient.

*Art Nouveau* was short-lived, (1895-1910), yet it profoundly stirred the imagination of artists in every line of endeavor. Japanese Art, beginning to come to the Continent through the recently open-door trade between East and West, generated the first spark that created the *Art Nouveau* movement. The Art Deco period, (1910-1929) was in reality an extension of *Art Nouveau* except that because of previously-mentioned factors, the designs changed from the sinuous curvilinear lines to a compromise between straight-stilted renditions and intervals of trills or frills of its parent-motif.

It was not until Art Deco reached maturity, (1920), that it completely broke away from *Art Nouveau* "apron-strings," and by 1925 Art Deco was newly named, "Art Moderne."

The latter nomenclature extended not only to jewelry and hatpins, but to all things industrial. As for the hatpin, what with bobbed hair and cloché hat the fashion, it became nothing more than an ornament which the Art Deco-ists and Modernists managed to vault into the annals of absurdities. But then 1925-1940 was an absurd age! It was much like an incubus emerging without knowing whether to crawl, walk, or fly. (So it did all three!) Examine some of the hat ornaments of the 1925-1945 era and you will have to agree!

In all fairness, Art Deco did not completely abandon the florals, fungals, insects, seaweed, billowing smoke, and other sensual motifs of the *Art Nouveau* period; rather it tamed their endless "wanderings" of curvilinear lines into strict obedience to the stylized motifs based on geometric renditions caged in borders of surreal motifs.

The conflict between machine and nature is evident everywhere in Art Deco youth and its Art Moderne maturity. There were no such confines in *Art Nouveau*, which is perhaps why it was so short-lived. It seems that anything without discipline will run wild and destroy itself by its own exhaustive free-for-all design.

But this child-like freedom, which by its very term is short-lived, is still so terribly touching in the rendition of *Art Nouveau* women with flowing locks; florals that seem moved by some invisible wind; insects that discard their biological garb

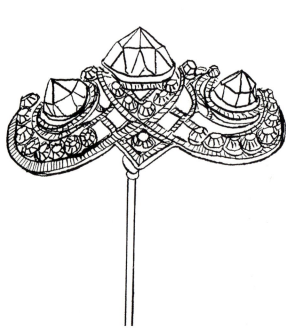

**Plate 200:** Detail of Plate 20.

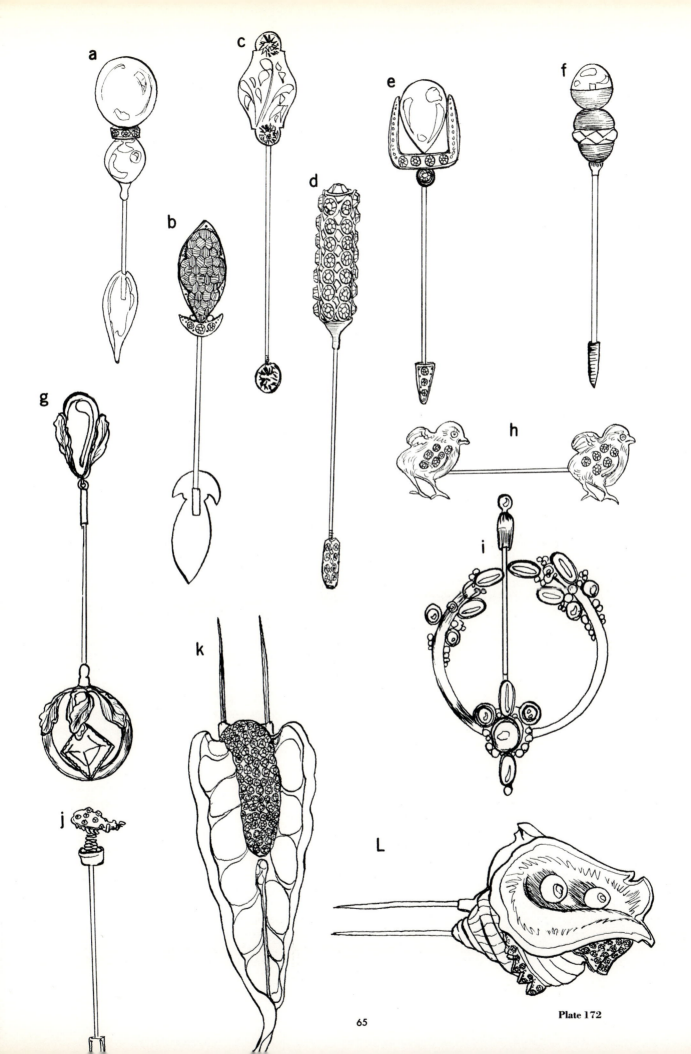

a

c

b

d

e

f

g

h

i

j

k

L

65

Plate 172

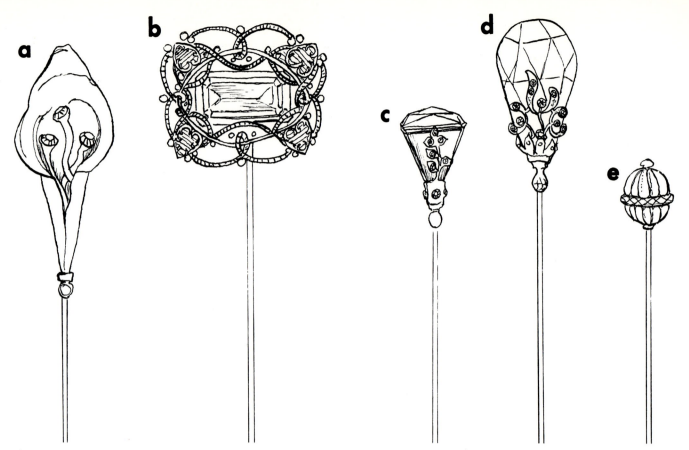

**Plate 168**

and embrace the once-scorned "inferior" gemstone or paste and combine with man-made enamels that challenge nature's ingenuity. The flames of *Art Nouveau* were bound to burn themselves out in the roar and intensity of newly ignited inspiration. Some inspired pieces are preserved for us and future generations in examples of hatpins and hat ornaments!

We have hatpins of other periods to cherish and preserve! Let us think for a moment back to the days before the advent of the motor-car, when cycling was the rage and costumes for women included those especially designed for this popular sport. There then lived a lady who had the reputation for growing the most beautiful roses. Although her name has since passed into oblivion, her talent for raising perfect roses and preserving them, has withstood the test of time.

By some secret process she preserved the bloom at the height of its beauty, when the petals were just beginning to unfold from the bud; somehow she eternized it with a secret formula which resembled gold lacquer. (See Plate 168.)

The flower was then affixed to the end of a hatpin to be worn as a decorative millinery accessory. It was a tribute to both nature and to this woman's ingenuity. I've been told that this process was once patented, but without a name or patent number, it was impossible for me to learn the secret which has since died with its inventor.

Today we have many dried flowers placed under glass away from the disintegrating effects of air, and other glycerine-treated blooms arranged in bouquets which are long-lasting. There is a chemical process, (patented *Ceramix*), which hobbyists use in preserving real flowers and corsages, but the final result differs greatly from the flower-topped hatpins. These rose-topped hatpins are unprotected, yet still remain mummi-fied on the end of a pin. Would that its scent could be thus preserved! But perhaps that's too much to ask.

Some of the most beautiful and sought after hatpins by collectors are those copied in design from antique jewelry, especially those of Roman and Greek gems. (See Plates 82, 89, and 131.) There may be slight variations from the genuine, but they are still beautiful in their own right.

Many of the settings for the gems and gemstones are baroque or tend toward the rococo of the 17th and 18th centuries, consisting of an imitation of shells, scrolls, leaves, and exaggerated florid design.

Others are neo-classic; several far advanced and more acceptable as abstract in today's evaluation of art. Others, with baton-cut stones cut in the shape of a long, narrow rectangle girdled at its lower edge by a mounting, could challenge the designs of Aubrey Beardsley and his graphic style of *Art Nouveau.*

Hatpins were often copied from the genuine gem-original-designs into elaborate heads of paste or colored glass. The colourless paste, not used until the late 19th century, was truly a substitute rather than an imitation of precious gems. These hatpins, made of non-precious materials, were much in demand to suit the prevailing fashions currently in mode. Some paste which contained a high percentage of lead could easily be mistaken for the natural diamond, especially when it was faceted with the extreme care of the expert craftsman.

This paste, or *strass*, was invented in the 18th century by a German goldsmith (jeweler) named Josef Strasser. But it was the French paste that surpassed that of other countries and the periods of Louis XV and XVI have been noted as "the golden age of paste," for it was worn by the aristocracy not so much

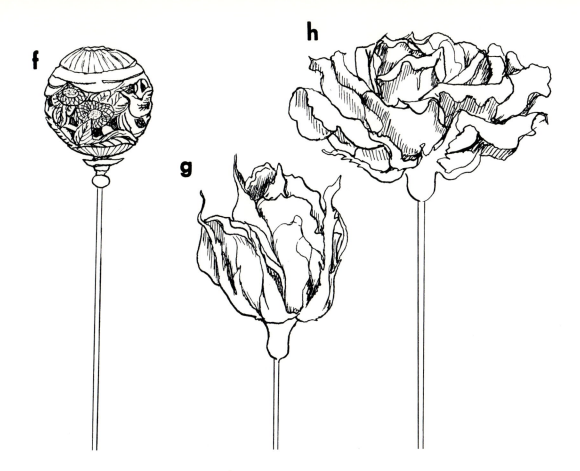

— as previously emphasized — as an imitation but as a substitute for the true gems. (Plates 21 and 23.)

Some stones in hatpins are set with bright polished foil, a thin leaf of metal placed in back of a gemstone or glass to heighten the brilliance or the color. It's sometimes difficult, unless one is an expert, to distinguish between diamonds, spinels, or paste.

Period hatpins are made with crochet ornaments, beaded heads, a braided or polished straw, woven raffia, fine needlepoint, and even hair of a loved one. The mountings are represented in geometric chased *pinchbeck*, (imitation gold, sometimes called *pom-pom*), most familiar during the early Victorian era. Then there is piercework of both delicate and daring artistry, openwork to challenge the most vivid imagination. The frivolous and the functional characterize most hatpin designs, even those of the pre-*Art Nouveau period*. (See Plates 37 and 127.)

Hatpin "gift sets," a very popular courting items of swooning swains, included paired hatpins, and matching collar and blouse studs, belt buckles, veil pins, and violet pins. (Plates 67 and 94).

The sea provided the abalone pearl in its familiar blister shape and startling iridescence, and the opalescent inner shell of pearl mollusk commonly called "mother of pearl." (See Plate 72 and 105.) These were combined with seed pearls or crystal or were set to advantage in a variety of mountings. Eventually, man-made pearls from the Bohemian area were shipped by the ton to fashionable Paris and London and were utilized in the hair and for dress decorations as well as for tops for hatpins. These imitation pearls had a wax-bead base.

Many hatpin settings can readily be detected as designs borrowed from all art styles of the past decades: Romanesque, Gothic and Renaissance. These were the main sources for all art of the Victorian, Edwardian, and *Art Nouveau* periods. (Plate 207.)

Robert Bishop, associate editor of *"Antique Monthly,"* defines the latter period: "Strictly speaking, *L'Art Nouveau* is the creation of a new style; it is a revolt against the classic, which throughout the nineteenth century artists and craftsmen have seen fit to do no more than copy."

Simply stated, *Art Nouveau* lines are sensuous and sensitive; Art Deco is stylized and stilted. Compare Plates 85, 93, 189, and 217, and the distinctiveness of each period, each with its own uniqueness, will become quite apparent. Both art forms were used by jewelers in designing the metal dies required for jewelry mountings — mountings which were then utilized in the manufacture of hatpin ornaments.

The *Art Nouveau* artists, swayed by the "new expression," lived and worked under the patronage of Monsieur Bing from 1892-1910, (considered the *Art Nouveau* period). From 1910, through the twenties and even into the early thirties, came the art-form named "Art Deco"; then right up to World War II arrived the newer term: "Art Moderne."

Today, hatpin collectors eagerly search out hatpins of these eras. The Plates throughout this volume will help the reader to identify different types according to a particular period. (*Art Nouveau*, Plates 167 and 205; Art Deco and Art Moderne on Plate 65.) Note the emphasis on Egyptian designs and motifs influenced by the opening of King Tutankamen's tomb in 1920.

It should be mentioned that right smack in the middle of the *Art Nouveau* period came the year 1887 when the conflagration against the configurations of hat-contours arose. Shall the hat be worn high or low? This was a serious issue for a fashion-conscious society not yet embroiled in political and social unrest. A compromise was reached which resulted in the wear-

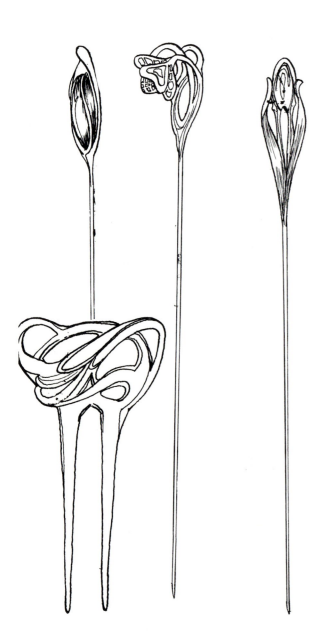

**Plate 217:** Maurice Dufrene's Early 1900 *Art Noveau* Designs rendered by Joyce Fairchild from exhibit catalog.

ing of both — the high crowned hats being called "three storeys," and the flat-crowned named "basement hat." Either design was worn upon puffed-up tresses and required the use of several long hatpins.

The elaborate hairstyles required so much artificial hair and "frizzettes," (custom-made toupees), that one company alone was reported to have filled orders at the rate of two tons of "hair-merchandise" a week!

Upon this bounty of real and artificial hair, rode a millinery "mast" anchored by several hatpins. Chapeaux were complimented with fur, fringe, braid and beads sewn in endless combinations along with silk, chenille, *moire*, damask, *gros grain*, metallic thread, and taffeta. One or more of these materials were gathered and stitched on felt, straw, heavy velvet . . . then the final fashion necessity of hatpins, hatpins, hatpins!

Other unusual hatpins which are rare finds for the collector are those carved in ivory and the 19th century art form of *Satsuma* with its mellow ivory tint. The fine enamel colours of Indian red, green, blue, purple, black and yellow with gilding and silvering, are excellent examples of the minutely painted hatpin ornament known as *Satsuma-ware*. (See Plate 99.) These hatpins are exquisite miniature paintings in their own right and are rather rare and difficult to find in the marketplace. (Also see Plate 78 and 111.) Many *Satsuma* buttons, knobs, brooches and such have been transformed into hatpin heads. Actually, the genuine *Satsuma* hatpin of china has a molded flange as part of the design into which the pin is inserted, or the china head is enclosed in a metal sleeve with its small tubular finding specifically made to accommodate the pin-shank.

Among other choice hatpins are the portraits in miniature, as on Plates 1 and 87. Then there are the beautiful baubles measuring more than two inches across. A hatpin in my own collection, is a life-size humming bird wrought in sterling silver. From its needle-like beak to its tailfeathers, it measures 5¼"! This beauty is pictured on Plate 2.

Hatpin-heads had changed in design from the popular Victorian hilt-headed pins with their two-or-three inch stone-studded and filigree swords, (Plate 207), to an almost limitless variety offered through catalogues, in millinery shops, and over jewelry counters.

Sears, Roebuck and Co. had more than a dozen assorted hatpins in their Fall 1903 "wish book," including a *"patented novelty"* of an imitation Pearl hatpin *"made of metal but lustred and unbreakable"*. Evidently the *"novelty"* wore off, because even at the low cost of 5¢ each, this type was not advertised again in any future catalogue.

Most hatpins advertised in Sears' catalogues appeared in either the jewelry pages or under "hat accessories." The latter included ribbons, plumes, flowers, and speciality 7" or 8" hatpins made up "three on a card," priced from 14¢ to 27¢ per card. Several of the designs thus offered are shown on Plates within this book and such hatpins are identified in the accompanying text of the Plate(s).

Other inexpensive types of hatpins were advertised in the jeweler's section of Sears, Roebuck & Co. catalogues dating from 1894-1913. Here is a sampling:

*Ladies Coin Silver Hat or Hair Pins. Very fancy bright cut — Engraved ball. Length 8 inches. Price each. 75¢*

\* \* \*

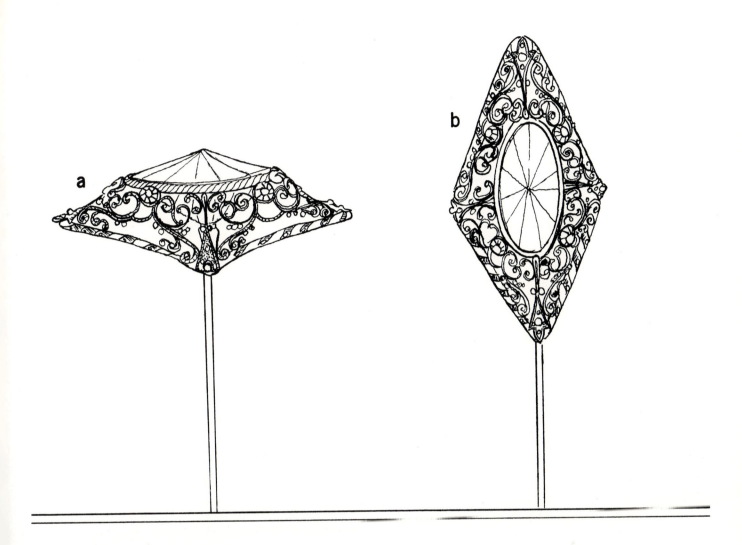

a

b

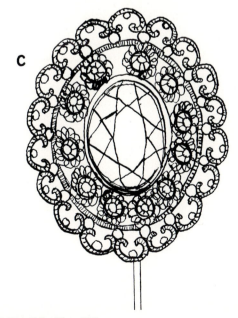

c

d

**Plate 199: Detail for Plate 194.**

*Jeweled Hatpin, New Fancy Design with colored set-*
*tings and rhinestone. Jewelry and millinery stores*
*sell them at 25¢. 7" length. Price, each . . . 15¢.*
*Postage extra. 2¢.*
(Note reference to sale of these items at *"jewelry*
*and millinery stores."*)

There's also a *"gold filled hat pin, Warranted 20 years,"* listed at $2.25 each. Described as *"very fancy engraved Roman gold sword handle; set with 6 imitation Diamonds, 1 imitation Ruby, 6½" long pin"* — this hatpin represents prices for gold objects on a much lower standard than the current market value of gold!

The aforementioned hatpins represent types of hatpins which were much desired by women of fashion just prior to the strong trend of *Art Nouveau*. It was the latter part of the Victorian and Edwardian years that the influential period of *Art Nouveau* design was born, nurtured, and then blossomed forth in startling profusion. Somehow this free-flowing, enchanting, almost mystical influence in design was "nipped in the bud" — meaning it was all too brief. But surely in the hands of a Lalique it had been cultivated to its full-flower potential!

During this *Art Nouveau* period all fashion became quite flamboyant in design and there was great freedom in decorating all objects, the hatpin included. The most characteristic expressions of the *Art Nouveau* of the late 19th century, particularly where it influenced jewelry and the period hatpin, is clearly explained with crystal-like clarity by jewelry historian, Zuzana Pesatova, historian for the Jablonec glass-works industry. In her words, *Art Nouveau* decorative style in jewelry is *"metal craftmen's articles shaped into intricate configurations out of the ribbon ornament, the insect elements and exotic flora."*

*"There was,"* she continues, *"a great deal of imitation both deliberate and involuntary. This . . . was the work of the school where exact copies were made of fashionable decorations (eg. jewels created by R. Lalique). There are quite a few features in the Jablonec goods of those days to remind you of the soft lines and ribbon interlacings of Peter Behrens of Duseeldorf, the subtle chains created by Ashbeen, or of the work done by Franz Bores of Stuttgart. In those days chief emphasis was laid on the clasp and the* **hatpin***, both being in harmony with the fashion of the time with its stress on a slim waist and its delight in enormous hats."* (See Plates 24, 90, 91, and 124.)

Contrasting the expensive hand-wrought hatpins made by jewelers catering to an exclusive trade, are the commonplace but not characterless celluloid or "French Ivory" hatpins which were sold in general stores and later in the five-and-dime established in 1879 by F. W. Woolworth.

Although many pressed-pattern glass hatpin heads are of American manufacture, the greater quantity and variety of glass baubles came from Bohemia. The jewelry manufacturing centers in Rhode Island and Massachusetts competed with metallic designs from England, France, and Germany. The great quantity of sterling products were English.

Molded and hand-cut imitations of oriental carvings in fake coral, ivory, and jade and other simulations of amber and onyx produced exciting results; as authors Gordon and Nerenberg point out, *"a great deal of plastic jewelry is not a simulation of other materials, but a working with and realization of what plas-*
tic itself can offer in the way of color, texture, and design." Plates 100 and 104 can testify to the accuracy of this statement. Unlike the "French paste" or pinchbeck which may well challenge both novice and expert with its deception, the plastics were certainly more easily detected for what they were. However, the common meeting ground of agreement is that imitations or substitutes eventually reached their true water-level in fashion and were socially acceptable by the masses. This was certainly success where it seems to matter most — the commercial aspect of selling the fad or fashion of the day.

From "Early Plastic Jewelry" by Eleanor Gordon and Jean Nerenberg, we read that plastics were used in ancient days and the word itself comes from the Greek, *plastikos*, meaning "to form." As collectors of the *"early plastic jewelry,"* the two authors are well versed and qualified to inform the novice regarding a material frequently used in period hatpins. They write:

*"The first plastics, that is moldable materials, were made from natural materials — horn and tortoise shell, soaked until bendable and then rolled, cut and pressed into desired shapes. Soon after these, came vegetable ivory (made from the large seed of the South American palm) and gutta percha, made from the rubbery gum of the Malaysian percha tree."*

The abovementioned excellent researchers state that Victorian buttons made of a plastic substance have proven to be a mixture of glue and fine sawdust which was almost comparable to the crushed paper-glue combination known as *papier-mache*. Interestingly and surprisingly noted is that despite the French moniker, *papier-mache* originated in China.

When we think of plastics we think today of man-made materials concocted from the chemist's tubes in scientific laboratories. Since much of the plastics were made in the latter 19th century during the heady height of the period hatpin, it's not surprising that many of the ornaments of the 1890-1925 era should have been of celluloid. These were manufactured as early as 1868 by the Hyatt Brothers of Newark, New Jersey.

"Celluloid" was first used as synthetic ivory in the manufacture of billiard balls. Just as early fashions were late in arriving from the Continent to America, so was the use of American-made fashion innovations postponed or slowly accepted on the Continent. This may well explain why most hatpin heads of plastic which were made to look like ivory, amber, mother-of-pearl, and tortoise shell, were not used until Victorian times. This is rather odd considering that before the early 1900's, the U.S. Patent Office had issued more than 1500 patents for plastic processes. Yet the Victorians of England and the *La Modes* of Paris did not favor plastic until the late 1890-1900 when it became the rage for innovative *Art Nouveau* jewelry, buttons, and accessories.

Most of the designs on plastic hatpin heads in the author's collection, and other collections I've seen, show that celluloid hatpin heads really came into their own during the Art Deco period rather than in the *Art Nouveau* era. As a point of interest, the later hatpins and hat ornaments in the 20's and early 30's were more properly "Art Moderne." This newcomer, plastic, expanded and expounded the original streamlined motifs of Art Deco. With "the sky the limit" (somewhat a literal expression inasmuch as the plastic industry made possible America's moon-landing), the Art Moderne stylists knew no bounds to self-expression. (See Plates 85 and 109.)

In "*The Yankee Peddlers of Early America*," J. R. Dolan tells how "*. . . a peddler was likely to arrive at the door . . . the peddler would have an amazing assortment of little things in his trunk. We think of them as little things because in size they are, but if we measure them in terms of downright usefulness they become gigantic — needles and pins . . .*"

The peddler, the town merchant, the catalogue and the city department store, each had a proper place within a growing America! It's doubtful that they really competed, for the peddler most likely only sold the cheapest ordinary glass-beaded hatpins (Plate 133); the town merchant or milliner catered to neighborhood tastes; the catalogues wooed both taste and pocketbook of those in remote places; and the lady in town patronized places which by its circumstance of location within a "metropolis" offered the "latest from Paris" to its fashion-conscious clientele.

The peddler's simple black-baubled hatpin differed greatly from the extravagant hatpins offered over the jewelry counters. Such a lovely pin is described by Margaret Page Hood in her novel, "*The Sin Mark:*"

"*. . . Her best hat with its limp ostrich plume, skewered to her pug by a lethal hatpin with* **a painted china head,** *rode nor'-by-east . . .*"

My own collection boasts such a "painted china head;" this example and some from other collections are shown on Plates 92, 98, and 132. The pearlized porcelain head was often claw-set, similar to the mountings used for gemstones in which tiny claws hold down the flat surfaces of the cut gem. (See Plate 69 for claw-type mounting.)

Several china or porcelain heads were more securely and artistically mounted in a "gypsy" setting so that the top scarcely appears above the level of the surrounding metal. (Plate 88.)

There seems to be no effort made in the above setting to make the ornamental head appear larger as is done in an "illusion" setting. Here the metal, be it only brass instead of precious ore, has its edges shaped so they appear to be part of the gem, thus aggrandizing the actual size of the stone. (Plate 118)

On Plate 118, note the most unusual dual setting of a cut crystal in an "illusion-type" setting which is then mounted in a full-figural bird's claw — not to be confused with an actual "claw-setting". (See Glossary)

Many other innovations were taking place in the shank or pin itself. A good example is the advertisement which appeared in the May 1906, "*Woman's Home Companion*":

*The New Revolving Spiral Hat Pin will hold your hat comfortably. Ask at hat pin counter or send 25¢ for handsome new design to Koy-Lo Co., 11 Broadway, New York.*" (This "spiral" or non-slip shank can be seen on Plates 8 and 17.)

It seems that once the new burst of freedom in design descended upon turn-of-the-century fashion, jewelers who once upon a time used pagan or religious symbols, and conservatively limited the gemstones to those of significance and superstition, now turned for inspiration to the Italian Renaissance and sought to reflect the art of that period. Jewelry became not only decorative and/or symbolic, but functional. And hatpins were not orphaned in this use of symbolism.

The bezoar, for instance, was set as a jewel because it was thought to be an antidote against poison; diamonds as victory over enemies; heliotropes for long life; sapphires for escape from danger; topaz to prevent harm; and turquoises for prosperity.

There has been from ancient times to our modern day a believed connection in the wearing of an adornment and the protection it gives as an amulet against supernatural elements and powers. Certain gemstones in pre-Christian times were believed to hold certain powers in the eerie, unearthly world of transcendentalism which borders on the occult popularized today.

The wonder of gemstones is especially credited by astrologers whose tenet teaches that precious stones are linked with the planets and are so-called "stones of the zodiac." We are familiar with "birth-month stones" and have popularized them more than ever in today's jewelry fashions. Period hatpins incorporated birthstones or "stones-of-the-month" and were exceedingly popular. The belief which emerged from the darkness of the Middle Ages that certain precious stones had a magical effect, either protective or healing, when worn upon the finger, has and probably always will persist in the minds of many. Today, more than ever, the "rings on all fingers" is fashionable; but it's not *fashion* that dictates the wearing of turquoise and amber and metallic insignia guaranteed to ward off the spell of evil spirits!

Jeweled hatpins and other touches of costume jewelry were worn as a mark of wealth and social status; but gradually, with mass production a welcome newcomer to commercial enterprise, hatpins and other "jeweled conceits" were a luxury even the "working stiff" could afford. And as the demand grew, more and more men took up the trade of jewelry-making. With mass production, came the inevitable shift from careful craftsmanship to commercial calculation of how much the masses could "consume." (Plate 169) Not only did the hatpin (and other works of the gemologist) become more functional, but they became trifling "doodles," rather gaudy — even vulgar. Some photographs of the era clearly show when jewels and such decoration were worn in great profusion! "Dance-hall" girls and stage actresses popularized the vogue of long, gaudy-colored bead necklaces — right back in style today!

Both gems and their imitations in glass were set with claws or in coronets with open backs so as to expose the stones to light from both behind and front, with an effect that was almost blinding! The foil gimmick was widely used in the manufacture of hatpins and hatpins became the MOST functional and decorative jewelry items next to, perhaps, the brooch. The latter had already become less functional with the introduction of the safety-pin, needle and thread, snaps, hooks 'n eyes, and other such devices to make the word "pinning" almost obsolete. While the brooch was delegated to the decorative class of artifices, the hatpin remained both functional and ornamental

**Plate 186.**

until the years following World War I — a changeover which will be discussed in greater length elsewhere in this chapter.

Several hatpins in my collection have gems signifying the virtues of the constellations; others were worn because they were believed to have therapeutic value; some were worn as talismans and amulets in hats just as the stones had once been worn around the neck or on the sword or crown. (Plates 91, 106 and 137.)

Hatpins with gemstones of lapis-lazuli or sapphire were favored by women because these and other blue stones were emblems of chastity; no doubt the women who fought for prohibition favored the amethyst which is supposed to counteract the effects of alcohol — the amethyst's name signifying the "sobering" gem. (Plates 37, 82 and 127.)

Of all the parts of the human figure, the head seems destined to be most adorned with jewels, from the hat badges or *ensieigne* worn in the early 16th century by men, to the pearls, laces, and *aigrettes* worn in women's hair or cap. These *aigrettes* were pins with jewels that supported a feather, or the jewels could be made to resemble a plume. Often as not, these imitation plumes were formed by intricate filigree work. (See Plate 159.)

The great portrait artists of the past have given us evidence of the famous and infamous men and women of their day resplendent in satins, velvets, furs, and jewels. Silver and gold wire, wreaths, strings of pearls, ribbons, garlands of flowers, fur caps — everything to adorn the heads of male and female. But alas, in all of the paintings from past to present, hardly a trace of a hatpin! Lesser than "blue book" artists have immortalized women in "transfer art" and lithography but there is no artistic evidence of how those cartwheel-sized hats managed to stay aloft atop upswept hair-styles.

In Lawrence Dietz' really enjoyable book about "*Soda Pop — The History, Advertising, Art and Memorabilia of Soft Drinks in America*," there appears a group of ads printed on paper and on tin trays. The ads feature the millinery styles of 1906, 1908, and 1912 — each hat defying gravity. Or so they seem, for not a hatpin in sight! The Pepsi Company issued a lovely tray in 1973 to celebrate the company's 75th anniversary. The typical "Lillian Russell" or "Mae West" outfit — take your pick — is complete with plumed, wide-brimmed hat roosting on top of a "Gibson Girl" hair-do. It would have required at least three to four good-sized hatpins to anchor

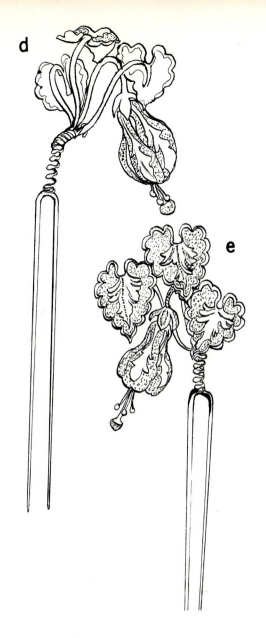

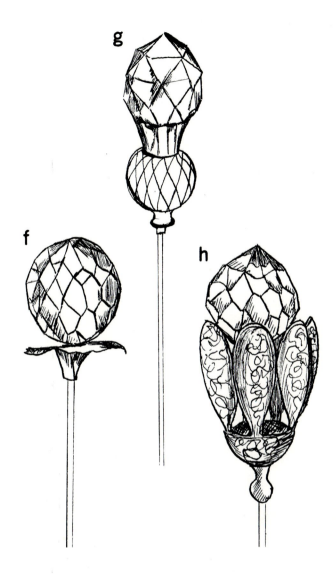

that chapeau! But not even a hint . . .

Those hatpins were there all right! Photographic evidence of more recent years belie the painter's canvas and his artistic license. (See Plates 211 and 213.)

Sometimes I'm tempted to classify the hatpin as nothing more than a glorified hairpin — a hair ornament that was first sharpened to go through the thickness of cloth, then lengthened to accommodate changing hair and hat fashions.

In both design and appearance, the decorative hairpin and hatpin are definitely related; the hatpin differs only after 1832 when the *manufactured* pin's length and thick gauged wire made it quite different than the hairpin of yesteryear. The *hand-wrought* ornamental hairpins *also* differ from the machine-made decorative hairpins which have heavy rather than thin shanks.

Although there has been some previous mention of the extraordinary lengths of some hatpins, I failed to clue the reader as to the actual sizes and weights of some of the fabulous hatpins in my own collection. (See Plates 16 and 20.)

One may rightly wonder how a fair damsel managed to hold her head erect with the weight of hat, hair, and hatpins! Considering that some hatpins are heavily encrusted with brilliants

and other gemstones, and weigh several ounces, this was quite an accomplishment. Even a 'good woman' would find it a challenge to hold her head up high under sumptuous hat, hair-rats and padding of mohair, plus veiling, hairpins, and hatpins! Sometimes the steel and jet ornaments incorporated in the design of the hat, contributed almost a quarter pound in weight! (For visual proof of jet-laden fashion and its weighty burden, see Plate 159.)

*Manufacturers' marks on hatpins do not appear until the later models of the 1900's. This is probably due to the fact that hatpins of earliest vintage were custom-made, but as the popularity and the necessity of fashion design increased the demand for pins, hatpins were *mass-produced* for the first time. (Manufacturers' marks are not to be confused with *Hallmarks* or artisans' *signatures*)

According to correspondence from Manufacturing Jewelers & Silversmiths of America, Inc., I have been advised by Executive Director, Mr. George R. Frankovich, as follows:

*Company trademarks, hallmarks, signatures and other marks may appear singly or in groups, all on same piece. (Plate 171)

**COLLARETTES AND ORNAMENTS** *(1.16.1892, p. 341).*
**Fig. l:** aigrette for the hair.
**Fig. m.:** necklace, brooch, and flower-pin
**Fig. n:** aigrette for the hair.
**Fig. o:** bertha and hair ornament of roses.

**Plate 158**

**Plate 169:** A jewelry shop, Long Beach, California, 1920. Note the women wear hat-pins as ornaments rather than out of necessity on "cloche-type" hats. Whether these are worn for possible "protective use" or merely for decoration, one must decide for himself. Photograph courtesy of Hogie's Antiques, Hermosa Beach, California.

**Plate 158** (Opposite) Feathered and jewelled **Aigvettes** were worn in hair and in hats. **( figs. l. & n.) Fig. M.:** Ornaments are also shown on Plates 12 and 17. Note the cape-pins with chanin (Plate 12), and an example of a flower-pin designed with hilt and sheath (Plate 17). The "collavettes and ornaments" circa 1892, represent a small portion of the extraordinary array of decorative "conceits" worn by women of the "Gay Nineties". *"Victorian Fashions and Costumes from Harper's Bazaar 1867-1898"*. Edited and with an Introduction by Stella Blum. Dover Publications, Inc., New York.

*"The suppliers of raw pins near the turn of the century included: Oakville Company, Oakville, Conn.; W. R. Cobb Company, 850 Wellington Ave., Cranston, R.I.; Geo. H. Fuller Company, 151 Exchange St., Pawtucket, R.I.; and F. H. Noble Company, 559 West 59th St., Chicago, Ill.*

*"The finished products were made by Brown & Mills, 100 Stewart St., Providence, R.I.; Waite Thresher, 10 Abbott Park Place, Providence, R.I.; Robert Barton, Providence, R.I.; Brewster Co., Attleboro, Mass.; T. W. Foster, Providence, R.I.; and S. & B. Lederer, Providence, R.I."*

It is to be noted that the above companies are represented in the *jewelry* trade and not in the manufacture of common household PINS such as the safety pin, straight pin, and the like.

Hatpins were definitely considered items of jewelry and were ordered from the jewelry sections of catalogues and brochures. Hatpins were not considered household items, such as needles and pins.

There are many hatpins which are clearly hallmarked. For an enlarged drawing of HALLMARKS, see Plate 171. This same hatpin holder (or stand), is shown in color on Plate 52. We know from the passant lion, (shown four feet in profile), that the piece is English.

Now this writer makes no attempt to decipher hallmarks since they are a study in a truly technical field. Books about hallmarks are available to readers who wish to pursue the subject in depth. Whenever possible, however, I give the benefit of accidental knowledge on the subject of "markings," tripped over while looking elsewhere for research closer to my theme.

A fabulous hatpin in my collection is an extremely rare signed hatpin executed by the famed French medalist, Armand Bargas. (See Plate 170.) The medal, a commemorative of Saint Jeanne d'Arc, was designed by Bargas for the 1904 Paris Exposition. Its *repousse* decoration in sterling exposes the finely done portrait in relief. The all-over size is about that of a silver half-dollar.

The mention of a silver half-dollar urges me to have the reader seek out Plate 20, in which the true size of some hatpin ornaments can be seen in contrast to an Eisenhower silver dollar.

My research and personal contact with antique dealers revealed other unique hatpins contributed during the hatpin period by Rene Lalique, (Plate 167), Louise Comfort Tiffany, (Plate 206), and Peter Carl Faberge, (Plate 206). Unfortunately, many of these magnificent type hatpins, which probably represent the epitome in hatpin-art, have been lost as hatpins. The bauble-heads have been guillotined on the jeweler's workbench, the spirit and soul reincarnated into another lifestyle of ring, brooch, pendant, charm, or trinket.

Mr. Tom J. Lawson, author of "Hatpinology," reported that a Reneé Lalique hatpin sold at the 1971 Sotheby's sale for 145 pounds, (approx. $450.). The hatpin is described in the Sotheby catalogue as follows:

*"Lot 29. A Lalique 'Pliqué-a-jour' Enamel Hat Pin modeled as a sprig of mignonettes, partly in cloisonne in pale green and rich orange, partly in pli-*

*qué-a-jour in darker green, 6¼"; 16 cm; marked Lalique and with gold marks; original fitted case marked R. Lalique 10 Cours La Reine, Paris. This piece probably dates from between 1901, when he moved to the Cours La Reine, and 1905 when he opened his shop in the Place Vendomé."*

A Faberge hatpin enameled with gold swags is pictured in Richard Falkiner's beautiful and informative book, *"Investing in Antique Jewelry."* Known simply as "Faberge," this wonderful artisan followed his father's footsteps as a goldsmith and jeweler in St. Petersburg, Russia, (1846-1920) — and although best known for his exquisite Easter eggs which were presented each year to the Czar, Faberge did not think the hatpin of so little importance, either! (See Plate 206.)

Louis Comfort Tiffany is represented in Graham Hughes', *"Modern Jewelry,"* by a small baubled but elegant hatpin. It is displayed alongside a necklace to show the length of the shank. There is a great similarity between this Tiffany creation and the hatpin in my own collection shown on Plate 12.

A substantial number of ornaments for pin-heads were made in sterling or oxidized silver, while a tremendous amount were made of *pinchbeck*, fake gold, or *pom-pom*. When brass, an alloy of copper and zinc, when contains 12 to 15 percent of zinc, it simulates the color of gold. This was the discovery in 1732 of a London clockmaker, Christopher Pinchbeck, who introduced a brass containing about 15% zinc for the manufacture of imitation gold jewelry. *Pinchbeck* was discarded several decades ago when electro-plating and other patented "gold-tone" were introduced and used in costume jewelry up to the present.

Colors of gold plated pins vary and can be found in yellow, green, red and white gold — all these produced by variations in the alloy. Silver and zinc tend to give a green color; copper offers red; and nickel produces white gold. Gold-filled pins are made by joining layers of gold alloy to a base metal and then rolling or drawing to the thickness required. The most common practice used today is gold electroplating — a method of depositing fine gold on base metal in a superior fashion.

Period hatpins should not be confused with corsage pins nor with hat ornaments of the 1925-1940 era. (See Plate 172.) Nor do they belong with the antique pins preceding 1832.

The function of the period hatpin is like no other accorded a member of the pin family.

The period hatpin was used primarily to keep hats firmly balanced — even in defiance of gravity — on women's heads at a time when radical changes in hair-styles were also adopted. The combination of mounting tresses and broadening brims could never have been attempted without the possibility

Plate 170 (left): Extremely rare signed hatpin: "A Bargas". Sterling, on 11½" pin. Ornament (1¼" round) is enlarged for detail. Armand Bargas, famed French medalist worked in the beginning of 20th century. He had an exposition in 1904, and this medal of Jeanne D'Arc was included.

Plate 171

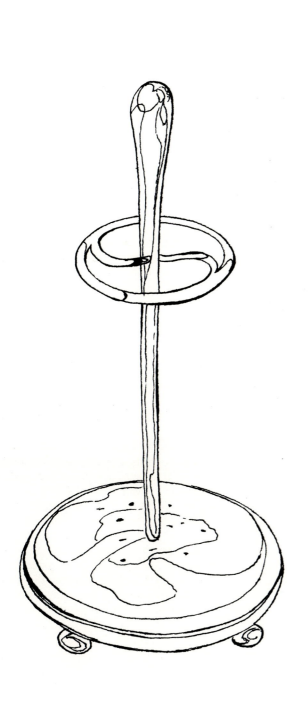

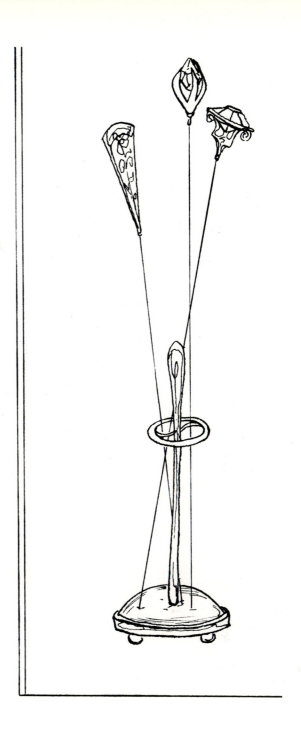

of the mainstay: the hatpin. Long pins were required and this necessity prompted the manufacture of the longest length "fashion wire cutting" in history. Once these long shanks proved functional, they entered into the realm of artistic device with no holds barred. The ornamental period hatpin was born!

But these period hatpins had two functions: to anchor and to be admired! After 1925, the cloche hat "dropped anchor," and almost out of habit, women continued wearing hatpins as ornamentation. So many of these ornaments bordered on the preposterous or on abstract absurdity. (See Plates 107, 113 and 116.)

These later ornaments, though technically hat-pins — hyphenated this time because they now have become decorative pins (or "badges") for a hat — were often a pinning tool which was added to an array of ribbons, feathers, veiling, or sashes. All these accessories were pinned to the cloche or tight-fitting styled crown. Hat and hair hugged the head. This was "the vogue" of the "roarin' twenties".

The evolvement from hatpin to ornament actually began slowly following World War I (1919); hatpins were already much smaller, until eventually they could be called little more than outright decoration. Some of these decorative hat-pins boasted no more than a 1½-2″ shank; others had a brooch-like pin or loop-shank (similar to that found on a button); these lat-

**Plate 174**

78

ter types were sewn as an accent right to the hat in conjunction with that feather, ribbon, veil, or gee-gaw.

Some hat-pin ornaments have a pin with either a plain, simple or removable "nib" (to guard against loss, not against sharp points), while others incorporated stylized "nibs" which were part of the all-over conception of the design. (See Plate 17, 107, 112 and 116.) I use the term "design" rather loosely here, for although there must have been some creative effort in the original drawing, the media used to execute same was, in most cases, without distinction. The exceptions, of course, were the rare ornaments conceived by the masters of the trade; most of these examples are now in private collections or are museum pieces. But by and large, the mass-produced articles were without proper motif and were readily discarded in favor of the next scheme off the drawing board.

I repeat, the simple or decorative "nibs" were no longer used as protection against injury or in obedience to the law, but rather to guard against loss. The hat-pin ornament was pushed through the fabric of the hat and once adjusted with the threaded "safety," remained put. It was *not pushed through hair, nor "rats," nor wires, etc.*; the hat-ornament *remained on the hat* when the hat was removed from the head.*

The *exact opposite* applies to the *period hatpin* which simply *had* to be removed in order *to take off the hat*. Since several of these pins may have been used to secure a hat to the head, it took a bit of doing to carefully remove the work of the milliner without messing the work of the hairdresser.
*"You'll have to be patient. I have three hatpins."* +

In addition to the hat-pins (hat ornaments), we did have actual hatpins in the 1925-40 era, but they were quite different than the *period hatpins* in that the shanks were much shorter and the ornaments necessarily smaller. Many of the hats worn during that period were not as deep-crowned as the *cloche* and were thus aided by the jab or two through the felt or straw of a small anchoring device which pinned the hat against several strands of hair. This time there were no cotton battings to combat, nor "rats" to skewer, nor wire to drill. It had become only "minor surgery" to insert one, or perhaps a pair of short hatpins into the crown of a hat and thus "suture," or unite the crown of the hat against the scalp. Plates 15 and 119 show to what extent the glory of the hatpin descended into almost another category — a corsage pin. The real difference between these commonplace hatpins and a corsage pin is that the latter usually has a pearl-ized head in either white or pastel shades. Corsage pins of the thirties and right up to the present time, are about 2-2½" long with approximately ⅛-¼" pearlized heads. These are a far cry from the violet pins or corsage pins of the Victorian era which were exceedingly beautiful and decorative. (See Plates 17 and 158m.)

Period hatpins had become a way of life, a part of daily living from 1890-1914. Edwin Post in his book about his famous mother, titled "Truly Emily Post," tells how Emily "... *perched high on a cushion, starchily shirtwaisted,* **with a broad-brimmed sailor made fast to her hair with pins** *and a spotted veil, drove the smart cob ... with great enjoyment to herself and others."*

Later on, Mrs. Post would climb down from the short-legged stocky horse with its fancy gait and climb up into the new fangled horse-powered motorcar. (How the automobile affected headgear and fashion and spelled doom for the hatpin will be discussed later in this book.)

In Emlyn Williams' autobiography, "George", the author tells how he sat through a sermon, "... *the test of endurance. I trained myself not to watch the clock for five minutes on end, for when watched it never moved; then, staring at the woman's hat in front, I tried to imagine her at home before the glass, settling it and spearing it, but I could not; she had sat there always."*

The date: December 1894.

And in Ralph G. Martin's "*Jennie: The Life of Lady Randolph Churchill,*" there's a footnote which reads: "*Also fashionable then were the wide-brimmed picture hats that seemed to float on the top of the head and were called hatpin heads (1895). Women skaters, however, had to be warned how to fall properly — falling on your back can drive your hatpin into your head."*

Finally, from the "*Young Ladies Journal,*" (Jan. 1890):
"*Hatpins are very fashionable at present, and are worn in every variety of form; they are sometimes of silver, gold, pearl, often very richly jeweled, others are of cut jet, garnets, or oxidized silver. In fact they are seen in every possible form."*

If the reader will study the many color plates and drawings in this book and within this chapter, just about every above-mentioned type of period hatpin may be found ... and then some!

Yes, the long hatpins were "settled and speared," being pushed through hat, bun, topknot, chignon, and miscellaneous "rats" and cotton batting which were worn under the hair to give it both height and the appearance of abundancy of tresses. Often the forelocks were dipped low over one side of the face then swept back over one or two bundles of cotton batting and secured in place with hairpins. Then the fanciful chapeau was placed atop all this and made secure with the aid of veiling, an extra ribbon-sash, and the all-important thrust of a generous sized hatpin ... sometimes two or three at that! (See Plate 175.)

Some of the later period hatpins had "guards" or "nibs" that were especially designed and manufactured for use on the extremely long hatpins. These "nibs" were the predecessors of the aforementioned decorative-type "ends" used on ornaments as security against loss. (Attleboro Mfg. Co., made "guards" of various designs similar to hatpin heads.)

The "nibs" became necessary because hatpin-points had proven dangerous to passerbys and also, perhaps, to gentlemen callers. If a suitor tarried too long, he feared not the rebuke as much as those sharp points as he leaned over to whisper "sweet nothings" into her ear! It has been suggested that period hatpins were the best chaperones possible, and now we can understand why. Just as the cumbersome corset must have saved many a maiden's virtue by giving her time to reconsider, so the huge hats with their long, sharp hatpins must have set up a sort of barbed-wire-barrier against certain advances — wanted or not! (But I've always maintained, where there's a Will, there's a May!)

There is such a multitudinous array of hatpins and hat ornaments that it's seldom collectors find duplicates. To the contrary, in both my own collection and in other collections I've

*For detailed drawings, see Plate 173.
+ (Line from "LOVE AMONG THE RUINS." See Plate 174.)

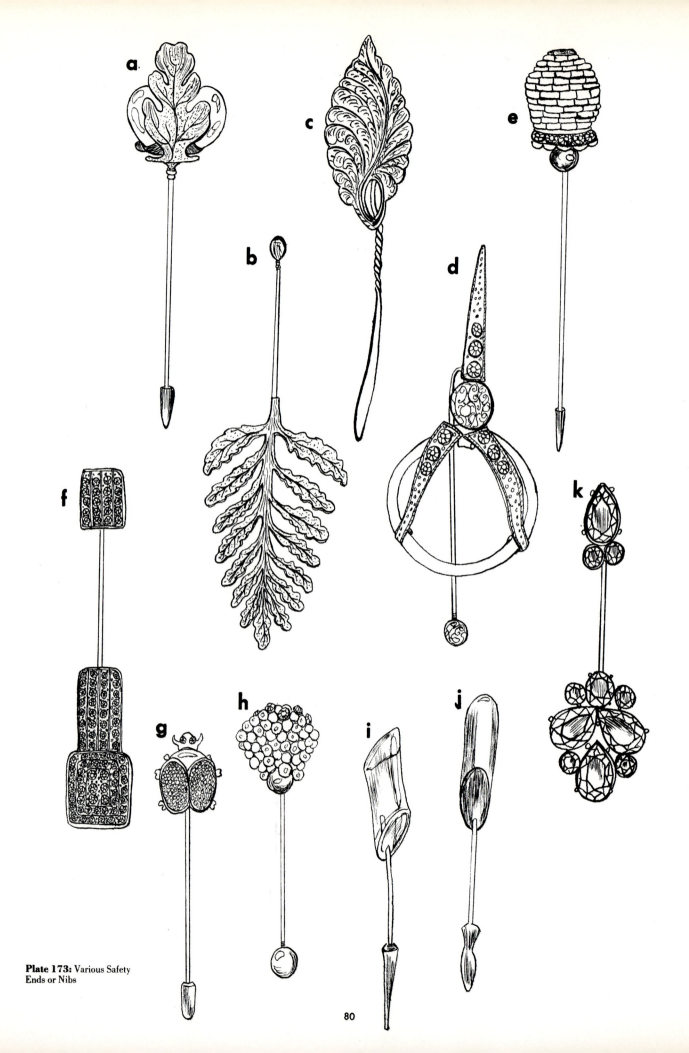

**Plate 173:** Various Safety
Ends or Nibs

80

seen, variety seems infinite and a duplicate breaks the rule of endless combinations of diversified forms of metallic art mounted on the end of a pin. Some of these metallic heads are flattered with turquoise, amethyst, topaz, pearls, opals, rubies, onyx, garnet, jade, rhinestones, French paste and other brilliants — all of which I've seen and handled with delight. Most are finely cut and polished; many would make beautiful rings and charm bracelets, were one inclined to destroy a fine example of a period hatpin.

Mrs. Elizabeth C. Martin, librarian for the Danbury Library, Danbury, Connecticut, wrote in her letter to me:

*"I have a collection of hatpins that were in my own family as some of the women wore sailors (hats) when I was a little girl. My mother was very proud of her gold topped pin which was open filigree with an oval top, beaded around the edge, with her monogram in the center — F.O.C. I now wear that top on my charm bracelet.*

*"I have one with a round piece of pottery top handpainted with pink roses. Three have amethysts and one a turquoise. One stone is cut like a crystal or obelisk, one is a small round ball set in etched silver and one is a large oval with a double silver frame around it. The ones that are etched gold balls I use a great deal as I have had the pins cut short.\* One that was a clear bright green stone I had made into a brooch for my young cousin. A friend tells me that she has one with the seal of Annapolis on it. Her cousin went there and gave it to her. It must have been a prom favor some years ago.*

*"I think women outdid each other with hatpins as men did with their stickpins."*

If one wonders why hatpins are becoming more and more scarce as collectibles, do remember that there are many women today who cut the pins, use the baubles as charms, or have brooches made from the heads of hatpins.

Precious stones are removed from the settings and used in pendants, rings, earrings, and other jewelry. And, unfortunately, it's usually the most perfect examples of period hatpins that suffer these fates.

A reputable jeweler and antique dealer on famous Royal Street in New Orleans, confessed that he's made several gorgeous "star pins" by joining six or eight hatpins — cut down to about 2½-3" — into a center cluster of gold resembling a nugget. Each point of the star is unique. Each brooch was then valued at more than $1500, for the heads of these re-set hatpins were of solid gold encrusted with diamonds, rubies, emeralds, pearls, precious lapis-lazuli, and similar gemstones.

The hatpins in the Royal Street antique shop represented a collection of pins which were not mass-produced but were custom-made by the "new breed" of designers and jewelers catering to the wealthy few who admired the new trends and could afford to patronize the salons brave enough to feature them.

This antique store in New Orleans caters today to those who appreciate the intricate designs and artistic concepts of these *Art Nouveau* hatpins, and who want to preserve each without altering shapes or stones when the cut pins are mounted in the contrived nugget-setting.

In the Smithsonian Institution, Washington, D.C., a pair of hatpins in precious ore and gems are on exhibit in the costume department. The gold pins are approximately nine inches long with heads of onyx imbedded with diamonds. I was told they were on loan from an important private collection of jewelry and were quite valuable from both an artistic and a monetary sense. The *rarity* of fine examples of hatpins places great importance on preserving such "implements" of the past. Regardless of intrinsic value, it seems almost tragic that the period hatpin has not been given more prominence in the collections of both costume and jewelry in various museums across country and throughout the world. I have received replies from certain museums (which shall remain anonymous), telling me that there is not even ONE example of this important accessory in their costume and/or jewelry exhibits — nor

**Plate 175:** "The Ladies' Field, May 14, 1904. F. P. Walkup Archives.

---

*\*Here is another example of the deliberate cutting of pins.*

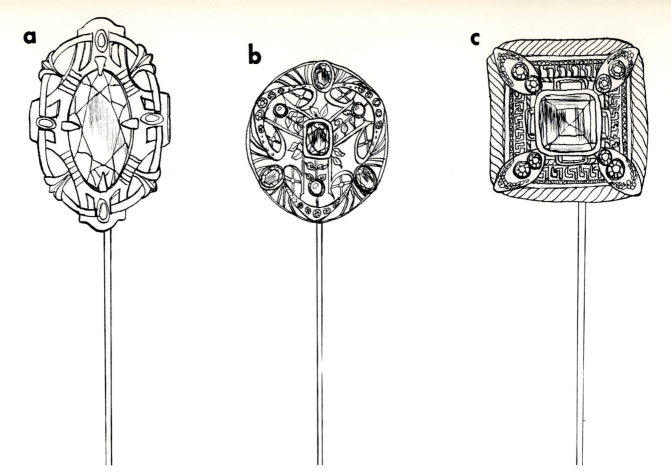

**Plate 177**

are there any stored away in the archives!

A researcher of period costume in a world-reknowned museum was almost apologetic at so meager a collection in her own department of costume and textiles. Another curator confessed that he "wasn't sure" there was a hatpin in the archives upstairs or downstairs, but happily there were a few found in a box in the basement. And he kindly unpacked them for study, for appreciation, and for final display in showcases along with costumes of the period.

Plates 164, 168, 176, 177 and 178, represent collections from museums which are identified in the accompanying text; hatpin collections typifying private treasure-troves are shown throughout the book and are acknowledged either with the Plate or under "Sources and Acknowledgements."

Unfortunately for the hatpin collector and for those seeking prize acquisitions for museums, too many of the more beautiful hatpins are being converted into other pieces of fine jewelry without retaining a hint of their former heritage of artistic-usefulness. Hatpins, having been outmoded or outlawed — as discussed in the special chapter on "Hatpins as Weapons" — have become jeweled "converts" to bracelets, rings, charms, and brooches.* I actually stood helplessly by as a magnificent

---

*"Authentic 1920 Art Glass from the Stephen Jourard Collection" is featured in a chain of Los Angeles department stores. Among the costume-jewelry thus featured, are HATPIN HEADS set into convertible brooch-pendant bezel-type mountings. The open-backed pieces plainly expose the molded glass "nub" into which the metal shank was inserted for hatpins. Several of the young salesgirls behind the jewelry counter seemed fascinated with the idea that they were actually seeing authentic period hatpins and promptly added to their own purchases just for the "novelty." As for the "1920 Art Glass" — the hatpin heads were an assortment of pressed and patterned glass of a full decade earlier — about 1910. That's when much of the "carnival" and other colored glass was popular as hatpin baubles. The hobnail pattern-glass hatpin head in cobalt blue, (Plate 8), is one of the glass-patterned heads utilized in the "Stephen Jourard Collection." Others are of molded jet glass, and a variety of multi-colored vitrics.

little solid-gold fox-head with diamond eyes was pulled from its gold stem. A gentlemen ordered the antique dealer, (who was also a jeweler), to make a ring of this enchanting bauble. Fortunately, I was able to prevail on both men to "save the animal from extinction" — and so the story has a happy ending, for the fox-headed pin has been restored on to its original shank and is now part of my collection. (See Plate 6, center pin.)

Although most hatpins were not of solid gold nor silver — since they were manufactured for the masses and required by the thousands — those of baser metals were still treated by their makers with artistic merit. Some of the inferior metals show details of such attention to ingenious workmanship that in many instances they challenge their counterparts in precious ore.

In many cases where high relief was required, the design was executed in bronze, the reddish colour of the metal providing a particularly well-suited base for gilding. Gilding was an excellent method of obtaining a very rich and simulated effect of enduring gold. Burnished metals also enhanced the overall attraction.

Strangely enough, the most difficult part of the hatpin to correctly plate is the pin or shaft, for there are no flat surfaces to adhere to but rather a continual cylinder from which the plating material slips and slides. The process for plating the pin itself is both interesting and amazing.

Many gold-plated (gilt) ornamental heads were used for engraving, and the hatpins with a shield or escutcheon for a monogram or crest design, seem to have been very popular. (See Plates 35 and 120.)

In addition, medallions and coat-of-arms and other insignia were much in demand. (Plates 30 and 83)

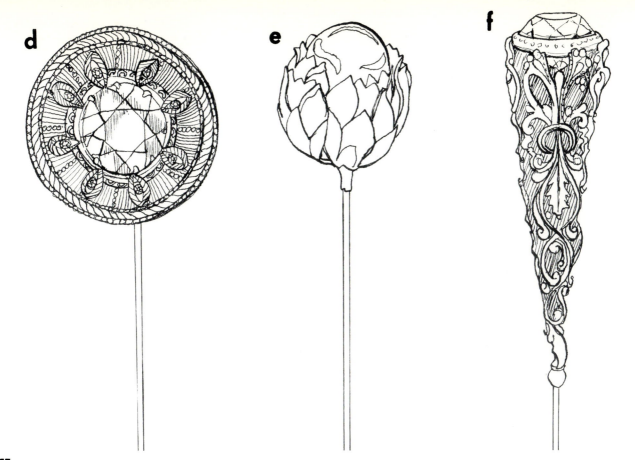

**d**  **e**  **f**

**Plate 177**

**Plate 176: ENGLISH HATPINS, EARLY 20th CENTURY,** *Left to right:* Hatpin, solid bead head made from black glass with blue yellow and pink floral design spaced between a fleck gilt scroll white metal pin. Hatpin, triple scroll made from silver and mounted on white metal pin. Hatpin, Poppy head made from metal and coloured in scarlet and green with black stamens, mounted on a gilt metal pin. Hatpin, Made of white metal consisting of 3 interlaced circles studded with turquoise beads surrounding a circular green glass head. Hatpin, Silver filigree — half dome surmounted by a nob and bordered with nobs set in twisted wire. Hatpin, Hollow ball made of silver filigree to which are applied small silver balls. By courtesy of The Victoria and Albert Museum, London.

his own conclusion.

Polished steel was mentioned in a fashion note of the early 19th century: ". . . *a brooch of polished steel confines the gown to bust and a very pretty woman appeared in public last week and all her numerous ornaments were of polished steel — immense in price and of beautiful workmanship.*"

An acquaintance of mine gifted me with a hair ornament made of polished steel. She purchased it as a hatpin, but the short, heavy-gauge shank, places it in the category of hair ornaments, for such thick shafts would puncture a good straw hat beyond repair, not to mention a fine felt or velvet! The polished steel ornament is pictured on Plates 17 and 48; it was found in a "flea market" in Madrid, of all places!

It was mentioned earlier that women for the first time ruled from the throne and eventually from the threshold. The latter was not heralded with sudden grace by men who were taken aback by the change in "the woman's place." The record shows the following homely lullaby printed in a 1901 newspaper: (See Plate 196.)

*"Hush-a-bye, baby, lie still with thy daddy,*
*Thy mammy has gone to the club;*
*She'll play herself broke, and call it a joke,*
*While daddy must stay home and scrub."**

*(Anon.)*

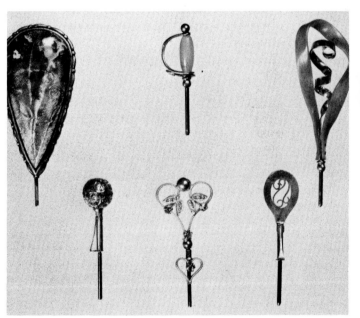

**Plate 216**

**Plate 181: WINTER AND SKATING COSTUMES** *(12.1.1894, p. 973)*
**Fig. a:** fur-trimmed cloth costume. **Fig. b:** velours du nord jacket.

Then there were the jeweled hatpins with metal and brilliants combined in designs characteristic of the period. Pins were topped with beads, pearls, coral, amber, marcasite, cinnabar, and the newcomer, crystal, which was sometimes worn even in the daytime. A hatpin rarity, that of mercury glass, is pictured on Plate 122.

Alistair Cooke stated in one of his famous essays about America, that Eli Whitney actually made hatpins. Were they handmade or made with a manufactured shank? Whitney's cotton gin was invented in 1792. It would be 40 years before the invention of the pin-making machine, so the reader may draw

First the "club-woman", then the "emancipated woman", and of course we must not forget the "sports-woman", — each dictating new manners and customs in decorum and dress. The period hatpins depict each change of mood and mode with their ornamental baubles. (See Plate 141 for the "sports-woman" attire — with hats, of course!)

Lawn tennis had become popularized by both sexes in 1870, and women wore hats advertised in *Scribner's Monthly*

*Pin Holder with squawling babies seemed a perfect tongue-in-cheek bit of illustrative material that could not be resisted by the author. (Plate 196.)*

(1878), as headgear especially designed for the "sportin' woman",

However, the "sportin' women" were still "fit matter for ridicule" well into the Nineties, and it's hardly a wonder when you visualize the female figure attired in 1895 garb:

> *"A costume recommended for skating is an under-petticoat of flannel, a silk undershirt, easy short corsets, a thick, warm pair of woolen stockings, a plain, short (at least three inches above the ankles), tweed or serge skirt, heavy enough to prevent it blowing up . . . As to hats, they should not be large, and feathers — at least ostrich ones — should be avoided as trimming."* (Plate 181.)

Small or large, the hats worn by "sportin' women" sat atop the puffed hair or Psyche knot, securely fastened in place with hatpins. By far the most popular sporting-hat was the sailor with its small low crown and very wide brim which was held straight on the head by a pair of hatpins — these pins often denoting the sporting event.

Even golfing became woman's fare as noted by the hatpins fashioned after the usual bag of cudgels. (See Plates 62 and 126.)

Hats were designed for all feminine sports, for no lady would ever be seen bareheaded on either the "lawn tennis courts" nor other "fields of play". The exception was met with newspaper comment (1897), at the first International Ladies' Hockey Matches.

Special uniform costumes were adapted for the English and the Irish teams. The English wore red; the Irish wore green. A white cap, similar to a man's cricket cap was worn by the English ladies, skewered in place by long hatpins. The Irish opponents judiciously dispensed with their headgear — to the horror of one reporter who wrote: *". . . in a game from which hatpins are debarred as dangerous, is apt to be a source of embarrassment."* The English team might have answered with the earlier retort spoken in the courtroom: *"After all, how was one to keep one's cap on, anyway?"*

Closer to home, it was reported in the town newspaper at Topeka, Kansas, Feb. 14, 1909, that *". . . the window fronts of four of the finest Kansas avenue saloons and drug stores were smashed in bits at an early hour this morning with an ax in the hands of Miss Blanche Boise, a disciple of Mrs. Nation."* (The legendary Carrie Nation, of course!) *"The smashing was done from the sidewalk. The damage will amount to hundreds of dollars. Miss Boise achieved notoriety some months ago by horse-whipping Mayor Parker and in several raids in times past with Mrs. Nation. She gives as her excuse for hatred of saloons that liquor ruined a favorite brother. She was arrested and placed in jail."*

I cannot help but wonder: when Blanche Boise was jailed, were her hatpins confiscated like those of her English suffragette sisters? Were her hatpins considered *weapons* too?

In any event, women began to primp and preen for club or game activities — no less social programs — and by the late 90s and early turn-of-the-century years, women were out to be seen and heard.

They began with frills and fluffs and the hat, a sign of true emancipation, became multiple layers of frosting. The cre-

**Plate 185:** Life-size drawing of ordinary hat pins.

85

ations of the milliners' art became a must for the fashion-conscious, fashion-hungry women of the "Gay Nineties". The style-setting Floradora Girls and Gibson Girls, who were in vogue, spotlighted the "new frontiers" of the emancipated woman who took to the stage or invaded the business world.

The "Floradora Girls" spun round the town in 1905 "open-air" Packards, their cartwheel-size hats securely anchored with long hatpins buried in flowers, plumes, and veiling.

As for "The Gibson Girl," one of Charles Dana Gibson's famous drawings depicts her with two exceedingly long hat-

George Waller.

It seems one summer at Saratoga, Miss Russell was *"challenged by a rising young charmer, Louise Montague, in a field in which Miss Russell considered herself nonpariel: picking winners at the race track."*

As the competition grew keen, stable owners, jockeys, trainers, and bookies allied themselves with one beautiful damsel or the other and supplied them with a succession of tips. One sultry August afternoon, as the horses came into the homestretch, Miss Russell claimed victory by a nose and used this as an excuse to celebrate. Miss Russell hosted a lavish party to

**Plate 203:** Photo Courtesy of Dr. L. A. Katzin, DDS.

pins in her mouth, and another poised for action as she adjusts her hat high atop mountainous tresses. Underneath the pen and ink drawing is the title: *"Dangerous: The Gibson Girl."*

In Mark Sullivan's 1932 publication, *"Our Times 1909-1914"*, there's a great picture of Lillian Russell (photographed in 1909), showing the belle of the ball with two enormous hatpins in her hat. Of all the many interesting stories connected with hatpins, one of my very favorites concerns Lillian Russell. It's related in *"Saratoga, Saga of an Impious Era,"* by

which "everybody who was anybody" attended.

Miss Montague, who had earlier suggested that her rival, Miss Russell, owed her reputation as a handicapper *"to blind luck in picking winners with a hatpin poked through the racing programs,"* arrived with due fanfare carrying a fancy-wrapped package from Tiffany's.

Miss Russell unwrapped it gaily enough and held up — for all the celebrants to see — an expensive three-tined fish fork.

*"Now you can pick them to finish first, second, and third all*

*at once,"* Miss Montague remarked.

There's no record of Miss Russell's reply, but methinks that this gift would have flinted a new feud fit for the great bard, Shakespeare. With a Miss "Montague," all that was required was a name-change from "Russell" to "Capulet"! Evidently, however, Lillian Russell emerged the victor, for she has remained remembered, while Miss-what's-her-name has gone down to oblivion.

While researching in an 1897 *Leslie's Weekly,* I came upon a photograph of Miss Russell in her parlor-car and dressing room. She's shown with large hats strewn here and there, and on a small table is a huge pincushion positively crowded with gorgeous hatpins! Her elbow leans on this table, and by using her arm as a measure, I judge the average hatpin jammed together in that cushion must have measured no less than ten inches long! No doubt they were of the "real McCoy," in keeping with the other luxurious fittings. According to the text which accompanied the photograph, Lillian Russell was *"An American Beauty, on the Stage and at Home."* To wit:

> *Lillian Russell is successfully touring the country this season in a kind of tailor-made confection, fitted to her resplendent personality in the guise of a comic opera, entitled "An American Beauty." Critics gen-*

**Plate 156:** Lecturer Fran Tucker models authentic mourning attire from her collection of turn-of-the-century clothing. Hatpin (author's collection), is jet-glass riveted hatpin; stones soldered to a wire construction. Craft reached perfection in the mourning period of Queen Victoria (1901). Hatpin from H. M. Supplier, Gebruder Feix, Albrechtsdorf (1850-1945), Jablonecer District, Czech. CREDIT: Photograph by Marilyn Zander

*erally have shied at this singular freak of stage composition, and we believe that even the members of the cast performing it have never been able to discover what it is about. Yet everybody is satisfied with Lillian Russell as the typical and perfect embodiment of the title role — and well they may be.*

*She quite lives up to the prospectus and to her own reputation, and so is doubly an American Beauty. Moreover, she sings better than ever.*

*Miss Russell's tours are always successful, so far as she individually is concerned. In consequence, she can afford the substantial luxury of a private car when she travels and, what is more to the purpose, has a perfect little nest of a home into which to settle down when she flits in from her professional migrations "on the road." This is the little bijou of a house which she owns, in West Seventy-something Street, New York City, overlooking the romantic Hudson near Riverside Drive. The superfluity of jewels with which she bedecks herself nightly in the dressing-room of the Casino or elsewhere, according to the requirement of her role, are only paste. But she can duplicate them in genuine stones if she so desires. Miss Russell's real diamonds never had to do "lost" duty, to revive flagging press notices. She finds a goldplated bicycle much more effective and up-to-date for that purpose.*

In *"The Big Spenders,"* Lucius Beebe describes this gold-plated bicycle which no doubt "revived" press notices.

*"While the cost of the run-of-the-mill Brady gold-plated bicycles is not at this remove, available, no such reticence surrounds the extra-special model that he (Diamond Jim Brady) ordered to be more than ordinarily heavy with gold for Lillian Russell and on which she dutifully made her regular Sunday appearance for the photographers in Central Park in a white serge cycling suit topped with a Tyrolean hat."*

(At this point I must insert that doubtless this hat was pinned with "genuine" diamond hatpins.)

To continue from Mr. Beebe's report:

*"The Russell wheel, according to Parker Morrell, had mother-of-pearl handlebars while the spokes of each wheel were encrusted with diamond chips, emeralds, rubies, sapphires, and other precious stones mounted so as to catch the rays of the sun and made the rider's progress a miniature display of fireworks. Miss Russell kept the bicycle in a blue plush-lined morocco leather traveling case and it went on tour whenever she took to the road. Once it arrived at Saratoga on a private car together with Brady's staff of thirty Chinese houseboys. It cost $10,000."*

All this flamboyance while war-clouds were gathering! With world events sobering the mind and the mind's-eye for fashion as well, came the submergence of frivolity in fashion — coinciding with the 1912 tragic sinking of the Titanic.

There has always been a superstition about having women aboard a ship. Sailors must have been terrorized during the height of the hatpin days, for in addition to their fear of women aboard ship, they also feared *pins* brought on board a vessel. Pins were considered "spiteful witches and ought never to be brought on board a vessel" because pins are the cause of "a leak, holes in nets, loss of gear at high sea . . .," etc. etc.

In view of the above, does one dare consider that the White Star Line's *Titanic* which struck an iceberg in the Atlantic on April 14, 1912, was ill-fated? Could it have been "cursed" at the height of the hatpin era, by women aboard who dared to wear hatpins in multiples in order to secure their hats against the stout ocean breezes? After all, hatpins are no ordinary pins, but pins at their greatest length and strength of superstitious power!

World War I came. With it arrived hat styles that were much too sobering to be flattering to many, and it was then that the period hatpin surrendered to the dictates of the times.

Since most hatpins were considered jewelry, they went the way of many ornaments that had become outdated or out-

**Plate 215:** Silver Hatpin. T. J. Lawson, Leicester, England, March, 1975.

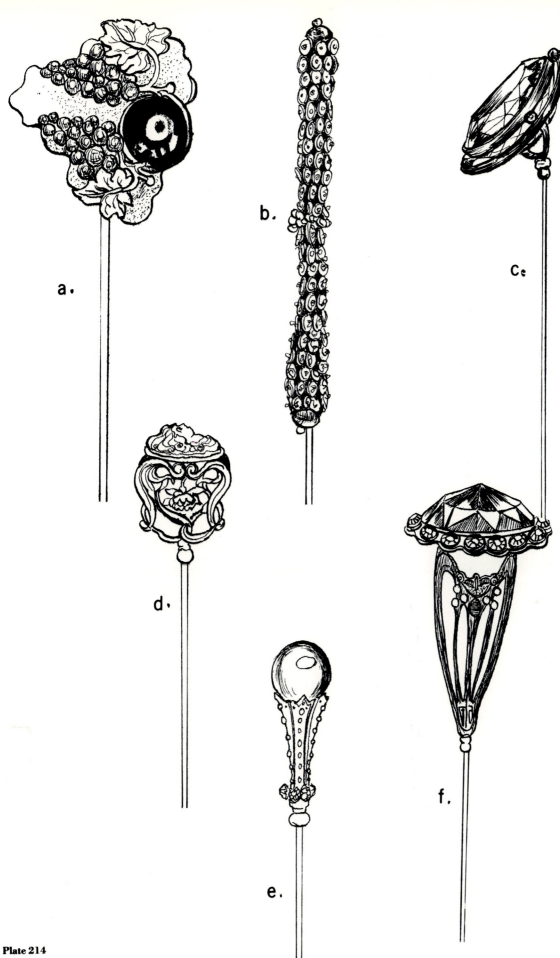

a.

b.

c.

d.

e.

f.

Plate 214

89

moded with the changes in fashion. Hatpins whose ornaments were made of precious metals were melted down to be recast; the precious or semi-precious gemstones were then reset in more current mountings.

A correspondent informed me that her mother's hatpins were donated — along with other metallic articles — to the United States Government during World War II, at which time there was an urgent call for scrap-material of any metal for the "war effort."

Fortunately, there have always been dedicated hatpin collectors preserving hatpins in holders and cushions to delight the aesthetic eye! One such collector is Mary Jo Marrese of York, Pa., whose assemblage was noted in a 1972 article published in *Antiques News:*

> *"Mary Jo's collection includes hatpins of pearls, silver, gold, silver filigree, gold filigree, onyx, oxidized silver, frosted gold, colorful stones of every color, porcelains with transfer patterns, porcelains with hand painted designs, moonstones, clamsbroth, cut jets, amethyst, cloisonne, pictured mourning pins, tortoise shell, compositions, turquoise, enamels, carnival glass, commemorative pins, dragon flies, soldier buttons, opals, ivory, jades, shells, straw weave, silver overlays, mineral stones, ruby, sterlings, gold, rhinestone, cameo, brass, pewter, ruby marquisette overlays, Art Nouveau, circus stone, polished coal, cut glass, emeralds, sandwich, aquamarine, topaz, alexandrite, satsuma and zircons."*

Her collection of over 500 hatpins was accumulated during a 12 year period! Search the Plates in this book and you're bound to identify at least one each of the above examples.

Jean J. Hepburn, former owner of the Whittemore-Durgin Glass Co., Hanover, Mass., has one of the world's largest collections and still deals in hatpins. How she became involved in hatpins was reported in April 1970, *Collectors News.* Seems a *"peculiar little old man who was operating a hatpin factory in a small town"* hadn't *"produced a single, solitary hatpin since 1910."* Still optimistic, he was *"hoping for a comeback and continued going down to the office every morning, hoping for some orders to come in the mail."* The eventual outcome: Jean Hepburn bought the business, "lock, stock and barrel," and then found herself a collector and dealer in hatpins.

For many, many years, to antique shows throughout the West and mid-West, came a couple with the *largest hatpin collection* in the world! Dr. L. A. Katzin and his late wife, Beatrice, often exhibited portions of their gigantic collection at antique shows where they sold and exhibited other antique merchandise as well. In 1963, their hatpin collection was reported to be the world's largest, in excess of 15,000-18,000 hatpins, with hardly a duplicate! When Dr. Katzin, a retired dentist and world-traveler lost his wife, he sold portions of the hatpin collection to many collectors, including myself. (Plate 203.)

I was fortunate to know Beatrice Katzin and was saddened by her death. She had been an encouraging force and most helpful in my research. It also seemed sad that such an extensive and marvelous collection of hatpins should be scattered once more from shore to shore.

My own collection has some fine examples of the early production of jet hair ornaments and hatpins (circa 1898), often described as "black glass jewelry". This type of jewelry has an interesting and fascinating background. Its history is really the story of glass jewelry and glass hatpins of Bohemian manufacture, and of the Land itself.

Six centuries of glass-production conditioned the growth of costume jewelry manufacture in Bohemia, of which in modern times, (little less than fifty years ago), evolved the prosperous glass-works in the region of Jablonec, in the interior of Bohemia.

Because suitable quartz is necessary in the making of Bohemian glass, manufacturers and tradesmen frequently dwelled in the forested foothills of these mountainous regions; it was these very inaccessible wooded countries close to the borders that kept the communities safe from the many wars and battles fought nearby. Because of this protected remoteness, the glass-works industry survived without influence and change — until the turn-of-the-century.

The Jablonec, (Czechoslovakia), village of glassworks was founded in 1785, and by the middle 1800s was successful on an international scale of manufacture and trade. Thus, right when the demand for exotic glass hatpins was at its height, the glassworks of Jablonec came forth with some of the most exquisite examples. (See Plates 96, 97, and 128.)

By the second half of the 19th century, Jablonec articles held practically a world monopoly in the jewelry trade from 1912-1950. In 1869, according to Jablonec historian, A. Benda, *"The Jablonec District became the California of Austria. Strangers flocked into the town from all parts seeking to make their fortune."* The population of that little village increased from its 1857 figure of 4,553, to 6,752 in 1869 — 2,878 "being foreigners."

Jewelry making not only involved the glassworks industry but involved independent trades such as the making of pins from wire, pressing, mould engraving, metal coloring, making of filigree parts, painting, waxing, mirror-coating, and many others.

Very seldom did a finished piece of costume jewelry (including period hatpins) issue from a single pair of hands. To the contrary, the hatpin was an assemblage of parts — from the pin, to the findings needed to anchor the ornament, to the mounting, and to the individual stones with their various combinations of cut, shape, and color.

It was the costume jewelry of the middle 19th and early 20th centuries that competed with the expensive jewels. Because of its low cost it allowed a greater variety of shapes and designs, since a worker can be much more daring in using sheet metal and glass than working with rare materials such as gold and precious stones. Most period hatpins coming from the glassworks industrial area of Jablonec had glass imitations of precious stones.

Costs were kept low because engraving metal dies, though tedious and time-consuming, were done by paying "starvation pay" to artists; they, in turn, used slightly differing modifications of the dies so an inexhaustible number of designs were produced; variations of these were then enlarged by using various combinations of imitation stones. By the 1890's, marcasite and Bohemian garnet came into vogue, and so did the black non-transparent glass called "blackwares", so often confused

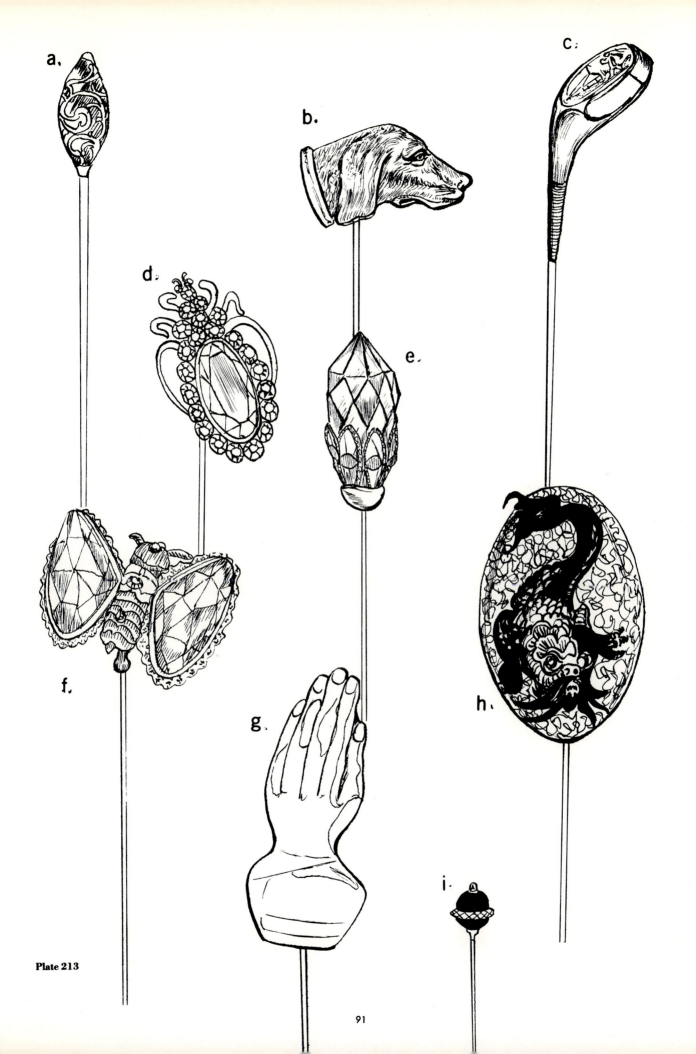

a.

b.

c.

d.

e.

f.

g.

h.

i.

Plate 213

91

with "jet". (See Plates 78, 79 and 128.)

The "black glass jewelry" was a highly skilled and specialized craft in which decorative pieces were made from cut stones put together on a wire frame. These stones ranged in size from 1/16″ to 2″ and were exquisitely cut and faceted stones. (See Plates 96 and 156.)

The glassworks produced imitation amber, alabaster glass, and glass decorated with lacquer or enamel. Glass was gilded, decked with girdlers' ornaments or finally lustred or irized. The finely faceted glass stones were combined with metallic mountings which in themselves incorporated the art of chiseling, stamping, pressing, embossing, and other types of metal-decorating. (Plates 23, 36, 77, 177 and 129)

While glass stones were being manufactured as imitations, there was also the world market for rochelle, bugle, and other type beads which were sold in the African trade. These glass beads were also used in hat ornaments and hatpins. (Plate 86.)

In 1864, the glass button won world position in fashion, and many hatpins resemble button-heads of the era. Glass hatpins were cut in variants and patterns, then refined by painting, cutting and polishing. (See Plates 24, 76 and 102.)

Also developed were hollow pearls and a method of silver-plating mirrors, thus creating a pearl-making industry that introduced inexpensive imitation pearls in hatpin ornaments.

*Glass* stones were cut with the same tools used for *precious* stones. Of course instead of "stones" there were rods of glass which were pre-molded with pressing tongs and polished on water-driven grinding machines. Those polished on a tin disc were considered the highest quality. These, were exported to Germany, France, Italy and Spain and were classified as Bohemian stones or "Bohemian diamonds".

The popular cutting-styles of genuine gems and gemstones most frequently imitated in the glassworks of the world-famous Jablonec region of Bohemian (Czechoslovakia), were carmoiseres, rosettes, routes, oval rosettes, square and rectangular shapes with sharp oblique corners, triangles, drop shapes, pointed elipses, etc.

Zuzana Pesatova, recognized Jablonec historian wrote:

> "The French Revolution had destroyed the feudal bears of the old culture and the jewel lost its exclusive character. The new revolutionary ideal of liberty permitted everyone to dress and deck himself at pleasure, irrespective of his origin or class."

The demands of the masses, then, were quite responsible for the *quantity* of jewelry produced, rather than the *quality*; for paste had long been accepted by the wealthy as a substitute for the real gems. Then came the "free-for-all" in the wearing of costume jewelry, and a tremendous commercial industry was — if not born — certainly accelerated! It became necessary, because of the demand, to use substitutes: precious stones were replaced by glass; gold by iron, tombac, or copper.

By the second half of the 19th century, the colour scheme in manufacturing beads included 200 variations in shades and about 19 various sizes. Iris and lustre had been discovered, and the bead-boom resounded throughout the fashion world. Coming on the horizon were those ropes and strands of beads which became larger and longer with the climax reached in those "roarin' twenties" when beads and banjos made music together.

The hatpins of that 1850-1920 production really outclassed all previous sources of inspiration for jewelry in its numerous forms, since it now had not only ancient art and art of other ages to be copied, but that most glorious inspiration for ornamentation provided by the Renaissance. Surpassing all other sources of inspiration, the Renaissance was a heritage not lost upon the artisans of the Victorian, Edwardian, and *Art Nouveau* periods. The jewelry of this latter era produced some of the most highly prized pieces for both collectors and museum acquisitions.

Inspiration, scientific discoveries, and inventive genius combined and merged and generated generations of fabricators who contrived, originated, and designed masterful jewelry decorations. The period hatpin was an unusual by-product — a device or contrivance which combined artistic merit, commercial enterprise, and utilitarian purpose.

The times of Lillian Russell (1851-1922) might well be called the "glorious era of jeweled hatpins". Right smack in the center of this era, bonnet ties were mere flutterings in the wind, and in many instances the bonnet was discarded in favor of the hat. And with the hat came the hatpins!

Some of these pins were made to hold the hat flaring up and off the face. (See Plate 134.) By 1907, hats became so exaggerated they lent themselves to parlor-car jokes and cartoons; but two things that were *not* overstated in caricature were the *size* of the hat and the *length* of the hatpins!

Women's head fashions had come full cycle, from the wearing of a hat as protection from the sun, to going bareheaded as "sun-lovers." The introduction of fast moving vehicles did away permanently with loose fitting bonnets or wide-brimmed hats. The "floppy-brim" has endured, but the stiff-straw six to ten inch brim is a thing of the past. Short cropped hair, the "natural look," and the long straight hair with its abandonment of hairpins or ties, make the come-back of the long hatpin unlikely. Tight-fitting "helmets", decorative hair-nets and "snoods", kerchiefs and headbands, seem to be traveling head attire of this century and the next.

Air travel and the close proximity of passenger airline seats,* necessarily dictates close-fitting hats, if any at all. Automotive travel in closed vehicles precludes the necessity of hats, ribbon-ties, and veiling. If a hat is worn, elastic bands, plastic combs sewn inside the lining, or a bobby pin, gives the same sense of security that hatpins once provided.

Hatboxes no longer carry *chapeaux*. They are now storage places for an extra wig or hairpiece. Even in large cities, hats are no longer common-place nor required by fashion. They seem to be conspicuous when worn but, in my opinion, have always seemed flattering to women. Even the Easter bonnet has been reduced to a fluff of veiling sometimes adorned with an artificial flower.

It would seem that the period hatpin is gone forever — except that I should like to leave my readers with words other than my own. They are words that urge me to shout:

> *"The hatpin is dead! Long live the hatpin!"*

---

*Perhaps contrary to some airline's advertising.*

From John Canaday's special report to the *New York Times*, datelined *Osaka, Japan*, (March 15, 1970):

"... but the ugliest thing at the fair, and one of the ugliest anywhere ever, is the monster sponsored by the Fuji Group, a combine of 36 of Japan's major companies. The Fuji Pavillion's enormous pneumatic sausage walls, plus numerous growths and excresences of inflated plastics throughout the fair give you the feeling that if you don't like the looks of the world of the future, the most effective weapon against it would be an old-fashioned hat pin."

*THE HATPIN IS DEAD! LONG LIVE THE HATPIN!*

\* \* \*

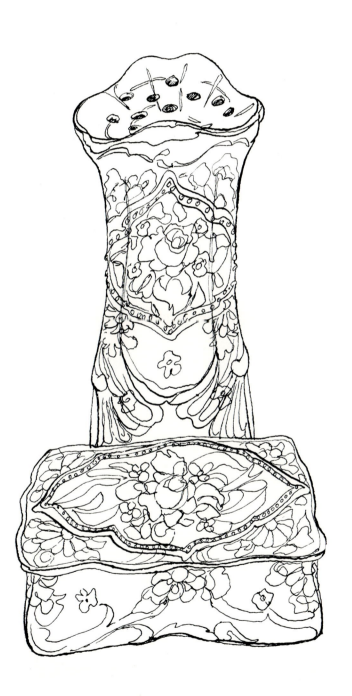

**Plate 209**

# Chapter IV
# THE PERIOD HATPIN ADDENDUM

While working on the final portions of this manuscript I allowed myself the luxury of a "break" in order to watch *Love Among the Ruins*", starring two stellar stage personalities — Katharine Hepburn and Lawrence Olivier. (See Plate 174.)

Advance publicity from IBM alerted me that the setting of 1911 was in the height of the hat and hatpin era.

The program, presented on ABC television, March 6, 1975, proved to be a rare gift for viewers. As for me, there was an extra bonus for it provided "much ado" about hats! In fact, hardly had the intriguing drama unfolded when Miss Hepburn was asked to remove her stunning chapeau.

"Don't you like it?" she asks.

The gallant Olivier assures her that he does but insists that its huge size shadows her face and he would like to see her better.

"Well," she replies, "you'll have to be patient; there are *three* hatpins!" And she proceeds to un-skewer the feathered headgear.

I must admit it's difficult to conceal my one disappointment of the evening; that is, I felt there should have been some spectacularly long hatpins of jet buried somewhere among the plumes. After all, the part called for the wealthy heroine to be "in mourning for two years." Instead, three quite miniature-sized pins were used and these were quickly removed from the hat and stabbed back into the crown.

There are three most conspicuous hatpins in a photograph of Lily Langtree, in James Brough's 1975 Book-of-the-Month selection, *"The Prince and the Lily"*. Such were the type hatpins I looked for in Miss Hepburn's costuming

The above must seem like "nitpicking" when considering the magnificence of the entire production of "Love Among the Ruins." But I mention these little flaws — little to some — only because they point to a sharper need for references regarding the proper use and design of accessories including the all-important hatpin. Perhaps this book will be such an aid to costumers and historians.

*"Love Among the Ruins"* set a new standard in television excellence and all those connected with its production deserve plaudits galore! My special thanks to Robert E. Jagoda, Program Manager, Advertising Services, IBM (International Business Machines Corporation), for providing the photographs of its brilliant stars, Hepburn and Olivier.

# Chapter V

# HOW TO RECOGNIZE AND AVOID FAKE HATPINS

There has been much altering and manipulation of hatpins in order to make their counterfeit results appear to be the genuine article. There are also reproductions being marketed under such misleading advertising banners as "uncirculated" hatpins.

Whether the misleading reproductions or the worthless imitations which are passed off as the genuine is more offensive to the collector is a question whose answer can only increase indignation when in both instances the article is sold as an authentic "period hatpin".

As the fascination for yesteryear artifacts increases, the interest in hatpins of the 1890-1914 period attracts more and more collectors. As the demand for these items leaps upward, it's part of the game that the unscrupulous will prey upon the

public, which in this case has been provided with little or no information regarding the period hatpin and its complimentary accessories. It's no wonder we find so many hatpin fakes being manufactured from antique brooches and buttons and from modern dress pins and jewelry.

Careful study of the drawings accompanying the text of this chapter, (Plates 136, 137 and 138), should provide an excellent guide and help in judging the authenticity of genuine period hatpins.

The drawings depict in detail the essential jewelers' *findings* utilized in authentic hatpin mountings.

Seldom has the writer discovered deviations in the typical mounting of the ornament on to the pin: the pin is always inserted into the center socket or patch portion of the pin, or

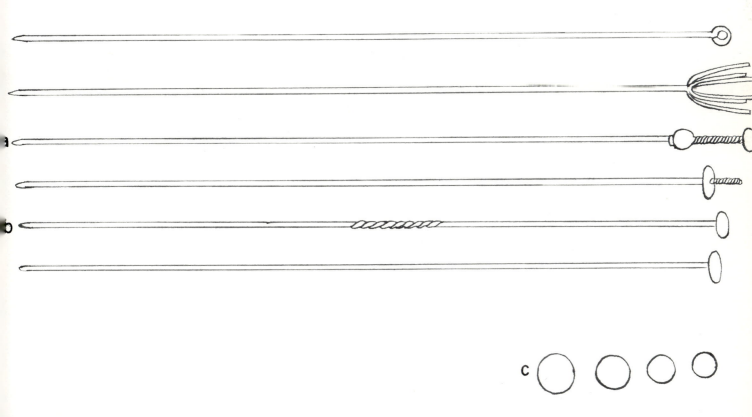

**Plate 137**

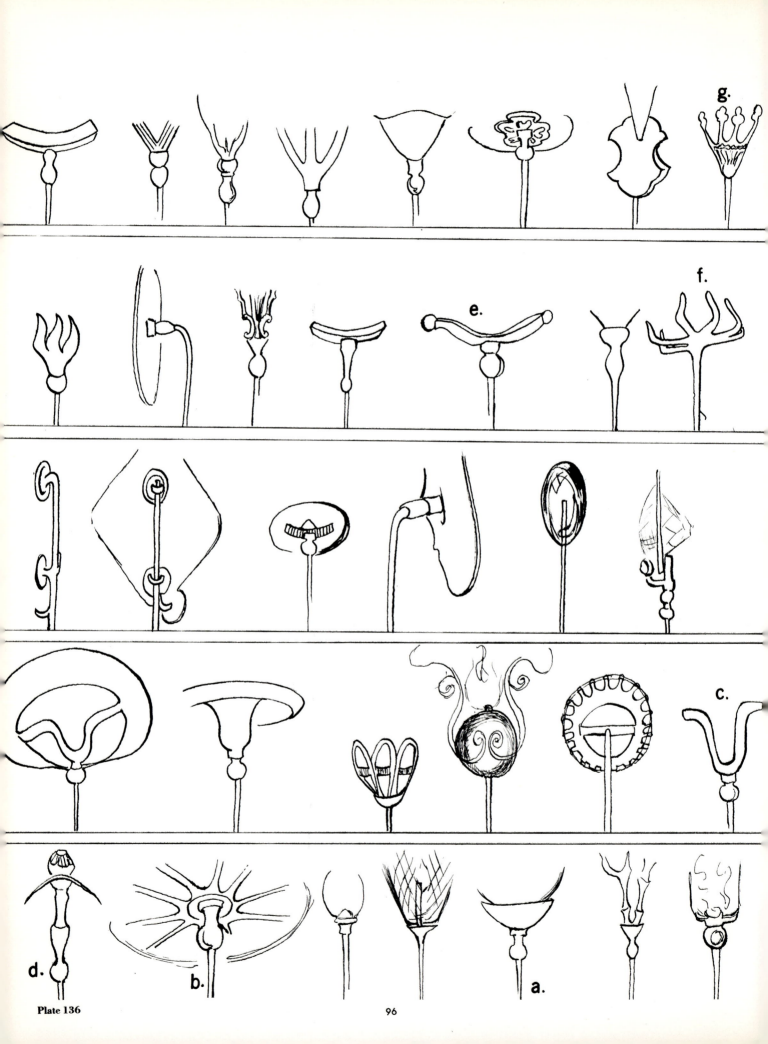

g.

f.

e.

c.

d.

b.

a.

Plate 136

96

else it is inserted into a finding which has been centered on the "bridge", "arc", or "span" which is used on the larger ornaments to balance it on the shank.

The ornaments are carefully fitted into the patch or sleeve-covering which is usually part of the device or design of the ornament head.

A small shank-piece separates the pin and the ornament and is actually used as a finishing joint to cover the place where the ornament and the pin are joined. This tiny tubular finding often aids in securing the bauble to the pin. If this small finding is missing between the pin and ornament, chances are the hatpin has either been repaired, is a "homemade" job, or is an outright fake.

There should never be visible adhesive on a genuine hatpin unless the genuine hatpin has been repaired. I would hesitate to buy any repaired pin unless it was one which had been damaged in my own handling, or if all the findings were complete and intact except for the insertion of the pin which had fallen out or had been loosened.

Since it is common for antique buttons and brooches to have metallic backings, silver solder and ordinary solder (lead and tin) have been used to cement long pins to such items. They are then "passed" as genuine period hatpins and purchased by collectors with an untrained and uneducated eye.

The rare exceptions to the above rule on adhesives are those ornaments which have been converted into hatpins such as a memento or souvenir which has then been utilized as a hatpin. Buttons and coins are typical examples of some hatpins which were manufactured as specialties; in most cases a custom mounting was wrought by a jeweler, and using his special drill, the pin was inserted without the use of unsightly adhesives. (See Plates 22 and 31.)

Concentrated study of the drawings will make the reader aware that where the pin is actually inserted or attached to the ornament it becomes by virtue of the jewelers' finding either an integral part of the design or an actual part of the mounting. The pin is *incorporated* rather than *added* on to the assemblage.

Seldom are decorative stones *pasted* into the mounting. They are SET in the many types of settings, such as "claw", "crown", etc. There are usually several prongs for support or the stone(s) are inserted into a deep well or metal sleeve rather than on a flat surface.

One must remember when looking for authenticity in period hatpins that the pin itself should be made of tempered steel, brass, or base metals — the latter often gilded. There are, of course, pins of precious metals such as gold carat or sterling silver.

There were no *stainless steel* pins used before the first quarter of the 20th century. Tin, copper, and pewter were not used in making pins due to the softness of the metals, although hatpin heads have been made of these materials and a particularly interesting one in pewter is in the writer's collection. (Plate No. 69.)

Today there are gold and silver colored metals used in costume jewelry which are remarkable for their permanence in color and in brilliance. So beware of any long pins that are "new" looking for they are indeed *new*, having been manufactured within the last fifteen years oftentimes with the express purpose of misleading those seeking antique hatpins. An

advertisement for hatpins "Circa 1950" is a prime example.

Over the counter today one may purchase small hatpins usually no longer than a corsage pin (2½"-3"), made with stainless steel pins.

These small hatpins are legitimately sold in better department stores and variety stores and have a small unimpressive bauble on the end. These modern-day ornaments are commonly *aurelias*, cheap paste, or glass beads. The stones are not usually prong-set but are merely pasted or wired into place; this make the hatpin inexpensive, (59¢-$1.00). Occasionally I have found one or more of these hatpins "roughed up" in an antique shop and being sold as an "original, old, hatpin from grandma's day."

Be especially wary of antique-type jewelry — often reproductions of genuine antique buttons and brooches — which has been soldered to a long pin or has had the pin pierced through into the flat side of the button or brooch. The solder conveniently covers the shank of the button. Where the fastener has been removed from a brooch, a genuine hatpin mounting with its familiar arc or span will cover the distance across the brooch, and solder is used to cover the two spots where the original brooch fastener or clasp had been joined.

Some disreputable dealers will explain that the hatpins have been repaired or "reinforced" but that the item is an "original". True, the ornaments may be antique or collectible but they are not original *hatpin* ornaments. Unfortunately, there are many such fakes flooding the market.

As with all antique merchandise, there are those few who will try to pass off articles as the real McCoy, but by and large it has been this writer's experience that most antique dealers are reliable and have been honestly duped themselves by individuals who are making period hatpins for profit.

It's become quite distressing to discover more and more of these fakes at some of the most reputable establishments and at recognized antique shows. As previously stated, most instances have proven pure ignorance or oversight. After all, until now there have been no guidelines for them to follow, and dealers cannot possibly know everything about everything! Whenever the opportunity has presented itself, this writer has tried to educate collectors and buyers on the subject of fakes.

Several sources have informed this writer that a few con-artists are buying up the plain old black or white glass-beaded hatpins with 8"-12" pins. By breaking off the simple glass marble with a hammer, the pins are then used in conjunction with old buttons and brooches and thus are converted into "old" hatpins.

Sometimes these longer pins are used to *replace* shorter pins on *genuine* hatpins of the period in order to *increase the selling price*. Hatpins with the longest pins are most desirable to collectors and are therefore higher priced.

In the case of the transfer or exchange of pin-lengths, the thing to look for is the difference in color between the ornamental head of gold or silver color as contrasted against the tempered steel pin which is greyish-blue in color. Well-crafted ornamental heads are seldom mounted on the same pins used for the cheapest black and/or white glass bead-type hatpins. Therefore, beware of the inconsistency between a gilt-headed pin mounted on anything other than a gilt, brass, or nickle-plated shank. The majority of pins are "silver-color", those with genuine stones used gilt shanks.

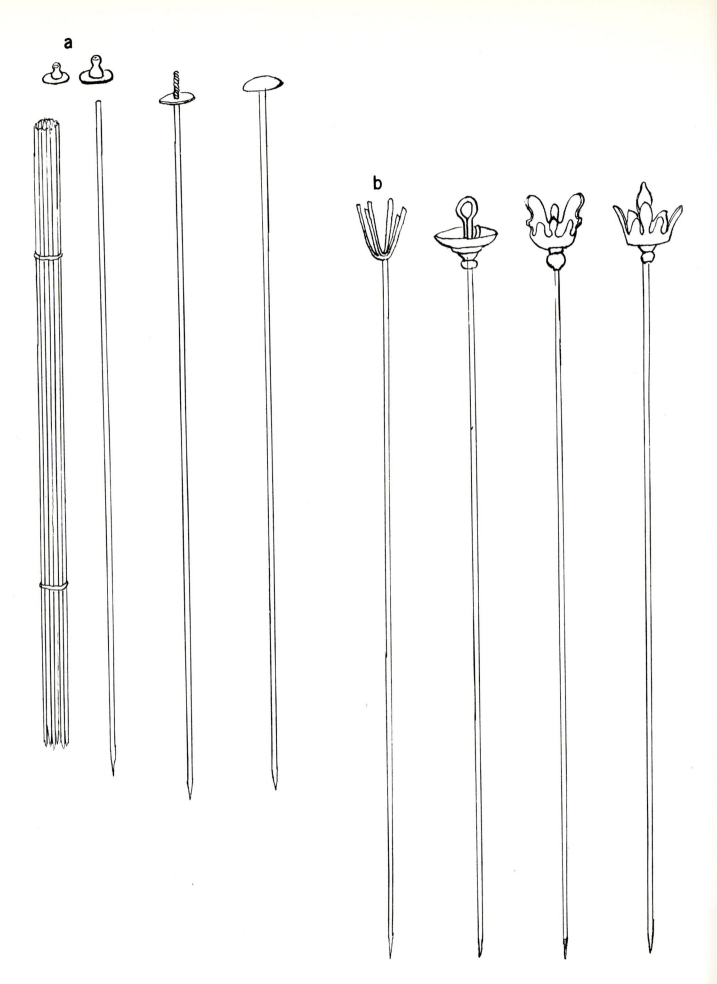

Plate 138

Upon close scrutiny, most collectors can see how fakes are accomplished and it is further suggested that the buyer always carry a magnifying glass for this purpose. Examine the pins and mountings carefully; some of these fakes are quite beautiful, for the buttons and brooches of the Victorian era were lovely and the *nouveau* most enchanting. Authentic hatpins of those eras may be found with similiar designs utilized on buttons and brooches. This is because the same jewelers who created other items of jewelry and decorative wear, also designed hatpin ornaments.

One can almost date the period hatpin by its length; that is, its length will dictate whether it was worn during the exaggerated period of hats and hair-styles (1890-1914) — give or take a few years on either side of the calendar. Short hatpins were worn with the more conservative millinery concoctions, and with hairdos that did not require more hair than that which was naturally endowed the wearer.

If you find an army button from "The Great War" (WWI) on an extremely long pin, buyer beware! Chances are it's been switched quite recently from its normally shorter pin to one "snitched" from an earlier hatpin with the longer and more popular shank. A purely commercial undertaking.*

Once again I urge the reader to study the drawings of the mountings, and how these mountings are attached to the bau-

*During the "hatpin crisis", many of the long pins were cut shorter so that women would not run afoul of the law. Some large baubles were obviously balanced on longer shanks in their original manufacture.*

ble. (Plate No. 136.) That is the best aid in determining the authenticity of period hatpins and is this writer's own determining factor in making a purchase. An advance collector will avoid any hatpin that's been repaired or has evidence of soldering material.

A rather deceitful trick is exercised by downright frauds who use old-time collar-buttons with the raw pins. How's the trick done?

A small hole is drilled in the end of the collar-button into which the shank is inserted. Then the flat disc top is adhered to a large ornament that was previously manufactured as a belt-buckle, clasp, clip, earring, button, or any number of other wearables.

Although the old-fashioned collar-button does *look* like one of the authentic findings used for hatpins, (See Plate No. 138a.), it can be easily detected because of its larger size and contrast in color from the ornament to which it is attached. Once you are familiar with this angle, such duped articles are readily spotted. If you've never seen an old-fashioned collar-button, it will be worth your while to search one out in the attic or antique shop and make a mental note of same.

Some hatpins with a simple small head made of glass beads, or faceted bauble of glass, were manufactured with just a tiny bushing or fitting that finished the hatpin off nicely. Once in a great while the marble-headed or glass bead has the pin imbedded into a small hole made by a drill and then glued for permanence. If the glue is crusty or yellow-looking, chances are it's an authentic hatpin that's been restored. But beware the newer non-smear, non-gooey adhesives of today which were not known at the time of period hatpins. If you do find a hand-

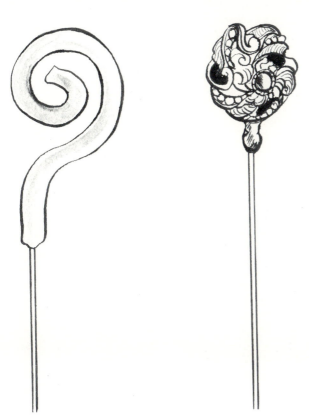

**Plate 210**

some hatpin that has been glued way-back-when, it's likely to be a home-made job rather than the work of a fine jeweler. Jewelers of the period hatpin era would have repaired the pin properly, using the required finding to complete the job. *Findings* are part of the "common-stock" of the jewelry trade.

Most cloth-covered decorated hatpins are the handiwork of Victorian ladies or of milliners who used small glass-beaded or tiny wooden-headed pins as the basis for their work.

One should be cautioned against purchasing silver-colored metal hatpins as *silver* unless they are hallmarked or have the word "sterling" imprinted on the head.

Gold and gold-filled hatpins are usually marked "karat" if made in America. If the pin is gilt, (gold color or gold plated), it is not usually marked. European hatpins are sometimes not marked "karat" but have numerals that are our equivalent, i.e.: 500=14K and 750=18K. Some very early gold pin-ornaments were unmarked. Karat gold is recognizable from mere brass because of the rich patina of the ore. Although there are some gemstones set in non-precious ore, gems such as diamonds, sapphires, rubies, and emeralds are set in other than precious metals.

When it comes to period hatpins, there's no such thing as an inflexible rule. It seems, in fact, that rules pertaining to hatpins are meant to be broken! However, as a *general* rule, period hatpins wrought in precious ore should be *marked* as to gold or silver content, since that was the practice (as well as a legal requirement) of recognized jewelers of the Trade.

Some gold or silver hatpin ornaments have pinshanks of matching color — either plated or filled. It's unusual to find a 14K bauble on a *steel* pin or a hallmarked "sterling" on a tempered steel greyish-blue shank. As stated before, there are exceptions, and some ornaments of precious ore and gems are found mounted on pins of steel or brass.

In my opinion, the abovementioned exceptions could be *replacement* pins for either broken shanks or for shanks that had been cut down.

The best advice in the end is to make your purchases from a reputable dealer, combining his and your accumulated knowledge and experience on the subject in conjunction with the information offered in this chapter. If purchasing from a private party, remember the ever-wise admonition: "When in doubt, do without!"

**Plate 202**

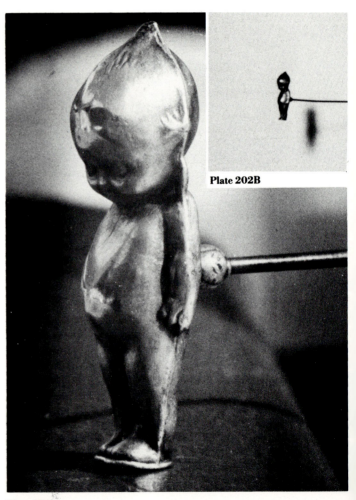

**Plate 202B**

**Plate 202A**

# Chapter VI

# HATPIN HOLDERS, INCLUDING LOOK-ALIKES AND REPRODUCTIONS — DRESSER SETS, PINCUSHIONS, AND OTHER RELATED ARTICLES TO THE HATPIN.

"*. . . upon lace doilies placed to save the beautiful rosewood top, lay a silver toilet set more magnificent than any Sara had ever seen. The mirror had a long slender handle. Even the glass hatpin case had a silver top.*" (*The Trembling Hills* by Phyllis A. Whitney.)

There are almost as many varieties of hatpin holders as hatpins, and like hatpins, one has a wide choice for they were made of many things: silver, gold, copper, crystal and all the standard glass and china of the period including cut, carnival, and jasper. The most popular seemed to be the hand-painted porcelains, or at least these are the holders which are found most plentiful today and were more easily afforded in yesteryear.

Hatpin holders were both cheap and expensive and were in identifying authentic hatpin holders from objects resembling other desirable collectibles and the reproductions which have innundated the antique market within the past three years. But first, let us explore *authentic* hatpin holders.

So little to date has been detailed regarding the unique hatpin holder, no wonder there's so much confusion!

Manufacturers' marks on hatpin holders testify that they were made in the mid-19th century and early 20th century. Most have European marks which is not unusual since the primary source of most china articles was either from the Continent or Britain, with the less expensive import-models coming from the Orient.

The holders were manufactured in brilliant cut, pressed, opaline, and carnival glass. They were beautifully executed in silver, pottery, ceramic, glazed porcelain and unglazed bisque.

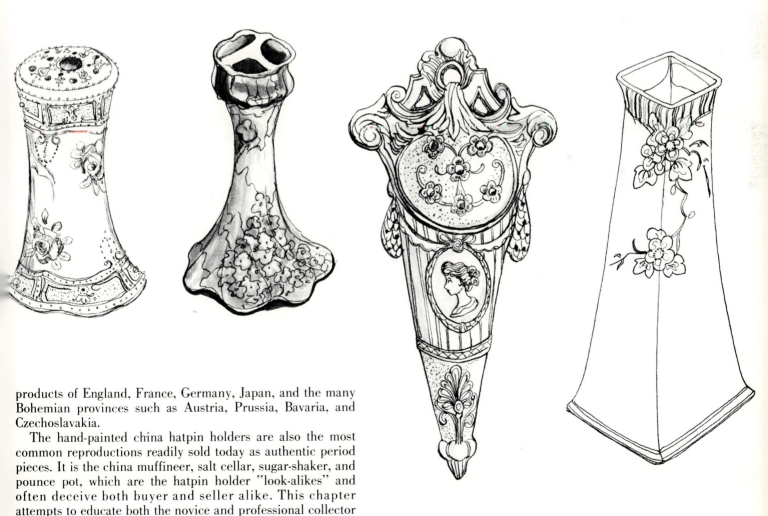

products of England, France, Germany, Japan, and the many Bohemian provinces such as Austria, Prussia, Bavaria, and Czechoslavakia.

The hand-painted china hatpin holders are also the most common reproductions readily sold today as authentic period pieces. It is the china muffineer, salt cellar, sugar-shaker, and pounce pot, which are the hatpin holder "look-alikes" and often deceive both buyer and seller alike. This chapter attempts to educate both the novice and professional collector

**Plate 192**

101

**Plate 182**

Many of the china holders were hand-painted by Victorian and Edwardian damsels, for china painting was a favored pastime. The factories also produced handpainted examples, but many others were decorated with transfer prints, embellished with beading, or enriched with designs in overlay paints.

The holders, signed and unsigned, may be found footed, flat, round, square, rectangular, and oval. Because some countries of origin no longer exist, trademarks of "RS Prussia", "Royal Rudolstadt", "Royal Bayreuth", etc. are highly collectible and rare. Their output was not as great as "Limoges" (France), "Nippon" (Japan), nor the stoneware and porcelain produced in the great industrial area known as Staffordshire (England).

Herman C. Carter, writing about *Milady's Dresser Accessories,* stated:

> *"The elaborate coiffure, the large and sometimes floppy hat, the hatpin, and the hatpin holder came in rapid fire succession. All of this to the great delight of the hairdresser, milliner, and the makers of ladies dresser sets. It was almost like a conspiracy against the man-of-the-house's pocketbook."*

But there were hatpin holders and dresser sets to fit all change-purses. (See Plates 13, 14, 44, 45, 46, 47, 57, 58, 60, 68, 74, 75.)

Just as it's wrong to generalize that hatpins "came in two standard lengths — nine and twelve inches," so we dare not limit the dimensions of the receptacles which held these pointed objects. Hatpin holders were made in every shape and form!

Some hatpin holders, molded as a single-piece accommodation for rings, hatpins, and tie-pins, (Plate 164 — left), are extremely hard to find. This particular example has often puzzled me. It seems that in a time when ladies' dressing rooms were "off-limits" to men, including their spouses, the *smaller* pin holder (referred to as a *tie-pin* holder) should more correctly be considered a holder for very short flower-pins, hairpins, and simple straight pins. There are small, *individual* pinholders that were used in men's dressing rooms, for scarf, cravat or tie pins. (Plate 48 and 59.)

It is also possible that the open-mouthed holders as shown on Plates 13 and 17, were used for the many decorative hairpins which had a *heavier guage shank* than hatpins, and would therefore not fit into the tiny pin-size holes of most hatpin holders. It seems almost certain that holders with larger than pin-prick size holes, such as are shown on Plates 39, 51, 52, and 53, were specifically designed to accept larger pin-shanks

**Plate 182**

such as hatpins with "nibs" or "protectors". (See Chapter III, "Hatpins as Weapons," regarding "nibs.")

Other than hatpins, women wore fan-pins, corsage pins (or violet pins, as they are sometimes called), a great variety of jeweled hair-pins, and lace pins. Many of these pins were double-pronged and usually measured from 4″ to 6″ in length. The ideal place for storage would have been the aforementioned holders with *large holes*, the *open-mouth* hatpin holder, or hatpin holders with a large center hole on top. This center hole has often been regarded as the "mold opening" from which the piece was removed from the mold. Some holders have these "mold openings" at the *bottom*; most hatpin holders, however, have *solid bottoms*. Many, many, holders have no more than pin-size holes on top; no doubt, they have an "applied" top or two-mold construction.

Since hats of the 1890-1914 period required the longest hatpins, it seems reasonable to assume that the tallest hatpin holders were made at that time. (See Plates 39 and 55.) Just about all hatpin holders made in the late 19th and early 20th centuries were manufactured to lodge the *manufactured* period hatpin, (post 1832).

However, since several hatpin holders are identified by marks as having been made early in the 19th century in Bavaria and Prussia, it's permissible, I think, to assume that

hatpins with *handmade* wire-pins were worn in the royal courts along with numerous other "conceits" so popular at the time. It's highly unlikely that hatpin holders would have been made *before* the advent or use of a hatpin. That would be like putting the cart before the horse! That is, unless the holders were made to house *other* types of decorative pins!

Regardless of speculation, there's no doubt that the largest quantity of hatpin holders were manufactured with the introduction of period hatpins on the fashion front. The dresser set or commode ensemble soon required a ring tree, earring hook, and the inevitable hatpin holder.

Most hatpin holders were made from 1860-1920 with the later models incorporating little saucers which were used for blouse pins, women's cuff-links, bar pins (for women's shirtwaists), and finally for the small "nibs" or "protectors".

Most hatpin holders have from six to eight pin openings as compared to tie-pin holders with their eight to sixteen pin-places. (See Plates 48 and 59.) This should dispel the notion, projected in a recent article stating: ". . . *At any rate, men did not have so many stickpins as women had hatpins so their holders could be smaller and have fewer holes in the top*".

Figural hatpin holders are a unique collection in themselves! Some of these are shown in Plates 38, 49, 53, 69 and 182. I have read of a figural holder depicting an elderly lady with a toothache, and I missed the sale of a grand hatpin holder which was a Santa carrying his sack. The pin-pricked sack was the receptacle for hatpins. Both lady and Santa were German bisque.

Hatpin holders and other pin-holders were decorated with flowers, vines, and foliage, as well as country scenes, portraits and souvenir issues. (See Plates 41, 54 and 70.)

Reed, raffia, straw, metallic thread, and other media were used in the handmade variety, (primitives), which were often hung from either a wood turning or mirror brace of dresser or vanity table. Some of these are illustrated in Plates 62, 119, and 187.

Marion T. Hartung, a first authority on Carnival Glass, has stated that the term "Carnival" ". . . *should properly be applied only to colored pressed glass, with iridescence fired on, as made in America between 1900 and 1925.*"

This information would therefore date hatpin holders in that media, as well as pinpoint the country of origin. Carnival glass hatpin holders are shown on Plate 55.

Storage for hatpins included silverplated and brass pincushion shoes, fashioned in the styles of footwear worn at the turn-of-the-century. There were also beaded cushions and the especially popular pincushion dolls which were in vogue just prior to World War I, and into the twenties.

These "half-dolls" are collectibles in their own right; several examples may be seen in Plates 9, 12, 56, and 195, accompanied by more detailed explanation.

Some writers expounding the subject of hatpin holders, suggest that salt-shakers which necessarily have cork-sized holes are "often confused with veil pin holders" — holders which are usually only three inches high. I, personally, have never seen a small tie or veil pin holder — considered authentic — that did not have a *solid bottom*. These miniature holders are scarce but occasionally one encounters an example at antique shops, shows, or in private collections. They are seldom for sale, being highly prized and used as props for tie-pins or delicate scarf pins.* Let me reiterate: salt-shakers have corkholes; authentic holders have solid bottoms.

The above is not necessarily true regarding authentic period *hatpin* holders. Some of these do have holes in the base. The holes are openings left where the pieces came off the mold. These holes may be irregular and occur in a base which is either perfectly flat or slightly concave.

A good way to judge whether or not you are looking at the "look-alike" china muffinier is to examine the shape and size. Muffiniers are plump around the middle, plump enough to hold at least a cup or more of sugar. Muffiniers have fewer and somewhat irregular-sized shaker holes; as a rule they have an oval or raised, dome. If the hole in the *base* is dime-sized or smaller, chances are it's not a muffinier but a hatpin holder. Condiment holders usually have a larger cork-hole set in a deep well, a depression which caught the excess or over-flow of sugar or spice, as the container was being filled. Thus, a sugar-shaker, salt-shaker, or muffinier would not have a *flat* base but rather a cave-like bottom with a cork-hole in the center.

I read an article recently which stated that many hatpin

holders were made of wood. From the description therein, I judge that the wooden product was another "look-alike" — namely, the pounce pot or sander.

The pounce pot usually measures from 2½″ to 4″ tall, and was used to shake pounce, a finely ground black sand. The sanding process was utilized in the 18th and 19th centuries as an aid in blotting glazed paper or for creating a more suitable writing surface.

Because pounce pots have solid bases and pin-sized holes in the top, they are easily mistaken for hatpin holders. Wooden pounce pots were hollowed out at the bottom, filled with sand, then plugged and sealed with the bases covered with fabric or paper. When the sand was gone, being used up, the pounce pots were simply discarded and a new one purchased. Many times the base shows advertising material, probably the name of the manufacturer. But one sure clue is its barrel-shape and the exceedingly deep *recessed* top. In addition, once empty, most wooden pounce pots are too lightweight to remain upright when hatpins are inserted into the top.

My own collection of hatpin holders has one unusual example that has a solid top with pinholes, no flat base whatsoever, and just an outer edge of porcelain to rest upon. One may well wonder what kept the sharp points of the pins from scratching the fine wood or marble of the dressing table. This "bottomless" hatpin holder, as with other varieties, was placed on a large comb-and-brush tray which not only gave protection from pin-scratches but became the catch-all for powder from the puff-box or loose hairs from the hair-receiver. "Bottomless" hatpin holders are a rarity. (Plate 39.)

In the *"Gentlemen's Magazine,"* (1764), we read that the King of Prussia *"at great expense"* established a porcelain factory and *"has already brought it to such perfection as to rival that at Meissen . . ."* Some of the most highly prized (and priced) hatpin holders are those marked "R&S Prussia" — not to be confused with the more plentiful holders marked "R&S Germany." (See Plates 38 and 40.)

The porcelain or china holders were usually made in a two or more mold process in which the top of the holder, a separately molded piece, was applied to the base. If the holder had an attached saucer, it would necessarily call for three separate mold-operations. All mold pieces are joined by "fettling" which smoothed the seams; then these seams were additionally camouflaged with applied gold decorative rings or beading. The decorative work was done after the first glaze was added; then another firing took place before the final embellishment. If the ceramic or porcelain is unglazed, it is called bisque-ware.

The subject of porcelain manufacture should be touched upon here, and the writer has taken the liberty of using excerpts from an anonymous dissertation which arrived in my mail-box in the form of an advertisement from The National Trust for Historic Preservation of which I became a founding member.

The non-copyrighted material is such an excellent exposition for the layman on the subject of *"How China Came to Paris,"* I felt compelled to use portions which will help the novice understand and appreciate what is entailed in the manufacture of beautiful hatpin holders of china and porcelain:

*Turn-of-the-century catalogues and brochures do not refer to men's scarf or cravat pins as "tie pins." Tie-pin is a modern term.*

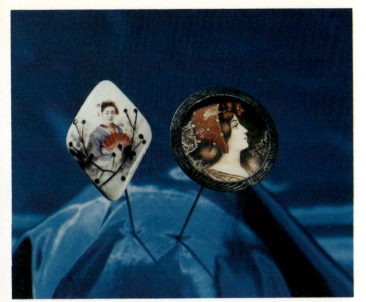

**Plate 1**

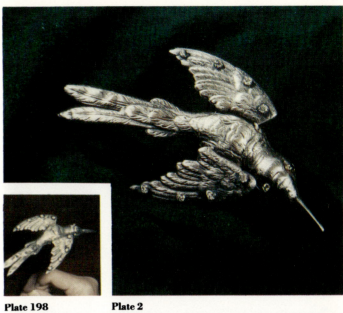

**Plate 198**   **Plate 2**

**Plate 3**

**Plate 4**

**Plate 5**

**Plate 6**

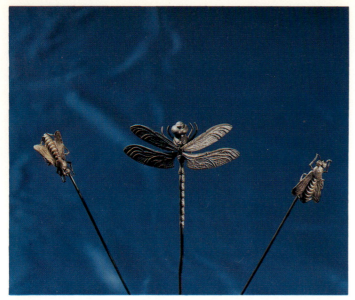

**Plate 7**

**Plate 8**

**Plate 9**

**Plate 11**

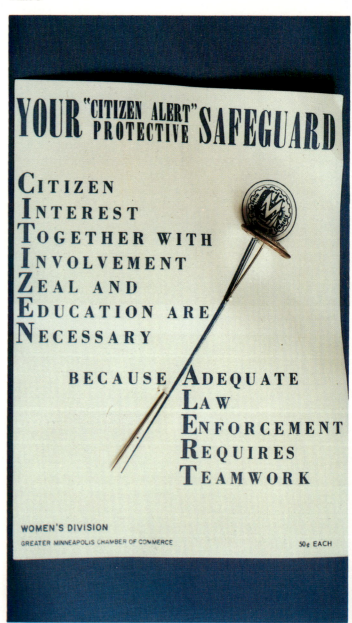

**Plate 10**

**Plate 12**

**Plate 13**

**Plate 14**

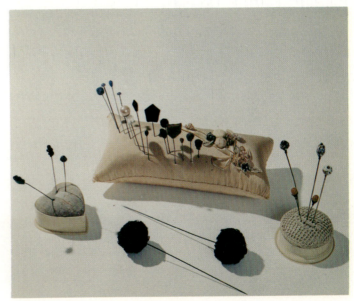

**Plate 15**

**Plate 16**

**Plate 17**

**Plate 18**

**Plate 19**

**Plate 20**

**Plate 21**

**Plate 22**

**Plate 23**

**Plate 24**

**Plate 25**

**Plate 26**

**Plate 27**

**Plate 29**

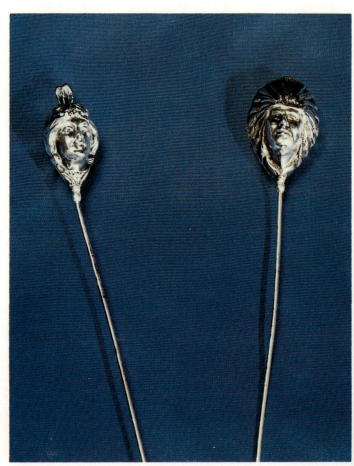

**Plate 28**

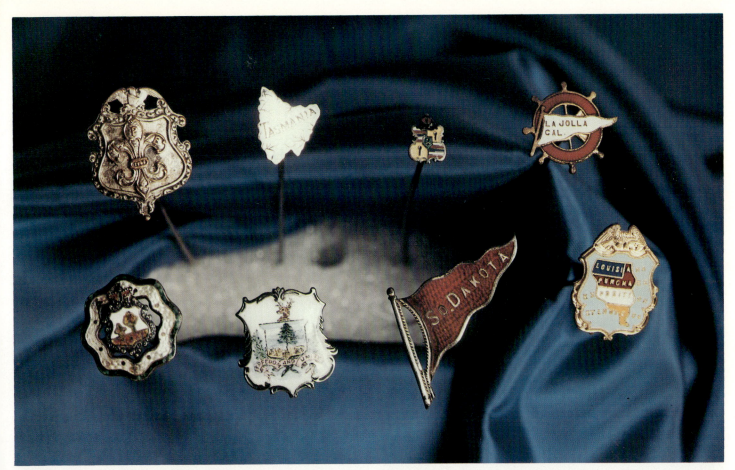

**Plate 30**

**Plate 31**

**Plate 32**

**Plate 33**

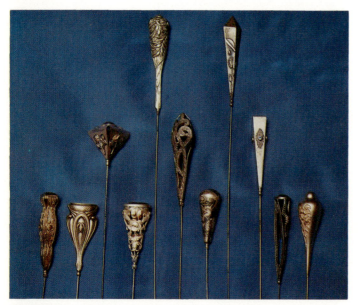

**Plate 34**

**Plate 35**

**Plate 36**

**Plate 37**

**Plate 38**

**Plate 39**

**Plate 40**

**Plate 41**

**Plate 42**

**Plate 43**

**Plate 44**

**Plate 45**

**Plate 46**

**Plate 47**

**Plate 48**

**Plate 49**

**Plate 50**

**Plate 51**

**Plate 52**

**Plate 53**

**Plate 54**

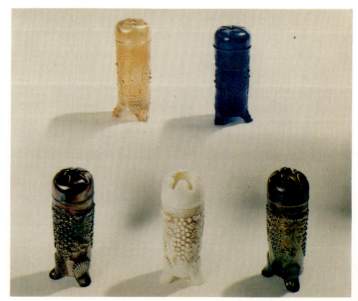

**Plate 55**

**Plate 56**

**Plate 57**

**Plate 58**

**Plate 59**

**Plate 60**

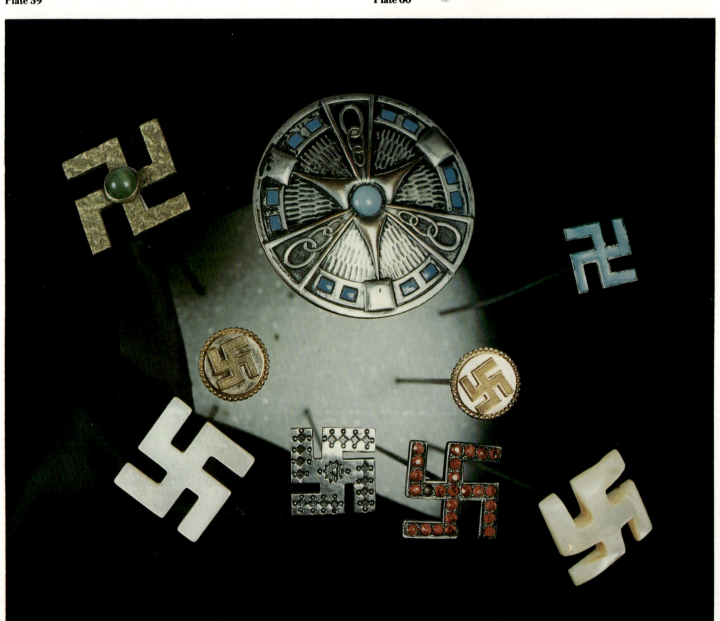

**Plate 61**

**Plate 62**

**Plate 63**

**Plate 65**

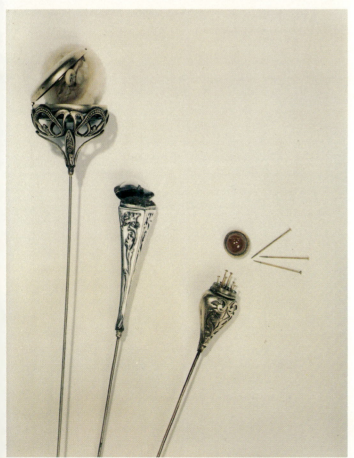

**Plate 64**

**Plate 66**

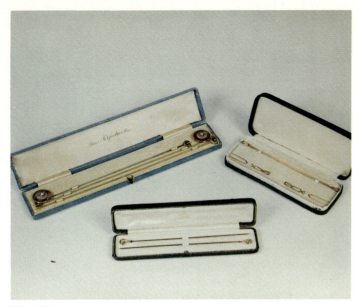

**Plate 67**

**Plate 68**

**Plate 69**

**Plate 70**

**Plate 71**

**Plate 72**

**Plate 73**

**Plate 74**

**Plate 75**

**Plate 76**

**Plate 77**

**Plate 78**

**Plate 79**

**Plate 80**

**Plate 81**

**Plate 82**

**Plate 83**

**Plate 84**

**Plate 85**

**Plate 86**

**Plate 87**

**Plate 88**

**Plate 89**

**Plate 90**

**Plate 91**

**Plate 93**

**Plate 92**

Plate 94

Detail from plate 94

Plate 95

Plate 96

**Plate 97**

**Plate 98**

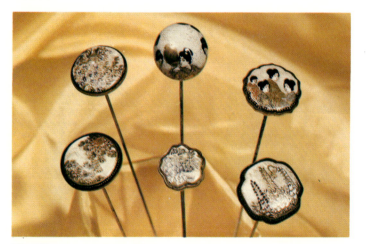

**Plate 99**

**Plate 100**

**Plate 101**

**Plate 102**

**Plate 103**

**Plate 104**

**Plate 105**

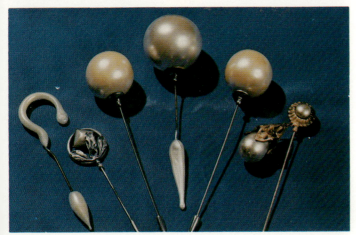

**Plate 107**

**Plate 106**

127

Plate 108

Plate 109

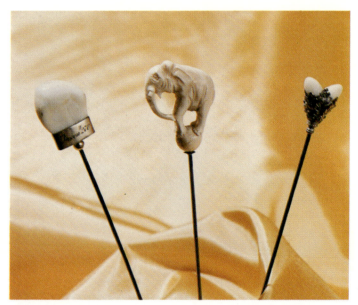

Plate 111

Plate 110

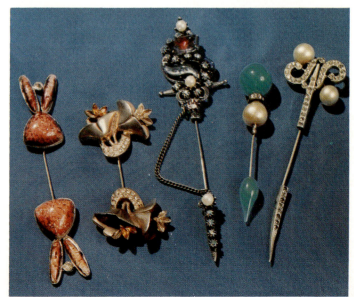

Plate 112

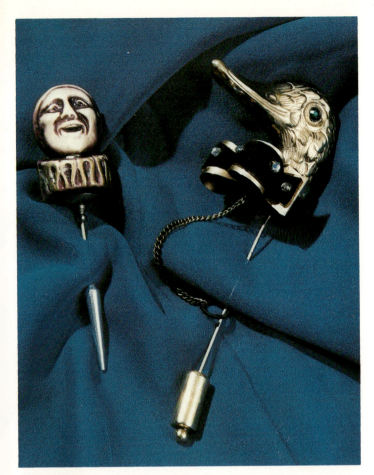

**Plate 113**

**Plate 114**

**Plate 115**

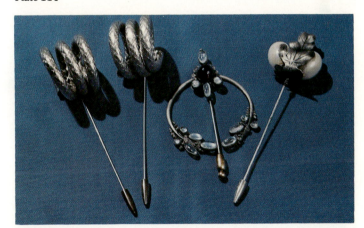

**Plate 116**

**Plate 117**

**Plate 118**

**Plate 120**

**Plate 119**

**Plate 121**

**Plate 122**

**Plate 123**

**Plate 124**

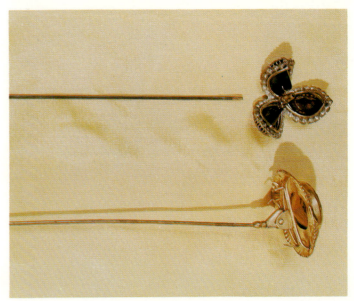

**Plate 125**

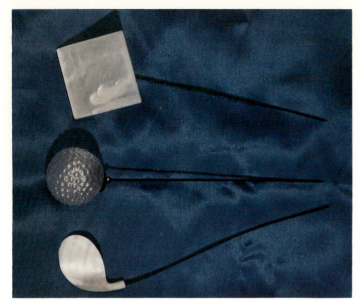

**Plate 126**

**Plate 127**

**Plate 128**

**Plate 129**

**Plate 130**

**Plate 131**

**Plate 132**

**Plate 133**

**Plate 160:** Jenny Lind Commemorative. Photo by George Castro.

**Plate 163a**
Judge or British Magistrate: "Guilty or Not Guilty"

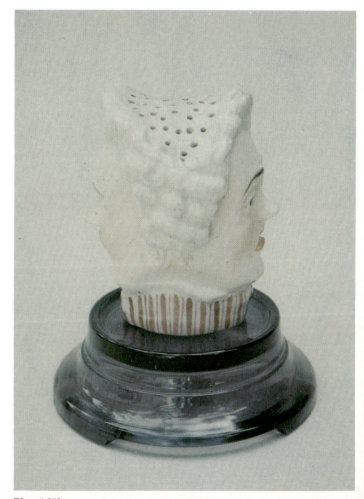

**Plate 163b**

**Plate 179:** Collection of Diane Malhmood, Rockville, Maryland.

**Plate 180a**

**Plate 163c**

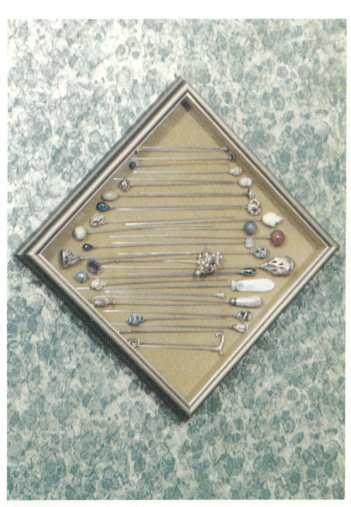

**Plate 180b**

**Plate 187a**

**Plate 187b**

**Plate 187c**

**Plate 189**

**Plate 193**

**Plate 194**

**Plate 195**

**Plate 196**

**Plate 197**

**Plate 205**

**Plate 206**

**Plate 207**

"Porcelain was named by Marco Polo after a shell called porcellana that has a white, translucent appearance. He had seen this marvelous product during his visit to the court of Kublai Khan in the mid-13th century. Although the Chinese had invented porcelain in the fifth century, Polo was one of the first westerners to learn of it.

"In the 800 years prior to Polo's visit, porcelain-making had been refined to the point of becoming a major art form, the pride of emperors. They made certain their factories were located in the hinterlands, safe from the prying eyes of visitors. Even the beloved Venetian traveler, a guest of the Khan's court for 17 years and a trusted deputy, did not learn the closely guarded secret of its manufacture.

"By the 15th century Ming porcelains reached Europe through the Saracens. A hundred years later, Portugese explorers returned from their voyages with porcelain in their holds. But the real impetus to the Chinese porcelain trade came in the 17th century when the East India Company began the commercial importation of domestic ware. Europeans called it 'china' after its country of origin.

"You can imagine how luxurious this fine, thin, white translucent material appeared next to the coarse earthenware that graced the tables of European king and peasant alike. But importation was slow and expensive, and could not begin to satisfy the demand. With such a vast market beckoning, virtually every kingdom and principality in Europe turned its alchemists to the task of unlocking the secret of porcelain.

"Years of experimentation finally yielded a Florentine 'soft-paste' porcelain, actually a form of glass. But no one could uncover the Chinese secret of hard-paste or true porcelain. Then, in 1706, Augustus The Physically Strong of Saxony, King of Poland, ordered his captive alchemist, Johann Bottger, to give up trying to make gold and find the secret of porcelain instead. Augustus shrewdly concluded that if he could fill the cupboards of Europe, he would also fill his depleted treasury.

"At the end of his first year in Meissen, Bottger glumly wrote, 'And God our Creator made a potter out of a gold-maker.' But by 1709 the 'potter' had made the first unglazed porcelain in Europe and in the following year he reported to his king that he could make a 'good white porcelain with the finest glaze and appropriate painting to such perfection that if it does not surpass, it is at least the equal of the East Indian.'

"Although China held the secret of porcelain 1200 years, Meissen kept it only 10. Some of its key workers were enticed with huge rewards to set up factories in Venice and Vienna. Security was tightened almost to the point of turning these early porcelain factories into prisons and the spread of the secret was stemmed for nearly a generation. Then other factories followed. Within another generation all of Europe was making porcelain.

"Between 1750 and 1780, 20 factories were built in Paris alone — among them, 'Porcelaine de Paris,' established by Jean Baptiste Locre on July 14, 1773, the year of our Boston Tea Party, and the same year Lafayette received his commission in the French army. (It is quite possible that when Lafayette arrived in America to aid and befriend George Washington, a piece of Locre's highly prized porcelain was among the gifts he bestowed upon the commander-in-chief.)

"By 1860 the sole porcelain factory in Paris was 'Porcelaine de Paris,' and today it maintains this enviable and unique position."

\* \* \*

The above reprinted advertisement is an education in understanding the complex nature and work of porcelain manufacturing. It goes on to tell about the materials used in making true or hardpaste porcelain which "are kaolin, a fine white clay; quarta; and feldspar. Kaolin is brought in from Brittany and Wales, carefully washed with water, and combed for traces of iron with huge electromagnets. Iron that slips by produces brown spots in fired pieces . . ."

"Kaolin is mixed with native feldspar, quartz and water to the consistency of heavy cream, then poured into the plaster mold. As the plaster absorbs the water, the form hardens and, finally, when firm, it is removed . . ."

"The form is placed in a drying kiln at 1000°C. It emerges as bisque, or buiscuit, and is flat white in color . . ."

From there on to the finished piece, the process differs depending on whether or not the piece is to remain bisque, enameled, or if transfers are to be used for decoration. The use of transfers is "an uncomplicated term applied to a highly intricate process called by its technical term, ceramic lithography." This process of "transfer" on porcelain or ceramic is often so expertly rendered as to make the piece look handpainted. And when actual overlays or decorative touches are added to a transfer, it sometimes takes an expert to decide where a transfer begins and the hand has taken over. This is particularly true in portraiture. (See Plates 54, 57, 60, 70 and 75.)

Surely one must admire the look and feel of a fine china or porcelain hatpin holder, after reading the history and handcraft required to make the article! And we have not taken into account the conception of design and human resource called "imagination" which enables production of hundreds of different receptacles for pins. (By the way, in the United States we call receptacles for hatpins, "hatpin holders"; in England they are called "stands" for hatpins.)

It is not surprising to find that hatpin holders are reported earlier on the Continent since hatpins were worn in European countries before the dictates of fashion came sailing across the ocean in the form of "fashion plates." Fashions in the "new British colony of America" were primarily copies of French and/or British designs. In an era when news traveled slowly, it often took fashion plates weeks and weeks to arrive from across the sea. Then came the equally slow process of copying and printing them in the first publications for women, such as Godey's Ladies' Book." Unlike our era of instant replay and "live" broadcasting via satellite, the changeover from one mode to another was extended for months and even years. Fashions would arrive "from the Continent," and would then require additional time and negotiations for the fabrics and other necessaries. We have air-travel to bring us these requirements; travel by boat and rail hastened how quickly new designs were adopted. In bygone days fashions became *stylish:* today, fashions are *fads* quickly adopted and just as quickly forsaken in keeping with our fast pace of living. (However, hang on to fashion long enough, and it will come back . . .)

*"Godey's Ladies' Book,"* the first fashion book in America, did not publish fashion plates until 1830, but it can be assumed that hatpins were worn in the United States before the "established" date of 1860 — a date agreed upon by most fashion authorities today as the earliest record of hatpins being worn in America.

However, since several hatpin holders were made *early* in the 19th century, it's permissible, I think, to assume that hatpins were worn sooner in the courts along with other ornaments so popular at the time. (In fact, I have a hatpin dated 1851 and another dated 1858. See Plate 29.)

*"The Ladies' Friend,"* (July 1872) stated, *". . . a great many ornamental pins are now worn in the plaits of hair, which are fashionable for evening toilets. These pins have either filigreed gold or silver heads. Some ladies wore antique pins with enameled heads of butterflies, flowers, etc. studded along the plaits . . ."*

The "antique pins" worn by ladies in 1872, could very well be the early *handmade* pins which were pushed into some form of *cushion* prior to the manufactured *china* receptacles. These early storage-places for pins were crochet, needlepoint, or silk cushions, handmade to accommodate such pins. There may also have been pin-holders in the form of fancy boxes in which were stored bent-wire hairpins or the "common" wire-pin which before 1832 was so extremely prized, because they were scarce, and expensive. These would not have been left laying carelessly around nor in clear sight of the servants.

Pins-boxes probably preceded porcelain holders for variety pins and hatpins; a collection of such boxes is a valid treasure-trove for the avid antiquer. A hairpin box, pictured in Plate 17, is a lovely example of the type "storage-box" used by grandmother, mother, and now me!

Some hatpin holders were little more than oversized pin-cushions, often embroidered with heavy silk and cotton thread, or velvet covered with elaborate glass-bead work. Some of these beaded beauties, inaccurately reported as being "made by the American Indian," weigh in excess of five pounds. Beadwork was a great pastime of the Victorian woman and was sometimes incorporated into needlepoint projects. I have a gorgeous mantle face-screen, used to protect a lady's delicate skin from the heat of a fireplace. It is a combination of petite-point and beadwork.

Beaded boots or booties were also utilized as holders. These types were made by the Indians. (See Plates 16 and 73.)

Many hatpin holders first perched on miniature chests of drawers designed as dressing tables of the earlier period, while others may have been kept on a small bureau or bedstand. As furniture styles changed, the highboy and robe-closet were replaced with a low bureau or dressing table, wide-topped

rather than narrow, and women resorted to more elaborate toilette sets consisting of a dozen or more pieces. These "dresser sets" were comprised of a comb and brush tray, puff box, hair-receiver, hatpin holder, ring tree, trinket boxes, the more mundane soap and washcloth dish, various sized pitchers, a bowl, and the toothbrush holder.

The toothbrush holder is another "look-alike," akin to the hatpin holder or ornamental pin holder. Toothbrush holders with drainage holes punctured in the base or sides of the holders are easily identified; but there are others that were made without such holes which might be correctly used interchangeably as a holder for other articles such as double-pronged pins or fashionable veil pins "in the shape of blocks, darts, and arrows."

Spiral-type heavier-gauge pins could be better accommodated in the "open-mouthed" holders, for the pin-holes in many hatpin holders were not large enough. Besides, the shorter length hairpins and other ornamental pins seem better fitted in these open-top holders than do the period hatpin with their extremely long shanks. Most open-mouth holders are seldom more than 4-5 inches tall and will easily topple if more than a few short pins are stored in them. (At least that's what my own experiments have proven.) But they are ideal for double-pronged or various wider-gauge shanks, such as are shown on Plates 7 and 17.

A dentist who wrote a report about his own collection of toothbrush holders, stated that the solid bottom vase-type holder is usually about 5½" high with mouth opening of approximately 2". This measurement conflicts with the actual sizes of the tops of most open-mouth pin holders which seem to average between 1-1½" across. I have placed a few toothbrushes into these small-mouthed holders and they do seem adequate. As stated by the dentist-collector, not all toothbrush holders had drainage holes nor had they open ends which sat on little drainage dishes. It's reasonable to assume that open-mouthed holders *could* have been used as toothbrush holders, decorative pin holders, and certainly for the scarf and corsage pins which had sheaths to cover their sharp points.

Was the toothbrush invented at the time hatpin holders were being marketed? My research indicated that Artemus Woodward of Medford, Mass., was the first manufacturer in America to set bristle into a handle for use as toothbrushes. Between 1834 and 1840, a dental society was formed and I deduce it was probably then that the toothbrush was introduced for general hygenic purposes. (The wooden toothbrush handle was eventually replaced by the less costly synthetic plastic handle; it wasn't until 1934, however, that nylon replaced the real hair bristles of the toothbrush). Wooden toothpicks were then invented in 1872, and it seems that between all this picking and sticking, a great number of holders and storage places came into being. All these made necessary by inventive genius, and all made *possible* by the slow-but-sure awakening of the giant "machine age!"

But I have digressed too far and must return to hatpin holders! Some of the most imaginative holders were created during the Victorian era. Say what you will of the excesses of Victorians, they at least grasped the meaning and mastery of "decoration" in its most lavish sense — utilizing to the fullest the principle of contrast in form and fantasy. It seems the Victorian could be both decorative and functional at one and the same time, something we "moderns" are not able to achieve very often in either our square sky-scrapers nor in our space-age furniture — not to mention the cold restraint used in the newer concepts of jewelry and art! Whatever we have that's warm and "free-wheeling," comes from reproduction of bygone eras, with particular emphasis on *Art Nouveau* and Art Deco.

Hatpin holders are a unique collection in themselves and some people eagerly collect them without special interest in the hatpins for which they were made. My own collection of holders grew out of the simple necessity of storing a treasury of hatpins.

The range of color, style, and design of the hatpin holder is endless, from a delicate porcelain, paper-thin example, measuring only 4″ high, (See Plate 41), to a heavier china hatpin holder 10″ tall which is best used for the long-stemmed hatpin beauties of the turn-of-the-century. (See Plate 70.)

The wealthy could afford commode articles in sterling and gold. For the more "common trade" there were the less expensive dresser sets and hatpin holders of stoneware, "French ivory" (celluloid), and base metals. Dresser sets or hatpin holders marked "Nippon" represented the least expensive china imports and until recently were rather snubbed by collectors.

Articles marked "Nippon," or the unmarked but obvious Oriental works, are some of the loveliest of all and should not carry the stigma often attributed to such merchandise. Not until recently have "Nippon" decorated wares gained the respect they deserve. Although "Royal Austria", "Germany", "Bavaria", "Limoges", and other favored marks are considered more valuable monetarily, they oftentimes cannot compete with the "Nippon" in design or beauty. (See Plates 51 and 187.)

An excellent book, particularly for identifying marks on NIPPON porcelains, including Hatpin Holders, is Paul and Candy Lima's reference work listed in the "Sources" section of this book.

Paul and Candy Lima write that the NIPPON PERIOD covers the period from 1858 until 1921, the years when Japanese porcelain represented "the tedious hand work which makes it, like other art forms of the period, so desirable to own."

"Nippon" is the Japanese word for *Japan* which translates into "place the sun comes from" or "Land of the Rising Sun." It's hard to believe that no merchandise was shipped to the United States from Japan until 1858! This is the year America entered into a trade agreement with the Japanese government at the request of Commodore Perry. Japanese art, imported as NIPPON, first came to our country during the Philadelphia Centennial Exhibition in 1876. Thus, when America celebrates its Bi-Centennial, it will also mark America's first 100 years of trade with the Japanese Empire!

After March 1, 1921, the word "Nippon" was ruled unacceptable as the country of origin for imports from Japan. It states in the aforementioned book on NIPPON: *"The requirements for country of origin marking imported into the U.S. first appeared in Section 5 of the Tariff Act of August 28, 1894 which provided that imported articles should be plainly and individually marked in legible English words to show country of origin."*

From this information, collectors will be able to date their hatpin holders — that is, those prior to 1894 when no restrictions were imposed, as against those *marked with country of origin* which would date them *after* 1894.

Oriental hatpin holders which are unmarked or are marked "Nippon," are 1921. "Made in Japan" dates after 1921.

Although Japanese wares for their own use were simple in design, those *exported* to the Continent and the United States were copied in more complicated designs after the *Art Nouveau* and European art forms. Ironically, while artists and craftsmen in European factories were imitating oriental motifs, (such as Blue Willow), so Japanese workers were busy copying pastoral scenes with Dutch windmills. (See Plates 51, 54 and 70.)

From 1900-1910, the manufacture of long, long hatpins was joined by the mass production of hair ornaments, both requiring holders of one kind or another. Varying shapes and sizes of ornaments and hatpin heads were fashioned of shell, amber, bone, hard rubber, horn and celluloid. Bent celluloid hairpins from two to four inches long were a good example of the transition from wire-made to wonderful science-blended imitations. Such plastics were a return to the ancient art of using natural products manipulated by man for woman. To *store* the abovementioned pins, *holders* were manufactured out of synthetics, too. (See Plates 15, 73 and 193.)

As a summation to hatpin holders, their "look-alikes" and "reproductions": as a general rule, most hatpin holders have solid bottoms with from six to twelve small pin-size holes on top to hold hatpins. The holders have tops with no visible mold-opening either top nor bottom. Hatpin holders have concave or only slightly domed tops, and seldom have the familiar "steeple" associated with the muffineer or sugar-shaker. If they *are* so shaped, they do not have a cork in the bottom, but are solid-bottomed. The hatpin holder is seldom as "plump" in design as its "look-alike."

Some hatpin holders have *applied* tops pierced with small holes which surround a dime-sized opening on the top which was used for removal from the mold. The bottoms of these type holders are always solid. As stated previously, most mold openings at the bottom of hatpin holders are either too small to successfully pour in a condiment, or the openings are too large or irregular to accommodate a cork. Most holders are altogether too slender to be practical for condiment use, or if big and round, have no possible way for filling from outside to inside. (Plates 41 and 51.)

Then there are the bud or vase type receptacles which have been featured in books and sold at antique shops as "open-top" hatpin holders. This type has been covered in preceding paragraphs. My inclination is to call them toothbrush holders because for some vague reason this toilette article has been overlooked as a common and usual item which would have been included in commode sets. Furthermore, logic dictates that during the era of "necessaries," bed-chamber pots and outhouses, there were few "inside" bathrooms or washrooms. Although some elite hotels had such accommodations inside, the average private dwelling-place did not. Thus, the toothbrush holder had to be an integral part of the indoor "appliances" such as the pitcher, bowl, soap dish, face-cloth-dish, "potty", "urinal," and other such necessary items which were

**Plate 188a**

**Plate 188b**

used *in*, *on*, and *nearby*, the familiar marble-topped bedroom commode or vanity.

Although some toothbrush holders had drainage holes in the bases, others did not. Some had a small saucer for drainage purposes. In any event, these holders have been wrongly identified, I feel, as being *positively* and *definitely* small vases or hatpin holders.

Experts in the field have overlooked the possibility that these open-top items could have been used for not only toothbrush holders, but for other items such as hairpins and pin-ornaments which could not possibly be housed in the pin-sized openings found in the majority of hatpin holders with closed tops. (Plates 17 and 40.)

Once this is clarified, authentic period *hatpin holders* can more readily be identified as the *closed-top receptacle* with pierced pin-holes. One thing is for certain: the pin-size holes in authentic hatpin holders could not be used for either toothbrushes nor for other articles such as double-pronged hair ornaments, heavy gauge hair-pins, nor sheath-type corsage and scarf pins. Some holders have larger-than-pin-size openings in the tops; these might well have been made for the many other type of pins besides hatpins, as mentioned above.

As an aside, the small pitcher which matched the larger ewer commonly stored inside the washbowl, was itself used for transporting hot water from the kitchen kettle. The larger ewer stored cold pump-water or sink-water. A small double-lipped container which resembles a handleless pitcher, was used to receive the spittle of mouthwash and rinse. All these items appear in Plate 43. Obviously, spittle had to be disposed of somewhere, and surely not out the window nor in the washbowl! This double-lipped container fits nicely over the mouth for asthetic, and sanitary use. After all, there were no bathroom sinks with drains nor flush-away facilities for unsightly waste!

Back to hatpin holders: Be wary of a dealer who tries to sell a china *pomadour* or pomander as a hatpin holder; also the dealer who produces a covered porcelain dish with small holes in its cover which was actually made to house perfumed soap. (Larger covered dishes, without holes in top, were another form of toothbrush holder.) The usual sales-pitch is that hatpins were pushed through the small holes into the soap. This was supposed to keep the pins "sharp", "upright", and "sweet-smelling." Fiddlesticks and hogwash! That's a soft-soap-sell if there ever was one! And considering there was no

stainless steel at that period, what about rusty pins?

Regarding hatpin holders with attached trays, be warned that several such hatpin holders are being reproduced in Japan. (See Plates 39 and 188.) Pictured are only a few reproductions of designs made for export to U.S.A. These are sold from $2.40-$3.95 RETAIL, and are unpainted. Each reproduction is made by a different Japanese firm and is currently being imported by American companies who deal with persons who buy for resale to collectors.

An R. S. Germany holder in white porcelain is being reproduced as shown on Plate 188. (Compare the authentic holder [Plate 40] with the reproduction.)

The "blanks" are imported, sold, and then hand-painted by today's enterprising women attending china-painting classes — also very popular in Victorian days. Some of the finished products are for personal use; others are peddled at antique shops and shows as *authentic* hatpin holders of an *earlier* period.

All the aforementioned reproductions are imported as "china blanks" with paper labels that are easily removed. The holders then have no identifying marks as to country of origin nor manufacture.

Veracious vendors of antiques and collectibles will tag such merchandise as reproduction; unfortunately, all sellers are not honest nor do they feel a responsibility to their trade. Unless you are buying from a reputable dealer who knows her inventory, it's suggested that the hatpin holder collector purchase only *imprinted trademarked* merchandise in the patterns pictured in this book. (Again, refer to Plates 39 and 188.)

Regrettably, there are *marked reproductions* being *newly produced* in England and offered for sale at gift marts across the country. Reproductions of both the "Wild Rose" and the "Romantic" patterns are being offered for sale in the wholesale market. It would again be up to antique dealers as to whether they represent the merchandise as authentically old or as newly reproduced.

The "flow-blue" *Romantic* pattern and the scenic *Wild Rose* are clearly marked on the botton: "Staffordshire, England." However, the *authentic old pieces* from which these have been reproduced, *also* show the *manufacturer's trademark* which is a lion and unicorn. The word "ironstone" is also imprinted.

The new hatpin holders in the *Romantic* pattern are marked: "flow blue," a *recent* phrase used by collectors refer-

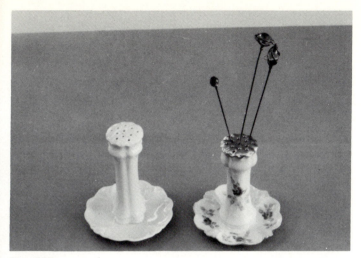

**Plate 188c**

ring to "old" china. It is now being coined by the company which is reproducing the old pattern. (See Plate 18 for authentic pieces now being reproduced.)

The new English reproductions are wholesaled at $4.50 (painted), but have been retailing from $12.50 to $35.00 — or whatever the trade will bear.

Now there's nothing wrong in buying beautifully executed reproductions of popular items, such as the *hatpin holder* which is coming into its own because of the demand for yester-year collectibles. What is so highly objectionable is the fradulent intent in selling such items as *original* or *old*. Unpardonable is their sale as *antiques*.

I recently received correspondence from an antique dealer residing on the East coast and who informed me that he has never seen nor heard of reproduction hatpin holders. He is fortunate! or else perhaps he's not as forewarned as he should be.

Reproductions are flooding the market on the West Coast, and I was able to purchase the Japanese "china blanks" from an antique dealer in Kansas! Thanks to her we have photographs to educate my readers. English reproductions are being sold at coast-to-coast gift shows.

Antiques have initially been an *Eastern* enterprise which has finally come West! Perhaps because the West is the "novice," the reproductions have been first *introduced* here instead of among the long-time experts.

My purpose in giving such a detailed report on "look-a-likes" and "reproductions" is to warn the buyer to beware at the marketplace — *buyer* meaning both the collector and dealer.

There are many photographs and drawings throughout this book which show off the various and lovely dresser sets complete with hatpin holder, of course. Note that some commode sets have candlesticks in size and pattern similar to the hatpin holder. Often a buyer is willing to pay a disproportionate share of the selling price of a complete or partially complete dresser set for the single item: *the hatpin holder*. It's no wonder, then, that so many toilet sets have important pieces missing — much to the frustration of collectors.

As a final commentary on the hatpin holder, I must add a charming note:

Surely after the 1861 publication of Isabella Mary Beeton's *"The Book of Household Management,"* sales of complete toilet sets must have risen sharply! For it is in her splendid record that we find a line that's become the "good housekeeper's maxim," and an apt description for the hatpin holder and related accessories discussed in this chapter:

*"A place for everything and everything in its place."*

# Chapter VII

# MEMOIRS OF A COLLECTOR

One day while rummaging through a neighborhood Thrift Shop, I observed an elderly woman sorting out a variety of glassware. As I approached she looked up from her task and welcomed me with a thin-lipped crescent that sent ripples of tiny wrinkles across her cheeks.

She was delighted when asked if she would share some of her remembrances of "hatpin days" — delighted that such a topic would interest one of my generation.

When I proceeded to talk enthusiastically about my hobby and to tell of my eagerness to learn as much as I could about the subject, she scooted from around the counter and practically shoved me into a wicker chair nearby.

"Those were the days . . ." she began — which is usually the way so many gentle souls begin to reminisce.

To bring her quickly round to the subject of hatpins, I commented that she was wearing hatpins that matched her felt hat which was a scuffed-up blend of wool and fur dyed a rich, royal purple. I timidly asked if she'd made the hatpins herself inasmuch as the hatpin heads were covered with the same material as her chapeau but enhanced by tiny sequins. These bitty-sized reflectors caught the gleam of the overhead light which was a dusty kerosene lamp — recently electrified — and the reflections bounced off the sequins like magical sunbeams each time she shook her head.

And she was shaking her head when she answered, *"No, this bonnet is probably older than you are!"* She smiled in an apologetic sort of way, as if to soften her next remark. *"They made materials to last in those days! These hatpins came with the hat right from the milliner's shop. Fact is, the milliner's shop was my neighbor's home down the road. But the general store in town had a bonnet counter with lots of goodies. Oh they made things to last in those days!"*

She repeated this statement with the same touch of pride typical of the tiny women of the turn of the century. She wasn't nearly so concerned with closing the "generation gap" between *us* as "depression kids" are with their children who were born in the "favored fifties" or "soft-on-the-paddle sixties."

I'm inclined to refer to these tiny women as *little* old ladies because strangely enough just about all I've ever met are quite petite. I'd judge their average height as not more than five-feet-two and they hardly outweigh a bushel basket of potatoes! That's why it seems even more absurd to imagine hatpins twelve inches long, with baroque heads sometimes ranging in size from four to six inches across, protruding from a hat perched on top of one of these little dynamic women! Had I not the physical evidence in my collection, I might have arrived at the conclusion that the hatpins appeared longer and larger because of the contrast in size to the wearer — but the truth is that although science reports that women at the turn-of-the-century were considerably smaller than today, women then did wear chapeaux measuring twice the distance across as around the female waist. The corseted waist boasted only 14-16 inches around — only an inch or two more than the hatpin worn in the same era (1880-1912).

Not all of my "little old ladies" could boast having lived a decade past Social Security age, yet none were more proud of their vintage than those *well over* seventy who could vaguely remember the final years of Queen Victoria's reign 1837-1901 — although they embellished their tales as if it were only yesterday!

Some recalled the lonely gas lamps in New York; some told how in the smaller towns when there was little moonlight, citizens who had to be out after dark carried lanterns for safety. Some recalled how their homes were lighted with candles and heated with cheap stoves; how running water from taps didn't exist, most depending on cisterns. Rainwater was the main supply in the large cities, but if one were wealthy he could buy water in special casks at the high cost of over a dollar a "hogshead" which was the equivalent of 63 wine gallons.

Most of my "little old ladies" were happy to live in our modern "times of improvement," but I remember accepting the invitation of one senior citizen who lived by herself in a large Victorian home with gables galore. She still did her own housework, gardening, and shopping — had for the past fifty-five years. This was the only home she'd ever known; had raised her seven children here. Indeed, she had been raised in this very same house herself! There were a few changes and improvements.

*"That is,"* she confided, *"if an inside lavatory be counted! But I'm not so sure of my gas stove. My old wood stove made a better bread."*

Throughout this house were signs of love's labor in crochet doilies, braided and hooked rugs, embroidered pillows, homey samplers, and intricate patchwork quilts.

I've found from experience that the hospitality of our senior citizen is boundless; rarely have I engaged one in conversation without the inevitable invitation to visit longer and "sup some tea." This lady was no exception.

She insisted on my tasting her own recipe for deep dish apple pie with open criss-crossed crust. It was served on a lovely old blue-willow plate of Holland design with a mulberry glaze rather than the traditional oriental blue.

*"I remember,"* she told me with her eyelids crimped tightly, as if to struggle inwardly for the memory, *"how we had a department store — Mother and Daddy, that is — and when it folded up after the crash in '29, Mother took as much as she could store of the merchandise and put it in a tall seven drawer chiffonier that stood upstairs in an extra bedroom we used as a guest room. Of course we had lots of guests then. Always an*

*aunt or uncle who was down and out. And it seemed no matter what we needed, Mother found it in one of those drawers! For the longest time I thought everything in the world could be found there — from underwear to hatpins nestled on the big horse-hair cushion on top. Matter of fact, I never knew what it was to buy anything store-made, save for the dinner table."*

Cautiously bringing the subject back to hatpins, I asked if she had any recollection of the type equipped with a "nodder," those small springs that made the bauble at the end of the pin bounce and jiggle. (See Plate 3)

Well, you should have seen my little old lady blush! She pulled out a lace handkerchief tucked in a frilly cuff that was beautifully buttoned with a small pearl stud. She snickered into it then leaned over towards me pursing her lips so she could whisper. Although we were alone in the house, she glanced around carefully before she tittered, *" 'Tis something that might shock you! I don't know exactly how to bring the meaning out clear, but I'll try. As I recall, the only hatpins dignified young ladies of respectable families wore were either black or white. Oh some of the saucy ones had to have some brilliants in theirs, but they seldom wore them except for a special social event or occasion or to boast about 'em. Some gentlemen indulged a few young girls with boxed hatpins much as a beau might bring a book or candy or flowers — but of course any gift of jewelry meant the man was in love and had serious intentions; but, oh my dear, those hatpins with the springers really marked a woman! Why to see them worn was to turn your head the other way. It was like, how would you call it — like a come on!"* She jerked her head sideways a few times. *"Know what I mean?"* (I believe she meant the head-movement as a "come-hither" look and I needed no interpreter to spell out the gesture.) She continued, *"And often as not, they were brazen enough to wear those hatpins in front of their hats, jiggling right along with a full bosom without stays. Or they wore them hatpins standing out rakish-like at the sides!"* She bit her lip at one corner and uttered a final *"tch, tch."*

I could well imagine the Gay Nineties "woman of the streets," with her tight corset boosting ample bosom until it fairly burst the buttons off her batiste or muslin blouse, with her plumed hat, topped by a large butterfly hatpin — a "nodder" — jiggling along with a *come on, come on,* motion!

(Oh, dear, I thought, shall I confess to my hostess that I dearly prize several of these hatpins in my collection?)

Within the very next week I met another woman, born at the turn-of-the-century, who well remembered a trip with her mother to a millinery shop in San Francisco. There they found a variety of ready-made hatpins, including some with springs, and others that were quite expensive because they were custom made by local jewelers.

Millinery shops were reputed to have the finest selection of one-of-a-kind hats as well as hatpins; if one recalls some early sequences in the film *Dr. Zhivago* there were several pin cushions steeped with long hatpins in the workshop owned by Lara's mother. The hatpins were quite prominent in the film, even to those not hatpin-conscious, and one became aware that hats were designed for the individual according to personal desire and taste.

Another lady clearly remembers a special excursion to San Francisco because her mother had chosen a black velvet hat on which was sewn a flamboyant feather almost sixteen inches

in length with a peacock's eye-feather in the center. Two matching jet hatpins surrounded by the finest French paste stones set off this beautiful creation. So taken was the father by this gorgeous chapeau, when he next visited Chicago he returned with a special gift for the mother — a solid gold hatpin with an enameled flower set with a baroque pearl, mounted on — of all things — a small gold spring that permitted the jeweled blossom to sway in the slightest breeze! This gem cost $35 back in the days when such an expenditure could well represent a working man's bi-monthly wages.

When I tactfully mentioned the tidbit about "springers" and "ladies of the streets," she pooh-poohed the tale as one that must have come from *"the mouth of a prude."*

*"Perhaps,"* she said, *"the lady you speak of could not afford the luxury of such a rare and expensive pin!"* However, lest she denounce one of her own generation — they are quite clannish in this respect — she added a bit conciliatorily, *"Maybe she was too modest to wear a bobbler because naturally it would draw a lot of attention and create comment."*

In J. F. Hayward's treatise on jewelry of the early Victorian Period, he describes such a setting as *"contrived with springs resulting in a waving or slightly oscillating motion when in use, which displayed to the fullest extent the brilliant colours of the stones."*

He does not mention who introduced the "nodder" nor who popularized its wear, nor does he suggest the intentions of the wearer or the jeweler who designed it.

However, in exploring old catalogues, I have seen *few* "springers" advertised: Sears' 1902 catalogue illustrates *two* out of a dozen with "vibrating tops," all twelve gold filled, "very fancy" with as many as forty-three brilliants. Since the 1902 catalogue stressed: "WE MAKE EVERY TRANSACTION WITH US STRICTLY CONFIDENTIAL," it would be difficult to pinpoint with whom they traded or the type clientele they served; but the truth in feminine fashion shows that more often than not it was the "brazen woman" who introduced change in mode and dress.

We see this even more and more today — the acceptance of outlandish apparel originally scoffed at by the conservative majority. Truth to tell, if a woman of reknown or of high society sets a new style, she's called daring or even an adventurous darling! Anyone else could be considered impudent, indecent, shameless or bold.

Put a *name-figure inside* a gown instead of a name on the label, and success is assured — at least from a monetary standpoint. Lillian Russell, Maude Adams, Carrie Nation, Marlene Dietrich, Katherine Hepburn and "Jackie" Kennedy, are names that stimulated sales of certain styles of women's-wear.

Many of the stories connected with hatpins are contradictory. Not only the aforementioned one regarding "vibrating tops," but those regarding the use of jet. My research shows that the use of jet was high fashion at the turn of the century, including jet that was enhanced by brilliants. Such jet ornaments with their brighter accents, followed the fashion of strictly black jewelry for the first months of mourning.

I was informed by one source that *dull,* unpolished black hatpins were worn only during strictest mourning. (See Plate 157 for example of dull, unpolished jet. Compare the hatpin's dull jet with the highly polished earrings and necklace worn by the model.)

The longest era of public mourning came with the death of Queen Victoria's Prince Consort, Albert, in 1861. The Queen popularized "black jewelry" for she wore no other in the 40 years she mourned the loss of her husband.

Still another informant of mine insisted that black was the favorite color for everyday, ordinary, hatpins.

English women "of carriage" wore the real jet — a mineral mined like coal but of a harder quality anthracite. The finest jet in the world is found at Whitby along the coast of Yorkshire, England. It was readily available for women who could afford it, and was worn when they were presented at court during the "mourning years," for the ladies were inclined to respect the Queen's request that no other type jewelry be worn.

It soon developed that all black jewelry was called "jet." Actually, some of the finest black *glass* hatpins were manufactured in France and the Bohemian countries from approximately 1870 to 1925. Real jet will retain its sparkling polish for many years while the "black glass" jewelry, although exquisitely executed and equally as attractive, will crack, scratch and become lackluster without the proper care.

When I confronted still another lady with this puzzlement regarding the wearing of black hatpins, she indignantly replied that there was a vast difference between the small insignificant black-knobbed hatpins and the larger jet hatpin ornaments. The ordinary black glass marble-types were literally a dime-a-dozen, while real jet or fine glass were sometimes enhanced with gemstones and could cost a dollar or more.

This same lady insisted that the plainer black pins were worn during mourning, but that later on some of the fancy jets (perhaps with a few brilliants), were adopted by younger widows almost as a consolation or contrast to the terribly staid styles of "widow's weeds." The intricately made "black glass" jewelry surely made the two-year period of "weeds," (imposed by formal etiquette up until 1914) seem less drab. Women — particularly in high social standing — wore black crepe dresses with matching bonnets, a very long veil to cover their faces in public, and black gloves. The all important Victorian jewelry was still worn, but it was black. Gradually the matching black bonnet became a large chapeau with yards of black veiling; the hat was secured to the top of the head with long, ornate-jet hatpins.

The tradition of wearing black is not completely outmoded. I remember when I was growing up I saw women dressed so. Nowadays, periods of mourning do not usually involve dress except for the most devout or traditional families. Even upon attending funerals today, one sees colorful attire instead of drab greys, browns, and blacks. This is hardly as disrespectful, may I comment, as is the use of freeways or express-ways enroute to the cemetery, as if one can't wait to get it over and done with. It seems to me that a slower procession on regular surface streets would lend more homage and dignity to the occasion.

After 1854, came the use of plate or rolled gold, and "pinchbeck" was ousted as the demand for low-carat gold increased at home and abroad. Many pins were gilded, and often the ornaments were of nine and twelve carat gold which had been legalized in England in order to compete with imports and to make the articles cheap enough to export.

Probably the most engaging creature I'd come upon in the pursuit of my hobby and interest in hatpins, was a lady who seemed to emerge right out of *"Arsenic and Old Lace."* She was introduced to me by a mutual acquaintance who warned me that this Mrs. G. was a bit of an eccentric.

Now why do some people label charm and independence as droll? True, Mrs. G. had never bobbed her hair and still wore her dress at mid-calf, but she was spritely, witty, and clearly loved company. She greeted me with a cheerful hello, her merry blue eyes twinkling with the expectation of the forever-young at Christmastide. And I suppose to her, living alone as she did, visitors were a special gift at that!

Now I'm especially enchanted by those who lived in the days of gaslights and quilting bees because they have a certain grace and charm belonging to another time. Mrs. G. must have sensed this for she warmed up immediately and begged me to be "patient with her ramblings." But in truth, I enjoyed her bubbling enthusiasm.

When I told her of my mission — which was to purchase her two hatpin holders of "old Vienna" vintage — she scurried away to get them from another room. While she was away from her parlor I took a moment to enjoy some of the lovely old pieces that graced a small mahogany drum table set off in a corner. Sunrays filtered through lace curtains obviously made by nimble fingers; the light darted and bounced off a diamond cut canoe-shaped fruit bowl.

Upon her return she surprised me by displaying a demitasse cup that matched one of the holders. *"It's all I have left of my mother's tea service,"* she said sadly. *"I broke the last of the saucers a long time ago. But I saved a cup!"*

I asked inquisitively, *"Why would a porcelain hatpin holder be decorated to match a china tea service?"* I was more than a little astonished! (Holder and demitasse cup shown Plate 19.)

She gave a small chirp and explained that when she was a young girl in Austria, her mother often invited women friends for afternoon tea on "receiving day." The women came calling in beautiful frocks with their hair dressed with two or three cotton "rats" adding height to the tower of tresses. On top of this seeming abundance of hair, were milliners' delights of satin, straw, velvet bows, and sweeping ostrich plumes. These gorgeously decorated hats were anchored with perfectly exquisite hatpins, each a showpiece of the jewelers' art.

Since parlor furniture was greatly influenced in design by the French Provincial of the day, and the *setees* or "love seats," as they were called, (because they could rarely seat more than two persons) were small and narrow, it was virtually impossible for even two *slim* ladies to be seated comfortably — unless they removed their huge hats! This they were invited to do — lest they bump heads — and it was done in a most gracious manner, with a flourish somewhat ritualistic.

Hatpins were removed and each lady carefully placed hers in the special hatpin holder on the center of the tea-table. Since each hatpin was more or less the lady's "trademark," being as personal as any custom-made brooch, none could mistake one for the other. Indeed, as is the fashion even today, many tried to outdo each other not only with their bouffant gowns, fantastic hats and coiffeurs, but with the unusual or unique in hatpins and other accessories. The women were as vain about hatpins as the men of the day were about cravat or scarf pins.

146

Picture, if you will, several society matrons of the era, sipping a *demitasse* with their Gainsborough-size hats resting gently against their skirts — lace petticoats exposed just a bit — in a position most attractive to the aesthetic eye, and engaged in lively but polite gossip. And there, on perhaps an inlaid coffee table, appearing like a bouquet of flowers, is a centerpiece of *pietre dure* mounted on the stems of long pins. What a charming and picturesque scene! And how many times I've seen just such women posed by artists for immortal canvases! (But no hatpins!)

The second hatpin holder which my Mrs. G. brought for my inspection and approval truly delighted me. Oval in shape, it was painted with soft green shadings and decorated with gold arabesques. Again, to my surprise and obvious pleasure, this hatpin holder had companion pieces: a *puff box, hair-receiver, trinket box, and small tray. It was a dresser set of almost incomparable loveliness.

"*. . . but I couldn't break up this set!*" exclaimed Mrs. G., as I lovingly fingered the hatpin holder. And she offered to sell it complete! So, I was fortunate to have this dear lady increase my personal collection with the addition of an entire Royal Vienna dresser set, including the much-sought-after hatpin holder. (Plate 45.)

Although many of my Lilliputian ladies insist the majority of hatpins worn by American or "pioneer" women were of the simplest kind with black or white knobs and tempered steel pins, they all agreed that women who lived in the larger towns and cities were more apt to "dress up" and be more lavish in their apparel and accessories. This was true even to the simplest brooch.

A country or farm woman would perhaps have one precious heirloom silver pin or cameo, whereas it was not uncommon to see the "city folk" with garnet necklaces, chains, glass beads, enameled gold set with pearls and semi-precious stones, or silver set with brilliants. Jade and ivory, lapis and pearls were much prized, too.

In Phyllis A. Whitney's, "*The Fire and the Gold*," she describes how "Papa arrived from the Orient with gifts to be exclaimed over — a jade pin for Mama, a brocade belt with an ivory buckle for Cora's small waist, a carved puzzle for Alec, hatpins with ivory knobs for Gran, and a coral ring for Melora."

I have seen an ivory-headed hatpin with a tiny hole at the top through which one may see Niagara Falls when held up to the light. Heads of hatpins were devised of the same materials as other popular jewelry. Onyx, carnelian, coral, agate, topaz, and turquoise were extremely prized as were the more common paste cameos of the period. Many hatpin heads were of two types of engraved gems; the intaglio on which the design is sunk into the stone, and the cameo on which the design is shown in relief. I have several examples of both types in my collection and have seen a few exhibited in other collections.

An exquisite cameo hatpin in my collection depicts the ancient Greek gods, Jupiter and Juno. (Plate 131.) With them is a peacock, the bird sacred to the queen.

Juno appears adorned with a crown and veil, appropriate to the goddess of marriage. Jupiter is bearded. The peacock is standing with spreading tail-feathers in gorgeous array. It is

*In scouting through old catalogues, I discovered that the covered dish that matches the size of a hair-receiver is called a "puff-box." The larger size covered box is a "powder-box."

entirely possible that this cameo was a heirloom which was set anew as a hatpin bauble, for it was no more uncommon for people to re-set precious heirlooms *then*, during the hatpin era, than it is to adapt heirloom jewels into modern settings today.

As if to cling to their European ancestry, habit of dress and hairstyle seemed dependent on the "stock" a person came from. Thus, it should not be strange that the tales of hatpins differ depending on the heritage of the lady telling the story, and which "side of the track" she came from.

For those who emigrated from small villages and hamlets and settled as farmers on the Illinois plains or Minnesota dairyland, their frugal way of life gave no cause nor merit to opulence in clothing nor the luxury of jewelry — including baroque hatpins. A hat, more aptly called a bonnet, was securely fixed on the head by ribbons tied under the chin. Fancy head-feathers were left to the "city folk."

In "*Godey's*," Dec. 1853, there's a bit of chitchat regarding the difference in head-coverings from the "town and city mouse":

It is almost impossible to describe them, as they are so varied in shape and texture. It is very rare in the city to see two bonnets precisely alike, or even approaching each other. It is not, as in the country place, Mrs. A's aim to copy Mrs. B. On the contrary, every lady abides by her own taste and judgement, aided by her milliner's advice, as to shape, material, and color.

. . . All will be found at the openings, or in the different show-rooms, and it is the purchaser's place to decide for herself, or to be persuaded by the milliner, as to what shape, size, or shade will be most becoming. There is nothing which annoys the practised eye more than the uniformity of a village congregation, where, in summer, every straw hat must have a bow on top, because Squire Thompson's wife had a bonnet trimmed so, and it is the fashion in New York, where the bonnet came from . . .

There is no fashion, strictly speaking in a large city, as we have often endeavored to impress upon our readers.

Although modest bonnets were the fashion of country maidens, "women of pleasure" often wore garish hats both in style, color, and decoration. Both salons and saloons provided ample evidence of this fact, and since head-feathers seemed to entice the male population, it wasn't very long before "ladies of polite society" began to adopt one or two in subdued hues — then proffering plumes and pinions equal to their "sisters under the skin."

I've seen examples of the modest straw hats once worn by country-folk out in the fields, with matching hatpins (covered with raffia), used to hold the hat so the prairie winds wouldn't sweep it away along with the bramble bush. But who can dispute that the knobs were not covered to enhance the otherwise unfashionable, functional, head-covering of straw?

Often as not, bandanas or scarves were tied around work hats, but for a trip to town a bit of veiling over the hat and face, bowed under the chin or coquettishly tied at the side, did the job of keeping road-dust off of the face and out of the eyes of Miss Dainty; but it was the hatpin that made the hat secure to the head with its stab in the crown — adding a touch of glamour, too, by a modest-sized ornament on top.

The Pennsylvania Dutch women and certainly the Mormon wives of Utah, with their flat, simplified hair-combs, had no need of hatpins, for they usually wore crochet caps or cotton Mother Hubbards to complement the utter simplicity in hair style and habit.

Contrasting this, of course, were those whose bloodline linked them to Paris, Vienna, London, or Prussia, to the horse and carriage days, to the days in town and court. Even servants in such courts, upon seeking their fortunes in the crowded towns and metropolises of the New World, copied their mistresses in perhaps less costly fabric, substituting *taffeta* for silk and satin and *velveteen* for the rich velvet and brocades of the ladies of fashion. Even the desire to own jewelry was satisfied with the substitution of brilliants or rhinestones for diamonds. And these women seeking a new life in the bustle of cities whose "streets were paved with gold," also sought a freedom in fashion and would not be denied such rights because of previous servitude. They copied and wore continental styles to their heart's content, according to their husband's indulgence, tolerance, and perhaps even his amusement. For many styles were really outlandish and uncomfortable — but when did these factors ever dissuade a determined woman bent on keeping "up with the style"?

I've often been puzzled by the absence of hatpins on the sumptuous hats of elegant ladies in paintings and in fashion plates, whereas in examining photographs of flesh-and-blood women wearing enormous hats of the period, hatpins are obviously used as essential implements for the security of the headgear — particularly in the 1890-1910 era. The inclusion of hatpins in illustrations were more or less limited to drawings of "Gibson Girls" and sardonic cartoons.

One answer to this mystery was provided very simply by a dear little soul who was nearing her 90th birthday. She quipped, *"Hatpins were worn in the back, and artists painted the front!"* Now why hadn't I thought of that? Yet, upon mentioning this point of view to another octogenarian, she sniffed, curled her lips downward and commented, *"Pshaw! I've seen 'em worn straight across the top like a bone through a cannibal's nose!"*

True, I've seen several photographs in which hatpins appear quite prominently, some with the bauble displayed by allowing the pin to be exposed several inches from the hat, that is, the decorated end of the pin and not the point\*. But as far as hatpins on portraits are concerned, they were completely ignored although other accessories of the day — not nearly as important — were included.

In all my hunting, digging, and snooping, I've yet to find more than a scarce few hatpins which are identical in both design and color, unless they are found in pairs or in a matched set which was gift-boxed. The more commonly found duplicates are those of molded glass, such as tinted pattern glass or carnival; the most frequently found — until recent years when they were "hunted down" for their shanks — are the ¼" marble-sized black or white glass-bead type which were

worn by the middling class and servants because of the low cost of such pins.

As for the ornate brass or gilded mountings, seldom have I discovered a duplicate in the thousands of hatpins seen and inspected by me in dozens of collections. This leads me to believe that hatpins with illusion style settings or claw mountings, and baroque or ornate fabrications — the sort of setting which rises above the simplest jeweler's findings — are deviations from the prototype or original die-casting, and represent the individual expression of the many prolific jewelers of the period. Each individually hand-wrought hatpin is a delightful work of art, extolling excellent craftsmanship, extravagant design, intricate metal-work, and often an almost inspired sense of "style." These craftsmen with creative cutting were able to achieve the desired brilliance from stones even if the stones were not of precious matter. Be it synthetic or glass, the "gems" sparkled from within their casings of scrolls, spirals, flourishes, interlacing, tooling, filigree, and fret-work. Skill and imagination were the chief tools of hatpin-makers!

In a letter from Jean J. Hepburn of Hanover, Massachusetts, I was referred to a March, (1970) issue of *"Silver-rama,"* which shows a series of Zodiac birth-month signs. These are embossed in brooches which have matching hatpins.

Sterling silver hatpins are some of the most desirable and coveted by collectors. Many of the ornaments show the influence of *Art Nouveau* in design and bear the mark of fine workmanship.

I have collected, among other fanciful hatpins, those worn with special attire such as garb for golf, tennis, fishing, etc. There is a set of sterling silver golf-clubs and a single hatpin with a bauble depicting the club-house and some of the activities surrounding it. (See Plates 62 and 126.)

Another category is the collection of sea-shells which are mounted on hatpins to be worn, I suppose, with the old-fashioned swimming caps of gingham and lace or with the floppy straw sunhats.

With regard to bathing, I found this advice to young ladies of "polite society":

> *Bathing calls for a costume of some material that will not cling to the form when wet. Flannel is appropriate, and a heavy quantity of mohair also makes a successful dress, as it resists water and has no clinging qualities. An oil-silk cap should be worn over the hair. The cut of the dress should be modest; the costume loose and full, and it should be made with a skirt. The neck should be cut quite high.*

The above advice was printed in 1896. By 1905, bathing attire had begun to be called "immodest," and the assortment of bathing-hats were as varied as shells on the beach.

One of my informants recalls buying such a shell-pin, as described previously, along the old boardwalk in Atlantic City. *"If one found a particularly pretty shell,"* she pointed out, *"there was a man whose business it was to wire it on to a hatpin as a souvenir or keepsake."*

For some it was a sweet reminder of the rare vacation away from the sweltering city where it was not uncommon at the

---

\* *"The Prince and the Lily" boasts a photo from the Bettman Archive which shows Lily Langtry with a real show of hatpins protruding from the back of her hat!*

turn-of-the-century — and before the "*horseless* carriage" — to find the poor innocent four-legged beast known as the "work-horse" fallen dead on the streets from heat prostration.

The shell mementoes of the sea must have been quite popular for they have been well preserved. Several varieties in my own collection and the favorites in other exhibits are shown on Plates 42 and 80.

Keepsake and souvenir hatpins were purchased right along with other commemorative or "reminder" pieces such as glassware and spoons offered to the public at historic sites, fairs, and the ever-popular expositions. There are commemorative hatpins with a cross or star, Masonic emblems, insignias of the GAR, (Grand Army of the Republic), B.P.O.E., (Benevolent and Protective Order of Elks), emblems for Women's Suffrage League, clubs, organizations, and those mementoes of vacation locales. (Plates 30 and 83.)

A treasured sterling silver hatpin in my collection is of the nation's capitol, with the Capitol Building engraved on one side and the White House on the other. Upon close scrutiny, one can date the hatpin to the early turn-of-the-century before the long steps to the Capitol were completed and the statuary placed at either side of the entrance. Who can dispute that this hatpin may have belonged to a famous "First Lady" of the land? (Plates 92 and 190.)

Souvenir enameled or gold hatpins from Niagara Falls, Prince Edward Island, and many states, and the ever popular initialed (monogram) hatpins in infinite variety are numerous. A pair of coins from the Hawaiian Islands, (before Hawaii became our 50th State), are dated 1883 and are unique in my collection. One coin shows "heads," the other "tails." (Plate 22, back row center.)

When I was in Virginia City, Nevada, enjoying a rare taste of early Americana, I was given a superb hatpin by a lady who owns an antique store there. She's a direct descendent of a family who originally settled in the "Mother Lode" country when it was the hub of the West.

The hatpin is made of nickel-silver mined from her grandfather's "claim." The woman, who has no other kin, felt it belonged in a collection such as mine. I will always cherish both the gesture and the hatpin's history. Imbedded in the patterned silver is a beautiful example of smokey quartz, mouse-color, with at least thirty-six facets, each shimmering with light. (Plate 115.)

Also in my collection is a hatpin reminiscent of the "wild west." It has a nugget of "fool's gold" mounted in what I like to call "tacky-Tiffany-type." (Plate 114, bottom right.) Can you imagine, as can I, that this hatpin was given to some glamorous creature in a frontier casino, perhaps like "Kitty" — the beautiful red-headed proprietess of the Long Branch Saloon in the T.V. program, "Gunsmoke." Isn't it easy to imagine some weary, hungry, bearded prospector riding into town astride his pokey mule with this special gift for Kitty? Not that she wouldn't know all along it was "fool's gold," but with a wink at her side-arm bartender, she orders a set-up of bottle and glass for the old coot and maybe a plate of dinner.

Part of the fun in collecting antiques of any kind is the castle-building, daydreaming, romantic reveries into the past. The speculation about what circumstance brought such-and-such pin to such-and-such place! And what kind of people were involved . . .?

Speaking of "Gunsmoke" and the West, my travels during the latter part of 1971 brought me through a half-dozen western States where I made many queries regarding hatpins and holders. During my three week journey I kept a detailed, comprehensive, day-to-day log. From this account comes this bit of exciting adventure:

*LABOR DAY, Monday, Sept. 6, 1971*
*. . . we pay another $2.00 to go out the East Gate of Yellowstone which is only 70 miles, in order for us to use that scenic route to Sheridan (Wyoming). But it's worth it because this is the section of Yellowstone which we had missed and is supposed to be the most lush and beautiful part . . . Just passed a passel of ducks taking a mist bath in a small pond. Open meadows with a mantle of frost glistening in bright early sunlight . . . saw two bears along West Thumb — a lonely duck all by itself on huge Yellowstone Lake — several cars loaded with elk horns . . . saw lots of snow and babbling brooks along the way to make it worthwhile. Cody is 52 miles away . . . clear as a bell with feathery clouds that look like they are there to dust it (sky) and keep it clean.*

*Cody is 13 miles East . . . peaceful and serene — mountains across the water (Buffalo Bill Dam) are snow-covered. Lots of campers round the bend. All the room in the world and they are camped two feet apart! "They are like animals at a watering hole; must like communal living," says my husband.*

*1:45 p.m. — welcome to Cody. "Howdy Partner" . . . this is a fantastic, lucky, stop, just five minutes from the world famous Cody Museum, and here we are eating in historic "Green Gables" restaurant . . . met world-renowned artist, (name withheld by request) and his wife, who have a hatpin collection of over 300 choice pins, including a gorgeous garnet, several portrait pins, ivory, enamels, and two Tiffany-glass pins. I met the couple through Richard I. Frost, Curator of the Buffalo Bill Cody Museum where I saw three hatpins belonging to Cody's eldest daughter. Mr. Frost opened the showcase so I could take pictures of the hatpins; unfortunately, the lighting was too poor and the photographs are not usable for reproduction.*

*Mr. and Mrs. (blank) displayed their hatpin collection in vases and several hatpin holders among which was a unique mushroom-shaped holder that was as modern in design as today. Mrs. _____ told me there were many hatpin collectors in the West and that a prominent collector lived in Casper, Wyoming. (Unfortunately, our itinerary did not include this community.)*

*. . . we are passing open range country with lush meadows, willows, rolling hillsides. Saw an adorable pinto pony with its mama. I can see where "wide-wonderful-Wyoming" earned its name. And the Texans have nothing on these people for friendliness . . . the sky is so wide and bright and clear it almost hurts your eyes.*

Throughout the West, where I encountered dozens upon dozens of antique dealers, I found that prices varied in each town and hamlet; one thing that *was* consistent, either a dealer had *neither* hatpins nor holders, or only a *small quantity* of each. Some dealers lacked interest and showed ignorance of the subject; others expressed concern because of the "rarity" of the items.

Later in the year, my travels took me cross-country and I toured the East coast from New York, New Jersey, Washington, D.C., and Virginia; then down to New Orleans delta.

My experiences, East and West, have brought me to the conclusion that there is no true "market-range" in pricing hatpins or hatpin holders. Prices seem to depend on the old law of "supply and demand." Since the interest in hatpins and holders has grown by leaps and bounds, prices have jumped and skyrocketed accordingly, until some are "out of sight." So, from careful calculation, I produced a "Price Guide" (available from Publisher), that provides a working formula which will establish a reasonable groundwork for the evaluation of hatpins.

Hatpins are such a little-thought-about object that a collector of hatpins stumped the entire panel of experts during a **1974** program of television's *"What's My Line?"*. My tele-

**Plate 157**

150

phone was kept busy *that* night! Each caller emphasized how both panel and audience were dumbfounded and fascinated when confronted with the few hatpin gems in the collection. Without doubt, this program influenced a new awareness and desire for this "collectible."

Among some of my most interesting pins of sentimental value are those that belonged to my mother. They are more than a half-century old; one, a large round wooden-topped globe arrived with her from the "Old Country." Another, a small dainty cluster of rhinestones set in a bowl of gilded bronze, looks like a tiny nosegay. This was one of her favorites. Still another resembles the Eiffel Tower turned upside down, with a large pearl in its base. Yet another is topped with a golden hilt like some ancient sword, similar to one I saw advertised in an old 1902 Sears' catalogue.

I had the good fortune to visit with an antique dealer in her home-shop combination in a lovely rural community just outside San Francisco. She fascinated me with some of her tales of the young Mother Lode country of California. She vividly recalled this scene of San Francisco when it had become the fashion metropolis for "gold prospectors" and settlers alike:

*"Throughout the thriving Barbary Coast, women wore velvet hats designed to perch upon a knot or bunion of hair, with billowing veils, ornaments of feathers and bows wired on in a variety of shapes. Long, fanciful hatpins, singly or in pairs, held the entire concoction firmly anchored against the stiff sailing breezes from the Bay. The ornamented sailing suits were made of warm materials that would withstand the sea water, but the hats were whimsical and impractical."*

At this same period, across the continent, outdoor sports, especially cycling, became the rage. Central Park, in New York, provided special bicycle paths not so much as homage to the sport but in consideration of the innocent strollers who had been "knocked-about" by this contraption which had "taken such a mighty grasp upon the land."

In an etiquette book of 1897, written by Maud C. Cooke, the following admonition appears: *"It is distinctly understood in the first place that 'cycling' is the correct word; the up-to-date woman dares not speak of bicycling nor of wheeling."*

Mrs. Cooke, a well-known and popular author of her day, included a complete chapter on "Bicycle Etiquette," some of which may be taken to heart considering today's upsurging interest in the sport:

*If in town, the early hours of the morning are chosen for a ride through the park . . . In the country the rules, both as regards cycling and driving, are not as rigid. The maiden, however, who is a stickler for form, does all her cycling in the hours which come before noon — unless there be a special meet, a bicycle tea, for instance, or a spin by moonlight.*

*Neither is it correct for a young woman to ride unaccompanied . . .*

*If one possesses such a commodity as a brother or a husband, he can always be made useful on a cycling excursion. Never is a man better able to show for what purpose he was made than upon such occasions . . .*

*Society insists on an upright position, with, of course, no attempt at racing pace. It also frowns*

*upon constant ringing of the bell — that will do for the vulgar herd who delight in noise. The well-informed wheelwoman keeps eye and ear alert and touches her bell rarely . . .*

*Very gallant escorts use a towrope when accompanying a lady on a wheeling spin . . . when he has finished towing he drops back to the lady's side, hanging the loose end of the cord over his shoulder, to be ready for the next hill. A gentle pull that is a bagatelle to a strong rider is of great assistance to a weak one up hill or against a strong wind . . .*

*Don't dress immodestly . . . sweaters worn like a Chinaman's blouse are almost indecent.*

By 1897, cycling was such a firmly established pastime that little comment was made upon the sport itself, but improved patent devices were continually appearing. The cycling costume, for instance, was *"in appearance an ordinary walking skirt, but in reality however, the back pleats were divided in the centre and lined half-way with separate pieces of the same material as the skirt which was on a la pantalon."* The cycling hat was still the ever-popular sailor perched flat on the head — much like our modern flying-saucer shape — and anchored by the decorative and functional hatpin(s).

In Mrs. C. S. Peel's, *"A Hundred Wonderful Years 1820-1920,"* there's an extract from an undated letter, which Mrs. Peel suggests was probably written in 1892, relating how the sight of a knickerbockered bicycling woman shocked old-fashioned people. The letter reports:

*. . . two ladies — or, as Granpapa says, two shameless females — in bloomers bicycled through the village yesterday, and some of the women were so scandalized that they threw stones at them. I didn't dare to say so but I thought they looked very neat, though I don't think I should quite like to show my own legs to the world like that. Still, it's all a question of what one is accustomed to. Why do old people always disapprove of anything which they didn't do when they were young?*

It was in 1869 that these baggy knickerbockers first appeared and were adopted by women cyclists. This modified form of trousers were called "bloomers," a name applied to the young ladies of that era who dared to imitate Mrs. Amelia Bloomer who first introduced the "outrageous" style in early 1851.

The "Bloomer-Girls" became known as those daring darlings of theatrical revues who drew forth cheers from the men but caused women of polite society to spread their fans and hide the blush.

An unnamed but eminent lady writer was quoted in a report of 1895, as saying that *"skirts are an abomination"* for cycling. Thus she stormed:

*In the first place let me condemn the skirt — not from prejudice, but from experience. Skirts, no matter how light, how trim, how heavy, are both a nuisance and a danger, (when cycling). A nuisance because they are always subject to entanglement in the wheel; because they fly up with every breeze and motion; because they have not the chic appearance of the properly made bloomer, and because, if they are weighted, like a riding habit, they make so much more to carry against the wind. And breeze makes weight.*

*They are a danger because with the constant pumping of the pedals the knee is required to raise too great a weight; this bears upon the body just below the back of the hips, giving backache; often more serious troubles. I wouldn't wear a skirt. I had one torn off me by the wheel; but I rode with them long enough to give a comparison of the merits of skirts versus bloomers.*

*Riding suits should be of fine, lightweight, navy blue or black materials, made with bloomers, and the blouse with tailor-made jacket. I wear the sweater myself in preference, because it is not so apt to leave one subject to changes of temperature. The Alpine hat or Tam O'Shanter is au fait for street, with leggings to match the bloomers and jacket, and low shoes made broad on the ball of the foot . . . bloomers should be made to fasten at the left side of the back, which leaves room for a pocket on the right side. Tinted leggings should always match the hat and gloves.*

*Tell the ladies to have their saddles built high and wide in the back, sloping away and downwards in front; and that if they pedal properly there is no reason why bicycling should not be a healthful, moral, modest and permanent form of exercise. For, mark it, the wheel has come to stay!*

It's been close to a decade since I began reading and collecting notes about the period hatpin, and each time a new book appears on the antique book market I search its pages hoping for additional enlightening information. I turn to the indexes of new fashion books on mode of dress and jewelry of the Victorian era through the present time, in hopes of finding "hatpins" listed along with other important accessories. I'm usually disappointed, for the information is often sketchy or it directs me to a photograph which lacks descriptive material.

I have dozens of "detectives" cluing me in on bits and pieces of information they come upon in magazines, books, newspapers, and shows (both film and television) with even the slightest hint or mention of the word "hatpin."

It was through one of my "informants" that I received a story from *The New York Times*, (Aug. 1952), which appeared reprinted in "Hobbies Magazine," a year later:

*"A true collector never throws anything away. The Rev. Earl E. Story . . . finding four hatpins left over from a church sale at his former Newport Church, and no ladies with hats needing pins, thereupon became a hatpin collector.*

*"The ladies of his church helpfully donated 21 more; he displayed his collection in a hobby show, and the well-liked minister suddenly found his collection increased to 100.*

*"Now he is in the advanced collector stage, and is*

*getting rare pins. One has a perfume box within its head. Another is a his-hers combination of matching hatpin and stickpin. Some eye-catchers have heads bobbing on springs, one is capped with a button from the Continental Army. Some are gem-studded . . ."*

Now the gospel truth is that every one of the hatpins described above, with the exception of the "his-hers," is represented in my own collection, from the perfumed top to the "springers" or "nodders"; they differ only in design, I'm sure. And when I have exhibited my collection, I've been fortunate to encounter "little old ladies" who donate hatpins and increase the variety in my collection. Too, I hear unusual and fascinating tales about hatpins and the hatpin era, some of which I've related in this chapter.

Besides ear-to-hearsay stories, I've received beautiful, sentimental, and interesting letters relating to the period when hatpins were such familiar everyday objects.

When I wrote to a company that made "novelty" articles of glass back in 1901, I hoped an answer would inform me that these novelties included hatpin holders.

The delightful reply was written by Elizabeth Degenhart, Ohio's "First Lady of Glass," who still supervises, purchases supplies, and is all-around manager of the Degenhart's Crystal Art Glass Company. At age 85, Mrs. Degenhart still drives her own car! She is one more example of the hearty and enduring "pioneer" stock that helped build America and provide its strong backbone!

Her letter gives such a vivid picture of hatpin-times, I must share it with my readers:

*"Cambridge Glass was built in 1901 and poured the first Glass in 1902. My husband aged 13 at the time! He drove the horse and buggy for A. J. Bennett, the owner, in 1901. April 1902, he worked in the first shop the first day Glass was made in 1902.*

*"I met him in 1906 and we were married in 1908. I worked at Cambridge Glass from 1905 to 1908 when I was married to John.*

*"In 1946, John and I started to build a small factory of our own and we made the first Glassware in April 1947. John passed away May 14, 1964 in his sleep. He would have been 80 in September.*

*"I am still operating the Factory and have tripled the business! I am 85. I do not recall the Cambridge Glass Company ever making hatpin holders. Nor did my factory ever make them . . .*

*"Hope this will give you some idea of our story."*

Throughout Mrs. Degenhart's letter, the word *glass* was capitalized — emphasizing the importance of the substance in her life!

How does one become a collector of hatpins? Mrs. Alice Getman of Michigan answered that query in interesting detail:

*"In the fall of 1960, I had surgery and a friend brought me a hand-painted holder with three hatpins and said, 'There! Now you have a hobby and are on the road to being a collector.'*

*"I had always admired the collections of others*

but had never really collected anything but trading stamps, myself. So I began in earnest. I worked at enlarging my group, both pins and holders. I found them in every imaginable place.

"People were very kind to me and helped me hunt. So many of the pins had a history or sentimental attachment I was surprised some would part with them, but they wanted them to belong to my 'collection'. It was always a great disappointment to hear about all the lovely pins they threw away because they were 'dangerous' to have in the house, especially with small children around. And so my collection grew until I said I had a 'corner' on all of them in southwestern Michigan.

"I kept them and their holders on open shelves so it became quite a chore to keep them all sparkling and beautiful . . .

"I have two small grand-daughters who may want my treasures some day so at present I have not entertained the idea of disposing of either the pins or about a dozen holders . . ."

(Portions of Mrs. Getman's collection of hatpins and holders are shown on Plates 180 and 187.)

A close acquaintance of mine decided to purchase "one or two hatpins" to complete the accessories required for her china toilet set which had a hatpin holder as well as the usual other pieces on the comb and brush tray. But like the potato chip commercial once you take a bite into the "hatpin habit," you're hooked! This gal now has dozens of magnificent examples of hatpins and holders, many of which are shown within the pages of this book. (See pieces marked, "private collection of Sybel Heller.")

Mrs. Joyce Roth, whose collection is well represented in this book, comes from a long-line of antique dealers; her mother is still in the trade back in Kansas. Joyce's interest and current obsession with hatpins came about after she was presented with a pair of hatpins for a Mother's Day gift from her eldest daughter who has inherited the love of "collectibles" right down the line!

Some people may scoff or look skeptical at my use of the terms "hooked" and "obsessed." For them I say, read on:

" . . . I'm so frustrated! I'm like a kitty who's been given a sniff of the prize trout! After meeting you and spending that one short hour with you, I'm dying to learn more about hatpins! . . .

"I've spent the past two Saturdays 'antiquing' and have bought a few hatpins. It's unbelievable how little the dealers know about them. I have told everyone about you and your book and they all say they don't know anything about hatpins because there's no information available! . . . I am itching for knowledge of the hatpin!

" . . . I saw a pin that I thought I'd tell you about. It's a little one with a one-inch head and six-inch pin. It's a World War I Military hat! It's in good shape with a 'bridge' mounting — as you taught me to look for. The dealer wants $35 for it; he says he's never seen another one and thinks it's rare . . .

"I went to Williamsburg, Virginia recently with my daughter's 4th Grade class. While visiting the restored area I went in the Millinery Shop to see the display of old hats and bonnets. I asked the Inn-keeper about hatpins — if they were used and what type. She knew nothing nor had any to show*. When were hatpins invented? What types? Is this information in your book? Oh . . .

" . . . Before I met you I was just interested in hatpins and thought they were sweet and pretty. Now I've become a hatpin maniac, craving for everything from beginning to end about hatpins! Lillian, I've decided that with your influence on people you should go into politics! . . ."

*Footnote: "Colonial" Williamsburg, Va. is an 18th Century restoration site, which pre-dates the era of the Period Hatpin; so there would be no hatpins at the Millinery Shop at Williamsburg.

**Plate 42**

153

The young woman who wrote me the above letter is so full of enthusiasm that one could feel it and her warmth "between the lines." Her subsequent correspondence to me certainly acted as a catapult for sinking morale — a battle all writers face on the field of research. She has been joined by dozens of young people I know who have been "pricked" with "hatpin disease."

Lest you think that only the female gender are subject to this "affliction," let me share some remarks from the opposite sex:

> "... I promised to tell you something about me as the collector. Once upon a time (in 1948) I entered the attic of my wife's parents' house and I discovered several cases with jewelry goods ... samples of the production of her great-grandfather and grandfather (he died in 1946 and was 86). They were jewelers who manufactured glassware, black glass jewelry, costume jewelry, brooches and hatpins, and they kept the interesting and important history of their work. I discovered the beauty of old hatpins and it pleases me to repair them ... or change them for other ones ... pins in lively colours, engraved, and _Art Nouveau_ ..."

The gentleman who wrote the above letter wished to remain anonymous, but I must mention that thanks to his generosity, some of my loveliest and rarest "mourning pins" came from his collection into mine. And it was through him that I was able to supply readers with the technical and historical information concerning these hatpins.

Another young man responded to my query: "... _two people who find collecting hatpin holders and hatpins as fascinating as we do certainly should call each other by our first names ..._"

He continued: "_It was about eight years ago that I started my collection. I'm sorry I can't give you any anecdotes. Oh, I do remember the time I asked a dealer for a better price and he did. It was $2.50 more than it was marked ..._"

Who said that collectors don't have a sense of humor? All I can say is that collectors had best have a good sense of humor when they get stuck with a "fake" or overpay on a "reproduction"!

Someday I hope to enlarge this chapter, "_Memoirs of a Collector,_" for I believe my reminiscences and experiences of the past decade would make a fascinating testimonial not only to people from every walk of life, but to collectors of hatpins and hatpin holders who are a breed deserving the shelter of kind, sympathetic, and understanding words from one of their own — words preserved for posterity.

From the above, one would imagine I allude to an "endangered species"; to the contrary, collectors, both young and old alike, are multiplying. This is one time I can say, "Happy hunting!" — and mean it with all my heart!

# Chapter VIII

# CONCLUSION: WITH REMARKS TO COLLECTORS OF HATPINS

A collector of hatpins need not necessarily be a collector of hatpin holders and vice-versa. But they do seem to go hand-in-hand and without doubt enhance one another.

However, just as a collector of fine prints need not necessarily store them in gilded frames, so those that amass either pins or holders need not deny the singular importance of *either* item as a collection.

But one cannot deny that the greater advantage in collecting *hatpins* is the conservation of space. Several dozen can make an impressive exhibit in either a small cabinet or on a corner tabletop. The latter is somewhat more suitable, for hatpins should be seen just below eye-level, looking down on their myriad of heads. (See Plates 43 and 208.) Too, hatpins should have close inspection for detail. Of course from a housekeeping point of view, safety for children, and theft, a *locked* china cabinet is the only way to go.

Authentic hatpin holders do enhance the showing of a hatpin collection as well as being the beautiful and intriguing items that they are. Holders come in such a variety of shapes and materials, a collector can "specialize" if he so desires.

Some hatpin collectors prefer exhibiting their treasures in pin-cushions, with pins darting in gorgeous array. (Plates 9, 15, 16, 56, 71 and 121.)

An effective and impressive display of hatpins is achieved by exhibiting them according to color of stone or by their category. For example, I have some of my silver-headed hatpins displayed in a silver hatpin holder; my thistle pins in a holder which itself has a thistle-stone accent.

My green simulated emeralds and other green glass hatpins are in the same color china hatpin holder or plush cushion, (Plate 194.); my topaz-color heads show off beautifully in a marigold carnival glass holder, just as the amethyst-color stones look elegant in the purple Northwood carnival glass, and so forth.

A collector friend of mine has a charming arrangement of hatpins and holders interspersed with small but elegant perfume bottles, small china dolls, and other charming bric-a-brac of the period.

A clever woman I know has taken assorted woven baskets, made a velvet cushion to fit inside each, and has her enormous collection of hatpins arranged like bouquets of flowers in every room of her house.

Another noteworthy advantage of collecting hatpins and holders, too, is the cost involved, since the novice collector can begin with the less ornate hatpins and *Nippon* or unmarked holders, which although less expensive than others are impressive and have great eye-appeal.

I must admit, however, that the prices of hatpins and holders have risen considerably in the past five years, as all antiques and collectibles have. This is due to the ever increasing interest in these curious objects and antiques and the sudden urge to return to the nostalgic past.

This urge seems strongest now in the younger generation. Whereas it was most common to see "dowdy" women, often considered eccentrics, collecting "junk" — now spelled JUNQUE, as if a derivative of ANTIQUE — there has always been a segment of the population interested in preserving and conserving things of the past. This segment used to consist of the "over 40" generation, but at last the gap has closed and young and old find a common meeting ground at the nearest antique shop or show.

It is believed that prices will continue to mount, making one's collection ever more valuable as an investment no less an intriguing hobby.

A collection is often defined as "an assemblage of works of art," and the collector as "one who performs the act." Although collecting or "antiquing" is a source of pleasure and a means of acquiring treasures, I must admit that my own reason for collecting hatpins is not altogether artistic.

I'm a person who's greatly influenced by an innate curiosity, an integral part of my nature. I'm wholly fascinated by such questions and puzzlements as:

Who wore such and such hatpin?

Was it a gift?

And for what occasion?

What kind of face was adorned by the hat skewered with hatpins?

What did the hat look like?

What kind of hands fingered the jeweled ornaments?

What went on under the hat and in the head?

What kind of labor did the hands perform?

Were they weak or strong hands that thrust the hatpin(s) in place?

Was the finger(s) ever pricked as was mine?

When was the hatpin made? And who conceived its design?

How much did it cost at the time it was first marketed? And how much did it cost at recent purchase?

And from whom and where was it bought — both past and present?

How far has the piece traveled?

Did it ever have its "day in court"?

Answers to these and dozens more questions prompted me to speak at great length to many, many, Victorian-born ladies. And it was from their many mad, merry, marvelous tales that the first format for this book evolved.

As I looked for further answers to historical and manufacturing queries, I found I had no place to turn. The usual reference sources were not helpful; my discovery of how terribly the subject of hatpins had been neglected spurred me on to writing a book, not only for self-satisfaction, but as an aid to other collectors. People with great diversified interests also spurred me on in my project and helped me along the way.

**Plate 208**

"Antiquing" brings people together with a common interest in linking the past to the present. I've found that collectors are a singular breed: innately romantic, "incurably green," insatiably curious, and intensely enthusiastic about antiques.

Whether one is a collector of primitive or provincial, collectors are birds of a feather flocking together at antique shows, rubbing elbows at swap meets, falling over each other at rummage sales, or out-bidding each other at auctions. And like the familiar adage about fishermen, they sit together afterwards moaning about "the one that got away!"

Robert Paul Smith's publication, *Lost and Found,* (Charterhouse, N.Y., 1973), lists the hatpin as one in a category of several things that have disappeared from the American scene.

Author Smith relates how he remembers the hatpin as being a *small stiletto* which his mother placed *between her teeth*; then, utterly fascinated by *one of those mysterious things*

*women could do,*" and get away with, he watched her place *the point on the hat . . . and drove six inches of cold steel straight into her skull . . .*"

Disregarding the fact that period hatpins came at a much later era, Smith suggests that Shakespeare should have armed Hamlet's mother, Queen Gertrude with such a vicious "stiletto" as the hatpin and do the King in!

Thus far, whether it be in life or literature, it seems that men are the real culprits when it comes to branding or brandishing hatpins! With this in mind perhaps my readers will forgive both the parody and my poetic license:

"Mary Doodle went to town,
Her pair of cobs high-steppin';
She'd stuck a hatpin in her hat
And called it *male-dubbed* weapon!

\* \* \*

156

# SECTION II

**Glossary**

**Supplement**

**Cross-index by Subject for Plates**

**Bibliography**

**Sources and Acknowledgements**

**Reference Notes and Appendix**

**Text for Plates**

**Numerical Index for Plates With Page Numbers**
    **(Credit and/or Source)**

# GLOSSARY

ABALONE — sea-shell creature of the Pacific Coast with an inner-shell lining of grey/pink natural pearlized substance. (See Plates 72 and 105.)

ACCENT — to accentuate an ornamental hatpin head with small brilliants, metallic design, natural elements, rattles or bells; anything added to enhance the ornament.

    *Beads* as accents, Plate 42.
    *Bell or rattle* as accents, Plate 205.
    *Brilliants* as accents, Plates 85, 91, 104.
    *Eyes* (Stone) as accents, Plates 2, 5, 6, 18, 65, 89, 91, 110, 123.
    *Gold,* Plates 41, 132.
    *Hand-painted,* Plate 87.
    *Metallic,* Plates 65, 91.
    *Natural Elements* as accents, Plate 21.
    *Pearl,* Plates 37, 206.
    *Stone,* Plates 2, 3, 5, 6, 11, 18, 34, 35, 65, 91.

AIGRETTE — hair ornament shaped like a plume or spray. (See Plates 142 and 158.)

ALFRED MEAKIN LTD., Tunstall, Staffordshire (England): from 1875 to present, manufactured many commode and toilet sets. The addition of "Ltd.," after 1897; word "England," introduced after 1891.

ALLOY — combination of metals fused together; a base metal mixed with a precious ore to make it workable, to harden it, or to change its color.

AMBER — a yellowish-brown fossil resin. (See Plates 104 and 114.) This fossilized resin, also found in black and varieties of brown and orange, comes from ancient forests of fir trees or mined from under the Baltic sea. The orange color amber comes from Sicily.

AMETHYST — a gemstone in shades from pale lavender to deep purple found in Russia, Brazil, Uruguay and Ceylon. (Imitation, Plates 37, 205; genuine gemstone, Plates 116, 206.)

ARABESQUES — flowing scrollwork in line, leaves, etc., often in low relief.

ART DECO — (1910-1941) A stilted, stylized design, a transition from *Art Nouveau*; found its influence in the 1925 (France) *Exposition Internationale des Arts Décoratifs,* as well as the art of the American Indian, ancient Egyptian, as well as Greek and Roman architecture. (Plates 77, 85, 112, 193.)

ART NOUVEAU — (1890-1910) Design incorporating undulating curves, spirals, and flowing lines. A short-lived art style introduced in the late 19th Century and ending in the early 20th. The influence of Japanese art forms is most apparent, and was popular-ized by the 1876 trade between Japan and the Continent. Art Nouveau was known in other countries as follows:

    *America, England, and France: L'Art Nouveau,* for the Paris establishment of Samuel Bing (1895).
    *Bohemia (Czechoslovakia):* "Recession" or "Secession" Period.
    *Germany:* "Judenstil," after the art magazine called, "Jugend," meaning "youth."
    *Italy: "Stile Liberty,"* after London's Liberty & Co., Regent Street Department Store.
    *Spain: "Arte Joven,"* meaning "young art."
    (See Plates 24, 32, 34, 35, 36, 64, 65, 93, 205, 207.)

BAROQUE — bold, ornate, "heavy-looking" ornament with elaborate frame. (See Plates 23, 36, 72, 77, 108.)

BAGUETTE — a rectangular cut stone. (Plate 37, back row.)

BAYREUTH — name of Bavarian town in the 18th and 19th centuries. (Porcelain is marked with name "Bayreuth") (Plate 182.)

BEAD — an ornament with a hole end-to-end into which a pin can be inserted. It is then "topped" with a jewelers' finding to prevent loss of ornament. (Plate 15.)

BERLIN PORCELAIN FACTORY — mark on porcelain, "konigliche porzellanmunt" — with orb, Prussian eagle, and/or "KPM."

BEZEL — groove or flange which holds a gemstone secure in its setting. (Plate 37.)

BILSTON — South Staffordshire (England) center for most of 19th Century pottery from England.

BISCUIT — porcelain, stoneware, or pottery after primary baking and before the application of a glaze.

BISQUE — china or porcelain without a glaze. (Plate 195.)

BLACK GLASS JEWELRY — imitation jet. (Plates 96, 97, 128.)

BONE CHINA — associated mainly with England. Bone china is animal bone added to porcelain mixture to make it soft — more sheer or translucent — than the harder paste.

BOBBLER — (See *Nodder*)

BOX SETTING — stone enclosed in a "box" with edges of metal pressed down to hold it in place. (Plates 36, 129.)

BRASS — yellowish-gold color which is primarily an alloy of copper, tin, zinc, or other base metal.

BRIDES — name commonly given to ribbons attached inside the brim of an open bonnet or broad-brimmed hat of the 1830 period. Ribbons were allowed to float free or were tied loosely under the chin.

BRILLIANTS — another term for less than ¼" stones of paste, strass, or rhinestones. (Imitation glass) Plates

85 and 91 show brilliants as accents; Plates 20, 21, and 23 show brilliants as ornamental hatpin heads.

BUGLE BEAD — long, tube-shaped bead. (Plates 15, 16, 86.)

BUREL GLASS — a Bohemian blown glass also known by its manufacturing term as "Hyalith." (Plate 25.)

CABOCHON — a stone without facets, shaped like a dome. (Plates 72, 82, 106, and 206.)

CAGE — (See *Mountings*)

CAMEO — conch shell, onyx gem, or coral, carved in relief. (Plate 131.) Also in molded synthetics or molded glass. (Plate 4.)

CARAT (or *Karat*) — standard unit of weight for gems or a measure for gold tabled at 1/24th part of pure gold in an alloy. Term *carat* used as symbol for unit weight of gems and gemstones; (ct.) as one carat diamond = 1 ct. # Symbol *K* used for gold: 24K = pure gold; 18K = 18 parts gold to 6 parts alloy, etc.

CARNIVAL GLASS — a pressed pattern glass made of iridescent colors: dark purple, cobalt, green, marigold, red, and white. Manufactured during 1910-1930 period by Northwood Glass Company, Martin's Ferry, Ohio; Imperial Glass Company, Bellaire, Ohio; Fenton Art Glass Company, Williamstown, W. Va. Often called "Poor man's Tiffany," it was sold by carloads at carnivals, and used as giveaways at movie houses, etc. It is strictly an American-made glass. (Plate 8, Hatpins; Plate 55, holders.)

CARTOUCHE — a shield or scroll with curved edges used particularly on silver for monogram, crest, or initial. (NOT same as *escutcheon*.) See Plate 83, for shield *cartouché*.

CAUL — a trellis-work coif or skull cap of silk thread or gold weave, sometimes lined with silk. Handmade pins were used to hold securely to head.

CELLULOID — (See *Plastic*)

CERAMIC TRANSFER — complicated and technical procedure in which designs are engraved on a copper plate, then inked; the impression on plate is transferred to a piece of tissue paper, then again transferred to a piece of pottery or porcelain to be decorated. The transfer design is then either left one color or handcolored with tinting. A permanent glaze is applied, fired in the kiln, and unless glaze is scratched, it retains original design intact. Transfer designs were applied in conjunction with handpainting on dresser sets and hatpins, and is most familiar on printed earthenware. (Plates 57, 75 and 130.)

CHANNEL SETTING — a series of stones set close together in a straight line; sides of mounting grip outer edges of stones. (Plates 21 and 23.)

CHAPEAU — (See *Fashions, Millinery*)

CHASING — the ornamentation of metal with grooves or lines with the use of hand-chisels and hammers. Flat or front chasing, *intaglio*, (Plate 90); chasing from back, *repoussé*, (Plate 89.).

CHIGNON — false hair, pre-styled and shaped in a particular hairstyle, fastened on a comb or with pins, to be worn in conjunction with headdress. Sometimes these were merely switches or braids of hair bound at one end to keep from unravelling. Chignons could weigh well over a ¼ pound.

CHINA — (See *porcelain*)

CITRINE — a pale lemon-color gemstone of quartz variety often mistaken for a topaz. (Plate 115.)

CLAMBROTH GLASS — a glass which is "cloudy" as clam-broth juice. (See Plate 122.)

CLAW-SET — tiny claws or prongs curved to hold down a stone into setting. (Plates 69, 72.)

CLOCHE — helmet-shaped woman's hat worn close to head. Popular from 1920-1930.

CLOISONNE — enameling in which thin wire is bent to form cells, *(cloisons)*, then filled with enamel. Each colour is in a separate compartment, each compartment separated by thin wire. (See *enamel*) Plates 29, 129, 206.

COBALT GLASS — a deep blue color. (See Plate 8.)

COMMODE SET — (also known as dresser sets, toilet sets) Victorian potters of highest skills worked on these dressing table and washstand sets. Many included the following: ewer and basin, chamber pot, slop pail, footbath, shaving mug, spittle pitcher, trinket boxes, comb and brush tray, pin trays, powder or puff boxes, talc shakers, ring trees, soap dishes, toothbrush holders, candlesticks, and other incidental but seemingly necessary items at a time when built-in bathroom accomodations were not known or in common usage. (Commode set, Plates 43 and 59.) (Dressing Table sets, Plates 13, 14, 44, 45, 46, 47, 57, 58, 59, 60, 68, 74, 75. With talc shaker, Plate 47; in miniature, Plate 59.)

CORAL — skeleton of the coral polyp. Victorian jewelry abounds with Mediterranean coral. (Genuine, Plates 12, 82; imitation, Plates 90, 207.) Molded coral roses, Plate 90 and 108.

CORSAGE PIN — (also known as "violet" or "flower" pin) (Plate 17.)

CORONAL — an arrangement of flowers or jewels worn as a crown.

COWRIE SHELL — 18th and 19th Century female sex symbol. (Plate 42.)

CRESPIN — (or *crespinette*) — a coarse net of silk or metal covering the hair.

CUT STEEL — used as beads or jewels, often mistaken for marcasite, (iron pyrite). Plate 48.

DAMASCENE — to inlay gold and silver into iron or steel in a decorative pattern. Characteristic of ornaments from Damascus. Plate 205.

DIE-STAMPING — to cut into metal for reproduction. This superceded hand-wrought and custom-made jewelry pieces, including hatpin heads.

DRAGON'S BREATH — simulated Mexican Fire Opal, popular 1910-1930. Plate 106.

ENAMEL — opaque glass fired to a gloss after it is applied to metal. The metal is dipped into molten colored glass, without wire dividers *(cloisons)* — which is what differentiates *"cloisonne"* from plain enamelwork. Plates 29, 83, 129.

EDWARDIAN — the era 1901-1910, the reign of Edward VII, which departed from Victorianism into an opulent, elegant period which was contrasted by a challenge in social values between the classes in England. The elegance in costume witnessed "millinery magic" and the height of the hatpin era.

ELECTRO-PLATING — a process which produced great quantities of gold jewelry; it replaced the old "pinchbeck" imitation gold.

EMERALD — commonly dark green color (but in varied shades of green); an "emerald-cut" stone is oblong or square cut since that is the usual treatment of a genuine emerald. Plate 34, 194.

ENGRAVING — cutting lines into metal which are either decorative or symbolic. Method used in monogramming on crest, cartouché, or escutcheon.

ESCUTCHEON — small metal plate used atop ornament for monogram or signet. Plates 35, 36, 77, 120, 129.

FACET(s) — small flat surfaces cut into stone, glass, or shell. Purpose is to refract light or enhance design. Plates 37, 122, 106, 206.

FASHIONS — styles of a certain era or period. (See Cross-index for Plates, under *Fashions*)

FIGURAL — (see *FULL*-Figural)

FIGURAL MOUNTING — a figural-form used to hold stone or artifact. (Not to be confused with FULL-FIGURALS.) Plates 35, 82, 89, 90, 91, 93, 110.

FILIGREE — to apply thread-like wire and decorate into a lace network. Plates 20, 21, 37, 89, 108, 207.

FINDINGS — metal parts used for finishing ornament or attaching hatpin head to pin-shank. Some of these findings are called "patch," "socket," "bushing," etc. Plates 136, 137, 138.

FLEUR-DE-LIS — French royal family crest; signifies life and power. Known as "flower of light," or Iris, which was named by the Greeks, meaning "rainbow" because of magnificent hues of color. Plates 82, 129, 206.

FOIL — silver, gold, or other color thin leaf of metal used to back imitation gemstones or faceted glass to improve color and provide greater brilliance. Most commonly used for rhinestones.

FLOW-BLUE GLASS — white china or glass in which color-blue is allowed to "flow" into random design or "over-flow" a set pattern. Mostly associated with china dishes; hatpin shown on Plate 84.

FRAME — (see *Mountings*)

FULL-FIGURAL HATPIN — an ornament consisting of a beast, bird, fish, flower, human, insect, or reptile, which is NOT A SPECIFIC MOUNTING FOR A STONE; stone accents may be used to enhance the ornament, such as stone eyes. Plates 2, 3, 5, 6, 7, 28, 65, 77, 81, 89, 91, 109, 111, 205, 206, 207. Examples in Glass, Plates 8, 78, 207.

"FRENCH IVORY" — an imitation of ivory tusk in grained celluloid. Plates 15 and 193.

GERMAN SILVER — metal which has no actual silver content but is an alloy of copper, zinc, and nickel, with the highest content of nickel to give it a silvery-white color. Used as a base for plating. Also called "nickel silver."

GILT — used after the invention of electro-gilding (plating).

A process of plating a die-stamped or hand-wrought piece of base metal to give it a real or pseudo-gold or silver color.

GLASS — (see specific type in Cross-Index to Plates)

GOLD — (also see *carat*) Precious metal ore containing alloys which vary depending on desired color and hardness. Gold colors range from green to dull yellow, to bright pink and even red. White gold (color of platinum or silver) is achieved by alloying nickel, a small percentage of platinum, to gold. Platinum is a 20th century discovery and was not used in Victorian jewelry. Gold is twice as heavy as silver which is perhaps the reason why SOLID silver (often "sterling")) was used, while gold was plated, filled, or rolled with inferior alloys. The term "carat" is for the fineness of gold; symbol = "K". Example: 18K or 750 equals 18/24 or 750/1000 which represents 75% pure gold content. Gold electroplating is a method of depositing fine gold on to a base metal. (For gold carat hatpins, see Plates 6, 67, 120, 156, 206.)

GOLD FILLED — joining a layer or layers of gold alloy to a base metal alloy, then rolling or drawing as required for thickness of material for particular manufacturing use.

GOLDSTONE — aventurine gemstone sparking with particles of gold-colored minerals; or man-made brown glass with specks of copper infused within. (Man-made, Plates 114, 206.)

GRANULAR WORK — gold or silver metal applied in decorative designs which resemble tiny grains or granules. Plate 206.

GUARDS — (see *Nibs, Point Protector*, etc.)

GYPSY SETTING — (also known as *Bezel*) Top of stone is exposed just above metal. Plate 106.

HAIR FASHIONS, accessories, etc. — see Cross-Index to Plates.

HALF-DOLLS — small figurines used in pincushions, powder boxes, tops of whisk-brooms, etc., manufactured 1900-1935 in Germany and Japan. (See *Bibliography*; also *Pincushion*). Plates 9, 12, 56, 195.

HALLMARK — an official mark (first adopted in England) which is incised, punched, or stamped on gold or silver to show quality and to signify purity of metal according to "sterling" or "Karat" standard. Other countries hallmarked to indicate origin, patent, manufacture, etc. (For detail of English Hallmark, see Plate 171.)

ILLUSION SETTING — a setting in which the stone is made to appear larger by cutting metal in shape of gem-table. Plate 37, 118.

IMITATION — to make out of other materials a substance resembling the natural element, i.e., paste or rhinestone for gems; rubber dyed and molded into coral-color flowers; plastic tortoise-shell; "French Ivory" grained celluoid which is an imitation of tusk or bone, etc.

IRIDESCENT — to give high lustre to glass or porcelain. Plates 8, 55, 117.

IMPERIAL GLASS — American manufacturer of glass,

including glass hatpin holders.

IRISH BELLEEK — porcelain with pearl-like lustre made in Fermanagh, Ireland since 1863. Mark: Tower, Dog, Harp, and word "Belleek." (Later reproduced or copied in America.)

JAPANNED — japanning is a process by which mourning pins made of iron wire were finished by immersing in black japan, a by-product of coal.

JARGOW-NIB — a nickname used in 1913 for point-protectors. Named for Berlin police-president vonJargold, who sought to enforce the wearing of hatpin "safeties" by law. (First report of use of "Jargow-nib" in *New York Times*, April 19, 1913.) See Cross-Index for Plates for various types of nibs.

JET — name given most black jewelry, whether it be genuine or glass. (See "Black Glass" Jewelry) Real jet will retain its sparkling polish for many years while "black glass" (also known as "French Jet," even though most glass came from Bohemia) will crack, scratch, and become dull. Genuine jet is a brown-black lignite in which the texture or grain of the original fossilized wood (of which this particular coal is comprised) can still be seen. It can be brought to a high polish and is thus easily imitated in glass. The finest genuine jet comes from Whitby (England) where over 200 workshops produced Victorian-era jewelry. Up to 1850, Jet was associated purely with mourning, although it had been used in ancient times for jewelry. (Genuine; Plate 157. Jet *glass*; Plates 78, 296. *Riveted Jet Glass* "mourning hatpins," Plates 96, 97.)

LALIQUE, R. — undisputed master jeweler and glassmaker in Art Nouveau style. (1860-1945). Examples of glass, Plates 205, 207; example of hatpin, Plate 167.

LAPIS LAZULI — deep blue containing gold-coloured specks of iron pyrites. Hornstone or jasper is sometimes artifically colored to represent Lapis gemstone.

LIMOGES — hard-paste porcelain manufactured since 1771 in the district of Haute-Vienne, France.

LUSTRE-WARE — decorated either partly or wholly with a shiny metallic glaze, sometimes pink or purple, silver, gold, or copper. The "silver" is actually platinum; the "copper" is obtained by using a solution of gold. Plates 87, 117, 126. (Most commonly associated with glazed pitchers or plates.)

MARCASITE — a white iron pyrite; if the ore is yellow, it takes on the appearance of "Fool's Gold." (Plate 114) Cut steel jewelry and Marcasites resemble one another in color and faceted treatment. (Marcasite, Plate 65; Cut Steel, Plate 17.)

MILLINERY — the art of designing headgear for women, with emphasis on originality and individuality of design for each patron. (See Cross-Index for Plates.)

MINTON — Founder, Thomas Minton, household name in English ceramics. (Marks: *M. and Co.* or *M. & H.*)

MOONSTONE — transparent, but more often translucent gemstone with pearly or opaline lustre. Plate 116.

MORIAGE — Japanese for "raised" and refers to pottery or porcelain decorated with raised forms or lines which comprise a series of white "strings" or "squiggles" in design. (Plate 51.)

MOSAIC — creating motif or design parquetry with minute pieces of colored glass (or stone) which have been set into plaster. Individual portions of design are sectioned by metal, similar to form used in cloisonne (cloisons). (Plate 33 and 206. Latter example does not use metal.)

MOTHER-OF-PEARL — differs from *Abalone* in color; it is the iridescent inner-shell layer of a pearl oyster. Plates 72, 79, and 126.

MOUNTING — the specific adaptation of a stone or artifact within a cage, frame, or setting usually comprised of metal. (Also see *setting*, and Cross-Index for Plates.)

MOURNING JEWELRY — black jewelry (either real or imitation jet) popularized during Queen Victoria's period of mourning on the death of the Prince Consort (Albert) (1861-1901 era). "Mourning" hatpins, Plates 96, 97.

MOURNING PINS — made of iron wire finished by immersing in by-product of coal, (japanning).

NIBS — small metal shafts used on the end of the pointed pin as a point-protector, shield or guard. (See Cross-Index for Plates for varied types.)

NIPPON — mark on Japanese exports from 1858-1921. (See Bibliography.) Plate 51.

NODDER — also called "bobbler," "springer," "trembler" — a short spring which causes ornamental head to bobble or bounce freely on top of pin-head. Plate 3.

NORITAKE COMPANY, LTD. — major exporter (1904) to Morimura Bros., (New York), who imported merchandise until 1941. (Mark: Wreath with an "M") (See Bibliography)

NORTHWOOD — American manufacturer of Carnival Glass, including hatpin holders. (Mark "N" in a circle) Plates 55, 182.

OPALESCENCE — a pearly sheen from inside a gem, such as Moonstone. Plate 116.

OPALINE — like an opal, translucent, milky variety of glass. Plate 32.

OPENWORK — (see Piercework)

PASTE — a superior glass containing oxide of lead used for jewelry to imitate gems and gemstones. Josef Strass perfected "paste," although paste was used since ancient times as imitations of precious stones.

PARURE — a set of matching jewelry.

PAVE SETTING — stones placed so close together that almost no metal shows between them. Plates 20, 23, 37.

PEACOCK EYE — a glass which resembles the "eye" of a peacock feather. Plates 108 and 123.

PEKING GLASS — sometimes called "poor man's jade," it is a light green glass. Plate 110.

PIERCE-WORK — die-cast frame which is cut and engraved with a great deal of open-work in metal. Plate 72.

PIN — origin of word thought to be from the Latin *spina*, a thorn found on the *Spina Christi* tree. Natural thorns are still used as pinning devices in some parts of the world. (See Cross-Index for Plates for various types of pins.)

PINCHBECK — a name used for the manufacture of imitation gold jewelry. Sometimes called "pom-pom," pinchbeck got its name from Christopher Pinchbeck, a London clock-maker who introduced 15% zinc into brass (1732) in a special process to resemble gold.

PLASTICS — term applied to a group of synethic chemical products with their distinctive quality which enables them to be molded into many shapes and sizes. (Also see *imitation*) Refer to Cross-Index for Plates for specific uses.

PINCUSHION — a piece of varied materials and designs utilized for safe-keeping of pins. (See Cross-Index for Plates.)

PLIQUE-á-JOUR — translucent cloisonne in which there is not metal *backing* for enamel. Plate 65 and 167.

MARKS — identifying trademark on porcelain for country of origin or manufacturer; anything marked "Made in —," was produced after 1914.

PUFF-BOX — china or glass (sometimes of precious metals), designed and utilized for storage of powder-puff. Usually part of a dressing table set. Plates 68, 74.

REPOUSSE — decorating metal by pushing out from behind or reverse side in order to create relief design. Plates 28, 89.

RHINESTONE — takes its name but no element from the River Rhine, Germany. It is a faceted glass stone, usually set with foil-backing to give it highlights. It is inferior to French paste or Strass and cannot be cleaned successfully; once the foil-backing is scratched or marred, it loses its lustre.

RIM — the outside edge of a set stone.

ROLLED GOLD — a thin leaf of gold used in plating lesser metals. Methods varied from rolling to electroplating a coat of gold over an inferior metal.

ROSE CUT — the faceting of a gem, genuine or imitation. See Plate 37, back row center amethyst; Plate 90, front row, amethyst and rear row amethyst.

ROUNDELS — tiny round beads or to be bead-shaped. Plate 86 (beads); Plate 206 (shape).

ROYAL DOULTON — English decorative porcelain. Term "Royal" used after 1901. Plates 54, 70.

RUFF — evenly arranged stiff linen as worn by *Periotte*. Plate 12.

SATSUMAWARE — hand-decorated and painted porcelain from the Orient. Plates 78, 87, 99.)

SCARABACUS — Form of a beetle, the Egyptian symbol of longevity. Plates 8 and 91.

SECESSION — the same as *"Jugendstill," "Art Nouveau,"* or an "anti-historical style" of modern jewelry from 1901-1920 coming from Bohemia. Plate 25.

SIGNET TOP — a hatpin with an escutcheon. Plates 35, 36, 77, 120, 129.

SETTING — (See Cross-Index for Plates) A specific type of design for incorporating stones into metal or other element. Bezel, Plates 36, 37, 106; Box, Plate 129; Channel, Plates 21, 23; Claw, Plates 69, 72; Crown, Plate 118, Gypsy (same as Bezel); Illusion, Plates 4, 5, 118; Metal Cup, (backing for rhinestones), Plate 125; Pavé, Plates 20, 21, 23, 37.

SILVER-DEPOSIT-WARE — Glass decorated with silver overlay. See hatpin, Plate 115. First made in 1880 but most popular in 1890s. Alvin Manufacturing Co., (founded 1886) Providence, R.I., specialized in silver-deposit-ware hatpins.

SILVER-GILT — silver with a thin coat of gold or yellow lacquer used to produce a rich golden color.

SLAGWARE — (Slag glass) made by glassmakers located near foundries. Comes in marbled form; purple, turquoise, opal, green, brown, etc. According to G. Bernard Hughes, "Victorian Pottery and Porcelain" manufacturing information, slag is a cross between glass and stone. Sometimes called "end of day," the "slag" floats upon the top of molten metal and was taken off at the end of day and sold to be mixed with flint glass and orychite which then produced a tough opaque material which can be colored and pressed into molds. Plates 95, 100.

STONE CHINA — called semi-china or semi-porcelain, but more commonly known as "Ironstone" for the original Mason's Ironstone (England). It is a heavy earthenware glazed to look like finer quality porcelains and manufactured to compete with bone china.

STONEWARE — a pottery mixture which is placed in a kiln at higher temperatures so that the product is tough and can be utilized in many ways. It can be decorated, polished, stained (as with Jasper), or cut and etched.

SPRINGERS — (see *Nodder*)

SQUARE CUT STONE — another design-cut for gems. Plate 36, 129.

STERLING — A British term referring to the highest standard of silver which has a fixed standard of purity, i.e., 925 parts of silver with 75 parts copper. The word originated with immigrant Germans who came across the Channel to England. They settled in a geographic area from which they took the name "Easterlings." These immigrant jewelers by trade were called upon to refine silver for coinage and in 1343 the first two letters were dropped from the word "Easterling," resulting in the nomenclature: "Sterling," which denotes the highest purity. All genuine British "Sterling" is hallmarked.

STRASS — (or Strasser) — brilliant lead glass perfected by Josef Strass for whom it was named. It is used in creating artificial gems or gemstones.

SWASTIKA — symbol in the form of a Greek cross with the ends of the arms extended at right angles all in the same rotary direction. However, this symbol may appear reversed. See Plate 61.

TAPESTRY CHINA — manufactured in Austria-Germany about 1890. It is a porcelain covered with fabric which has been stretched and decorated, then glazed. The finished product has a rough texture, very much like a piece of tapestry.

TEPLITZ — City in Bohemian province of Czechoslavakia when it was part of Austro-Hungarian Empire. (1880-1915). (Mark: "Teplitz," "Turn-Teplitz," or "Turn.")

TORTOISE SHELL — yellowish-brown grained substance which is the hard-plate shell from the back of a tortoise. Imitation tortoise-shell was manufactured from plastic. Plate 85.

TREMBLER — (Nodder), to mount ornament on spring or wire to cause motion.

TRIANGULAR CUT — shape cut for gemstones. Plate 90.

VANITY HATPIN HEADS — an ornament which contains items associated with a woman's "vanity," i.e., mirror, perfume, etc.; a hatpin head which contains an article of usage, such as small pins, watch, powder-puff, etc. Plates 64, 180.

VERMICELLI — Italian for "little worms," used to describe thin gold wire used in a decorative design which "squirms" like tiny worms. Plate 206.

VICTORIAN ERA — (1837-1901) The 64-year reign of Queen Victoria, during which there were vast political and social changes, a rapid growth of industrialization, but a retention of strict moral rules and decorum which was only challenged during the last half of her reign. "Victorian" now implies a "straight-laced," "old-fashioned" approach to both morals and religion. The Victorian era was, in fact, a time of great change from "the dark ages" to an age of enlightenment.

WEEPERS — ostrich plumes.

ZIRCON CUT — similar to faceted Rose-Cut diamonds. Plate 118.

# SUPPLEMENT

# GEMS, GEMSTONES AND NATURAL ELEMENTS POPULAR DURING THE HATPIN ERA

Abalone
Alexandrite
Amber
Amethyst
Aquamarine
Beryl
Bone
Cat's Eye
Chrysoberyl
Cinnabar
Citron
Copper
Coral
Diamond
Emerald
Fur

Garnet
Gold
Hair
Horn
Jade
Jet
Ivory
Lapis-Lazuli
Lead
Leather
Malachite
Marcasite
Moonstone
Mother-of-Pearl
Opal
Pearl, (cultured, fresh water, baroque/seed.)

Quartz variety: agate, jasper, onyx, rose etc.
Rock
Ruby
Sapphire
Sea shells
Silk
Silver
Spinel
Straw
Tooth
Topaz
Tortoise-shell
Tourmaline
Turquoise
Tusk
Wood
Zircon

# HATPIN HEADS OF MAN-MADE MATERIALS

Amber, (imitation)
Beads
Celluloid, (plastic)
Coral, (imitation)
China, (hand-painted porcelain)
Crochet threads
Felt
"French Ivory," (grained celluloid)
Glass, (simulated gems and gemstones)
Glass, art
Glass, blown
Glass, burel (Mfg. name, "Hyalith")
Glass, camphor
Glass, carnival
Glass, clambroth
Glass, cobalt
Glass, crystal (cut and faceted)
Glass, iridescent
Glass, mercury
Glass, milkglass (white, blue, etc.)
Glass, millefiori
Glass, molded

Glass, mosaic
Glass, opaline
Glass, paste (for brilliants)
Glass, pattern (pressed)
Glass, pearl-lustre
Glass, peking (Poor Man's Jade)
Glass, rhinestone (imitation diamonds)
Glass, slag
Glass, strauss (imitation gems)
Goldstone, (imitation)
Jet, (imitation)
Metallic thread
Pewter
Pinchbeck ("pom-pom," imitation gold)
Plastics, (imitation for natural elements)
Porcelain, (floral, decorated, portrait, scenic)
Satsuma-ware
Steel, (cut beads)
Tin
Velvet
Woven fabric

# POPULAR DESIGNS AND MOTIFS USED FOR HATPIN HEADS
## (1850-1920)

Animals
Archery

Baroque
*Beetles*
*Billowing Smoke*
*Birds*
Bulldog
*Butterflies*
Button Molds

Cameo

*Daffodil*
*Daisy*
*Damascene*
Dolphin
*Dragonflies*
Ducks

*Eagle*
Elephant
Emblems
*Eye of Horus (Egypt)*

*Falcon*
Fans
Fishing Equipment

*"Floradora"*
*Flowers*
Fox
*Frog*
*Fuchsia*

*Geometrics*
Golfing (Brassie, Cleek, Driver,
Putter and golfing activities)

Horses
Helmets
*Hibiscus*
Hockey Sticks
*Human torso*

*Insects*
*Iris*

*Leaf Motifs*
*Lotus Flower*

*Orchid*
*Oriental*
*Pagoda*
*Pharoah*
*Poppy*

Rabbits

Rams

*Sacred Asp (Egypt)*
*Scarab*
*Seaweed*
*Serpent*
*Sporting Activities*
Sporting Trophies
Storks
*Sun Disc (symbol)*
*Sweet Pea*
*Symbols (mystic)*

*Temples*
*Tendrils*
*Toad*

*Vines*
*Vulture*

*Water Lily*
*Wild Rose*
*Wispy Smoke*
*Women's Heads*

*Zodiac*

Italics = Art Nouveau and/or Art Deco
    (1895-1920)

# EXHIBITIONS AND EXPOSITIONS WHERE HATPINS AND HATPIN HOLDERS
# WERE EXHIBITED OR SOLD AS COMMEMORATIVE SOUVENIRS

1851    GREAT EXHIBITIONS OF THE WORKS AND INDUSTRIES OF ALL NATIONS — Crystal Palace, London.

1875    MASSACHUSETTS CENTENNIAL, Salem. (1775-1875)

1876    PHILADELPHIA CENTENNIAL, Philadelphia. (1776-1876)

1893    WORLD'S COLUMBIAN EXPOSITION (1492-1892), Chicago, Ill.

1897    THE DIAMOND JUBILEE OF QUEEN VICTORIA (1837-1897), London

1897    THE EXHIBITION OF ART NOUVEAU JEWELRY, Boston, Mass.

1900    THE PARIS EXPOSITION OF ART NOUVEAU ARTISTS

1904    ST. LOUIS WORLD'S FAIR

1925    *EXPOSITION INTERNATIONALE DES ARTS DECORATIFS*, Paris, France (Art Deco influence)

*1935    SILVER JUBILEE, KING GEORGE V., QUEEN MARY, London (1910-1935)

(Many local fairs and exhibits featured commemorative hatpins and hatpin holders. The above had an *international* influence.)

*Smaller hatpins in plastics or hatpin ornaments in base metals of "art moderne" designs were popular. Because of the depression years, the cheapest possible materials were utilized.

# CROSS-INDEX BY SUBJECT FOR PLATE(S)

| SUBJECT | PLATE(S) |
|---|---|
| *ACCENTS* (See *Glossary*) | |
| Beads as accents | 42 |
| Bells as accents | 205 |
| Brilliants as accents | 85, 91, 104, 205 |
| Eye-accents (glass or stone) | 2, 5, 6, 18, 65, 89, 91, 110, 123, 205 |
| Gold accents | 41, 132 |
| Hand-painted accents | 1, 87 |
| Metallic accents | 65, 91 |
| Natural elements as accents | 21 |
| Peacock-eye glass as accent | 123 |
| Pearl accents | 37, 206 |
| Porcelain w/gold accents | 132 |
| Stone (glass) accents | 2, 3, 5, 6, 11, 34, 35, 65, 91, 205 |
| *AIGRETTES* (See *Glossary*) | 142, 158 |
| *ART DECO* (See specific category and *Glossary*) | |
| *ART NOUVEAU* (See specific category and *Glossary*) | |
| *BOBBLER* (Same as nodder, springer, trembler) | 3 |
| *CABOCHON CUT* (See *Glossary*) | 72, 82, 206, 219 |
| *CAGE* (See *Mountings*) | |
| *CANDLESTICKS* (See *Dresser, Toilet and Vanity Sets*) | 46, 57, 60, 75 |
| *CHAPEAUX* (See *Fashions* and *Millinery*) | |
| *COMMODE SET* (Also see *Dresser, Toilet, and Vanity Sets*) | 43 |
| *COMMODE SET IN MINIATURE* | 59 |
| *CORSAGE PIN* (Also called violet or flower pin, etc.) | 17 |
| *DRESSER, TOILET AND VANITY SETS* (Also see *COMMODE SET*) | 13, 14, 44, 45, 46, 47, 57, 58, 60, 68, 74, 75 |
| *DRESSER, TOILET AND VANITY SETS* (miniature) | 59 |
| *FABERGE* | 206 |
| *FASHIONS* (Also see *Millinery*) | |
| Accessories | 158 |
| Aigrettes | 142, 158 |
| Combs (Tortoise-shell) | 139 |
| Costume (circa 1890s) | 213 |
| Costume (circa 1891) | 159 |
| Costume (circa 1894) | 184 |
| Costume (circa 1897) | 147, 191 |
| Costume (circa 1898) | 154 |
| Mourning attire | 157 |
| Sporting Dress (circa 1894) — Also see *Sporting Activity* under *Hatpin Heads* | 181 |
| Sporting Dress (circa 1896) | 141 |
| Sporting Dress (circa 1898) | 214 |
| *FINDINGS* (See *Glossary*) | 136, 137, 138 |
| *FOIL-BACKING* (See *Glossary*) | 20 |
| *FRAME* (See *Mountings*) | |
| *GEMS AND GEMSTONES AS HATPINS* (See *Hatpin Heads*) | |
| *GLASS HATPIN HEADS* (See specific type under *Hatpin Heads*) | |
| *GUARDS* (See *Nibs*) | |
| *HAIR* (Also see *Fashions*) | |
| Accessories (Also see *Aigrette*) | 139 |
| Combs (Tortoise-shell) | 139 |

Ornaments . . . . . . . . . . . . . . . . . . . . . . . . . . . . . . . . . . . . . . . . . . . . . . . . . . . . . . . . . . . . 7, 9, 48, 69, 107
Pieces ("Frisette") . . . . . . . . . . . . . . . . . . . . . . . . . . . . . . . . . . . . . . . . . . . . . 143, 144 fig. *f*, 158
Styles (1880-1910) . . . . . . . . . . . . . . . . . . . . . . . . . . . . . . . . . . . . . . . . 139, 143, 149, 175, 191
*HAIR-PIN BOX* . . . . . . . . . . . . . . . . . . . . . . . . . . . . . . . . . . . . . . . . . . . . . . . . . . . . . . . . . . . . . 17
*HAIR-PINS* . . . . . . . . . . . . . . . . . . . . . . . . . . . . . . . . . . . . . . . . . . . . . . . . . . . . . . . . . . . . . . . 17
*HAIR RECEIVER* . . . . . . . . . . . . . . . . . . . . . . . . . . . . . . . . . . . . . . . . . . . . . . . . 13, 68, 74, 75
*HAIR STYLES* (See *Fashions*)
*HALF-DOLLS* (Also see *Pincushions*) . . . . . . . . . . . . . . . . . . . . . . . . . . . . . . 9, 12, 56, 195
*HALLMARKS* (Detail drawing) (See *Glossary*) . . . . . . . . . . . . . . . . . . . . . . . . . . . . . 171
*HAT ORNAMENT* . . . . . . . . . . . . . . . . . . . . . . . . . . . 107, 112, 113, 116, 165, 172, 173
*HATPIN CARRY OR TRAVEL CASE* . . . . . . . . . . . . . . . . . . . . . . . . . . . . . . . . . . . . . 11
*HATPIN HEADS*
  Abalone . . . . . . . . . . . . . . . . . . . . . . . . . . . . . . . . . . . . . . . . . . . . . . . . . . 9, 72, 105, 106
  Amber . . . . . . . . . . . . . . . . . . . . . . . . . . . . . . . . . . . . . . . . . . . . . . . . . . . 63, 104, 114
  Amulet (Also see *Symbols*) . . . . . . . . . . . . . . . . . . . . . . . . . . . . . . . . . . . . . . . . . . 91
  Amethyst, (genuine) . . . . . . . . . . . . . . . . . . . . . . . . . . . . . . . . . . . . . . . . . 56, 116, 206
  Amethyst, (glass imitation) . . . . . . . . . . . . . . . . . . . . . . . . . . . . . . . . . . . . . 37, 125, 205
  Angel . . . . . . . . . . . . . . . . . . . . . . . . . . . . . . . . . . . . . . . . . . . . . . . . . . . . . . . . . . 123
  Animal (See specific type under *Hatpin Heads*)
  *Art Deco* design . . . . . . . . . . . . . . . . . . . . . . . . . . . . . . . . 65, 77, 85, 112, 193, 217
  *Art Deco* design in glass hatpin head . . . . . . . . . . . . . . . . . . . . . . . . . . . . . . . . . . . 24
  Art Glass . . . . . . . . . . . . . . . . . . . . . . . . . . . . . . . . . . . . . . . . . . . . . . . . . . . . . . . . . 9
  *Art Nouveau* design . . . . . . . . . . . . . . . . 24, 32, 34, 35, 36, 64, 65, 93, 167, 205, 207
  *Art Nouveau* design in glass hatpin head . . . . . . . . . . . . . . . . . . . . . . . . . . . . . . . . 24
  *Art Nouveau* portrait . . . . . . . . . . . . . . . . . . . . . 63, 65, 81, 93, 123, 124, 189, 205
  *Art Nouveau* women portraits . . . . . . . . . . . . . . . . . . . . . . . . 93, 123, 124, 189
  Baby (Child) . . . . . . . . . . . . . . . . . . . . . . . . . . . . . . . . . . . . . . . . . . . . . . . . . . . . . . 5
  Baroque . . . . . . . . . . . . . . . . . . . . . . . . . . . . . . . . . . . . . . . . . . . . . . . . . . . . . 82, 206
  Bead, Venetian glass . . . . . . . . . . . . . . . . . . . . . . . . . . . . . . . . . . . . . . . . . . . . . . . 15
  Bead, wooden . . . . . . . . . . . . . . . . . . . . . . . . . . . . . . . . . . . . . . . . . . . . . . . . . . . . 101
  Bead, with overlay . . . . . . . . . . . . . . . . . . . . . . . . . . . . . . . . . . . . . . . . . . . . . . . . . 15
  Beaded hatpin heads . . . . . . . . . . . . . . . . . . . . . . . . . . . . . . . . . . . . . . . . 16, 86, 194
  Beads, amber color . . . . . . . . . . . . . . . . . . . . . . . . . . . . . . . . . . . . . . . . . . . . . . . . . 63
  Beads, assorted . . . . . . . . . . . . . . . . . . . . . . . . . . . . . . . . . . . . . . . . . . . . . . . . . . . 16
  Beads, iridescent . . . . . . . . . . . . . . . . . . . . . . . . . . . . . . . . . . . . . . . . . . . . . . . . . . 86
  Beads, tiny bugle, roundels, seed, etc. . . . . . . . . . . . . . . . . . . . . . . . . . . . . . . . . . . . 86
  Beads, turquoise color . . . . . . . . . . . . . . . . . . . . . . . . . . . . . . . . . . . . . . . . . . . . . . . 4
  Beast figurals . . . . . . . . . . . . . . . . . . . . . . . . . . . . . . . . . . . . . . . . . . . . . . . . 5, 6, 89
  Bees . . . . . . . . . . . . . . . . . . . . . . . . . . . . . . . . . . . . . . . . . . . . . . . . . . . . . . . . . . 7, 8
  Beetle (See *Insect* and *Scarab*)
  Bird . . . . . . . . . . . . . . . . . . . . . . . . . . . . . 2, 3, 78, 90, 91, 109, 110, 133, 205
  "Black Glass Jewelry" Mourning Hatpins (See *Glossary*) . . . . . . . . . . . . . . . 96, 97, 128
  Black or white common variety hatpins . . . . . . . . . . . . . . . . . . . . . . . . . . . . . . . 133, 185
  Black or white common variety on card or paper . . . . . . . . . . . . . . . . . . . . . . . . 133, 185
  Blown or free-form glass . . . . . . . . . . . . . . . . . . . . . . . . . 15, 29, 32, 63, 84, 126
  Bohemian . . . . . . . . . . . . . . . . . . . . . . . . . . . . . . . . . . . . . . . . . . . . . . . . . . . . . . . . 84
  Bohemian art glass (Burel) . . . . . . . . . . . . . . . . . . . . . . . . . . . . . . . . . . . . . . . . . . . 25
  Bone . . . . . . . . . . . . . . . . . . . . . . . . . . . . . . . . . . . . . . . . . . . . . . . . . . . . . . . . . . . 78
  Brilliants (See *Glossary*) . . . . . . . . . . . . . . . . . . . . . . . . . . . . . . . . . . . . . . 20, 21, 23
  Bug (See *Insect* or specific listing)
  Burel ("Hyalith") Glass . . . . . . . . . . . . . . . . . . . . . . . . . . . . . . . . . . . . . . . 25, 26, 27
  Butterfly . . . . . . . . . . . . . . . . . . . . . . . . . . . . . . . . . . . . . . . . . . . . . . . . . . 3, 207, 208
  Cameo (molded glass) . . . . . . . . . . . . . . . . . . . . . . . . . . . . . . . . . . . . . . . . . . 94, 128
  Cameo, onyx . . . . . . . . . . . . . . . . . . . . . . . . . . . . . . . . . . . . . . . . . . . . . . . . . . . . 131
  Cameo, shell . . . . . . . . . . . . . . . . . . . . . . . . . . . . . . . . . . . . . . . . . . . . . . . . . . . . 131
  Cameo, synthetic . . . . . . . . . . . . . . . . . . . . . . . . . . . . . . . . . . . . . . . . . . . . . . 4, 131
  Camphor glass . . . . . . . . . . . . . . . . . . . . . . . . . . . . . . . . . . . . . . . . . . . . . . . . . . . 122
  Carnival glass . . . . . . . . . . . . . . . . . . . . . . . . . . . . . . . . . . . . . . . . . . . . . . . . . . . . . 8
  Caterpillar-moth . . . . . . . . . . . . . . . . . . . . . . . . . . . . . . . . . . . . . . . . . . . . . . . . . . . 81
  Celluloid (Also see *"French Ivory"* and *Plastics*) . . . . . . . . . . 65, 85, 100, 104, 109, 193

Ceramic (See *Porcelain*)
Ceramic transfer (See *Glossary*) . . . . . . . . . . . . . . . . . . . . . . . . . . . . . 1, 57, 75, 87, 98, 132
Charms (See *Symbols*)
China (Also see *Porcelain* and *Satsuma*) . . . . . . . . . . . . . . . . . . . . . . . . . . . . . . 87, 88
China, "Flow Blue" . . . . . . . . . . . . . . . . . . . . . . . . . . . . . . . . . . . . . . . . . . . . . . . 84
Citron gemstones . . . . . . . . . . . . . . . . . . . . . . . . . . . . . . . . . . . . . . . . . . . . . 115, 206
Clambroth glass . . . . . . . . . . . . . . . . . . . . . . . . . . . . . . . . . . . . . . . . . . . . . . 84, 122
Cloisonne . . . . . . . . . . . . . . . . . . . . . . . . . . . . . . . . . . . . . . . . . . . . . . . . . . 29, 206
Cloisonne (Plique-a-jour) . . . . . . . . . . . . . . . . . . . . . . . . . . . . . . . . . . . . . . . . 65, 167
Cobalt glass . . . . . . . . . . . . . . . . . . . . . . . . . . . . . . . . . . . . . . . . . . . . . . 8, 20, 81
Cock (Rooster) . . . . . . . . . . . . . . . . . . . . . . . . . . . . . . . . . . . . . . . . . 6, 8, 77, 81
Coin . . . . . . . . . . . . . . . . . . . . . . . . . . . . . . . . . . . . . . . . . . . . . . . . . 22, 89, 180
Colored glass . . . . . . . . . . . . . . . . . . . . . . . . . . . . . . . . . . . . . . . . . . . . . . . . . 8, 24
Commemorative (Keepsake, Memento, Souvenir) . . . . . . . . . . . . . 10, 22, 30, 31, 83, 89, 93, 105, 129, 160, 190
Common-type . . . . . . . . . . . . . . . . . . . . . . . . . . . . . . . . . . . . . . . . . . . . . . 133, 185
Common variety . . . . . . . . . . . . . . . . . . . . . . . . . . . . . . . . . . . . . . . . . 15, 119, 162
Copper . . . . . . . . . . . . . . . . . . . . . . . . . . . . . . . . . . . . . . . . . . . . . . . . . . . . 77, 79
Coral, (genuine) . . . . . . . . . . . . . . . . . . . . . . . . . . . . . . . . . . . . . . . . . . . . . . 12, 82
Coral, (imitation glass) . . . . . . . . . . . . . . . . . . . . . . . . . . . . . . . . . . . . 90, 108, 207
Coral, (molded synthetic rose) . . . . . . . . . . . . . . . . . . . . . . . . . . . . . . . . . . . 90, 108
Cross (Religious symbol) . . . . . . . . . . . . . . . . . . . . . . . . . . . . . . . . . . . . . . . . . . . 5
Crystal glass . . . . . . . . . . . . . . . . . . . . . . . . . . . . . . . . . . . . . . . 9, 63, 76, 83, 122
Decorated glass . . . . . . . . . . . . . . . . . . . . . . . . . . . . . . . . . . . 24, 76, 84, 91, 100, 102
Damascene . . . . . . . . . . . . . . . . . . . . . . . . . . . . . . . . . . . . . . . . . . . . . . . . . . 205
Diamonds (genuine) . . . . . . . . . . . . . . . . . . . . . . . . . . . . . . . . . . . . . . . . . . . . . . 6
Dog . . . . . . . . . . . . . . . . . . . . . . . . . . . . . . . . . . . . . . . . . . . . . . . . 81, 123, 218
Dragon . . . . . . . . . . . . . . . . . . . . . . . . . . . . . . . . . . . . . . . . . . . . . . . . . . 89, 218
Dragonfly . . . . . . . . . . . . . . . . . . . . . . . . . . . . . . . . . . . . . . . . . . . . 7, 8, 81, 165
"Dragon's Breath" glass . . . . . . . . . . . . . . . . . . . . . . . . . . . . . . . . . . . . . . . . . . 106
Egyptian motif . . . . . . . . . . . . . . . . . . . . . . . . . . . . . . . . . . . . . . . . . . . 65, 89, 91
Elephant, celluloid . . . . . . . . . . . . . . . . . . . . . . . . . . . . . . . . . . . . . . . . . . . . . 109
Elephant, ivory . . . . . . . . . . . . . . . . . . . . . . . . . . . . . . . . . . . . . . . . . . . . . . . 111
Emerald (green color glass imitation) . . . . . . . . . . . . . . . . . . . . . . . . . . . . . . . . . 194
Enameled . . . . . . . . . . . . . . . . . . . . . . . . . . . . . . . . . . . . 22, 29, 30, 67, 82, 83, 129
Enameled glass . . . . . . . . . . . . . . . . . . . . . . . . . . . . . . . . . . . . . . . . . . . . . . . . 24
Engraved glass . . . . . . . . . . . . . . . . . . . . . . . . . . . . . . . . . . . . . . . . . . . . . . . . 24
Escutcheon . . . . . . . . . . . . . . . . . . . . . . . . . . . . . . . . . . . . . . . . 35, 36, 120, 129
Etched . . . . . . . . . . . . . . . . . . . . . . . . . . . . . . . . . . . . . . . . . . . . . . . . 25, 26, 37
Faberge . . . . . . . . . . . . . . . . . . . . . . . . . . . . . . . . . . . . . . . . . . . . . . . . . . . . 206
Falcon . . . . . . . . . . . . . . . . . . . . . . . . . . . . . . . . . . . . . . . . . . . . . . . . . . . . . . 24
*Fleur de Lis* . . . . . . . . . . . . . . . . . . . . . . . . . . . . . . . . . . . . . . . . . . . 82, 129, 206
Floral . . . . . . . . . . . . . . . . . 35, 37, 52, 65, 81, 82, 90, 91, 93, 102, 112, 123, 132, 168, 176, 205
"Flow Blue" china . . . . . . . . . . . . . . . . . . . . . . . . . . . . . . . . . . . . . . . . . . . . . . 84
"Fool's Gold" nugget . . . . . . . . . . . . . . . . . . . . . . . . . . . . . . . . . . . . . . . . . . . 214
Fox . . . . . . . . . . . . . . . . . . . . . . . . . . . . . . . . . . . . . . . . . . . . . . . . . . . 6, 205
Fox and Grapes, (Aesop allegorical) . . . . . . . . . . . . . . . . . . . . . . . . . . . . . . . . . . 205
Free-form glass . . . . . . . . . . . . . . . . . . . . . . . . . . . . . . . . . . . . . . . . . . . . . 15, 95
"French Ivory" (celluloid) . . . . . . . . . . . . . . . . . . . . . . . . . . . . . . . . . . . 9, 109, 193
Frog . . . . . . . . . . . . . . . . . . . . . . . . . . . . . . . . . . . . . . . . . . . . . . . . . . . . . . 110
Full figurals (See *Glossary*) . . . . . . 2, 3, 5, 6, 7, 28, 65, 77, 78, 81, 89, 91, 109, 111, 129, 160, 194, 205-207
Full figurals, glass . . . . . . . . . . . . . . . . . . . . . . . . . . . . . . . . . . . . . . . . 8, 78, 207
Full figurals with escutcheon . . . . . . . . . . . . . . . . . . . . . . . . . . . . . . . . . . . . . . . 35
Garnets (genuine) . . . . . . . . . . . . . . . . . . . . . . . . . . . . . . . . . . . . . . . . . . . . . . 56
Gems and gemstones (genuine) . . . . . . . . . . . . . 5, 56, 65, 72, 76, 77, 91, 95, 106, 115, 206
Gift-boxed . . . . . . . . . . . . . . . . . . . . . . . . . . . . . . . . . . . . . . . . . . . . . . . . 67, 94
Glass beads . . . . . . . . . . . . . . . . . . . . . . . . . . . . . . . . . . . . . . . . . . . . . 15, 16, 63
Glass hatpins (See specific type glass under *Hatpin Heads*)
Glass with beaded overlay . . . . . . . . . . . . . . . . . . . . . . . . . . . . . . . . . . . . . . . . . 84
Glass with metal overlay . . . . . . . . . . . . . . . . . . . . . . . . . . . . . . . . . . . . . . . . . . 24
Glass with silver-deposit-ware technique . . . . . . . . . . . . . . . . . . . . . . . . . . . . 115, 218

Gold carat (karat) . . . . . . . . . . . . . . . . . . . . . . . . . . . . . . . . . . . . . . . . . . . . . . . . . . . . . . . . . . . .56, 206
Gold *color* ornamental head . . . . . . . . . . . . . . . . . . . . . . . . . . . . . . . . . . . . . . . . . . . . . . . . . . . . . . . .34
Gold color glass . . . . . . . . . . . . . . . . . . . . . . . . . . . . . . . . . . . . . . . . . . . . . . . . . . . . . . . . . . . . . . . . . .129
Gold Karat . . . . . . . . . . . . . . . . . . . . . . . . . . . . . . . . . . . . . . . . . . . . . . . . . . . . . . . . . . . . . . . . . .56, 206
Gold (gilt, plated, rolled) . . . . . . . . . . . . . . . . . . . . . . . . . . . . . . . . . .6, 56, 67, 120, 156, 206
Goldstone (imitation glass) . . . . . . . . . . . . . . . . . . . . . . . . . . . . . . . . . . . . . . . . . . . . . . . . . . . .114, 206
Golf Club (See *Sporting Activity* under *Hatpin Heads*)
Griffin (Mythological) . . . . . . . . . . . . . . . . . . . . . . . . . . . . . . . . . . . . . . . . . . . . . . . . . . . . . . . . . . . . . .35
Hat (Harlequin) . . . . . . . . . . . . . . . . . . . . . . . . . . . . . . . . . . . . . . . . . . . . . . . . . . . . . . . . . . . . . . . . . . .81
Holy Family on ivory, (miniature) . . . . . . . . . . . . . . . . . . . . . . . . . . . . . . . . . . . . . . . . . . . . . . . . .131
Human full figurals . . . . . . . . . . . . . . . . . . . . . . . . . . . . . . . . . . . . . . . . . . . . . . . . . . . . . . . . .5, 28, 220
Imitation gems and gemstones (glass) . . . . . . . . . . . . . . . . . . . . . . . . . . . . . . . . . . . . . .36, 37, 194
Indian full figural . . . . . . . . . . . . . . . . . . . . . . . . . . . . . . . . . . . . . . . . . . . . . . . . . . . . . . . . . . . . . . . . .28
Insect, (also see specific listings) . . . . . . . . . . . . . . . .7, 8, 81, 82, 89, 90, 123, 165, 206, 207, 208, 218
Iridescent glass . . . . . . . . . . . . . . . . . . . . . . . . . . . . . . . . .8, 16, 25, 26, 27, 32, 126, 130
Ivory . . . . . . . . . . . . . . . . . . . . . . . . . . . . . . . . . . . . . . . . . . . . . . . . . . . . . . . . . . . . . .78, 111, 180
Jade . . . . . . . . . . . . . . . . . . . . . . . . . . . . . . . . . . . . . . . . . . . . . . . . . . . . . . . . . . . . . . . . . . . . . . .61, 206
Japanned (See *Glossary* under *Black Glass Jewelry*)
*Jeanne d' Arc* . . . . . . . . . . . . . . . . . . . . . . . . . . . . . . . . . . . . . . . . . . . . . . . . . . . . . . . . . . . . . . . .89, 170
Jet beaded (glass) . . . . . . . . . . . . . . . . . . . . . . . . . . . . . . . . . . . . . . . . . . . . . . . . . . . . . . . . . . . . . . . . .86
Jet, genuine . . . . . . . . . . . . . . . . . . . . . . . . . . . . . . . . . . . . . . . . . . . . . . . . . . . . . . . . . . . . . . . . .12, 157
Jet, glass . . . . . . . . . . . . . . . . . . . . . . . . . . . . . . . . . . . . . . . . . . .17, 52, 78, 84, 128, 196
Jet, rivited (mourning hatpins) . . . . . . . . . . . . . . . . . . . . . . . . . . . . . . . . . . . . . . . . .79, 96, 97
Kewpie . . . . . . . . . . . . . . . . . . . . . . . . . . . . . . . . . . . . . . . . . . . . . . . . . . . . . . . . . . . . . . . . . . . . . . . .202
Lalique . . . . . . . . . . . . . . . . . . . . . . . . . . . . . . . . . . . . . . . . . . . . . . . . . . . . . . . . . . . . . . . . . . . . . . . .167
Lapis lazuli, (genuine) . . . . . . . . . . . . . . . . . . . . . . . . . . . . . . . . . . . . . . . . . . . . . . . . . . . . . . . . . . . . .58
Lapis lazuli, (imitation) . . . . . . . . . . . . . . . . . . . . . . . . . . . . . . . . . . . . . . . . . . . . . . . . . . . . . . . . . . . .69
Lion . . . . . . . . . . . . . . . . . . . . . . . . . . . . . . . . . . . . . . . . . . . . . . . . . . . . . . . . . . . . . . . .35, 52, 89
Lizard . . . . . . . . . . . . . . . . . . . . . . . . . . . . . . . . . . . . . . . . . . . . . . . . . . . . . . . . . . . . . . . . . . . .82, 110
Lustre glass . . . . . . . . . . . . . . . . . . . . . . . . . . . . . . . . . . . . . . . . . . . . . . . . . . . . . . . . . . . . . . . .117, 126
Madonna and Child . . . . . . . . . . . . . . . . . . . . . . . . . . . . . . . . . . . . . . . . . . . . . . . . . . . . . . . . . . . . . . . .5
Malachite, (genuine) . . . . . . . . . . . . . . . . . . . . . . . . . . . . . . . . . . . . . . . . . . . . . . . . . . . . . . . . . . .91, 95
Malachite, (imitation) . . . . . . . . . . . . . . . . . . . . . . . . . . . . . . . . . . . . . . . . . . . . . . . . . . . . . . . . .95, 193
Marbleized glass . . . . . . . . . . . . . . . . . . . . . . . . . . . . . . . . . . . . . . . . . . . . . . . . . . . . . . . . . . . . . . . . .119
Mercury glass . . . . . . . . . . . . . . . . . . . . . . . . . . . . . . . . . . . . . . . . . . . . . . . . . . . . . . . . . . . . . . . . . . .122
Metal alloys (copper, pewter, tin) . . . . . . . . . . . . . . . . . . . . . . . . . . . . . . . . . . . . . . . . . .69, 77, 103
Metallic, with or without stone accents . . . . . . . . . . . . . . . . . . . . . . . . . . . . . . . . . . . . . . . . . . . . . .124
Milkglass, blue . . . . . . . . . . . . . . . . . . . . . . . . . . . . . . . . . . . . . . . . . . . . . . . . . . . . . . . . . . . . . .84, 207
Milkglass, decorated . . . . . . . . . . . . . . . . . . . . . . . . . . . . . . . . . . . . . . . . . . . . . . . . . . . . . . . . . . . . . .32
Milkglass, (opaline) . . . . . . . . . . . . . . . . . . . . . . . . . . . . . . . . . . . . . . . . . . . . . . . . . . .32, 84, 102, 207
Milkglass, "thorn" design . . . . . . . . . . . . . . . . . . . . . . . . . . . . . . . . . . . . . . . . . . . . . . . . . . . . . . . . . . .32
Milkglass, white . . . . . . . . . . . . . . . . . . . . . . . . . . . . . . . . . . . . . . . . . . . . . . . . . . . . . . . . . .32, 84, 102
Millefiori glass . . . . . . . . . . . . . . . . . . . . . . . . . . . . . . . . . . . . . . . . . . . . . . . . . . . . . . . . . . . . . . . . . . . .56
Molded glass . . . . . . . . . . . . . . . . . . . . . . . . . . . . . . . . . . . . . . . . . . . . . . . . . . . . . . . . . . . . . . . . . .8, 100
Monkey . . . . . . . . . . . . . . . . . . . . . . . . . . . . . . . . . . . . . . . . . . . . . . . . . . . . . . . . . . . . . . . . . . . . . . . . . .5
Monogram or signet escutcheon . . . . . . . . . . . . . . . . . . . . . . . . . . . . . . . . . . . . . . . . . . . . . . . . .77, 186
Moonstone . . . . . . . . . . . . . . . . . . . . . . . . . . . . . . . . . . . . . . . . . . . . . . . . . . . . . . . . . . . . . . . . . . . . . . .116
Mosaic glass . . . . . . . . . . . . . . . . . . . . . . . . . . . . . . . . . . . . . . . . . . . . . . . . . . . . . . . . . . . . . . . . . .33, 206
Moth with peacock-eye accent . . . . . . . . . . . . . . . . . . . . . . . . . . . . . . . . . . . . . . . . . . . . . . . . . . . . . .123
Mother-of-Pearl . . . . . . . . . . . . . . . . . . . . . . . . . . . . . . . . . . . . . . . . . . . . . . . .62, 72, 79, 105, 126
Mourning jet (Also see *Japanned* in *Glossary*) . . . . . . . . . . . . . . . . . . . . . . . . . . . . . . . . . . . . .96, 97
Mythological griffin . . . . . . . . . . . . . . . . . . . . . . . . . . . . . . . . . . . . . . . . . . . . . . . . . . . . . . . . . . . . . . . .35
Natural elements, (abalone, amber, shell, wood, etc.) . . . . . . . . . . . . . . . . . . . . . . . .72, 78, 80, 114
Nugget, "Fool's Gold" . . . . . . . . . . . . . . . . . . . . . . . . . . . . . . . . . . . . . . . . . . . . . . . . . . . . . . . . . . . . .114
Nugget, rock . . . . . . . . . . . . . . . . . . . . . . . . . . . . . . . . . . . . . . . . . . . . . . . . . . . . . . . . . . . . . . . . .80, 114
Nugget, silver . . . . . . . . . . . . . . . . . . . . . . . . . . . . . . . . . . . . . . . . . . . . . . . . . . . . . . . . . . . . . . . . . . . .115
Opaline glass . . . . . . . . . . . . . . . . . . . . . . . . . . . . . . . . . . . . . . . . . . . . . . . . . . . . . . . . . . . . . . . . . . . . . .32
Oriental ceramic portrait . . . . . . . . . . . . . . . . . . . . . . . . . . . . . . . . . . . . . . . . . . . . . . . . . . . . . . . . . . . . .1
Oriental motif . . . . . . . . . . . . . . . . . . . . . . . . . . . . . . . . . . . . . . . . . . . . . . . . . . . .1, 78, 85, 87, 89, 99
Oriental symbols . . . . . . . . . . . . . . . . . . . . . . . . . . . . . . . . . . . . . . . . . . . . . . . . . . . . . . .100, 123, 218

Ornamental with small stone accents (Also see *Accents*) . . . . . . . . . . . . . . . . . . . . . . . . . . . . . . . . . . . . . . . . . . . . . . . . . .90, 91
  (Also see *Accents*)
Owl . . . . . . . . . . . . . . . . . . . . . . . . . . . . . . . . . . . . . . . . . . . . . . . . . . . . . . . . . . . . . . . . . . . . . . . . . . . . . . . . . . . . . . . . . .110
Pairs . . . . . . . . . . . . . . . . . . . . . . . . . . . . . . . . . . . . . . . . . . . . . . . . . . . . . . . . . . . . . . . . . .9, 67, 94, 107, 116, 206
Painted glass . . . . . . . . . . . . . . . . . . . . . . . . . . . . . . . . . . . . . . . . . . . . . . . . . . . . . . . . . . . . . . . . . . . . . . . . . . . . . . . . . .76
Paper portrait . . . . . . . . . . . . . . . . . . . . . . . . . . . . . . . . . . . . . . . . . . . . . . . . . . . . . . . . . . . . . . . . . . . . . . . . . . . . . . . . .1
Pattern glass (pressed/molded/blown) . . . . . . . . . . . . . . . . . . . . . . . . . . . . . . . . . . . . . . . . . . . . . . . . . . .8, 76, 84
Peacock-eye glass . . . . . . . . . . . . . . . . . . . . . . . . . . . . . . . . . . . . . . . . . . . . . . . . . . . . . . . . . . . . . . . . . . . . . . . . . . . .108
Pearl, (baroque) . . . . . . . . . . . . . . . . . . . . . . . . . . . . . . . . . . . . . . . . . . . . . . . . . . . . . . . . . . . . . . . . . . . . . . . . . .72, 177
Pearlized lustre . . . . . . . . . . . . . . . . . . . . . . . . . . . . . . . . . . . . . . . . . . . . . . . . . . . . . . . . . . . . . .87, 116, 117, 126
Pearls . . . . . . . . . . . . . . . . . . . . . . . . . . . . . . . . . . . . . . . . . . . . . . . . . . . . . . . . . . . . . .9, 37, 56, 77, 107, 205, 207
Peking glass . . . . . . . . . . . . . . . . . . . . . . . . . . . . . . . . . . . . . . . . . . . . . . . . . . . . . . . . . . . . . . . . . . . . . . . . .17, 110, 112
Pewter . . . . . . . . . . . . . . . . . . . . . . . . . . . . . . . . . . . . . . . . . . . . . . . . . . . . . . . . . . . . . . . . . . . . . . . . . . . . . . . . . . . . . . .69
Pharoh . . . . . . . . . . . . . . . . . . . . . . . . . . . . . . . . . . . . . . . . . . . . . . . . . . . . . . . . . . . . . . . . . . . . . . . . . . . . . . . . . . . .65, 89
Plastics, (also see *Celluloid*) . . . . . . . . . . . . . . . . . . . . . . . . . . . . . . . . . . . . . . . . . . .65, 85, 100, 104, 109, 193
*Plique-a-jour*, (see *Glossary*) . . . . . . . . . . . . . . . . . . . . . . . . . . . . . . . . . . . . . . . . . . . . . . . . . . . . . . . . . . . . .65, 167
Pod, (seed) . . . . . . . . . . . . . . . . . . . . . . . . . . . . . . . . . . . . . . . . . . . . . . . . . . . . . . . . . . . . . . . . . . . . . . . . . . . . . .80, 193
Porcelain . . . . . . . . . . . . . . . . . . . . . . . . . . . . . . . . . . . . . . . . . . . . . . . . . . . . . . . . . . . . . .1, 87, 88, 92, 98, 132
Porcelain, beading . . . . . . . . . . . . . . . . . . . . . . . . . . . . . . . . . . . . . . . . . . . . . . . . . . . . . . . . . . . . . . . . . .87, 92, 132
Porcelain, ceramic transfer . . . . . . . . . . . . . . . . . . . . . . . . . . . . . . . . . . . . . . . . . . . . . . . . . . . . . . . . . . . . . . . . . . . .98
Porcelain, gold overlay (accents) . . . . . . . . . . . . . . . . . . . . . . . . . . . . . . . . . . . . . . . . . . . . . . . . . . . . . . . . . . . . . .132
Porcelain, hand-painted . . . . . . . . . . . . . . . . . . . . . . . . . . . . . . . . . . . . . . . . . . . . . . . . . . . . . . . . . . . . . . . . . . . . . . .92
Porcelain, portrait . . . . . . . . . . . . . . . . . . . . . . . . . . . . . . . . . . . . . . . . . . . . . . . . . . . . . . . . . . . . . . . . . .87, 88, 98
Porcelain, scenic . . . . . . . . . . . . . . . . . . . . . . . . . . . . . . . . . . . . . . . . . . . . . . . . . . . . . . . . . . . . . . . . . . . . . . . . . . . .87
Portrait, *Art Nouveau* women . . . . . . . . . . . . . . . . . . . . . . . . . . . . . . .65, 89, 93, 123, 124, 160, 189
Portrait, celluloid . . . . . . . . . . . . . . . . . . . . . . . . . . . . . . . . . . . . . . . . . . . . . . . . . . . . . . . . . . . . . . . . . . . . . . . . . . . .65
Portrait, paper . . . . . . . . . . . . . . . . . . . . . . . . . . . . . . . . . . . . . . . . . . . . . . . . . . . . . . . . . . . . . . . . . . . . . . . . . . . . . .1
Portrait, porcelain . . . . . . . . . . . . . . . . . . . . . . . . . . . . . . . . . . . . . . . . . . . . . . . . . . . . . . . . . . . . . . . . . . . . . .87, 88
Portrait, metal with plastic frame . . . . . . . . . . . . . . . . . . . . . . . . . . . . . . . . . . . . . . . . . . . . . . . . . . . . . . . . . . . . . .89
Pressed glass, (See *Pattern* under *Hatpin Heads*)
Primitives, (felt-covered, hand-made, etc.) . . . . . . . . . . . . . . . . . . . . . . . . . . . . . . . . . . . . . . . . . . . . .15, 119, 162
Quartz gemstone, (genuine) . . . . . . . . . . . . . . . . . . . . . . . . . . . . . . . . . . . . . . . . . . . . . . . . . . . . . . . . . .3, 80, 106
Ram . . . . . . . . . . . . . . . . . . . . . . . . . . . . . . . . . . . . . . . . . . . . . . . . . . . . . . . . . . . . . . . . . . . . . . . . . . . . . . . . . . . . . . . . .81
Religious . . . . . . . . . . . . . . . . . . . . . . . . . . . . . . . . . . . . . . . . . . . . . . . . . . . . . . . . . . . . . . . . . . . . . . . . . . . . . . . .5, 131
Reptile . . . . . . . . . . . . . . . . . . . . . . . . . . . . . . . . . . . . . . . . . . . . . . . . . . . . . . . . . . . . . . . . . . . .81, 91, 116, 206
Rivited jet . . . . . . . . . . . . . . . . . . . . . . . . . . . . . . . . . . . . . . . . . . . . . . . . . . . . . . . . . . . . . . . . . . . . . . .96, 97, 128
Rock, (natural) . . . . . . . . . . . . . . . . . . . . . . . . . . . . . . . . . . . . . . . . . . . . . . . . . . . . . . . . . . . . . . . . . . . . . . . .80, 114
Rooster, (See *Cock* under *Hatpin Heads*)
Rose, (preserved, gilded) . . . . . . . . . . . . . . . . . . . . . . . . . . . . . . . . . . . . . . . . . . . . . . . . . . . . . . . . . . . . . . . . . . .168
Ruby, (red color glass imitation) . . . . . . . . . . . . . . . . . . . . . . . . . . . . . . . . . . . . . . . . . . . . . . . . . . . . . . . . . . . . . .129
Sapphire, (blue color glass imitation) . . . . . . . . . . . . . . . . . . . . . . . . . . . . . . . . . . . . . . . . . . . . . . . . . . . . . . . . . . .127
Satsuma-ware . . . . . . . . . . . . . . . . . . . . . . . . . . . . . . . . . . . . . . . . . . . . . . . . . . . . . . . . . . . . . . . . . . . . . .78, 87, 99
Scarab, (beetle) . . . . . . . . . . . . . . . . . . . . . . . . . . . . . . . . . . . . . . . . . . . . . . . . . . . . . . . . . . . . . . . . . . . . . . . . . . . . .91
Scarab, glass . . . . . . . . . . . . . . . . . . . . . . . . . . . . . . . . . . . . . . . . . . . . . . . . . . . . . . . . . . . . . . . . . . . . . . . . . . . . . . . .8
Scarab, (Scarabus or Bettle) . . . . . . . . . . . . . . . . . . . . . . . . . . . . . . . . . . . . . . . . . . . . . . . . . . . . . .8, 65, 91, 207
Shamrock . . . . . . . . . . . . . . . . . . . . . . . . . . . . . . . . . . . . . . . . . . . . . . . . . . . . . . . . . . . . . . . . . . . . . . . . . . . . . . . . . .180
Shell, *Art Deco* scallop in celluloid . . . . . . . . . . . . . . . . . . . . . . . . . . . . . . . . . . . . . . . . . . . . . . . . . . . . . . . . . . . .109
Shell, glass . . . . . . . . . . . . . . . . . . . . . . . . . . . . . . . . . . . . . . . . . . . . . . . . . . . . . . . . . . . . . . . . . . . . . . .32, 79, 80
Shells, abalone, cowrie, marine-life, mother-of-pearl, etc. . . . . . . . . . . . . . . . . . . . . . . . . . . . . .42, 72, 79, 80
Signed commemorative . . . . . . . . . . . . . . . . . . . . . . . . . . . . . . . . . . . . . . . . . . . . . . . . . . . . . . . . . . . . . . . . . . . . . .170
Silver, *Art Nouveau* design . . . . . . . . . . . . . . . . . . . . . . . . . . . . . . . . . . . . . . . . . . . . . . . . . . . . . . . . . . . . . . . . . . . .93
Silver, *Art Nouveau* women . . . . . . . . . . . . . . . . . . . . . . . . . . . . . . . . . . . . . . . . . . . . . . . . . .93, 123, 124, 189
Silver, baroque . . . . . . . . . . . . . . . . . . . . . . . . . . . . . . . . . . . . . . . . . . . . . . . . . . . . . . . . . . . . . . . . . . . . . . . . . . . . . . .93
Silver-deposit-ware . . . . . . . . . . . . . . . . . . . . . . . . . . . . . . . . . . . . . . . . . . . . . . . . . . . . . . . . . . . . . . . . . . . . . .115, 218
Silver, nugget . . . . . . . . . . . . . . . . . . . . . . . . . . . . . . . . . . . . . . . . . . . . . . . . . . . . . . . . . . . . . . . . . . . . . . . . . . . . . . .115
Silver, oxidized . . . . . . . . . . . . . . . . . . . . . . . . . . . . . . . . . . . . . . . . . . . . . . . . . . . . . . . . . . . . . . . . . . . . .89, 90, 94
Silver, (unmarked) . . . . . . . . . . . . . . . . . . . . . . . . . . . . . . . . . . . . . . . . . . . . . . . . . . . . . . . . . . . . . . . . . . . . . . . . . . .123
Silver, souvenir . . . . . . . . . . . . . . . . . . . . . . . . . . . . . . . . . . . . . . . . . . . . . . . . . . . . . . . . . . . . . . . . . . . . . . . . . .30, 93
Silver, sterling . . . . . . . . . . . . . . . . . . . . . . . . . . . . . . . . . . . . . . . . . . . . . . . . . . .2, 22, 52, 93, 123, 124, 207
Slag glass . . . . . . . . . . . . . . . . . . . . . . . . . . . . . . . . . . . . . . . . . . . . . . . . . . . . . . . . . . . . . . . . . . . . . . .95, 100, 108

Snake, (see *Reptile*)
Snowflake design . . . . . . . . . . . . . . . . . . . . . . . . . . . . . . . . . . . . . . . . . . . . . . . . . . . . . . . . . . . . .21
Souvenir, (commemorative, keepsake, memento) . . . . . . . . . . . . . . . . . . . .22, 30, 31, 83, 89, 93, 129, 160, 190
Spider . . . . . . . . . . . . . . . . . . . . . . . . . . . . . . . . . . . . . . . . . . . . . . . . . . . . . . . . . . . . . .8, 89, 193
Sporting activity . . . . . . . . . . . . . . . . . . . . . . . . . . . . . . . . . . . . . . . . . . . . . . . . . . . .62, 126, 218
Star-shaped . . . . . . . . . . . . . . . . . . . . . . . . . . . . . . . . . . . . . . . . . . . . . . . . . . . . . . . . . . . . . . .21
Sterling, (marked) . . . . . . . . . . . . . . . . . . . . . . . . . . . . . . . . . . . . .2, 22, 52, 93, 123, 124, 207
Sterling silver overlay, (also see *Silver-Deposit-Ware*) . . . . . . . . . . . . . . . . . . . . . . . . . . . . . . . .115
Stone, (natural rock) . . . . . . . . . . . . . . . . . . . . . . . . . . . . . . . . . . . . . . . . . . . . . . . . . . . .80, 114
Straw or raffia, (woven/polished) . . . . . . . . . . . . . . . . . . . . . . . . . . . . . . . . . . . . . . . . . . . . . . .16
Swastika . . . . . . . . . . . . . . . . . . . . . . . . . . . . . . . . . . . . . . . . . . . . . . . . . . . . . . . . . . . . . . . .61
Sword . . . . . . . . . . . . . . . . . . . . . . . . . . . . . . . . . . . . . . . . . . . . . . . . . . . . . . . . .112, 207, 221
Symbolic, (amulet, charm, religious symbol, talisman) . . . . . . . . . . . . . . . . .5, 8, 61, 91, 93, 123, 207
Thistle-cut genuine gemstone . . . . . . . . . . . . . . . . . . . . . . . . . . . . . . . . . . . . . . . . . . . . . . . . . .115
Thistle-cut glass imitation amethyst and topaz . . . . . . . . . . . . . . . . . . . . . . . . . . . . . . . . . . .52, 66
"Thorn" free-form design milkglass . . . . . . . . . . . . . . . . . . . . . . . . . . . . . . . . . . . . . . . . . . . . . .32
Tiffany . . . . . . . . . . . . . . . . . . . . . . . . . . . . . . . . . . . . . . . . . . . . . . . . . . . . . . . . . . . . . . . . .206
Tiger . . . . . . . . . . . . . . . . . . . . . . . . . . . . . . . . . . . . . . . . . . . . . . . . . . . . . . . . . . . . . . . . . . . .6
Tin . . . . . . . . . . . . . . . . . . . . . . . . . . . . . . . . . . . . . . . . . . . . . . . . . . . . . . . . . . . . .77, 79, 103
Tooth, (not tusk) — "Trophy" . . . . . . . . . . . . . . . . . . . . . . . . . . . . . . . . . . . . . . . . . . . . . . . . .111
Topaz, yellow color glass imitation . . . . . . . . . . . . . . . . . . . . . . . . . . . . . . . . . . . . . . . . . . . . . . .36
Tortoise-shell, imitation . . . . . . . . . . . . . . . . . . . . . . . . . . . . . . . . . . . . . . . . . . . . . . . . . . .76, 85
"Trophy" tooth . . . . . . . . . . . . . . . . . . . . . . . . . . . . . . . . . . . . . . . . . . . . . . . . . . . . . . .111, 197
Turquoise . . . . . . . . . . . . . . . . . . . . . . . . . . . . . . . . . . . . . . . . . . . . . . . . . . . . . . . . .56, 61, 77
Tusk, (ivory) . . . . . . . . . . . . . . . . . . . . . . . . . . . . . . . . . . . . . . . . . . . . . . . . . . . . . . . . . .78, 111
Vanity, (See *Glossary*) . . . . . . . . . . . . . . . . . . . . . . . . . . . . . . . . . . . . . . . . . . . . . . . . . . .64, 180
Venetian glass bead, decorated . . . . . . . . . . . . . . . . . . . . . . . . . . . . . . . . . . . . . . . . . . . . . . . . .15
Wax-Pearl, (glass) . . . . . . . . . . . . . . . . . . . . . . . . . . . . . . . . . . . . . . . . . . . . . . . . . . . . . .37, 205
With beading . . . . . . . . . . . . . . . . . . . . . . . . . . . . . . . . . . . . . . . . . . . . . . . . . . . . . . . . . . . . . .48
With detachable brooch . . . . . . . . . . . . . . . . . . . . . . . . . . . . . . . . . . . . . . . . . . . . . . . . . . . . . .161
With figural *mountings* . . . . . . . . . . . . . . . . . . . . . . . . . . . . . . . . . .35, 82, 89, 90, 91, 93, 110
With Marcasites . . . . . . . . . . . . . . . . . . . . . . . . . . . . . . . . . . . . . . . . . . . . . . . . . . . . . . . . . . . .65
With metallic mountings for stones (¼″ and larger) . . . . . . . . . . . . . . . . . . . . . . . . . . . .36, 37, 90
With nodders, (bobbler, springer, trembler) . . . . . . . . . . . . . . . . . . . . . . . . . . . . . . . . . . . . . . . . .3
Wood . . . . . . . . . . . . . . . . . . . . . . . . . . . . . . . . . . . . . . . . . . . . . . . . . . . . . . .78, 101, 103, 196
Wooden bead . . . . . . . . . . . . . . . . . . . . . . . . . . . . . . . . . . . . . . . . . . . . . . . . . . . . . . . . . . . . .101
Woven straw or raffia . . . . . . . . . . . . . . . . . . . . . . . . . . . . . . . . . . . . . . . . . . . . . . . . . . . . . . . .16
Zircon . . . . . . . . . . . . . . . . . . . . . . . . . . . . . . . . . . . . . . . . . . . . . . . . . . . . . . . . . . . . . . . . . . .56
HATPIN HOLDER, leather golf-bag for cudgels . . . . . . . . . . . . . . . . . . . . . . . . . . . . . . . . . . . . .62
HATPIN HOLDERS, (celluloid, china, glass, metal, and primitives) (Also see *Pincushions*)
American Belleek . . . . . . . . . . . . . . . . . . . . . . . . . . . . . . . . . . . . . . . . . . . . . . . . . . . . . . . . . . .38
*Art Deco* . . . . . . . . . . . . . . . . . . . . . . . . . . . . . . . . . . . . . . . . . . . . . . . . . . . . . . . . . .38, 41, 53
Art Glass . . . . . . . . . . . . . . . . . . . . . . . . . . . . . . . . . . . . . . . . . . . . . . . . . . . . . . . . . . . . . . . . .56
*Art Nouveau* . . . . . . . . . . . . . . . . . . . . . . . . . . . . . . . . . . . . . . . . . . . . . . . . . . . . .19, 41, 49, 50
Assyrian Gold . . . . . . . . . . . . . . . . . . . . . . . . . . . . . . . . . . . . . . . . . . . . . . . . . . . . . . . . . . . .187
Bavarian . . . . . . . . . . . . . . . . . . . . . . . . . . . . . . . . . . . . . . . . . . . . . . . . . . . . . . . . . . .39, 40, 41
Bisque . . . . . . . . . . . . . . . . . . . . . . . . . . . . . . . . . . . . . . . . . . . . . . . . . . . . . . . .38, 49, 73, 195
Blown Satin Glass . . . . . . . . . . . . . . . . . . . . . . . . . . . . . . . . . . . . . . . . . . . . . . . . . . . . . . . . . .56
Carmel slag, (Chocolate Glass) . . . . . . . . . . . . . . . . . . . . . . . . . . . . . . . . . . . . . . . . . . . . . . . .182
Carnival glass . . . . . . . . . . . . . . . . . . . . . . . . . . . . . . . . . . . . . . . . . . . . . . . . . . . . . . . . . . . . .55
Ceramic transfer . . . . . . . . . . . . . . . . . . . . . . . . . . . . . . . . . . . . . . . . . . . . . . . . . . . . . . . . . . .50
Ceramic-ware . . . . . . . . . . . . . . . . . . . . . . . . . . . . . . . . . . . . . . . . . . . . . . . . . . . . . .54, 69, 70
"Chocolate Glass," (carmel slag) . . . . . . . . . . . . . . . . . . . . . . . . . . . . . . . . . . . . . . . . . . . . . . .182
Cloisonne . . . . . . . . . . . . . . . . . . . . . . . . . . . . . . . . . . . . . . . . . . . . . . . . . . . . . . . . . . . . . . . .195
Commemorative, (also see *Souvenir*) . . . . . . . . . . . . . . . . . . . . . . . . . . . . . . . . . . . . . . . . .28, 41
Custard glass . . . . . . . . . . . . . . . . . . . . . . . . . . . . . . . . . . . . . . . . . . . . . . . . . . . . . . . . . . . . . .55
Cut glass, faceted . . . . . . . . . . . . . . . . . . . . . . . . . . . . . . . . . . . . . . . . . . . . . . . . . . . . . . . . . .182
Enamel and cloisonne . . . . . . . . . . . . . . . . . . . . . . . . . . . . . . . . . . . . . . . . . . . . . . . . . . . . . . .195
England . . . . . . . . . . . . . . . . . . . . . . . . . . . . . . . . . . . . . . . . . . . . . . . . . . . . . . . . . .54, 70, 182
European . . . . . . . . . . . . . . . . . . . . . . . . . . . . . . . . . . . . . . . . . . . . .40, 41, 49, 70, 73, 182

Figurals . . . . . . . . . . . . . . . . . . . . . . . . . . . . . . . . . . . . . . . . . . . . . . .38, 49, 53, 69, 163, 182, 195, 196
Floral . . . . . . . . . . . . . . . . . . . . . . . . . . . . . . . . . . . . . . . . . . . . . . . . . . . .38, 39, 41, 50, 54, 196
"Flow Blue" . . . . . . . . . . . . . . . . . . . . . . . . . . . . . . . . . . . . . . . . . . . . . . . . . . . . . . . . . . . . . .70
"Flow Blue" with ring-tree . . . . . . . . . . . . . . . . . . . . . . . . . . . . . . . . . . . . . . . . . . . . . . . . . . .18
For double-prong or heavy gauge wire pins . . . . . . . . . . . . . . . . . . . . . . . . . . . . . .13, 17, 39, 119
French . . . . . . . . . . . . . . . . . . . . . . . . . . . . . . . . . . . . . . . . . . . . . . . . . . . . . . . . . . . . . . .40, 41
"French Ivory" (celluloid) . . . . . . . . . . . . . . . . . . . . . . . . . . . . . . . . . . . . . . . . . . . . . . . .73, 193
German . . . . . . . . . . . . . . . . . . . . . . . . . . . . . . . . . . . . . . . . . .38, 39, 40, 49, 70, 73, 182, 195
German Silver commemorative . . . . . . . . . . . . . . . . . . . . . . . . . . . . . . . . . . . . . . . . . . . . . . . .28
Glass, blown art glass . . . . . . . . . . . . . . . . . . . . . . . . . . . . . . . . . . . . . . . . . . . . . . . . . . . . . . .56
Glass, carmel slag . . . . . . . . . . . . . . . . . . . . . . . . . . . . . . . . . . . . . . . . . . . . . . . . . . . . . . . . .182
Glass, carnival . . . . . . . . . . . . . . . . . . . . . . . . . . . . . . . . . . . . . . . . . . . . . . . . . . . . . . . . . . . .55
Glass, "chocolate" . . . . . . . . . . . . . . . . . . . . . . . . . . . . . . . . . . . . . . . . . . . . . . . . . . . . . . . . .182
Glass, custard . . . . . . . . . . . . . . . . . . . . . . . . . . . . . . . . . . . . . . . . . . . . . . . . . . . . . . . . . . . . .55
Glass, cut and faceted . . . . . . . . . . . . . . . . . . . . . . . . . . . . . . . . . . . . . . . . . . . . . . . . . . . . . .182
Glass, crystal-clear . . . . . . . . . . . . . . . . . . . . . . . . . . . . . . . . . . . . . . . . . . . . . . . . . . . . . . . .182
Glass, enamel (cloisonne) . . . . . . . . . . . . . . . . . . . . . . . . . . . . . . . . . . . . . . . . . . . . . . . . . . .195
Jasperware . . . . . . . . . . . . . . . . . . . . . . . . . . . . . . . . . . . . . . . . . . . . . . . . . . . . . . .49, 70, 182
Kewpie . . . . . . . . . . . . . . . . . . . . . . . . . . . . . . . . . . . . . . . . . . . . . . . . . . . . . . .49, 50, 182
Leather golf-bag holder for hatpins . . . . . . . . . . . . . . . . . . . . . . . . . . . . . . . . . . . . . . . . . . . . .62
Limoges . . . . . . . . . . . . . . . . . . . . . . . . . . . . . . . . . . . . . . . . . . . . . . . . . . . . . . . . . . . . . . . . .40
Metal . . . . . . . . . . . . . . . . . . . . . . . . . . . . . . . . . . . . . . . . . . . . . . . . . . . . . . . .28, 52, 69, 71
Metal stand . . . . . . . . . . . . . . . . . . . . . . . . . . . . . . . . . . . . . . . . . . . . . . . . . . . . . .52, 71, 171
Nippon . . . . . . . . . . . . . . . . . . . . . . . . . . . . . . . . . . . . . . . . . . . . . . . . . . . . . . . . . . . .51, 182
Open-mouth . . . . . . . . . . . . . . . . . . . . . . . . . . . . . . . . . . . . . . . . . . . . . . . . . . . . . . . . .17, 119
Oriental . . . . . . . . . . . . . . . . . . . . . . . . . . . . . . . . . . . . . . . . . . . . . . . . . . . . .51, 53, 70, 182
Primitives . . . . . . . . . . . . . . . . . . . . . . . . . . . . . . . . . . . . . . . . . . . . . . . . . . . . .62, 119, 187
Prussia, (not R.S. Prussia) . . . . . . . . . . . . . . . . . . . . . . . . . . . . . . . . . . . . . . . . . . . . . . . . . . . .40
R.S. Germany . . . . . . . . . . . . . . . . . . . . . . . . . . . . . . . . . . . . . . . . . . . . . . . .38, 39, 40, 70, 182
R.S. Poland . . . . . . . . . . . . . . . . . . . . . . . . . . . . . . . . . . . . . . . . . . . . . . . . . . . . . . . . . . . . . .182
R.S. Prussia . . . . . . . . . . . . . . . . . . . . . . . . . . . . . . . . . . . . . . . . . . . . . . . . . . . . . . . . . .38, 182
Reproductions . . . . . . . . . . . . . . . . . . . . . . . . . . . . . . . . . . . . . . . . . . . . . . . . . . . . . . . . . . . .188
Royal Bayreuth . . . . . . . . . . . . . . . . . . . . . . . . . . . . . . . . . . . . . . . . . . . . . . . . . . . . . . . . . . .182
Royal Doulton . . . . . . . . . . . . . . . . . . . . . . . . . . . . . . . . . . . . . . . . . . . . . . . . . . . . . . . . .54, 70
Rosenthal . . . . . . . . . . . . . . . . . . . . . . . . . . . . . . . . . . . . . . . . . . . . . . . . . . . . . . . . . . . . . . . .41
Shell, (see Pincushions)
Silver Stands . . . . . . . . . . . . . . . . . . . . . . . . . . . . . . . . . . . . . . . . . . . . . . . . . . . . . .52, 71, 171
Souvenir, (also see Commemorative) . . . . . . . . . . . . . . . . . . . . . . . . . . . . . . . . . . .41, 52, 54, 70
Stand, metal (detail drawings of hallmarks) . . . . . . . . . . . . . . . . . . . . . . . . . . . . . . . . . . . . . .171
Stands, metal hatpin holders . . . . . . . . . . . . . . . . . . . . . . . . . . . . . . . . . . . . . . . . . .52, 71, 171
Straw, (also see Primitives) . . . . . . . . . . . . . . . . . . . . . . . . . . . . . . . . . . . . . . . . . . . . . . . . . .119
Thistle-stone decorated metal stand . . . . . . . . . . . . . . . . . . . . . . . . . . . . . . . . . . . . . . . . . . . . .52
Wall hanging, (also see Pincushions) . . . . . . . . . . . . . . . . . . . . . . . . . . . . . . . . . . . . . . . . . . . .73
With attached covered pin-box . . . . . . . . . . . . . . . . . . . . . . . . . . . . . . . . . . . . . . . . . . . . .48, 209
With attached pin or trinket trays . . . . . . . . . . . . . . . . . . . . . . . . . . . . . . . . . . . . . . .48, 50, 180
With demi-tasse cup . . . . . . . . . . . . . . . . . . . . . . . . . . . . . . . . . . . . . . . . . . . . . . . . . . . . . . . . .19
With dresser, toilet, and vanity sets, (see Commode Set, and Dresser, Toilet, and Vanity Sets)
With sterling overlay . . . . . . . . . . . . . . . . . . . . . . . . . . . . . . . . . . . . . . . . . . . . . . . . . . . . . . . . .41
With various shapes of applied tops for pins . . . . . . . . . . . . . . . . . . . . . . . . . . . . . . . . . . . . . .192
HATS, (see Millinery)
HOLDERS, (also see Hatpin Holders and Pincushions)
For double-pronged hair-pins or ornaments . . . . . . . . . . . . . . . . . . . . . . . . . . . . . .17, 39, 53, 192
For scarf or tie pins . . . . . . . . . . . . . . . . . . . . . . . . . . . . . . . . . . . . . . . . . . . . . . . . . . . . . .48, 59
For veil pins . . . . . . . . . . . . . . . . . . . . . . . . . . . . . . . . . . . . . . . . . . . . . . . . . . . . . . . . . . . . . . .48
LALIQUE, . . . . . . . . . . . . . . . . . . . . . . . . . . . . . . . . . . . . . . . . . . . . . . . . . . . . . . . . . . . . . . .167
MANUFACTURE OF HANDMADE PINS . . . . . . . . . . . . . . . . . . . . . . . . . . . . . . . . . . . . . . . .135
METALLIC HATPIN STANDS . . . . . . . . . . . . . . . . . . . . . . . . . . . . . . . . . . . . . . . . . . . . . . . . .52
MILLINERY, (also see FASHIONS) . . . . . . . . . . . . . . . . . . . . . . . . . . . .134, 140 fig. c., 141, 142, 146, 148, 150,
151, 152, 153, 154, 155, 157, 159, 174, 175, 184,
191, 211, 212, 213, 214
MOURNING ATTIRE, (also see Hatpin Heads) . . . . . . . . . . . . . . . . . . . . . . . . . . . . . . . . . . . .157

*MOUNTINGS FOR HATPIN HEADS* (Also see *Settings*) . . . . . . . . . . . . . . . . . . . . . . . . . . . . . . . . 132, 219
  Arc-type finding . . . . . . . . . . . . . . . . . . . . . . . . . . . . . . . . . . . . . . . . . . 35, 36, 64, 65, 108
  *Art Nouveau* design . . . . . . . . . . . . . . . . . . . . . . . . . . . . . . . . . . . . . . . 23, 36, 77, 120
  Baroque . . . . . . . . . . . . . . . . . . . . . . . . . . . . . . . . . . . . . . . . . . . . . . . . . . . . . . . . 219
  Cage . . . . . . . . . . . . . . . . . . . . . . . . . . . . . . . . . . . . . . . . . . . . . . . . . . . . . . . . 5, 6, 36
  Chased . . . . . . . . . . . . . . . . . . . . . . . . . . . . . . . . . . . . . . . . . . . . . . . . . . . . . . . . . . 122
  Chased, flat (obverse) . . . . . . . . . . . . . . . . . . . . . . . . . . . . . . . . . . . . . . . . . . . . . . . 5
  Chased, *repoussé* (reverse) . . . . . . . . . . . . . . . . . . . . . . . . . . . . . . . . . . . . . . . 69, 72
  Claw . . . . . . . . . . . . . . . . . . . . . . . . . . . . . . . . . . . . . . . . . . . . . . . . . . . . . . . . . . . 118
  Crown . . . . . . . . . . . . . . . . . . . . . . . . . . . . . . . . . . . . . . . . . . . . . . . . . . . . . . . . 5, 36
  Engraved . . . . . . . . . . . . . . . . . . . . . . . . . . . . . . . . . . . . . . . 82, 89, 90, 91, 93, 110
  Figural (not FULL figural) . . . . . . . . . . . . . . . . . . . . . . . . . . 20, 37, 82, 177, 195, 199
  Filigree . . . . . . . . . . . . . . . . . . . . . . . . . . . . . . . . . . . . . . . . . . . . . . . 35, 120, 219
  For escutcheon . . . . . . . . . . . . . . . . . . . . . . . . . . . . . . . . . . . . . . . . . . . . . . . . . . . . 4
  Frame . . . . . . . . . . . . . . . . . . . . . . . . . . . . . . . . . . . . . . . . . . . . . . . . . . . . . . . . . . . 76
  Glass (rare) . . . . . . . . . . . . . . . . . . . . . . . . . . . . . . . . . . . . . . . . . . . . . . . . . . 32, 125
  Metal cup (backing for rhinestones, paste, etc.) . . . . . . . . . . . . . . . . . . 16, 114, 138
  Patch (with or without socket finding) . . . . . . . . . . . . . . . . . . 20, 36, 37, 90, 200, 219
  Pierced (open work) . . . . . . . . . . . . . . . . . . . . . . . . . . . . . . . . . . . . . . . . . . . . . . . 132
  Rim . . . . . . . . . . . . . . . . . . . . . . . . . . . . . . . . . . . . . . . . . . . . . . . . . . . . . . . . . . . 128
  Rivited . . . . . . . . . . . . . . . . . . . . . . . . . . . . . . . . . . . . . . . . . . . . . . . . . . . . . . . . 8, 88
  Sleeve . . . . . . . . . . . . . . . . . . . . . . . . . . . . . . . . . . . . . . . . . . . . 114, 136, 138, 219
  Socket . . . . . . . . . . . . . . . . . . . . . . . . . . . . . . . . . . . . . . . . . . . . . . . . . . . . . 136, 219
  Span, arc, or bridge-type . . . . . . . . . . . . . . . . . . . . . . . . . . . . . . . . . . . . . . . . 42, 80
  Wire . . . . . . . . . . . . . . . . . . . . . . . . . . . . . . . . . . . . . . . . . . . . . . . . . . . . . . . . . . . 157
*MOURNING ATTIRE, (also see Hatpin Heads)* . . . . . . . . . . . . . . . . . . . . . . . . . . . . . . . 157
*NATURAL ELEMENTS AS HATPINS* (See *Hatpin Heads*)
*NIBS, (same as "Jargow-nibs," guards, point protectors, safeties) — see "Jargow-nibs" in Glossary* 11, 16, 78, 107, 113, 116, 165,
                                                                                                            172, 173, 221
*NODDER, (same as "bobbler," "springer," "trembler") — see Glossary* . . . . . . . . . . . . . . . . . 3, 17, 186
*ORIENTAL* (see specific category)
*ORNAMENTS*
  Hair . . . . . . . . . . . . . . . . . . . . . . . . . . . . . . . . . . . . . . . . . . . . . . . . . . . . . . . . . . . . 69
  Hat, *(not hatpin)* . . . . . . . . . . . . . . . . . . . . . . . . . 17, 107, 112, 113, 116, 165, 172, 173
  Sword . . . . . . . . . . . . . . . . . . . . . . . . . . . . . . . . . . . . . . . . . . . . . . . . . . . . . . . . . . 112
*PAIRS OF HATPINS* . . . . . . . . . . . . . . . . . . . . . . . . . . . . . . . . . . . . . 9, 67, 94, 116, 206
*PATTERN OR PRESSED GLASS HATPINS* (see *Hatpin Heads*)
*PEWTER* (See *Hatpin Heads*)
*PIN, brass or gilt (gold color)* . . . . . . . . . . . . . . . . . . . . . . . . . . . . . . . . . . . . . . . . 205
*PIN, carat (karat) gold* . . . . . . . . . . . . . . . . . . . . . . . . . . . . . . . . . . . . . . . . . . . . . . 206
*PIN, detachable* . . . . . . . . . . . . . . . . . . . . . . . . . . . . . . . . . . . . . . . . . . . . . . . . 67, 125
*PIN, double-pronged* . . . . . . . . . . . . . . . . . . . . . . . . . . . . . . . . . . . . . . . . . . . . . . . . 17
*PIN, flower (corsage)* . . . . . . . . . . . . . . . . . . . . . . . . . . . . . . . . . . . . . . . . . . . . . . . . 17
*PIN, hair* . . . . . . . . . . . . . . . . . . . . . . . . . . . . . . . . . . . . . . . . . . . . . . . . . . . . . . . . . 17
*PIN, handmade wire* . . . . . . . . . . . . . . . . . . . . . . . . . . . . . . . . . . . . . . . . . 9, 15, 135
*PIN, hinged* . . . . . . . . . . . . . . . . . . . . . . . . . . . . . . . . . . . . . . . . . . . . . . 5, 125, 206
*PIN, manufacture of handmade* . . . . . . . . . . . . . . . . . . . . . . . . . . . . . . . . . . . . . . . . 135
*PIN, point protector* . . . . . . . . . . . . . . . . . . . . . . . . . . . . . . 11, 107, 113, 116, 165, 173
*PIN, scarf or tie-pin* . . . . . . . . . . . . . . . . . . . . . . . . . . . . . . . . . . . . . . . . . . . . . 17, 207
*PIN, scarf or tie-pin holder* . . . . . . . . . . . . . . . . . . . . . . . . . . . . . . . . . . . . . . . . . 48, 59
*PIN, shanks* . . . . . . . . . . . . . . . . . . . . . . . . . . . . . . . . . . . . . . . . . . . . . . . . . . . . . . 138
*PIN-TRAY, (also see Dresser, Toilet and Vanity Sets)* . . . . . . . . . . . . . . . . . . . . . . . . . . 48
*PINCUSHION HALF-DOLLS* (See *Glossary*) . . . . . . . . . . . . . . . . . . . . . . . 9, 12, 56, 195
*PINCUSHIONS* . . . . . . . . . . . . . . . . . . . . . 12, 15, 16, 42, 119, 121, 193, 194, 196
  *Art Nouveau* . . . . . . . . . . . . . . . . . . . . . . . . . . . . . . . . . . . . . . . . . . . . . . . . . . . . . 71
  *Beaded* . . . . . . . . . . . . . . . . . . . . . . . . . . . . . . . . . . . . . . . . . . . . . . . . . . . . . 16, 194
  Boot . . . . . . . . . . . . . . . . . . . . . . . . . . . . . . . . . . . . . . . . . . . . . . . . . . . . . . . . . 16, 73
  "French Ivory" (grained celluloid) . . . . . . . . . . . . . . . . . . . . . . . . . . . . . . . . . . 15, 73
  Fruit . . . . . . . . . . . . . . . . . . . . . . . . . . . . . . . . . . . . . . . . . . . . . . . . . . . . . . . . . . . 193
  Horn, carved . . . . . . . . . . . . . . . . . . . . . . . . . . . . . . . . . . . . . . . . . . . . . . . . . . . . . . 73

| | |
|---|---|
| Plush pear | 193 |
| Shell | 42 |
| Velvet | 15, 71, 196 |
| Victorian | 121 |

*PINS*, assorted shanks for hatpins . . . . . . 138
*PINS*, cape . . . . . . 158
*PINS*, flower (corsage, violet, etc.) . . . . . . 17, 158
*PINS*, handmade (c1825-1832) . . . . . . 15, 63, 207
*PINS*, japanned . . . . . . 25, 26, 27
*PINS*, with *flat* rather than round-shaped shanks . . . . . . 100
*PINS*, with spiral non-slippage feature . . . . . . 8, 17, 42, 56, 100, 137
*PINS*, with springs (nodders) also known as bobblers, tremblers, and springers . . . . . . 3
*PINS*, with threaded (detachable) ends . . . . . . 125
*PINS*, with wire hand-wrought before pin-*machine* (1832) . . . . . . 9, 15
*PINS*, veil . . . . . . 67
*PLASTIC HATPIN HEADS*, (see *Hatpin Heads*)
*POINT PROTECTOR*, (see *Nibs*)
*PORCELAIN, CHINA, CERAMIC HATPINS*, (see *Hatpin Heads*)
*PORTRAIT HATPINS* (See *Hatpin Heads*)
*PRIMITIVE HATPINS* (See *Hatpin Heads*)
*PUFF-BOX* (Also see *Dresser, Toilet and Vanity Sets*) . . . . . . 68, 74
*RING-TREE* (Also see *Commode, Dresser, Toilet and Vanity Sets*) . . . . . . 18, 46, 48, 52, 57, 75
*SAFETIES* (see *Nibs*)
*SATSUMA* (see *Hatpin Heads*)
*SCARF OR TIE-PIN HOLDER* . . . . . . 48, 59
*SETTINGS* (Also see *Mountings* and *Glossary*)

| | |
|---|---|
| Bezel | 36, 37, 106, 199 |
| Box | 129 |
| Channel | 21, 23 |
| Claw | 9, 69, 72 |
| Crown | 118 |
| Gypsy | 36, 37, 106 |
| Illusion | 5, 118, 218 |
| Metal cup | 125 |
| *Pavé* | 21, 23, 37 |

*SHELL OR SHELLS*, (see *Hatpin Heads* and *Pincushions*)
*SOUVENIR*, (Commemorative, Keepsake, Memento) see *Hatpin Heads.*
*SOUVENIR COMMEMORATIVE SET OF HATPINS AND HOLDER* . . . . . . 28
*SPORTING ACTIVITIES*, (see *Fashions* and *Hatpin Heads*)
*SPRINGER*, (see *Nodder*)
*STAND*, metal (See *Hatpin Holders*)
*SYMBOLIC HATPINS* (amulet, charm, religious symbol, talisman), see *Hatpin Heads.*
*SWORDS*, (assorted ornamental) . . . . . . 17, 71, 112, 207, 221
*TIE OR SCARF PIN HOLDER* . . . . . . 48, 59
*TIFFANY* . . . . . . 206
*TRINKET BOXES*, (also see *Dresser, Toilet and Vanity Sets*) . . . . . . 13, 57, 60
*"TROPHY" TOOTH WITH MATCHING GLOVE RING* . . . . . . 197
*VANITY HATPIN HEADS* (see *Hatpin Heads* and *Glossary*)
*VEIL PINS*, (also see *Pin* and *Pins*) . . . . . . 67
*"WEEPERS,"* (see *Millinery* and *Glossary*) . . . . . . 212

# BIBLIOGRAPHY

ADAMS, James Truslow, *"The Epic of America,"* Little Brown & Co., 1932.

ALLEN, A., *"The Story of Clothes,"* Roy Publishers, N.Y., 1958.

ARETZ, Gertrude, *"The Elegant Women From the Rococo Period to Modern Times,"* translated with a Preface by James Laver, George G. Harrap & Co., Ltd., London 1932.

*"Art Nouveau Jewelry & Fans,"* Gabriel Mourey, Aymer Vallance, et al. Dover Publications, Inc., New York, 1973.

*"Arthur's Home Magazine,"* T. S. Arthur & Co., Phila., Jan. thru Dec. 1866.

BAINRIDGE, Henry Charles, *"Peter Carl Fabergé,"* The Hamlyn Publishing Group, Inc., London, 1966.

BAKER, Lillian, *"Hatpin Holders,"* (Dec. 17, 1974) The Antique Trader, Dubuque, Iowa.

BAKER, Lillian, *"Hatpins"* (Sept. 17, 1974), The Antique Trader, Dubuque, Iowa.

BAKER, Stanley L., *"Collecting Art Deco,"* The Antique Trader, Dubuque, Iowa, Dec. 10, 1974.

BAUER, Dr. Jaroslav, *"A Field Guide in Color to Minerals, Rocks and Precious Stones,"* Octopus Books, London, 1974.

BEDFORD, John, *"Looking in Junk Shops,"* David McKay Company, Inc., N.Y. 1961.

BEDFORD, John, *"More Looking in Junk Shops,"* Max Parrish, London, 1962.

BINDER, Pearl, *"Muffs and Morals,"* William Morrow & Co., 1955.

BISHOP, Robert, *"Art Nouveau Influence Further Recognized in U.S.,"* Antique Monthly, Sept. 1974.

BOUCHER, Francois, *"The History of Costume and Personal Adornment — 20,000 Years of Fashion,"* Henry N. Abrams, Inc., N.Y.

BOWLES, Robert N., *"The Origins of 'Teplitz',"* The Antique Trader, Dubuque, Iowa, Dec. 10, 1974.

BRADFIELD, Nancy A.R.C.A., *"Historical Costumes of England,"* George G. Harrap & Co., Ltd., 1958.

BRADFORD, Ernle, *"English Victorian Jewellery,"* Country Life Limited, London.

BRUCE, John, *"Gaudy Century,"* Random House, N.Y., 1948.

BUCK, Anne, *"Victorian Costume and Costume Accessories,"* London, 1961.

BUEHR, Walter, *"Home Sweet Home in the 19th Century,"* Thomas Y. Crowell Co., 1965.

CARTER, Herman C., *"Milady's Dresser Accessories,"* The Antique Trader, Dubuque, Iowa, Jan. 29, 1974.

CHAFFERS, Wm., *"Marks & Monograms on European and Oriental Pottery and Porcelain,"* Edited by Frederich Litchfield, Bordon Publishing Co., Los Angeles, 1946.

CHALMERS, Helena, *"Clothes On and Off the Stage,"* Appleton, 1928.

COLE, Ann Kilborn, *"Old Things For Young People,"* David McKay Company, Inc., New York, 1963.

*"Hatpins Becoming Very Big,"* Collector's News, Grundy, Iowa, Apr. 1970.

CORSON, Richard, *"Fashions in Hair,"* Peter Owen, London, 1965.

CUNNINGTON, Dr. Phillis Cunnington, *"Costume in Pictures,"* E. P. Dutton and Co., Inc., 1964.

CURRAN, Mona, *"Collecting Antique Jewelry,"* Emerson Books, Inc. 1963.

CUSHION, J. P., *"English Ceramic Marks,"* Faber and Faber, 1954.

CUSHION, J. P., *"Handbook of Pottery & Porcelain Marks,"* Faber and Faber, 1956.

DOLAN, J. R., *"The Yankee Peddlers of Early America,"* Bramhall House, N.Y., 1964.

*"Dress, A Monthly Magazine,"* Vol. 1, No. 1, May 1887 through Vol. 2, No. 1, 1888; The Gallison & Hobron Co., New York and Jenness-Miller Publishing Co., New York.

E. V. RODDIN & COMPANY 1895, American Historical Catalog Collection, The Pyne Press, Princeton, N.J.

EARLE, Alice Morse, *"Costume of Colonial Times,"* State Book Co., New York 1924; Copyright 1894, Charles Scribner's Sons.

*"Early Victorian Period 1830-1860,"* Edited by Ralph Edward & L.G.G. Ramsey. Rainbird, McLean Ltd., London, 1958.

EICHLER, Lillian, *"The Customs of Mankind,"* Nelson Doubleday, Inc., Garden City, N.Y., 1924.

*"Encyclopedia Brittannica, 9th Edition,"* Charles Scribner's Sons, 1885.

EVANS, Joan, *"A History of Jewelry 1100-1870,"* Faber and Faber, London, 1953.

EVANS, Mary, *"Costume Throughout the Ages,"* J. B. Lippincott, Co., 1930.

FALKINER, Richard, *"Investing in Antique Jewelry,"* Clarkson N. Potter, Inc., N.Y., 1968.

*"Modes and Manners of the Nineteenth Century,"* Dr. Oskar Fischel and Max Von Boehn — translated from the

German, J. M. Dent & Sons, Ltd., London, 1927.

FLANAGAN, Barbara, *"Women Use Hatpins to Fight Crime,"* The Minneapolis Evening Star, Minn., Minnesota, Mar. 21, 1967.

FREGNAC, Claude, *"Jewelry From the Renaissance to Art Nouveau,"* G. P. Putnam's Sons, N.Y., 1965.

GARNER, Philippe, *"The World of Edwardiana,"* The Hamlyn Publishing Group, Ltd., London, 1974.

GERNSHEIM, Alison, *"Fashion and Reality 1840-1914,"* Faber and Faber, London, 1963.

*"Godey's Lady's Book and Magazine,"* Phila., Pa., Feb. 1853, Dec. 1853, Nov. 1858, May 1860, Aug. 1874.

GORDON, Eleanor and Jean Nerenberg, *"Early Plastic Jewelry,"* The Antique Trader, Dubuque, Iowa, Nov. 26, 1974.

HAMMERTON, J. A., *"Manners and Customs of Mankind,"* Vol. Four, The Amalgamated Press, Ltd., London.

*"Harper's Bazaar,"* March 1, 1873.

HARRISON, Michael, *"The History of the Hat,"* Herbert Jenkins Ltd., London, 1960.

HARTUNG, Marion T., *"Seventh Book of Carnival Glass,"* Emporia, Kansas, 1966.

HARTUNG, Marion T., *"Eighth Book of Carnival Glass,"* Emporia, Kansas, 1968.

HEINIGER, Ernst A. and Jean, *"The Great Book of Jewels,"* New York Graphic Society, Ltd., Boston, 1974.

HERBIG, F. A., *"Das Buchlein Der Tausend Kostume,"* Germany, 1961.

HERZBERG, Max J., *"Myths and Their Meaning,"* Allyn & Bacon, Inc., 1955.

HEUSSER, Audrey E., *"The Pindustry,"* 100th Anniversary Publication, History of The Star Pin Company.

*"Hobbies,"* June 1953 issue.

HORNUNG, Clarence P., *"A Source Book of Antiques and Jewelry Designs,"* George Braziller, N.Y., 1968.

HUGHES, Bernard, *"Victorian Pottery and Porcelain,"* Spring Books, London, 1967.

HUGHES, G. B., *"Horse Brasses and Other Small Items for the Collector,"* Country Life Limited, London, 1956.

HUGHES, Graham, *"Jewelry,"* E. P. Dutton and Co., N.Y., 1966.

HUGHES, Graham, *"Modern Jewelry,"* Crown Publishers, Inc., N.Y., 1963.

HUNT, William, *"Wooden Sanders,"* Spinning Wheel, April 1970.

JAMES, Bernice, *"Pin-Cushion Dolls Win New Interest,"* (Focus on Dolls, column), American Collector, Jan. 1975.

JAMIESON, Jack, *"English Silver Identifiable,"* Toronto Star Syndicate.

*"Jewelers Circular Weekly,"* 1913.

*"Jewelry, Watches and Silverware,"* E. V. Roddin & Co., 1895 Catalogue, American Historical Catalog Collection, The Pyne Press, Princeton, 1971.

*"Journal des Modes,"* 1786.

*"Journal des Tuxus Und der Moden,"* 1784.

KANE, Joseph Nathan, *"Famous First Facts,"* The H. W. Wilson Co., N.Y., 1950.

KELLY, Francis M. and Randolph Schwabe, *"Historic Costume 1490-1790,"* B. T. Batsford Ltd., London, 1929.

KILGOUR, Ruth Edwards, *"A Pageant of Hats, Ancient and Modern,"* Robert M. McBride, Co., N.Y., 1958.

KLOBUCHAR, Jim, *"Hatpins Liberate Women,"* The Minneapolis Evening Star, Mar. 29, 1967.

KOVEL, Ralph M. and Terry H., *"Dictionary of Marks — Pottery and Porcelain,"* Crown Publishers, Inc., 1967.

KOVEL, Ralph M. and Terry H., *"Know Your Antiques,"* Crown Publishers, Inc., New York, 1967.

KOVEL, Ralph M. and Terry H., *"Know Your Antiques,"* The Register and Tribune Syndicated column.

KUNZ, George Frederick, *"The Curious Lure of Precious Stones,"* J. B. Lippincott Company, Phila., Pa., 1913.

*"Ladies Home Companion,"* June 1897, 1901, 1906.

LANGNER, Lawrence, *"The Importance of Wearing Clothes,"* Hastings House, New York.

LAVER, J., *"Costume Through the Ages,"* Simon and Schuster, 1961.

LAVER, James, *"Victoriana,"* Hawthorn Books, Inc., N.Y., 1967.

LAWSON, Tom J., *"Hatpinology,"* Antique Collecting, Vol. 9; Number 8, London, Dec. 1974.

LEHNER, Ernst, *"The Picture Book of Symbols,"* Wm. Penn Publishing Corporation, N.Y., 1956.

LELOIR, M. Maurice, *"Histoire du Costume de l'Antiquite a 1914,"* Ernst Henri, Editeur, Paris, 1934.

*"Leslie's Weekly,"* April 8, 1897 — March 11, 1897.

LESTER, K. Monies, *"Accessories of Dress,"* Manual Press, Peoria, Ill., 1940.

*"Les Bijoux par Maurice Dufrene,"* Librairie des Arts Decoratifs, Paris, (Not dated, but attributed to artist's work of early 1900's)

LIMA, Paul and Candy, *"The Enchantment of Hand Painted Nippon Porcelain,"* Silverado Studios, Ca., 1971.

LONGMAN, E. D. and S. Loch, *"Pins and Pincushions,"* Longmans, Green and Co., London, 1911.

McCANE, John, *"Match Safes and Hatpin Holders,"* Better Homes and Gardens, Nov. 1965.

McCLELLAND, Elisabeth, *"Historic Dress in America 1800-1870,"* George W. Jacobs & Co., 1910.

McCLINTON, Katharine M., *"Registry of English Marks: The Complete Book of Small Antiques Collecting,"* Coward-Coward-McCann, Inc., New York, 1965.

McCLINTON, Katharine Morrison, *"Collecting American 19th Century Silver,"* Charles Scribner's Sons, N.Y., 1968.

MARION, Frieda, *"China Half-Figures Called Pincushion Dolls,"* J. Palmer Publishers, Newburyport, Mass., 1974.

MAY, Earl, *"Century of Silver 1847-1947,"* McBride, 1947.

MEYER, Florence E., *"Pins for Hats and Cravats Worn by Ladies and Gentlemen,"* Wallace-Homestead Book Co., Des Moines, Iowa, 1974.

MEYER, Franz Sales, *"The Handbook of Ornament,"* Wilcox & Follett Co., 1945.

MORRIS, Lloyd, *"Postcript to Yesterday, America: The Last Fifty Years,"* Random House, N.Y., 1947.

MORRISON, Don, *"Hatpin Project May Be A Stab in Hubby's Back,"* The Minneapolis Evening Star, Minneapolis, Minn., March 30, 1967.

NEIMAN, Kenneth E., *"Victorian Toothbrush Holders,"* Spinning Wheel, April 1970.

NORRIS, Herbert, *"Costume and Fashion Vol. III,"* E. P. Dutton and Co., N.Y., 1938.

PATON, James, *"Pins,"* Corporation Galleries of Art, Glasgow, Scotland, 1878.

PEEL, Mrs. C. S., *"A Hundred Wonderful Years, 1820-1920,"* Dodd, Mead & Company, 1927.

POESE, Bill, *"Victorian Stickpin Holders,"* The Antique Trader, Dubuque, Iowa, Jan. 21, 1975.

RAMSEY, L. G. G., (FSA), *"The Complete Encyclopedia of Antiques,"* Hawthorn Books, Inc., N.Y., 1962.

RICKETTS, Howard, *"Antique Gold and Enamelware in Color,"* Barrie and Jenkins Ltd., 1971.

ROBBINS, Russell Hope, *"The Encyclopedia of Witchcraft and Demonology,"* Crown Publishers, Inc., N.Y., 1959.

ROGERS, Agnes, *"Women Are Here to Stay,"* Harper & Bros., N.Y., 1949.

ROSE, Augustus F. and Antonio Cirino, B.S., *"Jewelry Making and Design,"* Dover Publications, N.Y., 1967.

SALA, George Augustus, *"Paris Herself Again,"* (Vol. I and II), Remington and Co., London, 1878-9.

SATER, Joel, *"A Heap of Hatpins,"* Antiques News, Dec. 1, 1972.

SCHMUTZLER, Robert, *"Art Nouveau,"* Harry N. Abrams, Inc., N.Y., 1962.

*"Scribner's Monthly,"* Year 1878.

SEARS, ROEBUCK & CO., catalogues (1894-1913).

SEVERN, Bill, *"Here's Your Hat,"* David McKay, 1963.

SJOBERG, Jan and Ove, *"Working With Copper, Silver and Enamel,"* Van Nostrand Reinhold Company, 1974.

SMITH, Robert Paul, *"Lost and Found,"* Charterhouse, N.Y., 1973.

STEINGRABER, Erich, *"Antique Jewelry,"* Frederick A. Praeger, N.Y., 1957.

*"The Delineator,"* April 1901.

*"The Ladies' Field,"* July 1872, Apr. 9. 1904.

*"The Lady's Friend,"* July 1872, Sept. 1872.

*"The Lady's Magazine,"* July 1866.

*"The Saturday Book,"* edited by John Hadfield, Hutchinson & Co., Ltd., 1966.

THE STAR PIN COMPANY, publication, *"The Pindustry,"* Shelton, Conn.

*"The Story of Jewelry,"* Marcus Baerwald and Tom Mahoney, Abelard-Schuman, London, 1960.

THOMAS, Diane, *"Milady's Hatpins Through the Years,"* Collector's Weekly, Vol. 6, No. 272, Dec. 3, 1974.

THOMAS, Diane, *"Variety Marks Hatpin Holders,"* Collector's Weekly, Vol. 6, No. 272, Dec. 3, 1974.

THORN, C. Jordon, *"Handbook of Old Pottery and Porcelain Marks,"* Tudor Publishing Company, N.Y., 1947.

URBAN, Stanislav and Zuzana Pestova, *"Jablonec Costume Jewelry — An Historical Outline,"* Museum of Glassware and Costume Jewelry in Jablonec, Orbis, Prague, Czechoslovakia.

*"Victorian Fashions and Costumes From Harper's Bazaar: 1867-1898,"* Edited and With an Introduction by Stella Blum; Dover Publications, Inc., N.Y., 1974.

*"Vogue,"* Feb. 1908.

von BOEHN, Max, *"Modes & Manners: Ornaments,"* E. P. Dutton & Co., Inc., 1929.

WALKUP, Dr. Fairfax Proudfit, *"Dressing the Part,"* Appleton-Century-Crofts, Inc., 1950.

WARREN, Geoffrey, *"All Color Book of Art Nouveau,"* Octopus Books, London, 1972.

WEINSTEIN, Michael, *"The World of Jewel Stones,"* Sheridan House, Inc., New York, N.Y., 1958.

WILCOX, R. Turner, *"Five Centuries of American Costume,"* Charles Scribner's, New York, 1963.

WILCOX, R. Turner, *"The Mode in Hats and Headdress, Including Hair Styles, Cosmetics, and Jewelry,"* Charles Scribner's Sons, 1959.

WILLET, C. and Phillis Cunnington, *"Handbook of English Costume in the Nineteenth Century,"* Dufour Editions, Phila., 1959.

*"Woman's Home Companion,"* May 1906.

WYLER, Seymour B., *"The Book of Old Silver — English — American — Foreign,"* Crown Publishers, N.Y., 1937.

* * *

## NEWSPAPERS

DAILY PICAYUNE, New Orleans, La., (1913-1914)

LONDON DAILY MAIL (1908)

LONDON OBSERVER (1909)

LOS ANGELES HERALD-EXAMINER (1970)

THE LONDON TIMES (1913-1914)

THE LOS ANGELES TIMES (1967)

THE MINNEAPOLIS EVENING STAR (1967)

THE NEW YORK HERALD (1919)

THE NEW YORK TIMES (1913-1914; 1952, 1970)

THE PARIS MAIL (1909)

THE SHENANDOAH HERALD-ASHLAND NEWS (1969)

THE VANCOUVER SUN (Len Norris, cartoonist) 1967-1975.

THE WALL STREET JOURNAL (1969)

TOPEKA DAILY NEWSPAPER (1909)

# SOURCES AND ACKNOWLEDGEMENTS

*My thanks to scores of persons and organizations, far and wide, who were kind enough to respond in a helpful way to my letters of query:*

ALLEN, Dorothy K., President, *F. H. Noble & Co.*, Chicago, Illinois, who also made available many old catalog pages of jewelers' findings.

BERGSTRAND, Ingrid, Asst. Curator, *Nordiska Museet*, Stockholm, Sweden, who also assisted my research correspondent in Sweden, Lena Rydin.

BERTSCHINGER, C., Secretary to Miss Deborah Kerr.

BETTMANN ARCHIVES

BONTE, Mme. M., *la Bibliothecaire, Union Centrale des Arts Decoratifs, Pavillon de Marsan Palais du Louvre*, Paris, France — and for her invaluable research on my behalf.

BLIZZARD, Bruce E., Publicity/Art Dept., *MGM Studios*, Culver City, Ca.

BOVIN, Murray, author of *"Jewelry Making,"* for his helpful "lead" in response to my inquiry.

BRIGHT, John, Still Dept., *Twentieth Century-Fox Film, Corp.*, Los Angeles.

CAREY, Bernard, State's Attorney of Cook County, Illinois.

CHAMBER OF COMMERCE, North Attleboro, Mass.

COLLINS, Robert T., Asst. Head, Correspondence and Mail Branch, *U.S. Department of Commerce*, Patent Office, Wash., D.C.

CONNICK, Anita, Asst. City Attorney, Parish of Orleans, La., for her invaluable assistance in researching the "hatpin war" in New Orleans.

de JONG, Miss M. C., *Kostuummuseum* (Museum of Costumes), *The Hague*, Netherlands.

DELIDA, Marjorie, Librarian-in-Charge, *Gardena Public Library*, Gardena, Ca.

DRAGOUN, K. *JABLONEX* Publicity Dept. 503, Jablonec n. Nis., Czech.

DWYER, Francis X., Associate Law Librarian, *The Library of Congress*, Wash., D.C.

EASTHOPE, W. R. A., Editor of the TIMES Archives, *TIMES Newspapers Ltd.*, Printing House Square, London.

FERREIRA, Maria Teresa Gomes, Chief Curator, (Gulbenkian Foundation), *Funda, cão Calouste Gulbenkian Servico de Museu*, Portugal.

FRANKOVICH, Geo. R., Executive Director, *Manufacturing Jewelers and Silversmiths of America, Inc.*

FRY, Mary Isabel, Reference Librarian, *Henry E. Huntington Library and Art Gallery*, San Marino, Ca. — for her "extra" service in accommodating me by mail and telephone, thus saving long trips.

GETMAN, Mrs. E. G., who not only made photographs available, but supplied information "in depth" regarding specific items.

GIARRUSSO, Jos. I., Supt. of Police (1968), New Orleans, La.

GLAZE, Miss Mary, Associate Curator, American Wing, *The Metropolitan Museum of Art*, New York.

GREENE, Ruth R., Asst. Curator, *North Attleboro Historical Society*, N. Attelboro, Mass.

HAGER, John, (*Picwic Bookshop, Dei Amo Branch*) for his cooperation.

HANISCH, Otto C., Pres., *Geo. H. Fuller & Son Co.*, Providence, R.I., for his correspondence which included an addition to my collection.

HARPER, William E., Mgr., Industrial Services Dept., *The Greater Providence Chamber of Commerce*, Providence, R.I.

HARRAH, Scherry, *Harrah's Automobile Museum*, Reno, Nevada, for her faith in the need for such a project, and the photographs which she made available for the book.

HARTUNG, Marion T., authority on Carnival Glass, who took time from her own work to answer several queries.

HEPBURN, Jean J., Hanover, Mass., for her helpful correspondence.

HOFER, M., JABLONEX, Publicity Dept. 503, *Jablonec n. Nis. Czech.*

*HOGAN, Ed, Publicity Director, Minneapolis Chamber of Commerce*, Minneapolis, Minn., who supplied information and a sample of the manufactured "weapon" for Minneapolis' fight against crime.

HUGHES, Graham, Goldsmith's Hall, London, E.C. 2.

JAGODA, Robert E., Program Manager, Advertising Services, IBM (International Business Machines), Armonk, N.Y., who provided the photographs from *"Love Among The Ruins."*

IRBY, Charles C., Jr. Asst. Curator, *The University of Texas*, for researching available Photographs from the archives.

JACK I. ELLERSTEIN CO., 37 West 39th St., New York 18, N.Y.

KATZ, Stephen R., Citizens' Aid Bureau, *The Commonwealth of Mass.*, Dept. of the Attorney General, for information on hatpin laws.

KOMBEREC, J., Czech., for his many letters and assistance in contacting persons who would be able to answer specific queries.

KOUGASIAN, Peter, *Brown & Mills Corp.*, Providence, R.I.

KOZAN, Adele, Archives, *Sears, Roebuck and Co.*, Skokie, Ill., for her research on my behalf.

LAND, Robert H., Chief, Reference Dept., *The Library of Congress*, Washington, D.C.

LANDERS, Ann, Syndicated Columnist.

LAVER, James, of England, for his helpful correspondence.

LARSEN, Robert V., Columbus, Nebraska, who willingly supplied text and photographs of his collection for incorporation in the book.

LASSEN, Erik, *Museum of Decorative Art*, Copenhagen, Denmark, who arranged for photographing the fabulous R. Lalique hatpin.

LAWSON, Tom J., of London, for invaluable research and assistance.

McNEIL, Donald S., Editor, *Jeweler's Circular-Keystone*, Phila., Pa.

MANUFACTURING JEWELERS & SILVERSMITHS OF AMERICA, INC., Providence, R.I.

MARTIN, Elizabeth C., Librarian, *The Danbury Library*, Danbury, Conn., who not only supplied research material but shared her personal "hatpin experiences."

MATERNOVA, Vera, Curator, *The Museum of Glass and Jewelry*, Jablonec nad Nisou, Czech., for her extraordinarily detailed letters.

MERMOD, JACCARD & KING JEWELRY CO., St. Louis, Mo., 1916 Catalogue.

MESSELL, Oliver, noted costume designer.

MILLIS, R. W., Mgr. Magazine Division, *Syndication International IPC, (Group Management) Ltd.*, London WC2.

MOORE, Doris Langley, *Museum of Costume*, Bath, England.

*MUZEUM SKLA a bizuterie*, JABLONEC NAD NISOU.

PHILLIPS, Mrs. Donald K., Chairman, *Attleboro Historical Commission*, Attleboro, Mass.

PORTER, Harold H., President, *The Star Pin Company*, Shelton, Conn., for his personal letters and assistance.

REFERENCE DESK, *Hawthorne Public Library*, Hawthorne, Calif., for the wonderful telephone assistance.

ROSEN, Myer, News Bureau, *Los Angeles Times*.

SEKULICH PRODUCTIONS, INC., for the courtesy of Press Passes to research in their sponsored antique shows in So. California.

THE MINNEAPOLIS EVENING STAR, Robert C. King, editor, for making available those marvelous stories of the "fight against crime."

THE NATIONAL HISTORICAL SOCIETY, Gettysburg, Pa., for the discourse on "How China Came to Paris" — one of the many advantages to membership in preserving our historic sites.

THE UNIVERSITY OF TEXAS AT AUSTIN, Humanities Research Center.

TINGLE, R. H., Product Mgr., *Scovill* (Oakville Division) Conn.

VICTORIA & ALBERT MUSEUM, South Kensington, London., for photographing their collection for my book.

YOUNGSTROM, Elizabeth, *Charles Scribner's Sons, Inc.*, for her reference work.

*To the following persons my heartfelt thanks for the personal contact (or via telephone), who enriched my experience and my book:*

BARLOW, Miss Genevieve, friend and author who listened to the first reading of the completed manuscript — and with her 25 years teaching seniority — "passed" me with good grades.

BERGMAN, William, Managing Editor, *"Yesteryear"* Magazine, Manhattan Beach, Calif., who hired me on as "antiques editor," and made available photographs from my first column on collecting.

BUNTEN, Donna, Library-aide, West Gardena Branch Library, Los Angeles County Public Library, who never frowned at a request.

BUTRUM, Beverly, *"One-of-a-Kind"* Shop, Disneyland, Calif.

CASTRO, George, Gardena, for his help and photography.

DREW, Walter R., Editor, *Antique Motor News*, Long Beach, Ca., who put me in contact with his Woman's Editor, Milly Orcutt.

FERRELL, Charlie, photographer, *Gardena Valley News*, for his service.

FRANK, Vera, gemmologist and gem expert, who gave of her precious time and talent to evaluate and separate gems from glass and thus help me correctly classify the hatpin heads photographed for this book.

FRICK, Mrs. Robert O., Pittsford, Vermont, who became a pen-pal over a period of years; a former editor, she continued to urge me on with my project, insisting success would come providing I continued to market the manuscript. Her words did wonders!

FROST, Richard I., Curator, *Buffalo Bill Cody Museum*, Cody, Wyoming, — big as the West itself in form and spirit — who was typical of "Western" hospitality during my visit to one of the finest museums in our country. He was instrumental in introducing me to a couple who collected nothing but "the real McCoy" in hatpin heads — unfortunately, the photographs were ruined.

GINNY of GINNY'S ANTIQUES ET CETERA, Gardena, Ca., — who put on that happy face even at my most preposterous requests, such as carrying away fragile porcelains for photographing (along with books from her personal archives). Happily for all concerned, no misfortunes! Her enthusiasm for my project was a shot in the arm — when I needed it most!

GOLDEN, John F., President, *Western Costume Co.*, Hollywood, Cal., who listened patiently as I explained my project and then made available the depleted collection of "original" hatpins from the vast costume departments of this world-famous house.

GOTTLOBER, Helen, former Librarian-in-Charge, West Gardena Branch, Los Angeles Public Library.

HARRISON, Nat, owner of *Dena Jewelers*, Gardena, for his able assistance in locating information on jewelry findings, manufacture, etc., making available private catalogs, and patient help in identifying specific mountings, settings, and technical terms.

HELLER, Sybel, for allowing me to photograph her extensive collection, and willingly preparing, delivering, and then picking up the hatpins — saving me such valuable time and effort.

HENDERSON, Bill, *Western Costume Co.*, 5335 Melrose, Hollywood, Ca., for his cooperation.

HENDRIX, Susan, who acted as my "scout" and "informant" — (as did others to a lesser degree) — and gave such continued encouragement.

HUSFLOEN, Kyle, Editor, *"Antique Trader Weekly,"* Dubuque, Iowa, who found my first articles based on my manuscript, publishable.

JONES, William, Director — Costume and Textire Dept. *Ahmanson Museum*, Los Angeles, for the use of the research library, and for providing the museum's collection of hatpins for illustration purposes.

KATZIN, Dr. Leon A., DDS, and the late Beatrice Katzin who left me a legacy of facts and a few artifacts for my collection.

McCURDY, Virginia — just for being herself when I needed her.

MAHLMOOD, Diane of Maryland who came for a visit, caught my "fever" and is now well into collecting! A novice collector when first we met, her collection has grown into quite an acquisition of silver hatpins, some of which she shipped for photographic purposes.

MARSHALL, Renee of Manhattan Beach, Ca., who even during the "gas crisis," drove back and forth for weeks on end to help with the technical clerical work involved in the price guide. Renee worked with persistence and endless patience — without complaint, with constant and consistent good humor, and all-out warm friendship. I'm in her debt for her devotion to tedious work and to my own accomplishment.

MOORE, Mr. and Mrs. R. T., Escondido, Ca. — for assistance in pricing, among many other things.

ORCUTT, Milly, Woman's Editor, *Antique Motor News*, for use of material from her personal archives — and for her encouraging letters.

RABBY, Otto, Manager, Merchandise Division, *Disneyland*, Anaheim, Ca., for his encouragement and help. Any person who knows Mr. Rabby would realize how warm his response to the needs of a writer.

REYHILL, S. W., owner, *Studio Art Metal Shop*, 5335 Melrose, Hollywood, who, with his wife, spared much time in explaining the process of electroplating, and allowed me to see his own project which was the manufacture of "jewels for the movie industry," including a hatpin for star, Julie Andrews, in "Darling Lili." Their personal collection of hatpins was made available for illustration.

ROBERTSON, Iola, *"One-of-a-Kind"* Shop, Disneyland, Calif.

ROTH, Joyce, who not only made available her private collection of hatpins and holders, but assisted in numerous other ways such as scouting antique shows and shops for current price information, buying trends, etc. In addition, Joyce helped in proofreading, and never lost faith in the ten-year project. All this, and friendship, too.

RYDIN, Lena of Sweden, who was my main research correspondent in London.

SAUNDERS, Bobbe, Library-Aide, *West Gardena Branch*, Los Angeles County Public Library, who aided so much and for so long!

SCHAEFFER, Debbie, Page, *West Gardena Branch*, Los Angeles County Public Library, who insisted on helping beyond the call of duty by delivering and picking up books enroute.

SCHROEDER, Bill and Meredith of COLLECTOR BOOKS, without whom this book would not be in print. And a special thanks for the "blind" confidence they placed in my "package" which they contracted for sight-unseen. A warm relationship began via telephone and letters, and for my part they have made a dream come true for me. It's my hope they shall find their just rewards, too.

SHWARTZ, Martin, Press Representative, Los Angeles Civic Light Opera., for his work on my behalf.

SKIPSEY, Eric, photographer, who expedited needed material.

SMYTHERS, Lois, former Library-Aide, *West Gardena Branch*, Los Angeles County Public Library, who pulled books from the aisle-cases I'd never have known about.

STAMBOOK, R. E., photographer whose conscientious efforts in photographing such a unique subject, were met with unstinting faith and good humor. He met every challenge — and demand — with a smile and a shrug, and then produced such fantastic results! He saved this author hours of exhaustive time and labor — and when recovering from illness, he became errand boy, so to speak. His cooperation is something to write home about!

TAM'S STATIONERS, Crenshaw and 156th St., Gardena, whose staff simply went all-out to serve: Margaret Saltus, Manager, Delores DeMarti, and Pat Fellows. If the Xerox-machine had a voice, it would sigh with relief at a project completed at last!

THE CHIMNEY SWEEP ANTIQUES SHOP in Solvang, Ca., whose owners responded so cordially to my requests.

THE NATIONAL TRUST FOR HISTORIC PRESERVATION, Wash., D.C.

WALKUP, Dr. Fairfax Proudfit, for the continuous use of her extensive personal library and archives, and for her most gracious addition to my book — the PRE-

FACE. To know her is to love her.

WARFIELD, Polly, Former Editor, *Gardena Valley News,* who for a full decade allowed me to sit at her elbow and learn the art of "blue-pencelling" while she edited my weekly columns and various other newspaper endeavors. In addition, she continually encouraged me with her persistent faith in the value of my writings. Above all, she has been a tried-and-true friend.

WIND BELLS COTTAGE ANTIQUES, and the "purple lady," Delma Peery, who gave encouragement and assistance all along the way.

YOUNG, J. Belle, friend and former librarian, who assisted in the proofreading. Her constant friendship and loyalty is valued by the author.

And thanks to the many collectors of hatpins who urged me to complete my project; to the many antique shop-keepers and "little old ladies" who stopped to chat and contributed bits-and-pieces that eventually fit so beautifully into the overall thesis of this hatpin history.

A very special thanks to Barbara Stewart, Taylor Publishing Company, Dallas, Texas, for understanding so beautifully the concept of this book, and for accomplishing the artistic layout, type and final composition of the end product.

* * *

My apologies to those whose photographs could not be used because of technical reasons. I do thank them for their time and effort on my behalf, and for the great words of encouragement. Writers do need that. When John Donne, the poet, wrote: "No man is an island, entire of itself . . ." he must have been referring to us — writers who depend so much on the assistance of others!

A final note: Writers should not edit their own work except under extraordinary circumstances which demands it. This *first comprehensive study of the subject* made such demands, and so the editing of this encyclopedia is solely the work and responsibility of the author — for better or worse.

# REFERENCE NOTES

TITLE

*Vol. IV, 15th Edition, 1975 Encyclopedia Brittannica,* Encyclopedia Publishing Co., Chicago, Ill.

*"MS" Magazine,* (Sept. 1972), "MS" Magazine Corp., N.Y.

*"Gone With the Wind,"* Margaret Mitchell, The Macmillan Company, 1936.

*"Aurora Leigh, Book VIII,"* Elizabeth Barrett Browning, Crowell Publishing, 1900.

*"Love Among the Ruins,"* ABC Theatre, Allan Davis, Producer.

*"Merry Widow,"* Franz Lehar, 1909.

*"Easter Bonnets of Yesteryear,"* Clarence T. Hubbard, The Western Collector, April 1968.

*"Partners in Crime — The Sunningdale Mystery,"* Dame Agatha Christie, Dodd-Mead & Co., 1929.

*"Belle of the Nineties,"* Paramount Pictures, 1934.

*"Extended Travels in Romantic America,"* Charles Dickens' notes, published by Edita, Lausanne, Switzerland.

*"The Man in Tower Ten,"* Mary Roberts Rinehart, Dell Publishing Co., Oct. 1969.

*"By Aid of the Stenographer,"* Edwin L. Sabin, "Ladies Home Companion," (Oct. 1901).

*"Roses From the South,"* Perceval Reniers, Doubleday & Co., Inc.

*"Upstairs, Downstairs,"* Masterpiece Theatre, PBS, Rex Firkin, Exec. Producer, John Hawkesworth, Producer.

*"The Men of the Alamo,"* (Poems of American History), published by Riverside Press, Cambridge, Mass.

*"A Prologue to Love,"* Taylor Caldwell, Bantam, 1973.

*"Strike Terror,"* Hy Steirman, Paperback Library, Inc., N.Y. 1968.

*"Darling Lili,"* Blake Edwards Production, 1970.

*"Death in Venice,"* Luchino Visconti film, 1971.

*"The Twenty-Seventh Wife,"* Irving Wallace, Simon and Schuster, Inc., N.Y. 1962.

*"Innocent in Alaska,"* John Springer, Coward-McCann, Inc., N.Y.

*"Witchcraft: Its Power in the World Today,"* Harcourt, Brace and Company, N.Y., 1940.

*"No Star Is Lost,"* James T. Farrell, Vanguard Press, Popular Library, 1938.

*"Gypsy,"* Arthur Laurents/Jule Styne/Stephen Sondheim; Theatre-Guild-American Theatre Society, Schubert Production, Los Angeles, 1974.

*"Three Sisters,"* A. Chekov; Center Theatre Group presentation, Los Angeles, 1973.

*"The Day After the Fair,"* Frank Harvey; Schubert Los Angeles, Sept. 1973 production.

*"The Streets of San Francisco,"* ABC, Quinn Martin, Exec. Producer; John Wilder, Producer.

*"The Hallelujah Trail,"* J. Sturges, Director/Producer, United Artists, 1965.

*"Gillian,"* Frank Yerby, Dell Publications, 1972.

*"The Good Old Days,"* David L. Cohn, Simon and Schuster, N.Y., 1940.

*"A Long Row of Candles,"* C. L. Sulzberger, Macmillan Company, N.Y., 1969.

*"The Year of the Horse,"* Eric Hatch, Crown Publishers, Inc., N.Y., 1965.

J. M. Barrie, author *"Peter Pan," "Little Minister,"* etc.

*"Gigi,"* Lerner and Lowe, The L. A. Civic Light Opera Association Production, Dorothy Chandler Pavilion, July 1973.

*"The Sin Mark,"* Margaret Page Hood, Coward-McCann, Inc., N.Y.

*"Soda Pop,"* Lawrence Dietz, Simon & Schuster, 1973.

*"Truly Emily Post,"* Edwin Post, Funk & Wagnalls Co., 1961.

*"George,"* Emlyn Williams, Random House, 1961.

*"Jennie,"* Ralph G. Martin, Prentice-Hall, Inc., Englewood, N.J.

*"America,"* Alistair Cooke; KCET 1974 series; PBS, Michael Gill, Producer.

*"Our Times 1909-1914,"* Mark Sullivan, Charles Scribner's Sons, New York, 1932.

*"Saratoga, Saga of an Impious Era,"* George Waller, Prentice-Hall, Inc., Englewood Cliffs, N.J., 1966.

*"The Big Spenders,"* Lucius Beebe, Doubleday & Co., Inc., 1966.

*"The Prince and the Lily,"* James Brough, Coward-McCann, N.Y., 1975.

*"The Trembling Hills,"* Phyllis A. Whitney, Ace Books, Inc., N.Y.

*"Dr. Zhivago,"* Carlo Ponti, Producer; David Lean, Director; MGM (1965).

*"Arsenic and Old Lace,"* Joseph Kesserling, Washington Square Press, N.Y.

*"The Fire and the Gold,"* Phyllis A. Whitney, Ace Books, Inc., N.Y.

*"Kitty,"* actress Amanda Blake in *"Gunsmoke,"* CBS; Exec. Producer, John Natley.

*"Gunsmoke,"* CBS, Exec. Producer, John Nantley.

*"What's My Line,"* TV Syndicated ½ hour; Goodson-Todman Productions.

*"Social Etiquette,"* Maud C. Cooke, J. R. Jones, Publisher, 1896.

# NOTES (Appendix)

*ALL COLOR PLATES WERE PHOTOGRAPHED BY R. E. STAMBOOK EXCEPT PLATES 160, 163, 179, 180, 182, 187, 189, 197, and 198.*

\* \* \*

*All Hatpins, Hatpin Holders, Accessories, and Artifacts are from the author's collection except:*

## COLLECTIONS FROM MUSEUMS AND SHOPS

AHMANSON MUSEUM, *Plate 168.*
CHARLES HORNER LTD., MUSEUM, *Plate 196.*
DISNEYLAND, "ONE-OF-A-KIND" SHOP, *Plate 197.*
GINNY'S ANTIQUES ET CETERA, *Plates 56 and 74.*
HARRAH'S MUSEUM, *Plate 164.*
KUNDSTINDUSTRIMUSEET, *Plate 167.*
STUDIO ART METAL SHOP, *Plate 177.*
THE CHIMNEY SWEEP ANTIQUES, *Plate 68.*
VICTORIA & ALBERT MUSEUM, *Plate 176.*
WESTERN COSTUME COMPANY, *Plates 172 and 178.*
WIND BELLS COTTAGE ANTIQUES, *Plates 17, 59, and 93.*

## *PRIVATE COLLECTIONS*

LOUISE ALEXANDER, *Plate 205.*
IRENE DUTKO, *Plate 64.*
MRS. E. G. GETMAN, *Plates 180 and 187.*
SHERRY GOLDWASSER, *Plates 206 and 207.*
SYBEL HELLER, *Plates 49, 63, 65, 66, 69, 71, 73, 76, 81, 82, 87, 193, 195.*
SUSAN HENDRIX, *Plate 59.*
DR. L. A. KATZIN, DDS and the late BEATRICE KATZIN, *Plate 203.*
RAY AND MAY KNOTT, *Plate 205.*
ROBERT V. LARSEN, *Plate 182.*
**TOM J. LAWSON,** *Plates 166, 215, and 216.*
MRS. G. W. McCURDY, *Plate 54.*
JO McFARLIN, *Plates 205, 206, and 207.*
DIANE MAHLMOOD, *Plates 5, 62, and 179.*
SALLY MARGOLIS, *Plate 208.*
RENEE MARSHALL, *Plates 9, 52, 53, 56, 115, 119, 178, 194, 195, and 196.*
JOYCE ROTH, *Plates 5, 42, 48, 49, 55, 61, 69, 70, 72, 73, 75, 77, 78, 79, 80, 83, 84, 85, 86, 88, 89, 94, 119, 193, 194, 195, and 196.*
DR. F. P. WALKUP, *Plate 31.*

# PLATES

**PLATE 1,** *page 105*

*l-r* — 6″ white pin w/ 2″ x 1½″ oriental ceramic transfer portrait w/hand-painted accents.

7¾″ white pin w/ 1¾″ transfer portrait highlighted w/gold accents. Celluloid w/ chased oxidized silver rim.

**PLATE 2,** *page 105*

8″ white pin w/ sterling life-size Hummingbird. 4½″ beak-to-tailfeathers w/ 2¼″ wingspread. Bird accented w/ 2 stone eyes and 8 brilliants.

**PLATE 3,** *page 105*

*Top Row, l-r* — 7″ gilt pin w/ 1¾″ chased figural butterfly with brilliant accents. Mounted w/ 1½″ "nodder."

5½″ gilt pin w/ ¾″ pierced and engraved gilt cage w/ five green brilliant accents mounted w/ ¾″ "nodder."

6″ gilt pin w/ 1¼″ ball and spring mounting. Figural American Eagle w/ 2″ wingspread and 9 brilliant accents and green color eyes.

*Bottom Row, l-r* — 5½″ gilt pin with 1″ "nodder" and ¾″ diameter pierced mounting w/ multi-color accents and ¼″ ruby color center stone.

5¾″ gilt pin w/ ¾″ ball and spring w/ ⅝″ claw mounted green stone.

4″ white pin w/ 1½″ spring and 1¾″ filigree figural butterfly.

3½″ gilt pin w/ ¾″ unusually heavy gilt spring w/ ¾″ chased and engraved *art nouveau* mounting w/ brilliant accents.

3½″ gilt pin w/ 1¾″ spring w ¾″ chased gilt mounting w/ claw-set ½″ cabochon-cut blue stone.

**PLATE 4,** *page 105*

*Top Row, l-r* — 8½″ gilt pin w/ 1¾″ gilt framed molded Cameo.

7¼″ gilt pin w/ 1¾″ *Art Nouveau* gilt frame, w/ turquoise color beads. ¾″ molded cameo set on "Wedgewood" blue glass.

*Bottom Row, l-r* — Pair, 8″ brass pins, w/ 1″ gilt simple frame, w/ 1⅛″ emerald color glass background for male and female ⅝″ molded Cameos.

Note typical wreaths of laurel and flowers adorning hair.

**PLATE 5,** *page 105*

*l-r* — 7½″ pin w/ 1½″ figural baby in high-button shoes and pinafore. Marked "925 Fine Sterling," plus hallmarks. Collection of Joyce Roth.

**PLATE 5,** *continued:*

9″ pin w/ 2″ sterling figural monkey on a hinge w/ garnet eyes. (Rear side shown to exhibit hinged pin.) Collection of Diane Mahlmood.

9½″ white pin w/ 1″ diameter highly polished onyx gemstone in illusion-type setting to enhance size of gemstone. Sterling silver mounting engraved with monogram.

8″ gilt pin w/ ¾″ x 1¼″ engraved gilt full figural symbolic cross.

7¾″ white pin w/ 1¾″ tall figural crowned Madonna and Child. Four joint pieces: front and back chased *repoussé* figures joined with an inserted 1″ tooled intaglio halo. Symbolic figural mounted on pin inserted into a ¼″ gilt unmarked base.

**PLATE 6,** *page 105*

*l-r* — 10½″ brass pin w/ 1⅛″ painted rooster, typical of copies of famous R. Lalique motif. Stone accent and ruby color eye.

4½″ gold pin w/ ¾″ 14K Florentine finish Fox full figural head w/diamond eyes.

8″ gilt pin w/ 1″ gold color full figural Tiger head w/ stone accent and ruby color eyes.

**PLATE 7,** *page 106*

Pair 6½″ gilt pins w/ 1″ brass figural Bees, *Art Nouveau* rendering.

Center pin is 5½″ gilt, figural chased Dragonfly w/ 2¼″ body w/ 2½″ wingspan, *Art Nouveau* design.

Pair of Bees have *sharp* points so as not to damage hat. *Abel Morrall Co.*, manufacturers of pins at Redditch, England, offered (Patent No. 1679), "Bayonet Pointed" hatpins as advertised in their early-nineteenth-hundreds catalogues.

"No more spoilt Millinery," they promised! *Morrall* pins ". . . penetrates easily, gives a firm hold and when withdrawn, leaves no unsightly holes."

Dragonfly pin is a *hair ornament* with a heavy gauge shank and dull point for piercing mohair or cotton batting which was worn to bolster-up hairstyle. The dull point could be used without endangering scalp.

(Compare difference in gauge wire between Bees and Dragonfly pins.)

**PLATE 8,** *page 106*

Carnival hatpins, unlike the glass button, have a "sleeve" which is part of the mold and specifically made to insert the long pin. Some Carnival Glass heads are domed or saucer-shaped or figural, and range in size from 1″-2½″ in diameter.

**PLATE 8,** *continued:*

According to Carnival Glass specialist and authority, Marion T. Hartung: *". . . a study of the jewelry sections of both wholesale and mail order catalogues from 1898 to 1916, it would appear that the Hat Pin vogue was at its height at approximately the same time that Carnival Glass was so much in demand." (Seventh Book of Carnival Glass)*

*Top Row, l-r* — 10¾″ steel pin w/ 1¼″ irridescent black Carnival molded figural Phoenix bird which is the Egyptian sign of immortality.

9⅛″ steel pin w/ 1¾″ oval black irridescent Carnival molded figural Dragonfly.

*Middle Row, l-r* — 8¾″ steel pin w/ 1⅜″ cobalt hobnail pressed glass head.

7⅛″ brass *spiral* pin w/ 1⅜″ purple Carnival grape pattern.

11⅝″ brass pin w/ 1⅝″ highly irridescent cobalt Carnival. Full-figural Scarab, the Egyptian symbal of longevity. (This "Beetle Hat Pin" is described in Hartung's 1966 *"Seventh Book of Carnival Glass"* as *". . . well molded, and on deep purple base glass. The dots are well raised and in parallel lines along the back. This is a light-weight piece, since it is hollow and is fitted with a tiny metal collar to hold the hat pin."*

*Bottom Row, l-r* — 8⅝″ steel pin w/ 1⅜″ pastel Carnival glass Gallic Cock, the French sign for courage.

9⅝″ steel pin w/ 1⅜″ pastel Carnival glass ornament.

5¾″ steel pin w/ 1⅜″ cobalt pattern glass. Bee in honeycomb.

8½″ steel pin w/ 1⅜″ molded green pattern glass. Bee in honeycomb.

7⅛″ steel pin w/ 1⅛″ purple Carnival Glass grape pattern.

8¼″ steel pin w/ 1⅛″ green Carnival Glass grape pattern.

**PLATE 9,** *page 106*

Photo by R. E. Stambook, Hatpins from PC Renee Marshall

Pairs of hatpins: Three pincushion dolls, *l-r* — Child half-doll in heavily beaded skirt. Pairs of pins: gold karat balls; claw-set pearls, rhinestone studded; gold sceptor heads; coronets; bezel-set gemstones; art nouveau silver; hand-made wire pins (circa 1835-40) w/ gold heads; gold chased box-shaped heads; chased gilt w/ bagette cut green stones, and lastly a pair red marbelize art glass in gilt illusion setting.

Center large porcelain pincushion doll in *moire* taffeta skirt w/ beaded waist. Exquisitely detailed hair and arms extended from body. Pairs of pins: oxidized silver chased mounting w/ multiple-faceted crystals; polished abalone, filigree mounted w/ rhinestone accents; highly polished mother-of-pearl; ¾″ round crystal balls; polished abalone; pear-shaped pears w/ rhinestones, and two large 1¼ hollow pearl dangle hatpins.

Two-piece pincushion doll consisting of torso and legs with ruffled lace skirts on silk cushion. Arms away from body. Pairs of pins: 1¼″ amethyst; pair of jet; brilliant-cut topaz; 4″ pierced imitation amber; 1 pr. twisted French Ivory plastic; button shape polished abalone in sterling; and a pair of 1½″ balls covered with sequins and beads.

Many pincushion dolls and novelty pin cushions were advertised in Sears' *Spring 1911* catalogue at 9¢ each.

**PLATE 10,** *page 106*

Photo by R. E. Stambook, Author's Collection

This is the *". . . four-inch hatpin, embossed with the Chamber Seal in attractive maroon and gold, I can protect my future, my life, and my sacred honor."* (From the 1968 story appearing in the *"Minneapolis Star"*)

**PLATE 11,** *page 106*

Photo by R. E. Stambook, Author's Collection

Black plastic hatpin carry-case. 7″ long x 1⅜″ round cylinder. 1″ x 2½″ mounted silver escutcheon embossed w/ inscription "Hat Pins".

Black leather travel-case for "Hat Pins". 4″ wide x 10″ long (closed); 14½″ (open); w/ 2 snap fasteners, fine felt lining, embossed on leather inside: "Brentanos-Paris-Importe".

Decorative Protective "Nibs" or interchangeable Hatpin ornaments: *l-r* — 2″ overall Baroque w/ ¾″ ball w/ four ¼″ ruby-color glass accents. Marked: "Pat. Mar. 1912".

1½″ overall w/ filigree pierced mounting w/ two ⅜″ emerald-color stones marked "Pat. Mar. 1912".

2¾″ overall Art Nouveau design, w/ one ⅜″ amethyst stone set in 2″ long pierced ornament. Marked: "Pat. Mar. 1912".

**PLATE 12,** *page 107*

Photo by R. E. Stambook, Author's Collection

*"China Half-Figures Called Pincushion Dolls"* by Frieda Marion, (J. Palmer Publishers, Newburyport, Mass. 1974), is an authoritative and informative book on the subject.

Mrs. Marion states that interest in these half-dolls and pincushions "has grown and prices have risen correspondingly."

*Top Row, l-r* — 4½″ tall porcelain flapper w/ sew-holes. Marked "4526 Germany". Possibly Dressel and Kister porcelain. The Flapper period was from 1925-29.

2¼″ high, carnival dressed little porcelain girl w/ mask. Sew-holes; marked "4950 Germany w/ "19" in black on inside glaze.

1⅜″ high, Pierrott, marked porcelain: "1413 Germany," 4″ tall, woman in feathered Gainsborough Hat, marked "23868". Red mark inside, possibly circa 1900.

*Bottom Row, l-r* — 2″ bathing beauty porcelain Flapper on 2″ pincushion. Sew-holes. Shown with 2″ cape pins. Pins have spiral safety pin, gold ball with embossed gold relief work w/ 12″ chain. Unmarked.

3″ pincushion doll w/ rose in hair, marked "16931 Germany", arms attached against body. Sew-holes.

3½″ long pincushion doll, porcelain Flapper dressed in black and white Pierrette fashion w/ yellow fan and shoes; marked "5987 Germany", signed on bottom, "Mary L. Campbell". Hatpins: 2½″ gold carat with genuine coral setting; 3½″ gold carat pin with diamond; 3½″ gold carat pin w/ dull onyx, faceted crystal and genuine pearl. Carnival figures, Pierrott and Pierrett, had wide ruff around neck and skull cap. *"Half-dolls were fashioned to please, to amuse, to distract and to titillate . . . surely not completely unworthy aims."* — Frieda Marion.

3½″ Madame Pompadour pincushion doll. Bisque. Unmarked.

2¼″ child pincushion doll, no sew-holes. "Most half-dolls had sew-holes but others had recessed portions just above base which fitted into the particular puff-box cover, small lamp base, and the like and was secured in place by drawstrings or heavy glue." — Frieda Marion. This charming child-doll is unmarked bisque — probably German.

Other half-dolls are pictured on *Plate 15* and an extraordinary example on *Plate 195.*

**PLATE 13,** *page 107*

Photo by R. E. Stambook, Author's Collection

Dresser Set: Hand-painted scenic oriental dresser set marked "Hand-painted, Nippon".

7½″ x 10¾″ oval tray; 3″ x 4″ oval covered trinket box w/ 1½″ tripod legs; 3″ x 4″ hair receiver and 4¾″ tall open-mouthed hatpin holder.

**PLATE 14,** *page 107*

Photo by R. E. Stambook, Author's Collection

Three piece unmarked oriental dresser set ornately hand-painted with heavy gold overlay.

7¾″ x 11⅞″ oval tray (repaired); 4½″ round covered hair-receiver and 4¾″ tall hatpin holder with solid base.

**PLATE 15,** *page 107*

Photo by R. E. Stambook, Author's Collection

l-r — 5″ x 11″ oblong pincushion covered w/ handmade ribbon silk flowers. (Shortest pins are cloth-covered pairs under 3″; taller pins are of a common variety worn during the twenties and thirties, and to the present time by our senior citizens, many of whom refuse to discard head-coverings when out in public.)

3¼″ heart-shaped pincushion of French Ivory, velvet covered 3″ hatpins have glass heads and are of common variety.

3⅝″ round French Ivory base covered w/ green silk and an overlay of crochet cotton. One pair of 2½″ handmade wire pins (Circa 1825) and three 5″ steel pins w/ Venetian glass beads. Note difference between thin gauge of *handmade* wire and *manufactured* shanks.

**PLATE 16,** *page 107*

Photo by R. E. Stambook, Author's Collection

Beaded Pincushions: *Top Row, l-r* — 8″ x 10″ beaded bird design w/ hanger, w/ 1″ beaded looped fringe.

5″ x 9″ beaded boot w/ hanger, w/ 2″ beaded tassels. Hatpins: 5¾″ steel pin w/ 2½″ lacquered straw head. 5″ steel pin w/ 2″ straw head.

11″ diameter beaded star w/ beaded crossed-flag motif.

*Hatpins in Foreground, l-r* — 1 pair 4½″ white pins w/ 2½″ two-color beaded heads.

12″ white pin (closest to ruler) w/ 1¾″ round multi-color hand-beaded design on silk cloth w/ metal frame. (For detail of head, see Plate 194).

10¼″ steel pin w/ 3″ purple irridescent glass beaded head.

7″ white pin w/ 1½″ purple irridescent glass beaded head.

4″ white pin w/ 2¾″ multi-color beaded head.

4″ white pin w/ 1″ jet beaded head set on patch-type metal mounting, w/ 12 rhinestones and screw-type "nib".

Stanley L. Baker's article, *"Beaded Indian Whimsies"*, (*The Antique Trader*, June 3, 1975), reports that the Museum of the American Indian in New York City, features beadwork as shown on this *Plate.*

The Mohawk Indians in Canada and the Tuscarora and Mohegan Indians tenting near the Niagara Falls and nearby Saratoga Springs, made such souvenir items for the tourist trade from 1890-1910 — *at the height of the hatpin era!*

**PLATE 16,** *continued:*

The article also clues us as to how to distinguish the parlor-work of the Victorian lady from Indian-craft. The Victorian damsel used sewing scraps such as velvet, satin, and silks; the Indian workers used a specially made cotton cambric in flesh pink or red color.

The pincushions shown on this *Plate* are all backed with that shiny fabric, with the exception of the velvet cushion designed with the patriotic flag-motif.

**PLATE 17,** *page 107*

Photo by R. E. Stambook, Author's Collection

Assorted Hairpins, Hatpins, and Corsage Pins with an *open-mouth* Holder.

*Top Left* — "Woman's Friend" hairpin box, silver-plate, marked: "Pairpoint Mfg. Co., New Bedford, Mass." Dated: "Aug. 22, 1893" Size, 2½″ x 4¾″. Author's Collection.

*Bottom, l-r* — 3″ hairpin w/ pearl tip. Author's Collection

2¼″ three-pronged Chinese hairpin. Sterling w/ gold wash over flowers and birds. Center bud has small ball inside that rattles. Collection of Delma Peery, Wind Bells Cottage Antiques, Hermosa Beach, CA.

5″ *spiral* heavy gauge hairpin w/ ivory dangle. Author's Collection.

3½″ double-pronged hat ornament on "nodder", w/ Fuschia in silver filigree w/ small ball inside closed petals w/ stamen. Author's Collection. (Refer to Plate 139 which shows this type hat ornament.)

4½″ white flat spiral pin w/chased silver feather design ornament, marked sterling. (Used w/ slit-opening in felt caps) Author's Collection.

3½″ Chinese hairpin w/ 1¼″ "peking glass", known as the "poor man's substitute for Jade". Collection of Delma Peery, Wind Bells Cottage Antiques, Hermosa Beach, CA.

3¾″ hairpin w/ 1½″ head w/ 2½″ dangle of steel beads. Author's Collection.

3″ Flower-pin or scarf-pin in sheath w/ 1½″ hilt w/ Persian turquoise and pearls. Author's Collection. (See Plate 158 fig. m. for illustration of 1892 flower-pin.)

4¼″ hairpin w/ 1¾″ pierced silver hilt. Author's Collection.

4″ white pin (hatpin) in jet sheath w/ 1⅝″ diameter jet ornament w/ 18 rhinestones w/ simple metal mounting. Author's Collection.

4¾″ open-mouth pin holder, marked "Hand-painted, Nippon". Note extensive gold overlay and beading. Also, Dutch Windmill scene as painted by an *Oriental* artist. Author's Collection.

**PLATE 18,** *page 108*

Photo by R. E. Stambook, Author's Collection

This popular "flow blue" Wild Rose pattern is being reproduced.

5″ tall hatpin holder marked "made in England — Staffordshire". Manufactured after 1914.

4″ x 5″ ring tree.

**PLATE 19,** *page 108*

Photo by R. E. Stambook, Author's Collection

Elaborately decorated *Art Nouveau* 5⅛″ tall hatpin holder with demitasse cup. Solid-base holder marked "hand-painted Alhambra" w/ two trademarks: one a winged crown; the other a crown and two crests. The latter w/

the words: "Vienna, Austria". The cup bears first trademark (above) and the word "Alhambra". Within a circle is marked "Austria".

**PLATE 20,** *page 108*

*l-r* — 10¾" white pin w/ 2" diameter round head w/ 200+ brilliants.

11½" white pin w/ 2½" diameter round head w/ 200+ rhinestones. Note: first and second pins have same quantity of stones but a variance in size of pins and mounting.

Rhinestones are mounted with foil-backing which often darkens with age or improper cleaning. A good paste or Strass retains its lustre and is commonly set without foil.

9½" white pin w/ 2" diameter. Filigree mounting w/ 40+ rhinestones and ¼" topaz color center stone. (Detail drawing *Plate 200.*)

12" white pin w/ 2½" diameter pierced mounting w/ four ¼" cobalt blue glass stones and 50+ rhinestones.

11½" white pin w/ 2½" oval metal backing w/ 30+ green and 60+ crystal brilliants.

Note contrast in size between hatpin heads and the U.S. Eisenhower *silver dollar.*

In setting this many small stones or brilliants, the jeweler used a variety of frames and cages with metal cups formed in rounds, ovals, stars or snowflake patterns. These cups were receptacles for the individual stones and provided solidity to the assemblage and design.

**PLATE 21,** *page 108*

*Back, l-r* — 10" gilt pin w/ 1½" pavé setting of 75+ rhinestones.

12" white pin w/ 2" snowflake design containing 40+ rhinestones.

6¾" gilt pin w/ 1¾" square filigree work w/ 75+ rhinestones.

11½" white pin w/ 2¼" six point star w/ 50+ rhinestones in pavé setting.

*Front, l-r* — 11" gilt pin w/ 1½" metal plate backing. Ornament set w/ four ½" mother-of-pearl accents and 50+ rhinestones.

12" white pin w/ 1¾" diameter set w/ six ¾" jet petals and 20+ paste stones.

6¾" gilt pin w/ 1¾" filigree square set w/ 75+ rhinestones.

11" white pin w/ 1½" filigree mounting set w/ 30+ rhinestones.

**PLATE 22,** *page 109*

*Front Row, l-r* — 6½" white pin with 2" overall enameled silver head. Reverse side marked, "Sterling". Inscribed: "Georgetown", accented w/ silver wreath. (Georgetown University memento)

9" steel pin w/ 1½" pierced and engraved mounting w/ ¾" square escutcheon. Escutcheon engraved with historic site and plate inscribed: "Entrance Gate, Gardiner, Mont." Top marked "sterling" w/ three heart-shaped hallmarks. (Engraving inside hallmarks worn and unidentifiable.)

7¼" gilt pin w/ 1½" one-half of a U.S. silver dollar, dated 1889.

*Back Row, l-r* — 10" gilt pin w/ 1¼" shield-shaped head w/ State of Utah crest inscribed "Industry" and "1847". "UTAH" appears on shield.

One pair 5¾" white pins w/ 1" Hawaiian coins ("head and tail"), dated 1883. Head: Portrait of former King of the Islands w/ inscription — "KALAKAUA I KING OF HAWAII 1883". Tail: a crest and inscription "UA MAU KE EA O KA AINA I KA PONO" (¼-D Hopaha)

9½" white pin w/ 1½" chased badge w/ head engraved with bank building. Reverse: "RUSTON STATE BANK, Ruston, La. Sutter Van Horn Co., New Orleans, La."

**PLATE 23,** *page 109*

*Back Row, l-r* — 7½" white pin w/ 1¼" ball. Pavé setting of 150+ rhinestones.

9" gilt pin w/ 2" pear-shaped head. Pavé setting of 150+ rhinestones.

8¾" steel pin w/ 2¼" gilt frame mounting. Crook ornament has channel setting of 75+ rhinestones.

10" gilt pin w/ 1½" gilt baroque mounting w/ 1" x 1¾" setting of 20+ brilliants.

*Front Row, l-r* — 11¼" white pin w/ 2" brass frame mounting w/ 20+ rhinestones.

7½" brass pin w/ 1" piercework mounting w/ 20+ rhinestones.

6½" gilt pin w/ 2" oval head w/ 250+ rhinestones in pavé setting. Note: pin on this large head had obviously been cut and resharpened.

**PLATE 24,** *page 109*

*Front, l-r* — 6¼" white pin w/ 1" Art Nouveau glass ornament.

8⅛" white pin w/ 1¼" decorated glass head.

6¾" white pin w/ 1⅛" Art Nouveau head.

5¾" white pin w/ 1" decorated glass head.

*Middle, l-r* — 6¼" white pin w/ 1⅛" Art Nouveau glass head.

8¾" white pin w/ 1¼" Art Nouveau irized glass head.

7⅞" white pin w/ 1" Art Nouveau head.

6¼" white pin w/ 1¼" oval decorated glass ornament.

*Back Row, l-r* — 6¼" white pin w/ 1¼" gilt bezel mounted Art Deco falcon. This bird is the Egyptian symbol for "Spirit of the Sun".

6¼" white pin w/ 1" Art Nouveau head.

9⅛" white pin w/ 1¼" irized glass Art Nouveau head.

8" white pin w/ 1⅛" blue and white decorated head.

These exquisite button-type Bohemian glass hatpins were produced during the *Art Nouveau* period, or "recession era", as it was called in Bohemia.

**PLATE 25,** *page 110*

*l-r* — 8¾" japanned pin w/ 2¾" Burel glass ornament.

5⅛" japanned pin w/ 2¼" Burel glass ornament.

9" japanned pin w/ 2½" Burel glass ornament.

These ornaments were manufactured by Jablonec Industries, Czech., under the manufacturing name of "Hyalith" Glass. They are hand-etched and are highly irridescent Bohemian art-glass.

**PLATE 26,** *page 110*

Photo by R. E. Stambook, Author's Collection

*l-r* — 9¼″ japanned pin w/ 3½″ Burel glass, hand-etched.

9⅝″ japanned pin w/ 3¼″ Burel glass, hand-etched.

9⅛″ japanned pin w/ 3¼″ Burel glass, hand-etched.

**PLATE 27,** *page 110*

Photo by R. E. Stambook, Author's Collection

5½″ japanned pin w/ 1½″ Burel glass, engraved ball.

9″ japanned pin, w/ 2½″ diameter bulb-shape Burel glass, engraved ornament.

6½″ japanned pin w/ 2″ reverse-teardrop shape bulb of Burel glass.

**PLATE 28,** *page 110*

COLOR, *page 110*: Photo by R. E. Stambook, Author's Collection; Black and White, *page 59*: Photo by Charlie Farrell

Metallic commemorative hatpin holder w/ pair of full figural Indian heads.

Holder: 6½″ tall w/ 1¼″ x 2¼″ solid base. Incised markings in metal on back side, "GSilver", a shield with letter "R", and words, "Pat. Apl'd For". Indian motifs in *repoussé*, includes Indian maiden and warrior.

Titled, "Hiawatha's Wooing", the Longfellow verse reads:

> FROM THE WIGWAM
> HE DEPARTED
> LEADING WITH HIM
> LAUGHING WATER
> HAND IN HAND THEY
> WENT TOGETHER
> THROUGH
> THE WOODLAND
> AND THE MEADOW

Marked "sterling", pair of Indian heads depict Hiawatha and his sweetheart, Laughing Water. 8½″ white pins w/ 1½″ two-mold (front and back) tooled *repoussé*.

It seems logical to speculate that this prized collectible was issued as a commemorative to the poet, Henry Wadsworth Longfellow, author of the epic narrative, "Hiawatha". Longfellow's death in 1882 — during the "hatpin era" — may have produced memorial expressions as shown on this *Plate*, as well as other forms of commemoratives.

**PLATE 29,** *page 110*

Photo by R. E. Stambook, Author's Collection

*l-r* — Three examples of high-style enamel and cloisonne of the period.

10″ white pin w/ 2″ engraved cloisonne head marked "sterling" and dated 1858.

6¼″ white pin w/ 1⅝″ decorated blown glass ornament. *Art Nouveau* floral design in gilt filigree cage w/ red enamel and silver overlay.

10″ white pin w/ 2″ chased and engraved cloisonne, marked "sterling" and dated 1851.

**PLATE 30,** *page 111*

Photo by R. E. Stambook, Author's Collection

*Bottom, l-r* — 8″ gilt pin w/ ¾″ enameled ornament w/ escutcheon. Marked "sterling", dated 1905, unidentified nation.

6½″ gilt pin w/ ¾″ enameled head marked "sterling", w/ trademark C.M.R. Inscribed: "Freedom and Unity". (Possibly a lodge insignia)

8″ gilt pin w/ 1¼″ enameled flag (So. Dakota). Marked "sterling".

8″ gilt pin w/ 1″ enameled head inscribed, "Louisiana Purchase Exposition, St. Louis '04."

*Top, l-r* — 8″ gilt pin w/ ¾″ head w/ *Fleur de Lis* escutcheon marked "L.P.E." dated 1903.

6″ white pin w/ ½″ marked "silver" head. Hallmarked, "F.A.B."

5⅞″ white pin w/ ⅜″ enameled head marked "sterling".

7″ steel pin w/ ¾″ enameled head inscribed "La Jolla, Cal."

**PLATE 31,** *page 111*

Photo by R. E. Stambook, Author's Collection

*Back Row, l-r* — 10½″ gilt pin w/ 1⅝″ chased gilt souvenir head. Escutcheon inscribed "PHILATHEA" Collection of Dr. F. P. Walkup

12″ gilt pin w/ 1⅛″ gilt souvenir head. Engraving of Niagara Falls, marked "Niagara".

7¾″ gilt pin w/ 1¼″ gilt head marked: "For Detroit Where Life Is Worth Living, 1910". (Reverse side marked: "B.P.O.E., Los Angeles 1909, Thiry's, Detroit".

10″ gilt pin w/ 2″ chased and engraved frame w/ shield escutcheon. 2″ overall gilt head engraved "Old Senate House — 1676" and "Kingston, N.Y."

*Front Row, l-r* — 6¼″ white pin w/ 1″ gilt uniform button monogrammed "GAR" (Grand Army of the Republic).

6⅝″ white pin w/ ⅝″ crown and anchor button (possibly regimental or private household livery button) mounted as hatpin ornament.

6″ gilt pin w/ 1¾″ full figural head. "USN" (United States Navy) in brass, escutcheon mounted on gold filigree. Symbolic rope tied to gilt anchor. Style and design of naval insignia outmoded by newer design of anchor.

6⅛″ gilt *square* rather than round stem with spiral. ⅞″ U.S. Army American Eagle uniform button marked on reverse side, "Horstmann, Philada." incised with star hallmark.

**PLATE 32,** *page 111*

Photo by R. E. Stambook, Author's Collection

*Top Row, l-r* — 4⅛″ steel pin w/ 2¼″ solid milkglass head.

6⅝″ white pin w/ 1¼″ blown and decorated milkglass w/ pontil set into patch-type mounting.

6⅝″ brass pin w/ 2⅝″ free-form "thorn" milkglass head.

9½″ brass pin w/ 1¾″ free-form "thorn" milkglass head.

**PLATE 32,** *continued:*

*Bottom, l-r* — 5¾″ white pin w/ ¼″ milkglass head.

3⅜″ brass pin w/ ⅞″ pear-shape milkglass head w/ four rhinestones in gilt metal cups. Socket mounting.

5⅝″ brass pin w/ 2¼″ twisted free-form milkglass head w/ hand-painted floral design.

7⅝″ steel pin w/ ⅞″ molded shell pattern irridescent opaline glass.

**PLATE 33,** *page 112*

Mosaics were much in demand in early Victorian days, declining slowly in popularity after approximately 1860.

*Top Row, l-r* — 6″ brass pin w/ 1″ oval w/ simple multiple design. Each pattern within a metal *cloison*. Filigree brass frame.

6⅝″ brass pin w/ 1¼″ button-type mosaic in metal-back frame. Looped *cloisons* separate repeated center design. Scalloped outer edge design, in individual *cloisons*, form a star.

5⅞″ gilt pin w/ 1″ simple single design mosaic, set in bezel-type solid-back mounting. Incised hallmark, "W.K.Co."

8¼″ white pin w/ ⅞″ two-sided mosaic head, each side has a simple multiple design.

*Bottom, l-r* — 9″ gilt pin w/ ⅝″ two-sided intricate multiple floral mosaic within a ⅞″ gilt filigree pear-shape mounting.

6¾″ gilt pin w/ ⅜″ six-sided cube. Each side has a varied floral design set into *cloisons*. The *cloisons* are mounted on gilt box frame.

6½″ brass pin w/ 1⅛″ oval. Twelve brass *cloisons*, each with intricate variations of multiple floral designs. Chased brass frame.

**PLATE 34,** *page 112*

*Top Row, l-r* — 9¾″ gilt pin w/ 3¾″ chased brass ornament w/ 2 small oval cut topaz either side.

10″ white pin w/ 3″ gilt *Art Nouveau* ornament.

*Middle Row, l-r* — 10″ white pin w/ 1¼″ x 1¾″ *Art Nouveau* ornament w/ ½″ rose-cut amethyst.

10¾″ gilt pin w/ 3″ brass piercework ornament.

10″ gilt pin w/ 2½″ simple frame w/ initial "M" engraved on top. Brilliants in filigree as accents.

*Note typical use of leaf patterns in Art Nouveau designs.*

Bottom Row, l-r — 11¼″ white pin w/ 2⅝″ *Art Nouveau* ornament w/ ½″ square cut topaz on top w/ 4 smaller topaz accents.

8½″ white pin w/ 2¼″ *Art Nouveau* ornament w/ escutcheon top.

10″ brass pin w/ 2″ *Art Nouveau* ornament w/ 1″ oval topaz.

12″ gilt pin w/ 1¾″ chased and engraved ornament.

10″ white pin w/ 2¾″ piercework ornament w/ ½″ amethyst on top.

9¾″ gilt pin w/ 2¾″ *Art Nouveau* ornament.

**PLATE 35,** *page 112*

*Top, l-r* — 6½″ white pin w/ 1″ gilt *Art Nouveau* mounting using a figural Griffin circling a lily pad. The Griffin is the mythological sign for Vigilance. Mounting has decorative escutcheon initialed "L.M.".

4″ gilt pin, (obviously shortened) w/ 1″ gilt baroque mounting w/ decorated escutcheon, initial "S".

7″ white pin w/ 1″ gilt *Art Nouveau* figural mounting of pair of lion heads. Decorated escutcheon w/ initials "A.L.P."

*Bottom, l-r* — 7½″ white pin w/ ¾″ gilt piercework frame w/ decorative escutcheon w/ initial "L".

8″ white pin w/ ¾″ gilt *Art Nouveau* floral mounting, Daffodil, w/ decorative escutcheon. Initials "C.G."

8″ gilt pin w/ 1¼″ gilt *Art Nouveau* floral mounting, Fuschia. Plain escutcheon. Initial "P".

8″ gilt pin w/ ¾″ gilt piercework frame w/ plain escutcheon and two ruby color accents. Initials "A.R.A."

8″ gilt pin w/ 1″ gilt *Art Nouveau* floral, Laurel Wreath w/ decorative bow. Two ½″ sapphire color stones, decorated escutcheon, initials "L.E.T." (For detailed drawing of this pin, see *Plate 186, fig. a and b.*)

**PLATE 36,** *page 112*

*Top, l-r* — 9″ gilt pin w/ ¾″ gilt *Art Nouveau* mounting w/ ¾″ oval topaz stone bezel-set in escutcheon.

9¾″ gilt pin w/ 1″ gilt *Art Nouveau* mounting w/ ⅝″ oval topaz stone bezel-set in escutcheon.

8″ steel pin w/ 1″ gilt baroque mounting w/ 1″ oval topaz stone bezel-set in escutcheon.

8½″ gilt pin w/ ⅜″ gilt simple frame w/ 1″ round topaz stone.

*Bottom, l-r* — 12″ steel pin w/ 1″ gilt chased frame w/ ¾″ x 1½″ rectangular topaz stone.

5½″ gilt pin w/ 1½″ gilt *Art Nouveau* mounting w/ ¾″ square topaz.

11⅝″ steel pin w/ gilt chased frame w/ 1″ round topaz.

All of these tin-wheel cut and faceted stones are of the finest paste and would require an expert gemologist to distinguish between the real and imitation topaz.

**PLATE 37,** *page 112*

*Back, l-r* — 8½″ gilt pin w/ 2⅛″ gilt mounting w/ filigree backing, floral design, set w/ 75+ amethysts and 150+ rhinestones.

11⅛″ steel pin w/ 1½″ gilt filigree mounting w/ ½″ center amethyst, four ¼″ amethysts, and 90+ rhinestones.

11″ white pin w/ gilt plate backing. Head set w/ six ⅜″ amethyst baguette-cut stones and 75+ rhinestones.

8⅞″ gilt pin w/ 1⅞″ plate backing; head set w/ fifteen ¼″ stones, sixteen brilliants and 30+ purple brilliants.

*Front Row, l-r* — 10¾″ steel pin w 1¼″ amethyst in simple frame w/ 20+ simulated pearl accents.

**PLATE 37,** *continued:*

10¾″ gilt pin w/ 1⅞″ gilt *Art Nouveau* mounting w/ 1″ oval amethyst and 16 rhinestones.

8⅝″ white pin w/ ⅞″ simple frame w/ ½″ amethyst and 4 rhinestones.

10″ steel pin w/ 1¼″ gilt claw-mounted amethyst.

**PLATE 38,** *page 113*

Photo by R. E. Stambook, Author's Collection

*Top Row, l-r* — 5½″ tall hatpin holder, (red mark) "R. S. Prussia". Solid base. Hand-painted floral.

5″ tall figural hatpin holder, (as Art Deco as it can come) — solid base with two separate pin-holders for the shorter stems of the twenties. Note sassy applied green glass feather on brim of hat. Base marked: "Roulogne, France".

6½″ tall steeple-shaped highly pearlized porcelain holder w/ solid base. Silver overlay. Marked "Belleek, Sterling". (American-made circa 1880).

*Bottom Row, l-r* — 4½″ tall open-base urn-shaped holder with applied handles. Hand-painted floral. Marked "R. S. Prussia" (red mark). Unusual shape.

5″ tall bisque holder with ½″ jasper cameo insert. Solid base marked with "R" inside a crown.

4½″ tall hand-painted floral solid base footed holder marked "R. S. Germany"

**PLATE 39,** *page 113*

Photo by R. E. Stambook, Author's Collection

*Top Row, l-r* — 5″ tall hand-painted holder in barber-bottle shape. Solid bottom unmarked.

7″ tall solid bottom pearlized porcelain holder w/ hand-painted flowers. Marked "Germany". (Unusually tall.)

5¼″ tall unmarked rectangular base w/ mold opening. Note triangular holes cut for heavy gauge wire pins and ornaments.

*Bottom Row, l-r* — 5¾″ solid-base hand-painted highly irized porcelain w/ exquisite hand-painted flowers. Marked "Germany".

5″ tall fully open-base holder w/ delicate pastel glaze. Marked "Favorite Bavaria".

4½″ tall solid-base holder. Marked "R. S. Germany". Undecorated, this shape holder has been reproduced in white glaze or has been decorated with ceramic transfers for today's market. This holder has authentic "R.S. Germany" mark.

5½″ tall hand-painted and gold decorated holder marked with crossed swords and crown and words, "Royal Germany".

**PLATE 40,** *page 113*

Photo by R. E. Stambook, Author's Collection

Note variation in design of applied tops of hatpin holders.

*Top, left* — 4¾″ tall solid-base holder with hand-painted unusual treatment of flowering tree. Marked: "P. L. Limoges, France".

*Top, right* — 5″ tall solid-base hand-painted holder marked "Bavaria".

Hatpins shown are described on other plates within this book.

*Bottom, l-r* — 5″ tall solid-base holder with hand-painted floral marked "Prussia".

**PATE 40,** *continued:*

4½″ tall solid-base holder with hand-painted magnolias with numerous pin-holes. Marked "R. S. Germany".

4″ tall solid-base holder with three large openings at top to accommodate pins with nibs, heavy-gauge stems, or double-prongs. Marked: "P. L. Limoges, France".

4½″ tall solid-base holder with hand-painted roses. Numerous pin-holes. Marked, "R.S. Germany".

4½″ tall solid-base holder with *Art Nouveau* treatment of hand-painted flowers. Numerous pin-holes. Marked: "R. S. Germany".

**PLATE 41,** *page 113*

Photo by R. E. Stambook, Author's Collection

*Top Row, l-r* — 5½″ tall souvenir hatpin holder, solid-base marked "Willow Art China, Longton". Hand-painted words: "Hat Pin" w/ ceramic transfer design inscribed "Jerusalem".

Same holder as above except ceramic transfer is a crest with coat-of-arms designated as "Bridlington".

5″ tall solid-base holder with hand-painted violets (badly worn). Base marked w/ crown and crossed swords and "Rosenthal" — "Gebrauchemusterschutz". Also signed and dated "M. L. Snyder, 07".

*Bottom Row, l-r* — 4¾″ tall solid-base holder. Exquisite hand-painted *Art Nouveau* motif w/ heavy gold overlay on top. Painting initialed by artist: "HR". Base marked "Hand-painted China, W. A. Picard — N & Co. — France". (The stylized treatment of the lily and design represents the transition period of late *Art Nouveau* into Art Deco.)

4¾″ tall solid-base holder. Hand-painted Art Deco floral w/ heavy gold overlay. Trademarked "hand-painted china, W. A. Picard — Rosenthal — Gebrauchemusterschutz".

5″ tall unmarked solid-base holder. Heavy silver overlay. Marked on floral motif: "Sterling".

4¾″ tall solid-base holder. Art Nouveau decorated and signed by artist, "T. Hyatt". Base marking: "Z. S. and Co., Bavaria".

**PLATE 42,** *page 113 and 153*

Photo by R. E. Stambook, Author's collection

5½″ Conch shell marked "Souvenir St. Louis" improvised as a pincushion with heavy 2¾″ bronze base. Collection of Joyce Roth.

Half-Clam shell with assorted shells as base, topped by a murex shell with plush cushion set in its opening.

9 variations of marine-snail shells as ornamental heads for hatpins:

*l-r* — 6½″ brass pin w/ 2″ shell. Brass wire woven to represent sword hilt.

7½″ brass pin with 1½″ shell, wire-mounted.

8″ brass pin with claw-mounted 1½″ shell.

8½″ brass pin with 1½″ claw-mounted shell fragment.

8½″ brass pin with 1″ shell. Wire and beads form a hilt.

7½″ brass pin with 1¼″ wire-mounted shell.

7½″ heavy gauge white pin with 2½″ shell.

*Bottom Two Pins, l-r* — 5¼″ square *spiral* brass pin with 1½″ shell decorated with filigree wire.

**PLATE 42,** *continued:*

5½″ brass pin with 1½″ shell and brass wire forming hilt.

A twelve inch ruler gives visual proof of extraordinary length of some hat-pins worn in the extravagant hats of the 1901-1910 era. The charm of sea-shells has never been challenged by era; the variety of forms and mountings are countless. Souvenir of a summer at a beach, each is displayed in a unique pincushion crafted from assorted shells. Note spiral twist of pin in the center hatpin; this was introduced to keep pins from slipping and to hold hat more securely to hair and head.

**PLATE 43,** *page 113*

An ironstone commode set of English manufacture. Unmarked. Twelve pieces with assortment of hatpins in a Christmas arrangement.

*Center:* ewer and basin — (commonly known as a pitcher and bowl) — pitcher measures 9″ x 12″ with applied handle; basin is approximately 16″ diameter.

*Left:* 9½″ x 13″ comb and brush tray; covered trinket box; powder jar; double-lipped pitcher; small saucer or pin tray; hatpin holder with open-mold base.

(Hatpins are shown on plates throughout this book.)

*Right:* Uncovered container (missing lid), filled with an array of hatpins; two-piece dish with drainage hole for holding soap or washcloth.

Two factors imply that this commode set is of turn-of-the-century or before: *1.* unmarked china or stoneware, without country of origin, indicates pre-1910; and *2.* the numerous outmoded "necessaries" included in assorted toilet articles suggests pieces utilized before the convenience of "indoor" plumbing and running water.

**PLATE 44,** *page 114*

Six piece Vanity Set. Hand-painted with gold overlay. Each piece with trademark: crown and crest with initial "B", imprinted "Prussia, Royal Rudolstadt".

*l-r* — 3¼″ covered hair receiver; 5″ solid-base hatpin holder; 3¼″ covered puff box; and 8½″ x 11½″ tray with reticulated china work.

Delicate, almost translucent china, denotes fine exports of Prussian porcelain. The Rudolstadt family learned their trade at Meissen. Although comparable workmanship, competition from the older established firms in Meissen prematurely closed the Rudolstadt production of fine wares.

**PLATE 45,** *page 114*

Two Dresser Sets, *l-r* — 8-piece set hand-painted with heavy gold beading and overlay. Pieces marked, "O. E. & G. — Royal Austria".

5½″ x 8½″ comb and brush tray; 4¾″ tall open mold base hatpin holder; 2¾″ covered trinket box; 3¼″ covered puff box; and 3½″ covered hair receiver. Note unusual oval-shape of holder.

6-piece set hand-painted with gold accents, marked "Germany".

7″ x 9¾″ tray; 5¾″ tall solid-base hatpin holder; and 3½″ each covered puff box and hair receiver.

**PLATE 46,** *page 114*

Two Dresser Sets, *l-r* — 7-piece set hand-painted green porcelain marked "Germany"; 8″ x 12″ tray; 5″ tall solid-base hatpin holder; 3¾″ hair receiver, and covered trinket box with applied knob-handle; and 2¾″ x 3½″ ring tree base w/ 1¾″ tall tree.

6-piece set, European orange lustre (pearlized) porcelain: 8¼″ x 11¼″ tray w/ handles; 4½″ tall open-base hatpin holder; 3″ covered hair receiver, and a pair of 5¼″ tall candlesticks.

(The lack of trademark or country of origin and the inclusion of candlesticks dates this as pre-1900.)

**PLATE 47,** *page 115*

Here are hand-painted pieces reflecting the transitionary period of *Art Nouveau* to Art Deco (1910-1920):

Although each piece in the set is obviously painted by the same artist, the china "blanks" were of different manufacturers per marks:

Seven pieces include:

From Bavaria: 3¾″ x 6″ pin tray and a 4½″ talc shaker marked "H C Royal Bavaria Pat. applied for".

From France: 2¾″ x 4½″ covered soap dish or trinket box, base marked: "Haviland"; and a 4½″ solid base hatpin holder marked: "PL Limoges, France".

From Austria: A large 5½″ covered and footed puff box, marked: "O. & E. G. Royal Austria".

**PLATE 48,** *page 115*

*l-r* — 4¼″ holder w/ 2¼″ x 4″ attached covered pin box w/ hand-painted beading. Author's collection.

4½″ x 5½″ tray, 3¾″ holder, 1½″ scarf or veil pin holder. Hand-painted w/ beading. Shown: 2 scarf pins and 1 hair ornament w/ steel beads. Author's collection.

2″ tall ring tree w/ 3½″ base, unmarked; 4¼″ hatpin holder w/ *open* bottom mold. Unusual. Collection of Joyce Roth.

**PLATE 49,** *page 115*

*Top, l-r* — 4½″ tall green Jasperware "Kewpie" hatpin holder. Solid-base with incised marking, "Rose O'Neill, Kewpie, Germany". Collection of Sybel Heller.

5½″ tall solid-base pearlized bisque *Art Nouveau* hatpin holder with heavily applied glass beading and enameling. Unglazed hand-painted bisque stylized portrait. Base marked with incised crown and sunburst with letter "R". Attributed to "V-Rudolstadt".

4½″ tall blue Jasperware "Kewpie" hatpin holder. Incised mark "Rose O'Neill Kewpie, Germany" and also marked with the same abovementioned crown and sunburst seal with letter "R". Collection of Joyce Roth.

**PLATE 49,** *continued:*

*Bottom, Left* — 5¼″ tall transitional *Art Nouveau* hatpin holder w/ 2¾″ solid-base incised with crown and sunburst and initial "R". Fashioned with exquisite detail, this figural is as enigmatic as the Sphinx. This holder may be dated with the opening of the Egyptian tombs (1920). Collection of Joyce Roth.

A glazed and unglazed example of the above hatpin holder with same markings. Center holder is highly glazed, while holder on right is unglazed, unpainted bisque.

**PLATE 50,** *page 116*

Seven hatpin holders with various designed and attached trays for "nibs", small pins, chains, and miscellaneous trinkets.

*Top Row, l-r* — 5″ tall highly pearlized porcelain hand-painted w/ *Art Nouveau* butterflies, solid base tray incised w/ numerals and signed "L. Kriege".

4½″ tall hand-painted holder w/ 4¼″ diameter attached tray; two ring or earring loops applied to holder. Incised numerals on solid base.

4½″ tall holder w/ 4½″ diameter attached fluted tray. Holder is a reproduction of an earlier model and is hand-painted w/ "Kewpies" (See *Plate 49*) Signed by artist, "G. May".

*Bottom Row, l-r* — 4½″ tall holder w/ delicately painted flowers. 3″ diameter attached tray, solid-base signed by artist, "C. Baker".

4″ tall hand-painted floral holder w/ heavily applied gold overlay and beading w/ deep 4″ diameter tray. Unmarked but probably Nippon.

4½″ tall handpainted floral holder; quaint shape, w/ small 3″ diameter attached tray, unmarked by mfg. on solid-base, but signed by artist, "R. Fuller".

4½″ tall holder combination with hand-painted and ceramic transfer design with 4″ diameter attached tray. Solid-base with unidentified trademark and word "Schwarzburg".

**PLATE 51,** *page 116*

A dozen assorted Oriental hatpin holders.

*Top Row, l-r* — 4″ tall holder marked "Japan" with artist's signature in Oriental caligraphy. Rare blue and white Dutch windmill scene.

4¾″ tall holder with exquisitely executed oriental scene depicting teahouse, garden, bridge, and strolling Geisha. Heavy gold beading and overlay. Artist's signature in gold within red square. This style of signature denotes approval for export; in addition, it was limited to artists of recognized scope and stature by the Emperor. (Unmarked Oriental wares designate early export.)

4″ tall holder hand-decorated with heavy gold filigree-type overlay with purple accents. Highly irridescent. Solid base marked: "Hand-painted Japan, Mikado Extra" and trademark.

4″ tall holder hand-painted, with elaborate gold overlay and beading w/ blue and red enameling and high-lustre glaze. Solid-base marked "hand-painted" and oriental sign for artist's insignia.

3¾″ tall holder w/ beautifully detailed and decorated applied top. Porcelain portion of holder hand-painted with red roses; upper and lower portions of bisque highly decorated with applied multiple color beading and overlay. Solid base marked "hand-painted Nippon".

4″ tall holder unmarked with oriental figures; typical early Nippon export.

**PLATE 51,** *continued:*

*Bottom Row, l-r* — 4″ tall holder marked "Japan", with trademark insignia. Hand-painted floral with elaborate beadwork.

4″ tall holder with 3¾″ solid base marked "hand-painted Nippon". Heavily applied gold decoration. The fine quality and design might easily be mistaken for Limoges.

6″ tall holder with 3½″ diameter solid bottom and applied top. Unusually large ¼″ pin hole openings which could accommodate heavier shanks used on decorative hairpins or hair ornaments. Marked "hand-painted Nippon".

5″ tall holder, hand-painted scenic depicting forest, rocks, stream, mountains and solitary figure. Gold overlay and heavy beading with detailed decorative top. "Made in Japan" with artist's oriental signature.

5″ tall holder with highly lustrous porcelain, hand-painted with flowers with gold accents. Marks on solid base: "hand-painted Japan" within trademark insignia.

3¾″ tall holder marked "Made in Japan". Oriental decoration typical of hand-painted export chinawares such as vases and tea sets.

(See book text for details regarding Oriental exports and Nippon wares.)

**PLATE 52,** *page 116*

Hatpins from the collection of Renee Marshall:

*l-r* — Sterling *Art Nouveau* pin; two Thistle pins; and jet glass pin w/ sterling floral overlay.

From Author's collection: *l-r* — 5¾″ silverplate hatpin stand with topaz thistle w/ 2½″ base, velvet covered cushion.

8″ tall w/ 3½″ base, silverplate hatpin stand. The bottom of base is marked: "UNTERSTUTZUNGSVREIN der GASTWIRTE und HOTELIERS WIENS", "19 9/2 12" (Sept. 2, 1912). Inscription names a club formed by owners of restaurants who evidently had a convention at which this souvenir holder was given to participants.

6½″ sterling footed w/ 2″ base, pierced *Art Nouveau* design hatpin stand w/ ring or earring holders.

5″ tall w/ 2½″ base hatpin stand accented w/ 4½″ round ivory balls. Three hallmarks plus registry number and "S.M.&Co.". Tallest pin is unusual treatment of Thistle design. (See *Plate 171* for detail drawing of hallmarks.)

**PLATE 53,** *page 116*

*Top, l-r* — 6″ figural unmarked holder with 3½″ solid-base with four ½″ pin openings. Almost ironstone quality glazed china. Large pin holes could easily accommodate pairs of cape pins used with rain apparel. Openings descend through stem of holder to solid base.

3″ tall with 2½″ solid base with hand-painted figural holder. Three inch tall reclining winged figure with four ½″ pin openings. Unmarked.

*Bottom, l-r* — 5″ tall comic dog figural with small mold opening at base. Hand-painted on poor quality china and marked "Made in Japan".

4″ tall hand-painted holder with 4¼″ diameter solid-base tray. Art Deco carnival-garbed masked figure.

7″ tall novelty figural duck solid-base holder with four ¼″ pin holes. Hand-painted. Unusual oriental treatment of Art Deco. Marked "Japan".

**PLATE 54,** *page 116*

*Top Row, l-r* — 5″ tall holder, hand-painted with solid base. Unmarked, heavy ceramic ware.

4¾″ tall holder hand-painted hunt scene (man on horseback). Marked: "Royal Doulton." Impressed trademark is circa 1902-1922: "Lambeth and Burslem Co., England". Collection of Mrs. G. W. McCurdy.

4½″ tall unmarked heavy ceramic souvenir holder. Solid base. Inscribed, Front: "Good Luck" — "From British Empire Exhibition, Wembley." Reverse: inscribed above Passant Lion (British Symbol) "A present from British Empire Exhibition, Wembley".

*Bottom Row, l-r* — 4½″ tall elaborately hand-painted floral holder. Marked on solid bottom, "Handpainted, manufactured by Thos. Till & Sons, Burslem, England, Estb. 1825". (All this imprinted in ¾″ x 1½″ rectangle.)

4¼″ tall solid-base holder marked with a cobalt blue stroke and green color initial "P".

4″ tall footed holder with solid base. Hand-painted floral with gold highlights. Unglazed heavy ceramic with incised numerals.

4½″ tall unmarked souvenir solid base holder. Pearlized porcelain commemorative with ceramic transfer portrait: "H M King George V".

**PLATE 55,** *page 116*

*Top, left* — 6¼″ tall footed marigold carnival glass holder in orange tree pattern. (Northwood) Collection of Joyce Roth

*Top, right* — Same holder except in cobalt blue carnival glass.

*Bottom, l-r* — 6¼″ tall footed Northwood purple carnival glass in grape pattern. Collection of Joyce Roth

Same dimensions and pattern hatpin holder in custard glass.

Another carnival glass holder in green color. Collection of Joyce Roth

**PLATE 56,** *page 117*

Miniature half-dolls of intricate design and figurine-quality. Skilled hands are required to complete these many-molded dolls, the finest of which are attributed to the Dressel and Kister Company, Germany.

Note the applied decorations, such as tiny flowers with each petal perfectly shaped and true-to-life coloring.

Quality craftsmanship is evident in the first pincushion half-doll (left) from the collection of Ginny's Antiques Et Cetera. Hatpins stored in this pincushion: *l-r* — 1 pr. 4½″ 14 karat gold filigree with faceted rock crystal; 5⅞″ filigree square; 6″ pin with gold Karat ball; 5″ pin with 14 Karat gold filigree with amethyst color faceted crystal; 5½″ gold with Persian turquoise; 6″ 10 Karat monogram head, and 6″ pin with ⅝″ engraved head.

*Center* — Rare satin glass holder with heavily decorated and embossed gold overlay with hand-applied beading. Possibly Bohemian or German. 5½″ tall with 3″ base with polished pontil.

**PLATE 56,** *continued:*

Seven hatpins in satin glass above holder: 7⅛″ pin with 1⅛″ gold interlaced scroll with turquoise; 6½″ pin w/ ⅝″ gold escutcheon; 7⅞″ pin w/ 1⅜″ *Art Nouveau* mounting w/ stone accent; 8″ pin w/ 1″ *Art Nouveau* head accented w/ rose zircon; 7¾″ pin w/ ¾″ head w/ 3 garnets; 7½″ pin w/ ¾″ baroque 14K top; and 7¾″ pin w/ 1″ chased gold mounting w/ green stones. Collection of Renee Marshall.

*Right* — Pincushion half-doll with movable body and feet from the collection of Ginny's Antiques Et Cetera. Hatpins from author's collection: 3¾″ gilt spiral pin embedded with Bohemian garnets; 6″ pin w/ ⅜″ gold filigree head w/ faceted topaz; 5½″ pin w/ ½″ pierced cage w/ cabochon amethyst; 5″ pin w/ 1⅛″ head w/ oriental jadite in gold karat; 4⅞″ pin ¾″ baroque gold set w/ tiny fresh-water pearls and genuine amethyst; and 3⅛″ pin w/ rare millefiori glass ornament.

**PLATE 57,** *page 117*

Eleven piece dresser set with hand-painted flowers. Marked "Czechoslovakia".

8½″ x 11½″ embossed and reticulated porcelain tray with ceramic transfer of playful cherubs.

4¾″ tall pair of swirled scalloped-base candlesticks and matched-mold 4½″ tall hatpin holder completely open base.

Dainty 2¼″ x 3″ ringtree with incised numerals; one 3″ and two 2¼″ covered trinket boxes with fancy finial lids.

This set has heavy hand-applied gold overlay.

(Hatpins, collection of author, shown on other plates in this book.)

From Sears' *Spring 1911* Catalog: ". . . *Bureau or Toilet Set, containing one 12½″ comb and brush tray . . . Made of first quality china with embossed scalloped edges, hand-traced with gold. Decorated with a border of pink roses and green foliage.*" This could almost describe set pictured in Plate.

Many other types of catalogues feature "*tinted Bureau or Dresser*" sets such as "*Dresden pink rose decoration on ivory tinted background*", or "*white china, gold traced,*" or simply, "*imported fancy hand-painted china*".

**PLATE 58,** *page 117*

9 piece vanity set with hand-painted roses, pierced handles, pearlized porcelain with gold overlay. Heavy cobalt blue trim. Exceptionally large 6½″ x 21½″ comb and brush and trinket tray with incised numerals. Incised numerals seldom oriental manufacture but are of European origin.

5¼″ tall hatpin holder; single 6″ candleholder; 3¾″ hair receiver, and a pair of 3¼″ covered trinket boxes.

(Hatpins pictured on other plates except for center pin which has a genuine 1″ stone of polished lapis lazuli).

**PLATE 59,** *page 118*

The importance of vanity and toilette accessories is emphasized by the inclusion of such items in Victorian turn-of-the-century miniaturia.

A finely feathered miniature millinery creation, scaled an inch-to-the-foot, designed and sewn by Susan Hendrix, rests against the full-scale author's gold and turquoise thimble. This combination will allow the reader to contrast the one-inch-to-the-foot scale of the toilette and vanity sets hand-crafted and painted by ceramist Norma Johnston. Properly scaled hatpins, by Susan Hendrix, are from her own collection of miniatures.

Standing tall, rear center, is a rare hand-painted full-size 2¼" tall Meissen scarf (tie-pin) holder from the collection of Delma Peery, Wind Bells Cottage Antiques.

**PLATE 60,** *page 118*

*Photo by R. E. Stambook, Author's Collection*

11 piece unmarked china dresser set of English origin. Oriental influence on decoration of the period is most apparent in the European artistry of hand-painted flowers embossed with raised "slip" work, which was the method of applying an overlay of ceramic to china, porcelain, bisque or any other type of earthenware. This raised design gives an almost three-dimensional quality to the flowers, vases, and pattern.

10½" x 14" tray; 5" tall hatpin holder; pair 3¼" tall candleholders with 4" base; one each 4½" covered hair receiver and puff box; 4" covered footed trinket box; and 4" footed open pin dish.

**PLATE 61,** *page 118*

*Photo by R. E. Stambook, Author's Collection*

These are examples of both right and left rotary arms used in the design of the symbolic swastika. The word, a derivative of Indian Sanskist, *svasti*, denotes well-being. When arms extend at right angles, it takes on the form of a Greek cross. However, when *tilted* and worn as an insignia on an armband or uniform, it represents the Nazi regime beginning in 1933 with Adolph Hitler's rise to dictatorship in Germany.

Prior to World War II, there was no ugly connotation associated with this ancient mystic symbol which had been used by early American Indian tribes, and in Persia, Japan, and in India. From "Indian Mythology", by author Veronica Ions, (Paul Hamlyn, London publishers), we read that the swastika is "a symbol of fortune, bringer of good luck. The swastika, *whose arms could be turned in either direction*, became associated in Hinduism with the sun and also with Gansea, the pathfinder whose image is often found where two roads cross." (My italics.)

In several early jewelry sales catalogues, the swastika is shown as hatpin heads and the symbol appears in *either* right or left rotary movements. However, it is assumed that were this symbol to become popular again, (which is doubtful because of the Nazi connotation), the rotary would be to the *left*.

The 1963 Library Guild, Inc. publication of "Webster's New Twentieth Century Dictionary of the English Language (unabridged)", illustrates the swastika with rotary arms counter-clockwise — to the left — and states that the *right* angle rotary was used as a Nazi symbol.

*Top, l-r* — 7¾" pin w/ chased gilt ¾" head set with ¼" cabochon-cut Jadite. Collection of Joyce Roth

11½" white pin w/ 1¾" round symbolic design set with genuine turquoise.

8" white pin w/ ½" turquoise enameled head. Marked "sterling" on reverse side.

*Center* — Pair 7⅞" gilt pins. Each ⅝" button-type head mounted with swastika symbol.

*Bottom, l-r* — 8" white pin w/ 1" hand-cut and polished mother-of-pearl swastika. Collection of Joyce Roth.

8" white pin w/ ¾" chased and engraved swastika. Marked "Sterling".

8" white pin w/ ¾" swastika channel-set w/ 24 red brilliants. Marked "sterling".

8" white pin w/ ¾" hand cut and polished mother-of-pearl swastika.

**PLATE 62,** *page 119*

*Photo by R. E. Stambook*

An embossed leather golfbag Hatpin Holder w/ two irons and one wood golf-club. Collection of Diane Mahlmood.

Shown in golfbag, *l-r* — Iron golfclub w/ white pin. Overall 8½" w/ ⅞" iron head. Author's collection.

Wood golfclub, 8¼" overall. Marked: "silver pin", w/ 1" Wood head. Space for monogram on one side w/ engravings of club house and golfer. Author's collection.

7½" overall Iron golfclub marked "silver pin" w/ ⅞" Iron head. Author's collection.

8" white pin w/ 1¾" Mother-of-Pearl wood head. Collection of Diane Mahlmood.

8" white pin w/ 1" finely molded and polished amethyst glass wood head golfclub in sterling w/ hallmark. Author's collection.

6" brass pin marked "sterling top" w/ 1" head engraved w/ four different golfing activities. Author's collection.

7" overall white pin w/ 1" wood head golfclub marked "sterling." Author's collection.

**PLATE 63,** *page 119*

*Photo by R. E. Stambook*

*l-r* — 4⅝" white pin w/ 1¼" blown glass head w/ filigree. Gilt chains w/ 2" blue bead dangles. Collection of Sybel Heller.

5½" white pin w/ ¾" gilt *Art Nouveau* portrait w/ 8 amber-color beads. The use of brass or gilt for this type ornament is rare. Collection of Sybel Heller.

Pair, 3½" *handmade* brass-wire pins, w/ 1" blown crystal glass, gold decorated and washed, w/ ⅜" dangling glass ball. (Circa 1825). Author's Collection.

Note difference in gauge of wire between pair of *handmade* pins and *machine-made* pins.

**PLATE 64,** *page 119*

*Photo by R. E. Stambook*

*l-r* — 10" white pin w/ 1¾" brass *Art Nouveau* mounting w/ 1½" monogram on top lid of powder compact, complete w/ lamb's wool puff w/ ivory loop; inside lid is convex mirror. Marked inside bottom: "Pat. Pending". Author's Collection.

7" white pin w/ 3" *Art Nouveau* ornament; 1" velvet cushion for perfume fragrance. Marked "sterling". Author's Collection.

7¾" pin w/ 1½" *Art Nouveau* motif of scrolls, leaves, and flowers. Threaded screw top set w/ gemstone. Ornament contains ten 1" brass pins in ½" opening. Collection of Irene Dutko.

**PLATE 65,** *page 119*

*Photo by R. E. Stambook*

*l-r* — 7⅝" pin w/ 1¼" *Plique-a-Jour* work, (cloisonne without metal backing), accented with marcasites and green gemstone. Hallmarked and inscribed "*Depose*" which is the French term similar to *patent* or *trademark*. Author's collection.

**PLATES 65,** *continued:*

8″ pin w/ ½″ x 1″ *Art Nouveau* brass mounting set w/ ¾″ amethyst. Collection of Sybel Heller.

4½″ gilt pin w/ rare 2-piece celluloid mold. 2¼″ painted pierced mold and ¾″ painted pattern and portrait mold of the Pharoh. Unusual metallic accent of 2″ brass Art Deco *Scarabaeus* which is the Egyptian symbol of longevity. Note the typical geometric Art Deco lines used in this hatpin. Author's collection.

8″ pin w/ ¾″ brass filigree portrait w/ initial. Collection of Sybel Heller.

8½″ gilt pin w/ 1⅜″ full figural oxidized metal Water Lily. Note the flowing lines of *Art Nouveau.* Floral head accented with two ruby color and two rhinestone brilliants. Author's collection.

6¾″ pin w/ 1″ triangular brass double-sided portrait head. Collection of Sybel Heller.

**PLATE 66,** *page 119*

Photo by R. E. Stambook, Author's Collection

*l-r* — Two 8″ white pins w/ 1″ each leaf, chased and engraved in repousse. ¼″ thistle-mold faceted amethyst glass. Second pin set with topaz color stone.

9¾″ pin w/ 1½″ x 1″ thistle-designed head, marked "sterling". Hallmarked. Collection of Sybel Heller.

6″ pin with 1¾″ looped ornament with ½″ thistle-mold faceted amethyst. Marked "sterling" and hallmarked. Collection of Sybel Heller.

7⅝″ white pin with 1¼″ *Art Nouveau* ornament set with one each ¼″ and ⅜″ thistle-mold faceted amethyst glass stones. Sterling hallmarked, "CH".

8″ white pin/ 1″ looped ornament w ¼″ thistle-mold faceted topaz glass. Sterling hallmarked, "CH".

8″ white pin w/ 1¼″ diameter stylized leaf motif. ½″ thistle-mold faceted amethyst glass. Sterling hallmarked, "CH".

**PLATE 67,** *page 120*

Photo by R. E. Stambook, Author's Collection

Three gift-boxed sets of Hatpins.

*Center* — 1⅝″ x 8¼″ velvet and satin lined gift box, inscribed inside top lid: "J. C. Vickery, 179. 181. & 183. Regent St. W." (England) Marked 9ct gold w/ two each Persian turquoise on either side of crook-design pin. Pair pins are 8″ overall w/ ¾″ head.

*Top, left* — 2¼″ x 12¾″ silk and velvet lined imitation leather-covered box. Patent "Perfectus" Pins, sold by Dean Marburg Ltd. 1⅛″ pair of pin heads w/ tinted mother-of-pearl. ¼″ white zircons, marked "Patent — Gilt". One 9″ white steel pin and two 12″ brass pins with patented clip-on hinges for detachable heads.

*Top, right* — 2⅞″ x 7⅜″ gift box, simulated leather, with velvet and silk lining. Unmarked. Pair of 6″ hatpins w/ ½″ ornament. Pair of veil pins, gold plated brass measuring 2½″ w/ ½″ ornamental top.

Not shown: A pair of gift-boxed hatpins w/ hinged heads that lock at right angles for flat storage, and include bar-pin and short studs, is owned by another avid collector.

**PLATE 68,** *page 120*

Photo by R. E. Stambook

Six piece Bavarian dresser set is fine example of hand-painted and reticulated china, with hand-holes in tray. Collection of The Chimney Sweep Antiques, Solvang, California.

**PLATE 69,** *page 120*

Photo by R. E. Stambook

*l-r* — 2½″ high metal boot, 3″ toe to heel, w/ 1½″ Bulldog seated inside. Dog has glass eyes and 16 pinholes. Collection of Sybel Heller.

3¾″ tall ceramic holder w/ 4″ heart-shaped base w/ 2 dividers for trinkets, "nib" and/or small pins. 2¾″ Bear figural. Unmarked. Collection of Joyce Roth.

8¼″ tall Bird figural w/ attached stump hatpin holder, open base but solid closed pin-holder insert. High glaze. Applied glass eyes. Marked with a Crown and "N" for Noritake. Collection of Joyce Roth.

Note: Pins and ornaments in holders are from author's collection.

*l-r* — 4¼″ white pin w/ ¼″ diameter head of *pewter* w/ 4 brass decorative accents and ½″ synthetic lapis stone.

4¼″ heavy gauge pin, hair ornament, w/ ⅛″ circular coiled snake w/ 3 rhinestones in dangles.

4¼″ heavy gauge pin, hair ornament, w/ ⅝″ metallic ball hugged by a ¾″ claw.

Inside stump hatpin holder w/ perched bird: 6″ pin w/ 1¼″ ornate brass crown mounting w/ ¾″ pearl. 8″ pin w/ 1¼″ claw-type mounting w/ ½″ *gemstone.* 8⅝″ gilt pin w/ 1¼″ claw-type mounting w/ ¾″ *gemstone.* Last two pin heads show use of reduction or variation in same metal-dies used for mountings.

**PLATE 70,** *page 120*

Photo by R. E. Stambook, Collection of Joyce Roth

*Top Row, l-r* — 5″ tall souvenir holder, hand-painted with gold beading. Crest insignia. Base marked "Alexandra".

4″ tall holder, hand-painted scenic with figure. Oriental artist's mark on base.

4¼″ tall flow-blue decorated holder. Solid-base marked "Pekin" and trademark. Also imprinted on base: "Thos. Till & Sons, Burlsem, England".

*Bottom Row, l-r* — 5″ tall high-glaze heavy ceramic holder. Marked "Aller Vale N1". Pennsylvania-Dutch type painted motif. Other side inscribed: "A PLACE FOR THE HAT PINS".

4½″ blue Jasperware holder with three ¼″ pin holes. Applied shield with castle and word: "ADVANCE" with motto: "SANDOWN — 1 — W". Solid-base inscribed: "Tunstall, England" — "Adams, Estb. 1657" and initials "J.C."

5½″ tall holder with 4″ solid base marked "Royal Doulton, England". The term "Royal" was used after 1901. Reverse side: hand-painted scene depicts an Inn with a hanging fish-shape sign inscribed "The Gallant Fishers".

7″ tall holder with 13 pin holes. Delicately hand-painted floral typical of the mark, "R. S. Germany".

**PLATE 71,** *page 120*

Photo by R. E. Stambook, Collection of Sybel Heller

*l-r* — Sterling silver pincushion holder, 4½″ overall height. 3¼″ stem set into 2½″ base w/ purple plush velvet cover. Signed: "W. D." and three hallmarks.

Pincushion, 4¼″ x 5¼″ base w/ pierced sterling *Art Nouveau* cover, w/ Medusa (woman w/ snakes), florals, curved design and birds. Each 1″ bird imposed on mounting.

**PLATE 72,** *page 121*

*Top Row, l-r* — 8" white pin w/ 1¼" oblong baroque pearl w/ silver filigree.

4¾" gilt pin w/ green mottled stone in 2" baroque frame.

3½" white pin (broken), w/ 3" abalone feather-shaped head.

*Bottom, l-r* — 8" gilt pin w/ 1" gilt claw mounting set w/ agate gemstone.

9½" white pin w/ 1½" oval mother-of-pearl w/ rhinestone accents.

6" white pin w/ claw mounted abalone.

9" gilt pin w/ claw mounted mother-of-pearl head.

**PLATE 73,** *page 121*

*Top Row, l-r* — 9" deeply incised and engraved horn. Floral design with 9" chain. 2½" diameter, royal blue velvet cushion. Collection of Joyce Roth.

6½" celluloid hanging cone-shape holder with 8" silk cord with matching loop. Advertised in *Spring 1911* Sears' catalog as *"White French Ivory (grained celluloid) . . ."* Top of holder has pin holes around the rim, while center of holder has plush velvet cushion.

4½" beaded boot-shaped holder with ½" tassels and 2" beaded hanger. Heavy ornamentation of crystal and green rocail, bugle and other beads.

5" beaded boot with 1½" dangles. Full beading in rose, green, blue, yellow and brown crystals.

*Bottom Row, l-r* — 7" hand-painted wall-hanging cornucopia. This "horn of plenty" was the symbol of "bountiful things showered upon mortals by such friendly personages as Plutus, Fortuna, and others". Hatpins and holder. Collection of Sybel Heller.

7" hand-painted holder, same as above but signed on back, "N. Oggle — 1906".

Pair of 6¾" bisque wall-hanging holders with Jasperware cameos. Back incised with numerals and trademark of crown and sunburst with letter "R". Attributed to V-Rudolstadt factory.

**PLATE 74,** *page 121*

Six piece dresser set marked Limoges, France. Delicately hand-painted floral porcelain. Collection of Ginny's Antiques Et Cetera.

**PLATE 75,** *page 121*

Eleven piece vanity set marked: "Victorian China — Czechoslovakia". Floral with varied ceramic transfers of mythological figures and scenes.

A dressing table set shown in Sears' *Fall 1915* catalog is advertised as follows: *". . . Louis XIV hand-painted, elaborately embossed and richly outlined with gold. Decorated with love scenes in relief. Hand-painted in delicate colors on ivory background."* (An apt description of above 11 piece set.)

Collection of Joyce Roth

**PLATE 76,** *page 121*

*Top Row, l-r* — 9½" gilt pin w/ 1" crystal set w/ ¾" pink accent stone. Author's collection.

10⅛" white pin w/ 1½" heavy cut crystal w/ ¾" polished black stone accent. Author's collection.

6" steel pin w/ 1⅛" metallic sleeve mounting of faceted jet glass w/ ¾" cabochon glass accent. Author's collection.

*Bottom, l-r* — 9½" white pin w/ 1⅞" pressed pattern amethyst color glass. Collection of Sybel Heller.

9½" white pin w/ 1⅜" oval pressed glass, decorated w/ gold. Author's collection.

12¼" white pin w/ 1½" square pressed pattern amethyst glass w/ gold decoration. Collection of Sybel Heller. (This is one of the longest shanks seen by author.)

11¾" white pin w/ 1¾" oval gold-plated metal insert mounted in glass w/ *Art Nouveau* pattern-work. Author's Collection.

11½" white pin w/ 1½" round mock tortoise w/ celluloid patch and socket mounting, w/ Art Deco transfer pattern resembling stained glass. Author's collection.

**PLATE 77,** *page 121*

*Top Row, l-r* — 4½" pin w/ 1½" pearl-dangle grape cluster.

8½" pin w/ 1" Art Deco enameled fan-shape head.

7¼" pin w/ ¾" round escutcheon set w/ 5 round turquoise.

9" pin w/ 1¼" escutcheon set in 1¾" diameter baroque mounting.

7½" pin w/ simple looped mounting set w/ turquoise. Note typical tubular socket joining pin to ornament. (Socket is a Jeweler's "finding".)

*Bottom, l-r* — 8" pin w/ 1" oval gold plated escutcheon. Monogram head.

9¾" pin w/ 2" full figural Gallic Cock, French sign for Courage. Molded in silver color metal.

10" pin w/ 1¼" rare round black painted tin head w/ floral *Art Nouveau* motif. Made to resemble jet.

7¾" pin w/ ¾" flower petal head in copper (rare). Copper, for centuries, (and to the present day), is worn to ward off certain illnesses.

**PLATE 78,** *page 122*

*Top Row, l-r* — 8" pin w/ ¾" cut bone rosebud (rare).

8½" pin w/ ¾" carved ivory ball.

7" pin w/ ¾" carved floral ivory.

1 pr. 6" overall w/ 2½" "nib" ends of black wood w/ "umbrella" handle shape heads.

**PLATE 78,** *continued:*

5″ pin w/ 2″ jet glass figural bird ornament w/ brass applied beak and glass bead eyes. (rare)

*Center Front* — 8¾″ pin w/ 1½″ scalloped frame mounting. Satsuma-ware w/ Tiger Lilies. Back incised mark on metal.

**PLATE 79,** *page 122*

Photo by R. E. Stambook, Collection of Joyce Roth

*Top, l-r* — 8½″ pin w/ 2½″ Art Deco ornament, hand-painted on tin. (rare)

11½″ pin w/ 2″ heart-shaped faceted jet w/ jet accents riveted to wire frame.

9½″ pin w/ 1¼″ button-shape mother-of-pearl with pierced floral silver color metal accented by brilliants. Ornament attached to pin w/ adjustable hinge.

*Bottom, l-r* — 11½″ pin w/ abalone shell in two bezel-type mountings of copper. (unusual)

11½″ pin w/ 3″ faceted jet w/ small cut jet accents on riveted frame. Large center stone has japanned metal backing.

12″ pin w/ 2½″ two-color pierced *Art Nouveau* mounting w/ 1″ rose zircon.

8½″ pin w/ 1½″ jet scallop shell which signifies "Good Luck".

9½″ pin w/ 1¾″ Oyster Shell w/ several hallmarks on small metallic mounting attaching pin to ornament. First hallmark (Lion passant) denotes pin is of English origin.

**PLATE 80,** *page 122*

Photo by R. E. Stambook, Collection of Joyce Roth

Natural elements as Hatpin Heads.

*Top Row, l-r* — 8¾″ pin w/ 1″ wired marine-life shell.

6½″ pin w/ 1″ wired shell fragment.

7½″ pin w/ 2″ mounted twist of abalone.

6½″ pin w/ 1″ wired cowrie shell.

*Bottom, l-r* — 7¼″ pin w/ 1″ natural unpainted pod wired to pin.

7½″ pin w/ 1″ quartz nugget, prong mounted.

7″ pin w/ ¾″ round polished multi-colored rock.

7¼″ pin w/ ¾″ brown buckeye pod.

**PLATE 81,** *page 122*

Photo by R. E. Stambook, Collection of Sybel Heller

*Bottom Row, l-r* — 7¼″ white pin w/ 1″ x 1″ Art Deco Ram figural. Unmarked silver.

11″ white pin w/ ¾″ Carnival or Harlequin hat. Hallmarked "*silver plate*".

7″ white pin w/ ¾″ figural dog's head, marked "Pat. applied for" and "sterling".

7¼″ white pin w/ 1½″ design of wings and snakes w/ amethyst stone setting.

**PLATE 81,** *continued*

10″ white pin w/ 1¼″ chased frame mounting w/ applied metal rooster and amethyst color stone accent.

10½″ white pin w/ 2¼″ brass *Art Nouveau* Dragonfly w/ pink and white brilliant accents.

8″ white *hinged* pin w/ 1″ figural Raven perched in silver circle. Hallmarked.

*Top Row, l-r* — 6½″ white pin w/ 1″ *Art Nouveau* portrait w/ pansies. Marked "*sterling front*".

7¾″ white pin w/ 1⅛″ *Art Nouveau* portrait. Marked "*sterling front*" and incised w/ 5 point star.

7¾″ white pin w/ 1¼″ *Art Nouveau* curved Caterpillar-Moth. Marked sterling.

5½″ white pin w/ 1¼″ *Art Nouveau* portrait. Marked "*sterling front*" and incised w/ 5 point star.

9″ white pin w/ 1⅛″ *Art Nouveau* portrait w/ Lily. Marked "sterling", plus two hallmarks.

**PLATE 82,** *page 122*

Photo by R. E. Stambook, Collection of Sybel Heller

Many period hatpins were set with stones but others depended on design alone for appeal and beauty.

*l-r* — 4¾″ pin w/ 2″ gilt *Art Nouveau* floral Lily w/ amber bead accents.

9½″ pin w/ 1¾″ gilt filigree *Art Nouveau* mounting accented w/ amethyst stones.

4½″ pin w/ 2″ chased and engraved gilt head w/ *Fleur de Lis* (the Flower of Light).

8″ pin w 1″ x 1¼″ pierced baroque mounting w/ escutcheon.

7″ pin w/ 3″ gilt *Art Nouveau* ornament set w/ a cabochon-cut amethyst set into both sides of ornament.

9″ pin w/ 1″ oval chased frame w/ enameled Lily of the Valley.

9½″ pin w/ 2¼″ polished coral w/ 2 chased and engraved lizards as figural mounting. Lizards are a symbol of "Good Luck".

**PLATE 83,** *page 122*

Photo by R. E. Stambook, Collection of Joyce Roth

*Top, l-r* — 10″ pin w/ 1¾″ silver head marked on back, "S. D. Childs & Co. Chicago". Front: Jug inscribed "Green River". Head: "She was bred in old Kentucky".

7″ pin w/ ¾″ floral mounting w/ escutcheon engraved "Ferry Hall, Lake Forest, Ill."

12″ pin w/ 1″ embossed head inscribed, "St. Johnsbury, Vt."; "St. Johnsbury Academy"; "Instituted 1842".

9″ pin w/ ¾″ cloisonne Canadian Maple Leaf. Reverse marked "sterling" and "R.H.".

*Bottom, l-r* — 7¾″ pin w/ 1″ banner ornament enameled Maple Leaf and "Vancouver".

7½″ pin w/ marked "sterling" head. Shield inscribed: "St. James Hotel, Sapulpa, Okla."

**PLATE 83,** *continued:*

6″ pin w/ ¾″ enameled signet head inscribed "SIGILL: COLL: YALEN: NOV: PORT: NOV: ANGL" on outer blue rim.

10″ pin w/ 1″ enameled Maple Leaf, rear marking "sterling" and "R.H.". Maple Leaf is national motif for Canada.

7½″ pin w/ ¾″ enameled and incised shield w/ unidentified hallmark.

**PLATE 84,** *page 123*

Photo by R. E. Stambook, Collection of Joyce Roth

*Back Row, l-r* — 7½″ pin with ¾″ round Bohemian glass head with gold overlay and beading.

7½″ pin with spear-shaped ½″ amethyst color glass with multiple facets.

9¾″ pin with 3″ blown amber-color glass ornament.

9¾″ pin with 2½″ white milkglass "thorn" ornament.

*Front Row, l-r* — 8″ pin w/ 1¼″ patterned crystal ornament with gold painted overlay. Silver foil backing for extra highlight.

9″ pin with 1½″ patterned black glass head with four ⅜″ exposed hearts on green and gold painted background.

7½″ pin with 2″ oval pressed-pattern "clambroth" glass. (rare)

7¼″ pin with 1¼″ diameter round "flow blue" china ornament. (rare)

9½″ pin with 1″ diameter round *blue* milkglass ornament. (rare)

**PLATE 85,** *page 123*

Photo by R. E. Stambook, Collection of Joyce Roth

*l-r* — One pr. 4″ pins w/ 2½″ black painted celluloid, Art Deco design, accented w/ rhinestones.

4½″ pin w/ 3½″ molded celluloid, hand-painted w/ oriental motif.

4½″ pin w/ 2″ molded turquoise-color plastic.

9½″ pin w/ 2″ simulated tortoise. Pierced celluloid mold, reticulated flower.

4″ pin w/ 5″ pierced molded celluloid, amber color diamond-shaped head.

3″ threaded pin w/ 4½″ two-mold plastic hat ornament. Molded coral color feather w/ molded jet accent w/brilliants.

One pair 3½″ pins w/ 3″ imitation tortoise. Hand-painted celluloid w/ rhinestone accents.

Note: Compare *Art Nouveau* 9½″ reticulated flower with shorter stemmed Art Deco pins of the twenties and thirties.

**PLATE 86,** *page 123*

Photo by R. E. Stambook, Collection of Joyce Roth

*Top, l-r* — 6½″ pin w/ ¾″ black beaded head.

9″ pin w/ 1½″ round head combined w/ steel and jet beads.

6″ pin w/ ¾″ round jet beaded head.

**PLATE 86,** *continued:*

*Bottom, l-r* — 7″ pin w/ jet beaded head, accented w/ four 2¼″ Art Deco dangles.

One pair 7″ pins w/ 3″ lustre bead heads.

9″ pin w/ 3¼″ elongated head of purple lustre beads.

7¾″ pin w/ 2¾″ jet beaded head.

**PLATE 87,** *page 123*

Photo by R. E. Stambook, Collection of Sybel Heller

*Top pin* — 7¾″ pin w/ ¾″ hand-painted porcelain portrait accented w/ hand-painted flowers.

*Bottom, l-r* — 6¼″ pin w/ 1½″ round scenic Satsuma-ware, incised hallmark on back.

8″ pin w/ 1½″ ceramic transfer on pearlized porcelain w/ hand-painted gold accents.

6″ pin w/ 1″ ceramic transfer on pearlized porcelain, hand-painted accents. Ball mounted on gilt filigree cage.

7¾″ w/ 1¼″ round Satsuma-ware Dragonhead, hallmarked on metal back.

**PLATE 88,** *page 123*

Photo by R. E. Stambook, Collection of Joyce Roth

*Center pin* — 9″ pin w 1¼″ round ceramic transfer portrait.

*Clockwise, l-r* — 7″ pin w/ 1¼″ round hand-painted floral porcelain in brass mounting.

9″ pin w/ 1¾″ round ceramic transfer. Mythological scene, similar to transfer used on fancy toilet set shown on Plate 75.

8″ pin w/ ¾″ miniature portrait head w/ *Art Nouveau* pierced mounting. Transfer has hand-painted overlay accents.

7¼″ pin w/ 1¼″ round transfer portrait highlighted w/ gold and china beading.

7¼″ pin w/ 1″ oval floral porcelain, enclosed in metallic sleeve.

**PLATE 89,** *page 123*

Photo by R. E. Stambook, Collection of Joyce Roth

*Top, l-r* — 5½″ pin w/ 1¼″ full figural spider.

9″ pin w/ 2½″ long figural mounting. Two dragons circling polished coral. (The dragon is the Chinese symbol for Royalty and Good Fortune.)

*Middle, l-r* — 4¼″ pin w/ 1″ portrait head, reverse marked "sterling front" and incised star hallmark.

6¾″ pin w/ 1¾″ diameter head of green painted celluloid w/ brass *Art Nouveau* portrait with unusual type mounting.

10″ pin w/ 1¼″ full figural lion, open mouthed w/ ⅛″ brilliant. Head accented w/ green glass eyes.

*Bottom, l-r* — 7¼″ pin w/ 1″ 1904 Liberty Head silver quarter. Reverse marking: "Pat. Aug. 11. 08".

12″ pin w/ 1¾″ round intaglio portrait. Art Deco Pharaoh in unusual copper and brass combination metals.

8″ pin w/ 1″ full figural. Helmeted Jeanne d'Arc. Reverse marking: "sterling front".

**PLATE 90,** *page 124*

Photo by R. E. Stambook, Author's Collection

*Top, l-r* — 11½″ white pin w/ 2″ full figural molded synthetic coral roses w/ gilt metal leaf accents.

10¼″ white pin w/ 1¾″ gilt chased and engraved mounting w/ triangular stone and other brilliant accents.

9½″ white pin w/ 2″ gilt *Art Nouveau* figural mounting w/ ½″ oval bezel-set amethyst. Bird has red stone eye.

10″ gilt pin w/ 1½″ gilt pierced mounting w/ filigree overlay and 12 red and 13 green brilliants.

*Bottom, l-r* — Two 11½″ white pins w/ 1½″ oxidized silver color floral figurals each w/ ⅜″ stone accents and three brilliants.

11½″ white pin w/ 1¾″ chased oxidized silver *Art Nouveau* figural floral w/ ¼″ Tiffany-type mounted amethyst w/ 12 brilliants set in stem of Iris. (The Iris flower is the model for the French *Fleur de Lis*)

10″ gilt pin w/ 2″ chased rectangular mounting w/ four heart shaped pierced corners, bezel-set center stone w/ 4 brilliants.

**PLATE 91,** *page 124*

Photo by R. E. Stambook, Author's Collection

*Top, l-r* — 7¼″ white pin w/ ⅝″ oval hand-carved Malachite ancient scarab. Rear of stone carved with Egyptian signs. These ancient talisman-artifacts were often buried with the dead as a symbol of eternal life.

6¾″ brass pin w/ 1″ *Art Nouveau* oxidized silver head. Floral figural Lily Pad w/ frog and water snake coiled around brilliant accent.

7¾″ white pin w/ 1″ coiled snake figural mounting. ½″ round amethyst in bezel mounting.

*Bottom, l-r* — 7¾″ white pin w/ 1¼″ full figural Art Deco Phoenix Bird w/ ½″ bezel-mounted green stone as body. Red brilliant eye. This bird is Egyptian symbol of Immortality.

10¼″ white pin w/ ⅞″ diameter molded glass head w/ red and gold enameled Art Deco scarab. (Compare this scarab to the ancient carved stone Malachite (top row) and note the stylized treatment of the design which is so typically Art Deco.)

10″ brass pin w/ 1⅞″ gilt figural lion w/ topaz stone accent in mouth. Fluted frame w/ topaz brilliants.

**PLATE 92,** *page 124*

Photo by R. E. Stambook, Author's Collection

*l-r* — 11¼″ steel pin w/ 2¼″ porcelain head, w/ hand-painted roses and beading, w/ high lustre.

7⅞″ steel pin w/ 1″ ball-type porcelain, w/ hand-painted roses. (Attributed to Limoges)

**PLATE 93,** *page 124*

Photo by R. E. Stambook, Author's Collection

Metal was twisted, draped, curled, overlaid — anything to make the head a thing of beauty.

*Top, l-r* — 8″ brass pin w/ 1¼″ *Art Nouveau* floral motif. Marked on pin: "Sterling Top".

7″ brass pin w/ ¾″ *Art Nouveau* floral nosegay w/ four genuine garnets. Marked on pin: "Sterling top".

**PLATE 93,** *continued:*

7¾″ steel pin w/ 1″ souvenir head. Escutcheon top for monogram. Marked "sterling". Engraved on one side: "THE U.S. CAPITOL"; Reverse: "WHITE HOUSE". (See detailed drawing *Plate 190.*)

5¼″ white pin w/ 1¾″ baroque top marked on pin "sterling top". Note: Compare this baroque-type ornament w/ typical *Art Nouveau* pins on bottom row.

*Bottom, l-r* — 7″ white pin w/ ⅞″ symbolic figural winged lion w/ halo and book. Unmarked silver. This is the Christian symbol for St. Mark.

6¾″ brass pin w/ 1″ *Art Nouveau* portrait marked on pin "sterling top".

8″ brass pin w/ 1″ *Art Nouveau* portrait w/ escutcheon monogram "F.S.". Marked on pin, "sterling top".

7″ white pin w/ ¾″ Baroque top, marked "sterling" on head.

**PLATE 94,** *page 125*

Photo by R. E. Stambook, Collection of Joyce Roth

11½″ long satin and velvet lined gift box w/ snap-lock, containing pair of 10¼″ *threaded* white pins, w/ 1¼″ each oxidized metal silver color ornaments, accented w/ 20 brilliants per hatpin.

10¾″ white pin w/ 1¼″ glass molded amethyst-color Cameo.

9¾″ gilt pin w/ 1¼″ x 1½″ oval molded Cameo in gilt gypsy setting.

**PLATE 95,** *page 125*

Photo by R. E. Stambook, Author's Collection

*Back, l-r* — 7¾″ gilt pin with 1⅜″ genuine malachite gemstone.

7⅛″ white pin w/ ½″ imitation polished malachite glass head accented by seven brilliants.

*Front, l-r* — 5¾″ white pin with 2″ overall two-piece dangle of free-form marbelized glass.

8″ white pin with 2″ overall simple brass frame with 1¾″ green slag glass rimmed by brilliants.

**PLATE 96,** *page 125*

Photo by R. E. Stambook, Author's Collection

*l-r* — 3½″ japanned pin w/ 5¼″ jet riveted ornament soldered to a wire construction.

3½″ japanned pin w/ 3″ x 5″ spray ornamental design.

Note: Both pins show perfection of riveted jet jewelry.

**PLATE 97,** *page 126*

Photo by R. E. Stambook, Author's Collection

*Top to bottom* — 9″ japanned pin w/ 1″ box-shaped ornament.

11¼″ japanned pin w/ 2¾″ ornament.

8¾″ japanned pin w/ 1¾″ diameter circle.

7¼″ japanned pin w/ 1¾″ diameter ball.

*Front Row, l-r* — 10½″ japanned pin w/ 3¾″ ornament.

10¾″ japanned pin w/ 2½″ pear-shape ornament.

10¾″ japanned pin w/ 3″ ornament w/ rhinestone accents.

**PLATE 98,** *page 126*

*Back Row, l-r* — 8⅜″ steel pin w/ ¾″ round porcelain, w/ ceramic transfer portrait.

7½″ steel pin w/ ¾″ round porcelain, w/ ceramic transfer portrait.

*Front Row* — 7¼″ steel pin w/ 1¼″ diameter ceramic transfer head, w/ cobalt blue porcelain mounting set into small metallic sleeve attached to pin.

**PLATE 99,** *page 126*

*Top Row, l-r* — 11¼″ gilt pin w/ 1″ round head w/ metal backing. Scenic Satsuma-ware.

8″ gilt pin w/ 1″ ball portrait. Satsuma-ware.

8¾″ gilt pin w/ 1″ scalloped metal framed ornament. Oriental hallmark. Satsuma-ware portrait head.

*Bottom, l-r* — 7¾″ gilt pin w/ 1″ diameter metal backed floral Satsuma-ware. Oriental hallmark.

7¾″ gilt pin w/ ¾″ scalloped metal frame. Floral Satsuma-ware.

7¾″ gilt pin w/ 1″ badge-shaped head w/ 2 Oriental hallmarks on metal frame. Floral Satsuma-ware.

**PLATE 100,** *page 126*

*l-r* — 12″ unusual square rather than round brass pin w/ spiral at center of shank. 3/16″ simple gilt frame (damaged). 1¾″ bezel mounted molded glass ornament, painted w/ gold accents. (Same design as pin on right)

8″ brass pin w/ 1⅝″ brass bezel mounted molded plastic head w/ oriental symbols.

8¼″ white pin w/ 1¾″ oval molded marbelized brown slag glass w/ gold painted accents. Cranes in pine tree and tortoise are both Chinese symbols of longevity. Pin to left is identical except for painted overlay.

**PLATE 101,** *page 126*

*Back Row, l-r* — 7½″ steel pin with ¾″ cut and polished wooden bead.

11½″ steel pin with ¾″ diameter polished wooden ball-head.

*Bottom, l-r* — 7⅛″ gilt pin w/ 1¼″ diameter round wooden ball with painted overlay. (Worn protective coat of lacquer appears as a stain on hat-pin head.)

7″ brass pin with 1¼″ black painted wooden ball with gold painted oriental motif and symbolic swastika. (See *Plate 61*.)

11¼″ steel pin with 1¼″ diameter black painted and lacquered wooden ball.

**PLATE 102,** *page 126*

*Top, l-r* — 9¼″ white pin w/ 1⅛″ *Art Nouveau* painted milk glass. Pattern mold w/ gold accents. Metal bushing connects pin to head.

**PLATE 102,** *continued:*

10¼″ steel pin w/ ⅝″ *Art Nouveau* pattern black glass w/ white applied glass design.

6¼″ steel pin w/ 1¼″ pressed milk glass w/ gold accents. Ox-eye Daisy.

*Bottom, l-r* — 9⅜″ white pin w/ ⅞″ button-type molded milk glass pattern hand-painted w/ metal bushing attaching head to pin.

10″ brass pin w/ 1¾″ oval milk glass w/ prong mounting and gilt metal back.

6⅛″ steel pin w/ 1¼″ pressed pattern milk glass hand-painted w/ raised gold beading and decoration.

**PLATE 103,** *page 127*

*l-r* — 4¾″ white pin w/ 4¼″ black painted and lacquered wood ornament.

11¼″ steel pin with 1⅝″ cut, painted, and lacquered wooden head made to resemble jet.

11″ brass pin with 1½″ painted tin head machine-molded to resemble faceted jet. (Note arc-type mounting)

4½″ steel pin with a 5¼″ black painted and lacquered wood ornament with hand-painted floral design. ½″ socket-mounting.

**PLATE 104,** *page 127*

*l-r* — 8½″ brass pin w/ 3⅛″ molded plastic imitation amber head.

5⅛″ white pin w/ 2¾″ polished dark amber head w/ 150+ rhinestones drilled and set into natural resin element.

7″ white pin w/ 1½″ polished light natural amber w/ hand-painted and hand-cut drape design accented with 19 rhinestones.

**PLATE 105,** *page 127*

*Top, l-r* — 6¾″ white pin w/ 1⅛″ abalone head, bezel mounting, marked "sterling".

3⅝″ gilt pin w/ 3½″ abalone in ¾″ pierced gilt mounting.

6″ brass pin w/ ⅜″ heart-shaped mother-of-pearl in silver mounting.

*Bottom, l-r* — 6″ brass pin w/ ½″ oval bezel mounted mother-of-pearl, marked "sterling".

6⅜″ brass pin w/ ⅞″ flat button-type abalone in bezel mounting, marked "sterling".

8″ brass pin w/ ¾″ cabachon cut abalone, bezel mounting, marked "sterling".

7½″ brass pin w/ 1⅛″ oval mother-of-pearl in bezel mounting. Marked "sterling". Souvenir pin engraved on back with City, Organization, and Date. "LOS ANGELES G.A.R. 1912". (Grand Army of the Republic).

**PLATE 106,** *page 127*

*Center, Bottom Pin* — 8½″ brass pin w/ 1⅝″ hand-carved abalone shell head.

*Center* — 6⅝″ pin w/ 1″ gemstone claw-set in 1⅛″ oval chased cage mounting. (Cracked stone)

**PLATE 106,** *continued:*

*Clockwise, l-r* — 11¼″ pin w/ ⅞″ Rose Quartz gemstone, bezel set in silver.

5¾″ white pin w/ ¾″ imitation Mexican Fire Opal oftentimes called "Dragon's Breath" (See GLOSSARY). Bezel-set in silver, this type art glass was made from 1895-1920. Marked "sterling".

10″ pin w/ ⅝″ bezel mounted synthetic gemstone.

6½″ pin w/ ¾″ oval bezel mounted Agate gemstone.

8″ pin w/ ⅝″ oval gemstone, of Quartz family.

10″ brass pin w/ ⅞″ round opaline glass w/ foil backing in brass bezel mounting.

These pins represent examples of genuine and imitation gemstones. It is important to have such pins appraised for true value. Regardless of whether stones were genuine or imitation, workmanship reflects the excellence of the craftsman in the jeweler's trade.

**PLATE 107,** *page 127*

*l-r* — 4⅛″ ornament w/ 1½″ head and 1⅛″ screw-type "nib".

3⅜″ overall *Art Nouveau* ornament w/ 1⅛″ head. 1″ dangle with screw-type "nib".

One pair 3½″ white pins w/ ¼″ hollow pearl heads w/ ½″ threaded "nib".

5″ overall ornament w/ 1⅞″ pearlized pear-shape w/ 1½″ threaded hollow ball. Note: unusual that the *head* of the ornament should be threaded rather than the "nib"-end.

4½″ overall ornament w/ ¾″ *Art Nouveau* gilt head w/ 1½″ gilt dangle, w/ ½″ threaded "nib".

**PLATE 108,** *page 128*

*Top Row, l-r* — 8″ white pin w/ ⅞″ gilt *Art Nouveau* mounting w/ ¾″ oval aquamarine stone.

9″ white pin w/ 1¼″ gilt *Art Nouveau* mounting w/ ⅞″ molded coral color rose.

9¾″ white pin w/ 1″ *Art Nouveau* mounting, w/ ½″ coral cabochon cut stone. Hallmarked "Sterling".

*Bottom Row, l-r* — 7¼″ white pin w/ 1″ gilt *Art Nouveau* mounting w/ ⅝″ turquoise color ball.

9⅝″ white pin w/ 1¼″ gilt *Art Nouveau* mounting, w/ 1⅝″ pink slag glass.

8″ white pin w/ ¾″ gilt mounting w/ ⅝″ peacock-eye in crown setting.

**PLATE 109,** *page 128*

*Top, l-r* — 5½″ white pin (one of a pair) w/ 2¼″ full figural celluloid molded elephant head.

5⅛″ white pin w/ 1¾″ Art Deco geometric plastic head.

5⅛″ white pin w/ 1¾″ ivory celluloid simulated scallop shell in Art Deco design. The scallop shell is a symbol for safe travel.

**PLATE 109,** *continued:*

*Bottom, l-r* — 4⅝″ white pin w/ 2¾″ patterned plastic hand-painted Art Deco.

5½″ white pin w/ 2¾″ *Art Nouveau* "French Ivory" w/ marbelized plastic insert.

4″ white pin w/ 3⅛″ pierced and formed *Art Nouveau* plastic molded bird and Four Leaf Clover.

**PLATE 110,** *page 128*

*Back, l-r* — 7½″ brass pin w/ ⅝″ chased brass Owl with seed-pearl eyes. This figural mounting sets off a 1½″ cut and polished fragment of mother-of-pearl shell. The "quality and virtue" of the Owl is *wisdom.*

7½″ brass pin w/ ½″ brass figural mounting consisting of four frogs forming a crown to hold a ⅜″ x ½″ escutcheon mounted art glass stone.

*Front* — A pair of 6⅝″ white pins. A ⅝″ figural mounting shows twin lizards, (signifying "Good Luck"), which form a claw-mount for a piece of 1″ polished peking glass. Peking glass is called "the poor man's jade".

**PLATE 111,** *page 128*

Favored amulets of old were elephant tusk, walrus teeth, elks teeth, perforated shells and other such elements — each guaranteed to "drive away" evil spirits.

*l-r* — 6″ pin w/ 1″ trophy walrus tooth mounted in gold, engraved "Queen #270".

8¼″ white pin w/ 1½″ carved full figural ivory elephant balanced on ivory ball.

6¾″ pin w/ ¾″ sterling silver filigree mounting w/ pair-of trophy teeth of the Chamois. This hatpin has a matching glove-ring. See *Plate 197.*

**PLATE 112,** *page 128*

*l-r* — 4½″ overall size ornament w/ plastic simulated stone.

3⅛″ overall size ornament, abstract flower design in Art Deco.

5½″ overall size sword ornament typical of the forties, marked "© Florenza", (similar type may be seen in 1898 Sears' catalogue).

3½″ overall size ornament w/ pearl and "peking" glass.

4¾″ overall ornament, typical of the twenties and thirties, incised "#18".

**PLATE 113,** *page 129*

*l-r* — 2″ pin w/ plastic figural Art Deco styled "Pierrott". Hat ornament. Overall size, 3½″ w/ 1″ screw-type "nib".

2″ pin w/ Art Deco brass Duck figural w/ emerald color eyes. 4¾″ overall, w/ 3″ gilt chain. Velvet bow-tie w/ 5 brilliant accents. Rare ⅞″ *cork-filled* metal "nib".

*Pierrott's* costume is distinguishable from the diamond-patterned tights worn by *Harlequin,* by his baggy pantaloons and especially Pierrott's wide ruff atop a loose fitting blouse. Pierrott wears a skull cap as close-fitting as the "spit-curls" plastered against his cheeks.

**PLATE 114,** *pag 129*

*Top Row* — 7⅜″ white pin w/ ¾″ gold carat illusion-type setting of polished rock.

8½″ steel pin w/ 1⅝″ overall layers of varied color rocks separated by thin metal strips and capped by diamond-shaped pewter at top and base.

9½″ white pin w/ ½″ cube of glass "goldstone", drill-set into socket mounting.

*Bottom Row* — 7⅝″ white pin w/ 1¼″ pear-shape amber in socket mounting.

6½″ white pin w/ 1½″ natural pyrite rock in wire-claw mounting.

8″ white pin w/ ¾″ natural rock of "fool's gold" in wire-claw mounting.

**PLATE 115,** *page 129*

Silver was utilized in many different ways:

*Top, l-r* — 8¼″ heavy gauge handmade and hand-sharpened pin w/ ⅝″ sterling silver nugget with two deeply incised hallmarks.

8¼″ steel pin w/ 1″ unfaceted crystal w/ chased spiraled silver mounting. Marked "sterling" w/ hallmark and date "1900". Collection of Renee Marshall

6⅝″ pin w/ 1″ *Art Nouveau* sterling mounting for jet. Collection of Renee Marshall

*Bottom, l-r* — 6″ white pin w/ ¾″ chased and engraved mounting w/ ½″ faceted gemstone (citron). Detail of this thistle-cut many-faceted gemstone is shown on *Plate 186*, *fig. g*.

4″ white pin w/ 1″ green glass head w/ sterling silver overlay. Incised star hallmark on small socket mounting.

7⅝″ white pin w/ ⅞″ amethyst glass with sterling overlay. Hallmarked.

**PLATE 116,** *page 129*

*l-r* — One pair 4½″ white pins w/ 1⅛″ x 1⅝″ coiled chased snakeskin design ornamental heads w/ ⅝″ threaded "nibs".

3⅜″ overall ornament w/ ⅜″ cabochon-cut genuine amethyst and 13 moonstones.

3⅛″ white pin w/ 1⅞″ *Art Nouveau* mounting w/ two ¾″ pearlized glass stones. Threaded "nib".

**PLATE 117,** *page 129*

6″ gilt pin w/ 1¾″ head of hand-painted lustre glass, pearlized finish similar to that used on lustre-ware china tea-sets. Heavy hand-painted overlay of gold accent at base and set into gilt simple ball and socket mounting.

**PLATE 118,** *page 130*

*l-r* — 6¼″ steel pin w/ ⅜″ gilt crown mounting w/ ¾″ faceted diamond color stone in illusion setting.

8⅜″ steel pin w/ ¼″ gilt crown mounting w/ ⅝″ faceted stone in illusion setting.

**PLATE 118,** *continued:*

8½″ gilt pin w/ 1¼″ figural bird's claw mounting combined with an illusion setting of ½″ topaz color stone.

8″ steel pin w/ ⅜″ gilt crown mounting w/ ⅝″ topaz color stone.

8⅝″ steel pin w/ ⅝″ gilt crown mounting w/ 1″ rose color rhinestone.

**PLATE 119,** *page 130*

*Top, l-r* — 3½″ x 5″ trophy hoof w/ green plush velvet cushion. Author's collection.

5″ tall china open-mouth holder w/ woven metallic threads covering ceramic container. Solid bottom. Collection of Renee Marshall.

*Front* — 11″ overall hatpin holder, ribbon silk covering w/ hanger. 6″ glass tube insert for pins. Collection of Renee Marshall.

*Center* — 10″ woven straw primitive hanging hatpin holder. Collection Joyce Roth.

Pins displayed in hoof: *l-r* — 3″ steel pin with purple marbelized head; 2½″ white pin w/ light green pearlized head; 5¾″ white pin painted black metal head; 3¾″ white pin painted black wooden head; three 4¾″ steel pins w/ black glass beaded heads; one pair 2⅝″ white pins w/ ¾″ painted heads. All from author's collection representing pins of the twenties and thirties.

**PLATE 120,** *page 130*

*Top, l-r* — 7¾″ gilt pin w/ 1″ chased mounting w/ decorative escutcheon. Monogram "A".

8″ gilt pin w/ 1″ *Art Nouveau* mounting w/ plain escutcheon. Initials "K.O."

8¾″ gilt pin w/ 1″ *Art Nouveau* mounting w/ plain escutcheon. Initial "F".

11″ gilt pin w/ ¾″ baroque mounting w/ ⅞″ convex plain escutcheon w/ monogram "L".

7⅛″ gilt pin w/ ¾″ pierced mounting w/ concave decorative escutcheon w/ initial "S".

*Bottom, l-r* — 8″ gilt pin w/ 1″ *Art Nouveau* mounting w/ ⅞″ decorated escutcheon. No initials in signet.

10″ gilt pin w 1″ pierced mounting w/ ¾″ plain escutcheon. No monogram.

8″ gilt pin w/ 1⅜″ *Art Nouveau* mounting w/ ¼″ x ⅜″ rectangular plain escutcheon. Not engraved.

**PLATE 121,** *page 131*

Late Victorian — pin cushion with stand. *Art Nouveau* period.

7″ x 10″ diameter tufted silk cushion sewn on gilded frame. Frame decorated with gilded 1½″ leaves and a 5″ gilded bird with 3″ wingspread. Laurel wreath in beak. 1″ x 2½″ bevelled glass mirror accent.

**PLATE 122,** *page 131*

Left Group: *l-r* — 7″ white pin w/ ¼″ faceted crystal w/ brilliants.

8½″ white pin w/ ⅝″ faceted crystal ball.

**PLATE 122,** *continued:*

7⅞″ brass pin w/ ½″ pierced gilt mounting set w/ ¾″ clambroth glass ball.

8½″ white pin w/ ⅞″ mercury glass ball. (rare)

*Center: l-r* — 8″ white pin w/ ⅛″ silver chased mounting w/ ¾″ faceted crystal.

7″ white pin w/ ⅞″ faceted crystal.

8″ white pin w/ 1⅛″ faceted crystal.

7¼″ white pin w/ 2″ faceted crystal.

*Right Group: l-r* — 3¼″ white pin w/ ¼″ gilt claw mounting w/ 1½″ faceted crystal.

4″ brass pin w/ ⅛″ x ⅝″ gilt chased mounting set w/ 1⅝″ etched and faceted crystal.

4⅞″ brass pin w/ ⅝″ silver color *Art Nouveau* frame w/ 1⅜″ blown free-form camphor glass. Metal frame accented w/ 9 crystal brilliants.

7½″ steel pin w/ ⅝″ gilt rim or bezel-type mounting w/ ⅝″ faceted crystal. Dangle is accented w/ ¼″ stone.

**PLATE 123,** *page 131*

*Front Row, l-r* — 6⅞″ white pin w/ ¾″ figural English Bull Dog w/ ruby color eyes. Unmarked silver.

6½″ white pin w/ ¾″ Oriental "Good Luck" symbol. Unmarked silver.

7⅞″ white pin w/ 1″ *Art Nouveau* daisy figural. Marked "sterling *front*".

*Back Row, l-r* — 7½″ white pin w/ ⅞″ figural angel. Marked "sterling".

10″ white pin w/ 1¼″ figural moth w/ ⅜″ peacock-eye accent. Unmarked silver.

7½″ white pin w/ ¾″ *Art Nouveau* portrait. Marked sterling.

**PLATE 124,** *page 131*

Hatpins of precious metals were usually elaborately chased, embossed and/or engraved as on these examples:

*Top, l-r* — 10″ white pin w/ 2″ *Art Nouveau* head marked "sterling".

7⅛″ white pin w/ 1½″ *Art Nouveau* head, hallmarked "P&B" and marked "sterling".

*Bottom, l-r* — 5⅝″ brass pin w/ 2″ *Art Nouveau* head marked "sterling".

9¾″ white pin w/ 2½″ *Art Nouveau* head marked "sterling".

8″ white pin w/ 2⅛″ *Art Nouveau* head marked "sterling" and "KEENE".

**PLATE 125,** *page 131*

*Back Pin:* 11½″ white pin w/ 1/16″ threaded end which screws into the head. 1½″ ornamental top consists of three ¾″ gilt claw-mounted faceted amethysts. Top has threaded socket. The amethyst glass is accented by 54 magnificent paste brilliants individually metal-cupped.

**PLATE 125,** *continued:*

*Front Pin:* 12″ gilt pin w/ 1½″ diameter chased and engraved Art Deco frame, bezel-mounted with a 1″ faceted topaz. A 1½″ applied hinge allows the head to be angled at various degrees.

**PLATE 126,** *page 132*

*Top Pin:* 7⅞″ brass pin w/ 2½″ diagonal measure mother-of-pearl w/ socket mounting.

*Center Pin:* 7½″ brass pin w/ 1½″ irridescent glass blown in the mold w/ pontal set into socket mounting.

*Bottom Pin:* 7¼″ brass w/ 2″ mother-of-pearl golf club.

**PLATE 127,** *page 132*

Multi-faceted glass came in all colors of the rainbow to match other fashion accessories; however, the use of blue stones (sapphire color) seems to be far and few between. Here are some:

*l-r* — 7½″ brass pin w/ ¾″ pear-shaped faceted sapphire color glass.

7¼″ white pin w/ 1¾″ chased gilt frame w/ pavé setting of 15 diamond color and 3 sapphire color brilliants.

6″ brass pin w/ 1¼″ triangular gilt bezel set 1″ faceted sapphire color glass w/ 12 brilliants in metal cups and gilt cage.

7¾″ white pin w/ ¾″ faceted stone bezel set in silver color mounting.

7⅞″ steel pin w/ ½″ oval gilt frame w/ bezel mounted 1¼″ faceted stone. Arc-type mount for attaching ornament to pin.

**PLATE 128,** *page 132*

Jet-glass riveted hatpins with stones soldered to a wire-construction. Craft reached perfection in the mourning period of Queen Victoria (1901). Hatpins from H. M. Supplier, Gebruder Feix, Albrechtsdorf (1850-1945), Jablonecer District, Czech.

*l-r* — 9¾″ japanned pin w/ 2¼″ convex faceted head.

12″ japanned pin w/ 1⅝″ bezel mounted jet-glass cameo set in a japanned metal sleeve.

10¼″ japanned pin w/ 2¼″ diameter riveted wire frame w/ 1⅛″ center faceted stone.

**PLATE 129,** *page 132*

*l-r* — 8″ brass pin w/ 1¼″ souvenir head. An enameled *Fleur-de-Lis* inscribed: "ST. LOUIS '04". This pin is one of several from the world famed exposition held at St. Louis, Mo. The *Fleur-de-Lis* is the French symbol for life and power. This "flower of light" is designed from nature's Iris.

11¼″ white pin w/ 1½″ chased bezel mounted 1″ red faceted stone. Outer rim of gilt is beautifully enameled. The superior enameling on this pin hints of Faberge craftsmanship.

10¼″ brass pin w/ ¾″ enameled escutcheon mounted on 1⅛″ chased and pierced gilt frame.

Photo by R. E. Stambook, Author's Collection

*Back Pin:* 7⅝" steel pin w/ 1½" triangular faceted glass. Irridescent, with 3" faceted glass dangling accent.

*Front Pin:* 8¼" gilt pin w/ 2¼" pear-shape faceted irridescent glass in simple ½" gilt sleeve-type mounting.

Although the hatpins are highly irridescent, they cannot be categorized as "carnival" since they are European.

**PLATE 131,** *page 132*

Photo by R. E. Stambook, Author's Collection

Cameos of mythological characters were considered talismans, as were the scarab, cat, snake, spider, frog, and many more symbols from the animal kingdom.

*l-r* — 7" brass pin with ⅞" gilt chased and pierced mounting, with ½" molded cameo.

6⅝" steel pin with ⅝" Holy Family miniature portrait hand-painted on ivory.

9⅝" white pin with ⅞" oval onyx gemstone cameo, bezel mounted in gold karat. The intricately carved cameo depicts Queen Juno and Jupiter, (father of Gods and Men). Juno, goddess of marriage has the appearance *"of a beautiful majestic woman of middle age, large and attractive eyes, and a grave expression commanding reverence."* She is shown wearing the familiar crown and veil, with the peacock in gorgeous array, and the cuckoo (herald of springtime). Both birds were considered sacred to her.

**PLATE 132,** *page 133*

Photo by R. E. Stambook, Author's Collection

*l-r* — 6½" white pin w/ 1⅛" hand-painted flowers on porcelain w/ gold accents.

7¼" gilt pin w/ 1⅛" piercework mounting. Hand-painted floral on porcelain, w/ gold overlay and blue beading.

7¾" gilt pin w/ 1½" hand-painted floral on porcelain w/ gold accents.

8⅛" white pin w/ 1⅛" scenic transfer on porcelain w/ metal rim sleeve.

8" white pin w/ 1¼" hand-painted porcelain w/ gold decoration and beading. Metallic rim is attached to pin w/ arc-type jeweler's finding.

**PLATE 133,** *page 133*

Photo by R. E. Stambook, Author's Collection

*Original* Hatpins on *Original* selling cards and/or paper.

*l-r* — 1 pair 6" gilt pins w/ figural Blue Birds; enamel on gilt. 1" wing-spread.

10" steel pins w/ 3 white ¼" glass-bead heads. *Reverse* side of card reads: "HANEUSS (trademark) *Aix-La-Chapelle*", and shows young children on wooden bridge tossing pebbles into water. A charming lithograph.

10" tempered steel pins w/ black glass-beaded heads. Six on card.

9" pin w/ black glass-beaded head. *Reverse* of card reads: "Every Pin of Warranted Steel, MORRIS AND YEOMANS, England". And, "Hat Pins Made at our own Factory". — "Ladies will find these pins the cheapest because they are the best." (This slogan disproves our modern adage: "You get what you pay for!")

8" pin on *"BONNET PIN"* paper, imprinted "Germany". (Rare)

**PLATE 134,** *pages 24 and 25*

"After A Fashion," October, 1974 issue
Courtesy Milly Orcutt, Women's News Editor:
*Antique Motor News,* Long Beach, CA

1910 *"The Ladies Home Journal"*, featured a rare *fashion plate* showing the much-needed hatpins without which the *"New Velvet Hat — The Shirley"* could hardly nestle safely nor securely on the hair and head.

**PLATE 135,** *pages 2 and 3*

Reproduced from "The Pindustry," Courtesy: The Star Pin Company, Shelton, Conn.

The history of the pin and pin-making machine.

**PLATE 136,** *page 96*

Drawings by Joyce Fairchild

Typical mountings incorporating jewelers' *findings* as shown on a variety of hatpins from author's collection:

*A.* Sockets; *B.* Patches; *C.* Span; *D.* Bridge-type; *E.* Arc-like mounting; *F.* Prongs; *G.* Crown.

*A., B., C., D.,* and *E.,* were used to mount the ornamental top of the hatpin to the pin-shank.

*Finding E.,* is typical of type used for *larger* and *heavier* baubles.

*Findings F.,* and *G.,* were sometimes the only metallic portion of an ornamental setting for stones.

Many hatpins elaborate metal castings were attached to their pin-shanks in the various ways illustrated.

**PLATE 137,** *page 95*

Drawings by Joyce Fairchild

Jewelers' *findings* from F. H. Noble & Co. *Pins, patches,* and *prong mountings:*
    *A.* Sizes of *patches* used on hatpins ranged from ¼" to ½". Stock pins were offered in sizes 8", 9", and 10".
    *B.* A "spiral" pin.

*Pintongs* were offered in twelve separate sizes, as advertised in Noble's 1898 catalogue.

*Pins* offered in sales catalogues were gold, gold filled, gold or silver plated, gilt, and silver.

Artist's drawings by permission of F. H. Noble & Co., from their advertising catalogues dated prior to 1923.

**PLATE 138,** *page 98*

Drawings by Joyce Fairchild

Drawings from the original pages of F. H. Noble & Co.'s Catalogue of Jewelers' Findings, 1898-1928, by permission F. H. Noble & Co.

a. Polished steel; steel (gold plated); nickel silver pins — with patches and sockets. Raw pins with typical jewelers' findings, including round patches with screw-top insertion at top of pin, and collar-button-type sockets often found in "fake" mountings. Sockets were brass or steel, unlike the gold, gold-filled, or gold-plated collar button used in counterfeit findings.

b. Porcelain hatpin mountings with gold plated pins.

**PLATE 139,** *page 15*

"Victorian Fashions and Costumes from Harper's Bazaar: 1867-1898"
Edited and with an Introduction by Stella Blum.
By permission of Dover Publications, Inc., New York

**PLATE 139,** *continued*

Tortoise-shell combs and hair-pins were used to secure the puffs, switches, braids, curls, hairnets and chignons. Besides hatpins for security and ornamental purposes, the hat was additionally weighted with an assortment of hat ornaments such as buckles, bows, festoons of flowers, etc. (May 14, 1887 issue, *Harper's Bazaar*)

**PLATE 140,** *page 22*

"Victorian Fashions and Costumes from Harper's Bazaar: 1867-1898"
Edited and with an Introduction by Stella Blum.
By permission of Dover Publications, Inc., New York

Note on fig. c., that the *fashion plate* actually shows the application of a hatpin spearing through the brim into the chignon of hair at the back of the head. The front crown is already "settled" by what appears to be a pair of hatpins. This is a rare showing of hatpins on *fashion plates* of 1898.

**PLATE 141,** *page 19*

"Victorian Fashions and Costumes from Harper's Bazaar: 1867-1898"
Edited and with an Introduction by Stella Blum.
By permission of Dover Publications, New York

Sporting costumes each required various types of fashionable headgear. Some are shown in this 1896 *fashion plate*. But where are the necessary hatpins?

**PLATE 142,** *page 13*

"Victorian Fashions and Costumes from Harper's Bazaar: 1867-1898"
Edited and with an Introduction by Stella Blum.
By Permission of Dover Publications, Inc., New York

Examples of embellished fabrics for hats, using feathers, flowers, bows, ribbons, and *aigrettes*, etc. (Fashion Plate Oct. 4, 1896, "*Harper's Bazaar*".)

**PLATE 143,** *page 20*

Photo by George Castro, Courtesy Dr. F. P. Walkup archives

"*Toupees, Transformations, and Accessories at Lichtenfeld's*" — Hairstyles (1904) issue May 28, 1904, "*The Ladies' Field*".

To keep the hair in place and wherever fullness was required in the hairstyle, padded rolls were worn and kept in place by pins and combs.

**PLATE 144,** *page 14*

"Victorian Fashions and Costumes from Harper's Bazaar: 1867-1898"
Edited and with an Introduction by Stella Blum.
By permission of Dover Publications, Inc., New York

The "frisette" was popular from 1850-1900. (See Fig. f) The tightly curled affair helped camouflage thinning forelocks. (Oct. 8, 1881 issue *Harper's Bazaar*)

**PLATE 145,** *page viii*

Courtesy: Milly Orcutt Archives

Frontispiece.

**PLATE 146,** *page 58*

Photograph by Eric Skipsey

Miss Agnes Moorehead as Aunt Alicia in "*Gigi*", Los Angeles Civic Light Opera Production, 1973.

**PLATE 147,** *page 4*

Photo by George Castro, Dr. F. P. Walkup archives

Hair, hats and hatpins are prominent in this fashionable promenade in Dupont Circle, Washington, D.C. (From *Leslie's Weekly*, April 1897.) A hatpin depicting the Capitol and White House is shown on color Plate 93, with a detailed drawing on Plate 190.

**PLATE 148,** *page 38*

Photo courtesy Mr. Edward Parkinson, Publicity Director for The Schubert Theatre

Miss Deborah Kerr as "Edith" in "*The Day After the Fair*". Play covers period of three months in summer 1900 . . . during the height of the hatpin era.

**PLATE 149,** *page 21*

Photo courtesy of Still Dept., Twentieth Century-Fox Film Corporation

Barbra Streisand wearing an extravagantly plumed chapeau from the film, "Hello, Dolly!" This hat is representative of types requiring long, long hatpins. Usually between two and three hatpins were utilized in cocking the hat against the *Gibson Girl* hairdo. Ornament from one hatpin glitters from center brim of hat.

**PLATE 150,** *page 54*

Photo by George Castro, Dr. F. P. Walkup archives.

From "*The Ladies' Field*", (July 16, 1904). This lovely true-to-life portrait might well be called, "the finishing touch" to milady's toilette!

**PLATE 151,** *page 21*

Photo courtesy of Still Dept., Twentieth Century-Fox Film Corporation

Barbra Streisand in fabulous cartwheel-size hat for role in "*Hello, Dolly!*" Hatpins lie buried in flurry of feathers, but are obviously required to keep chapeau secure.

**PLATE 152,** *page 20*

Photo courtesy Imogene Chapman

The late comedienne, Geraldine Rollins, traveled with the May Robson Touring Company across the U.S.A. in what was called "The Chautauqua" circuit. Mrs. Rollins is shown wearing a hat typical of the 1898-1908 era which required several hatpins to keep it in place.

This beautiful portrait was taken around 1904 and is especially noteworthy because it records the costume and accessories worn during the Edwardian era (1900-1910). A decade earlier, during the Victorian age, a woman traveling and performing "blackface", (as did Mrs. Rollins), would have been unheard of. But with the flamboyant King Edward, many of the tight-laced restrictions were lifted, and the gay "playboy" era entered the scene with eyebrow-raising permissiveness.

**PLATE 153,** *page 21*

Photo courtesy of Still Dept., Twentieth Century-Fox Film Corporation

The "Merry Widow" hat, with its befeathered concoctions was worn high on the pompadour hairstyle. Barbra Streisand's "Hello, Dolly!" chapeau is brimming over with "willows" of Ostrich plumes.

**PLATE 154,** *page 23*

Portrait by F. Collier Lankford, Photo courtesy, Mrs. Scherry Harrah

1898 costume from the collection of *Harrah's Museum*, Sparks, Nevada. Model, Mrs. Scherry Harrah.

**PLATE 155,** *page 23*

Portrait by F. Collier Lankford, Photo courtesy, Mrs. Scherry Harrah

Turn-of-the-century costume complete with necessary hatpins, modeled by Mrs. Scherry Harrah. From the costume collection at *Harrah's Museum*, Sparks, Nevada.

**PLATE 156,** *page 87*

Photograph by Marilyn Zander

Lecturer Fran Tucker models authentic mourning attire from her vast col-

**PLATE 156,** *continued*

lection of turn-of-the-century clothing. Hatpin, from the author's collection, is jet glass riveted and soldered to a wire construction.

**PLATE 157,** *page 150*

Photo by Marilyn Zander, Hatpin from Author's Collection

Fran Tucker, fashion coordinator, lecturer, model, and collector of authentic old-fashioned clothing and headgear, models typical plumed wide-brimmed hat with popular jet jewelry (1901). Hatpin is unpolished jet with stones soldered to a wire construction. 11½″ japanned pin with 2″ diameter head. (Compare dull jet ornamental hatpin head to the polished jet earrings and necklace worn by model.)

**PLATE 158,** *page 74*

"Victorian Fashions and Costumes from Harper's Bazaar 1867-1898"
Edited and with an Introduction by Stella Blum.
By permission of Dover Publications, Inc., New York.

Feathered and jeweled aigrettes (*figs. l.* and *n.*) were worn in hair and hats.

On Plate 12, *bottom row*, is a pair of cape pins with chain as shown *fig. m.*

Plate 17 is an example of the flower-pin with hilt and sheath as shown on *fig. m.* The "Collarettes and Ornaments" of 1892 were only a small portion of the extraordinary array of decorative "conceits" worn by women of the Gay 90s.

**PLATE 159,** *page 63*

"Victorian Fashions and Costumes from Harper's Bazaar: 1867-1898"
Edited and with an Introduction by Stella Blum.
By permission of Dover Publications, Inc., New York

The popularity of jet is best illustrated by this June 6, 1891 cover story in *Harper's Bazaar.* Somewhere in *"the hat, from the Maison Virot . . . of transparent black horse-hair . . ."* are one or more anchoring hatpins . . . probably with ornamental jet-heads!

**PLATE 160,** *page 134*

Photo by George Castro, Author's Collection

Front and side view commemorative hatpin, "Jenny Lind".

6¾″ steel *replacement* pin. 1½″ Art Nouveau portrait of Jenny Lind, marked "sterling" plus hallmarks.

(With *original* sterling pin-shank)

**PLATE 161,** *page 17*

Drawing by Joyce Fairchild

7¼″ gilt pin w/ 1½″ detachable brooch. Gift to author by Otto C. Hanisch, Pres., Geo. H. Fuller & Son Co., manufacturers of jewelers' findings.

Where cross-pin is attached to the brooch, solder material is covered by small oval finishing patch or plate, known as a finding.

Note detailed country-scene engraved and chased on novelty brooch-hatpin. (Rare)

**PLATE 162,** *page 26*

Photograph courtesy Jablonec Corp., Czechoslovakia

Display used during jewelry exhibition by Jablonec Corp., famed manufacturers and world-wide exporters of jewelry. Jablonec designed many of the beautiful glass hatpin ornaments of the period. (Some are shown on other plates within this book.)

**PLATE 163,** *page 134*

Photo by George Castro, Author's Collection

3¾″ tall, 3½″ from "nose-to-nose", two-faced figural hatpin holder depict-

**PLATE 163,** *continued*

ing a British judge in his formal court wig. *Frown* might possibly indicate "guilty" verdict and *smile*, vice versa, but this is the author's assumption. There has been much speculation as to the intent of the artist who conceived the piece; nevertheless, it is a wonderful bit of illustrative material for the chapter, "Hatpins as Weapons, etc.", particularly for the courtroom episodes.

Unmarked, hand-painted porcelain.

**PLATE 164,** *page 29*

Photo courtesy Mrs. Scherry Harrah

The period hatpin collection as displayed at *Harrah's Museum*, Sparks, Nevada. Exhibit shown in conjunction with the costume display on Main Level.

**PLATE 165,** *page 43*

Drawing by Joyce Fairchild

This is a detailed drawing of figural Dragonfly on *Plate 7.*

Two types of safety "nibs" or protectors are shown: a threaded "nib" and a "plunger" type. The latter type is easily lost but is also the quickest and easiest to remove from hat. The *threaded* "nib" was the accepted type utilized on most decorative hat ornaments following the Post World War I change of fashion in hair and hat styles.

**PLATE 166,** *page 57*

Photo courtesy Tom J. Lawson, England

Collection of hatpin cards, some with original hatpins intact, including the patented Abel Morrall's *"Bayonet Point"* (no. 1679). These items are rare finds as most were discarded as would any outside wrap or carton. (Collection Tom J. Lawson).

**PLATE 167,** *page 62*

Photographed by Ole Woldbye, Copenhagen, Denmark — Kunstindustrimuseet

Hatpin in gold, silver, diamonds, horn and glass. The sunflower is a carved opal by Rene Lalique, acknowledged leader of the *Art Nouveau* movement. The hatpin was purchased from Lalique for 1,500 French francs at the Paris World Fair, 1900, by the Kunstindustrimuseet, Copenhagen. (This hatpin may be seen in full color in *"The Art of Jewelry"* by Graham Hughes, 1972 edition.)

**PLATE 168,** *page 66*

Drawings by Joyce Fairchild, Courtesy William Jones, Costume and Textile Dept
The Ahmanson Museum Collection, Los Angeles.

A: 11¾″ brass pin, gilded Lily w/ three stamens each accented w/ brilliants.

B: 11½″ brass pin, chased and filigree gilded cage w/ topaz stone in gypsy setting.

C: 6″ white pin w/ faceted crystal stone set between metallic leaves and accented w/ rhinestones.

D: 6¾″ brass pin with faceted crystal. Fancy filigree encasing stone, with 11 brilliants set into small claw with chased socket.

E: 7″ gold filled pin with two-piece molded camphor glass on either side of faceted amethyst. Tiny seed pearl tops this elegant pin. (Similar hatpin in author's collection, *Plate 12.*)

F: 10⅜″ white pin with ornately carved ivory. Leaves, tropical flowers and bird set in patch-and-socket mounting.

G&H: 10¾″ white pins with gilded roses.

**PLATE 169,** *page 75*

A jewelry shop, Long Beach, Calif., 1920.

Note hatpins worn as ornaments rather than out of necessity on cloche-type hats. Whether these were worn for "protective" use or merely for decoration, one must decide for oneself.

**PLATE 170,** *page 76*

Rare, signed hatpin: "A. Bargas". Sterling on 11½" pin. 1¼" ornament is enlarged to show detail and signature. Armand Bargas, famed French medallist, worked in the beginning of the 20th century. This medal, depicting Jeanne d'Arc, was included in his 1904 Exposition. (Author's collection)

**PLATE 171,** *page 77*

A detailed drawing for Plate 52, showing hallmarks: Lion Passant = England; Sheafs of Wheat and Sword = town mark of Chester; punched letter "C" signifies date 1903-4.

**PLATE 172,** *page 65*

Assorted hat ornaments with varied "nibs" and double prongs for guard against loss. Figures g and i are details for Plates 107 and 116.

Figures a thru h from the author's collection.

Figures *j*, *k*, and *l* are from the collection of Western Costume Company, Hollywood, Calif.

**Fig. j:** 2" brass pin w/ "nib". Ladybud accented with red and crystal rhinestones on spring "nodder".

**Fig. k:** 4" long gold leaf-shaped pin clustered with rhinestones.

**Fig. l:** 2" shell-shaped gold plated frame set with two small pearls and accented with rhinestones.

Note the variations from simple to decorative "nibs". In some instances, the ornamental head and "nib" are identical as on fig. b and h. Figs. *a, c, d, e,* and *g*, have nibs that are extensions of the design of the ornamental heads.

**PLATE 173,** *page 80*

These hatpins and hat ornaments have various safety "nibs", except for fig. *C*, with its flat, unpointed spiral stem. This chased silver feather-design ornament and fig. *E*, are shown on color Plate 17 — as is fig. *E*.

**Fig. *A*** is a detail drawing for pin on Plate 116, and shows unusual type of chased and engraved leaf-motif mounting.

**Figs. *B*** and **C** have simple type "nibs"; **Figs. *D*, *F*, *H*, *I*, *J*** and **K** have decorative "safeties" which are an extension of the ornamental head design.

**PLATE 174,** *page 78*

Miss Katharine Hepburn and Sir Laurence Olivier are the romantic pair in *"Love Among the Ruins"* (ABC-TV production, March 6, 1975).

**PLATE 175,** *page 81*

From *"The Ladies' Field"*, May 14, 1904: flowers, feathers, ribbons, veiling,

**PLATE 175,** *continued*

and *aigrette* with rhinestone or steel bead buckles, adorned various type crowns and brims of Gay 90s *chapeaux*. The popular Gibson Girl hairstyles were worn by many, but so was the *coif* pillowed at the nape of the neck.

**PLATE 176,** *page 83*

All English, early 20th Century.

Hatpin, solid bead head made from black glass with blue, yellow, and pink floral design spaced between a fleck gilt scroll.

Hatpin, triple scroll made from silver and mounted on white metal pin.

Hatpin, Poppy head made from metal and coloured in scarlet and green with black stamens, mounted on a gilt metal pin.

Hatpin, made of white metal consisting of 3 interlaced circles studded with turquoise beads surrounding a circular green glass head.

Hatpin, silver filigree — half dome surmounted by a nob and bordered with nobs set in twisted wire.

Hatpin, hollow ball made of silver filigree to which are applied small silver balls.

**PLATE 177,** *pages 82 and 83*

**Fig. a:** pierced gilt *Art Nouveau* mounting with amethyst stone.

**Fib. b:** filigree head with chased cage; 4 amethysts, 3 pearls, and 5 rhinestones set in each *Art Nouveau* type design.

**Fig. c:** gilt chased mounting enameled border with filigree work centered with blue stone. Each chased metal leaf and four corners accented with rhinestones.

**Fig. d:** gilt pin with chased and embossed frame with large blue center stone. Individual brilliants set in chased cup mounting.

**Fig. e:** A cluster of brass and gilt leaves provide setting for black baroque pearl.

**Fig. f:** large *Art Nouveau* gold plated pin head with escutcheon top set with faceted amethyst.

These authentic period hatpins serve as prototypes for various artistic improvisations of hatpins recreated for the movie industry. For example, Mr. Reyhill designed the extraordinarily long-stemmed ornamental hatpin used by Julie Andrews in "Darling Lili", (Twentieth Century Fox production). Hatpin was carefully boxed and flown to Paris where filming took place.

**PLATE 178,** *page 60*

*Fig. 1, a thru e:*
*a:* 12" steel pin with 2" antiqued silver top embossed with floral scroll design.

*b:* 12" steel pin with 1½" wheel-shaped filigree gold head set with four pink stones and multi-assorted rhinestones.

*c:* 6" steel pin with 1½" free-form blown glass head.

*d:* 12" steel pin with 5" amber color celluloid head set in gold socket.

*e:* 12" steel pin with 2" shield-shaped antiqued silver top with filigree. Three large rhinestones with center cluster of matching size multi-rhinestones.

**PLATE 178,** *continued:*

*Fig. 2, a thru c, l-r:*
**a:** This unusual jet plastic hatpin is a detailed drawing of pin on Plate 193 shown in plush velvet pear cushion. The combination of plastic, metal and brilliants is not commonly used in such ornaments. Author's collection.

**b:** This is a detailed drawing of the claw-mounted gemstone as shown on Plate 69 in figural china bird hatpin holder. Author's collection.

**c:** Mythological carved stone cameo in rare gold floral setting accented with brilliants. Collection of Renee Marshall.

Collection of Western Costume Company, Hollywood, California. Western Costume Company's collection of hatpins serve as patterns for reproductions used for stage, screen and television. This large company is world-renowned for costuming either the individual or an entire army which can be outfitted from the gigantic inventory of period attire housed on five floors!

**PLATE 179,** *page 135*

Collection of Diane Malhmood

A bouquet assortment of *period hatpins* in astounding variety. The plush cushion is a favored receptable of many hatpin collectors since it does not limit the size of display as does the *china* receptacle with its usual six to twelve pin holes. The large pincushion allows the collector ample storage in a limited area.

**PLATE 180,** *page 135*

Photos by Dana Getman, Collection of Mrs. E. G. Getman

A. Hatpins mounted in a wall-hanging box. Display includes Mrs. Getman's favorites from a collection of over 700 hatpins.

B. Hatpin holder with attached tray containing some unusual hatpins such as: *Art Nouveau* pierced portrait compact with mirror; an ivory chick in shell; an 1884 Indian Head penny; and a Shamrock set with three genuine green jade stones.

**PLATE 181,** *page 84*

"Victorian Fashions and Costumes from Harper's Bazaar: 1867-1898" Edited and with an Introduction by Stella Blum. By permission of Dover Publications, Inc., New York.

The illustration from *Harper's Bazaar* is dated December 1, 1894. Within a year — 1895 — the recommended skating outfit had a *"short (at least three inches above the ankles),* tweed or serge skirt . . .".

**PLATE 182,** *pages 102 and 103*

Collection of Robert V. Larsen.

*Top Row, l-r* — Seven R. S. Prussia (Red Mark) scenic and floral hatpin holders: "Mill and Water Wheel with Maiden", 4½" tall w/ 2½" tri-footed base; "Winter Scene: Trapper, Wigwam, Polar Bear and Wolf", 3¾" tall w/ 2¼" base and 13 pin-holes; "Blue Birds", 4½" tall w/ 2½" six-sided and footed base and 19 pin-holes; 4¾" tall w/ 3½" base floral bulbous w/ 13 pin-holes; tri-footed 4½" tall w/ 2½" base floral; 4" tall w/ 3½" base and 16 pin-holes, floral poppies; 4¾" tall w/ 3" base floral w/ ½" center hole surrounded by 12 small pin-holes.

*Middle Row, l-r* — R. S. Prussia (Red Mark) floral, 4¼" high w/ 2¼" base, six-sided and footed w/ 19 pin-holes; R. S. Prussia (Red Mark), 4¾" tall w/ 3¼" base, floral w/ two-handles and 13 pin-holes; R. S. Germany (rare RED MARK), six-sided and footed floral, 4¼" high w/ 2¼" base and 19 pin-holes; another rare (Red Mark) R. S. Germany floral, 4½" tall w/ 2" base; R. S. Poland (Red Mark) three-handled floral, 4¾" tall w/ 3½" base and 16 pin-holes; R. S. Germany (Blue Mark), floral, 4¾" tall w/ 3" base and 13 pin-holes; R. S. Germany (Green Mark), six-sided and footed, floral 4¼" tall w/ 2¼" base on 19 pin-holes.

*Bottom Row, l-r* — Four Royal Bayreuth and an English Jasperware: "Colonial Couple" in Royal Bayreuth (Blue Mark) Tapestry, 4½" high w/ 2" base

**PLATE 182,** *continued:*

and 15 pin-holes; another Bayreuth (Blue Mark) Rose Tapestry, 4½" tall w/ 2" base and 15 pin-holes; (Blue Mark) Royal Bayreuth Sunbonnet Babies, 4¾" tall w/ 3½" base and 16 pin-holes; Dark blue Jasperware with white Crest, signed "Adams", 4¼" tall w/ 2½" base and three large pin-holes; Royal Bayreuth (Blue Mark) "Cavalier Musicians", (signed "Dixon"), 4½" tall w/ 3" square base and 17 pin-holes; Royal Bayreuth (Blue Mark) "Goose Girl", 4¾" tall w/ 3½" base and 16 pin-holes.

*Top Row, l-r* — Rare Carmel Slag (Chocolate Glass), Orange Tree pattern, 7" tall w/ 2½" base; Clear Glass (turning purple), w/ 1 large opening surrounded by 6 slits, 6¼" tall w/ 2½" base; signed Rose O'Neill Kewpie (same as *Plate 49*); rare size signed Rose O'Neill Kewpie, only 4" high w/ 2" base w/ 8 pin-holes — both Kewpie holders in blue jasperware; extremely rare Cut Glass (Diamond Octagon cutting), 5½" tall w/ 2¾" base, w/ ½" center hole surrounded by 5 smaller pin-holes; Carnival Glass, purple, same as Grape and Cable pattern shown *Plate 55*; R. S. Germany (Green Mark) floral, 7" tall w/ 3" base and 13 pin-holes.

*Middle Row, l-r* — Five Royal Bayreuth Figurals, (Blue Mark): "Oyster and Pearl", four-footed, white in color, 5" tall w/ 2½" base and 13 pin-holes; "Owl", brown in color, 4" tall w/ 3¼" base and 16 pin-holes; "Clover", 4½" tall w/ 2½" base, light and dark green w/ pink blossom and 13 pin-holes; "Lamplighter", 4½" tall w/ 2¼" base, green in color w/ 16 pin-holes; "Poppy", 4½" tall w/ 3½" base, w/ 11 pin-holes, green body w/ white blossom.

*Bottom Row, l-r* — Clown Figural, (Marked Germany), 7" tall w/ 3" base, grey and green in color, trimmed in red, w/ 10 pin-holes; "Pigs at Pump", (Marked Germany), pink pigs w/ green color base, 4½" tall w/ 3" base and 8 pin-holes; "Peasant Girl", 4½" tall w/ 2" base in floral pinafore dress, 16 pin-holes; Comic Man's Head w/ Fly on end of nose — 4½" tall w/ 2" long base and 24 pin-holes; Pink Pig, 2½" tall w/ 4" long base and 18 pin-holes. (Latter three hatpin holders are unmarked). Figural Pitcher, (Nippon), 5½" tall w/ 2¾" base, pink roses and much gold overlay, w/ 16 pin-holes.

**PLATE 183,** *page 28*

Drawing by Joyce Fairchild

Flat-brimmed *sailor* worn with yards of veiling to protect the face and neck of the daring female drivers of the newfangled open motorcar. (1904-1908) The celebrated Emily Post was one of the admired women who gave up her "cob and carriage" to ride in the new *horse-powered* roadsters.

**PLATE 184,** *page 32*

"Victorian Fashions and Costumes from Harper's Bazaar: 1867-1898" Edited and with an Introduction by Stella Blum. By permission of Dover Publications, Inc., New York

The "lady who travels alone" was given advice in *"Godey's Lady's Book"*. The "unprotected female" was cautioned on personal decorum upon her arrival at the hotel. Note the profusion of ribbons and flowers in the stiff-brimmed hat. There is a *hint* of hatpins, if one looks close enough — but the *need* for hatpins is quite evident!

(Fashion Plate from *Harper's Bazaar*, Sept. 29, 1894)

**PLATE 185,** *page 85*

Drawing by Joyce Fairchild

The ordinary common household hatpin shown on its original paper holder. Glass heads were often irregular in size and shape — not the perfect marble-round as found in beads. Tempered steel pin-shanks are grayish-blue in color.

**PLATE 186,** *pages 72 and 73*

Drawings by Joyce Fairchild

*Fig. a:* Detailed side-view of hatpin shown on Plate 35, *Bottom Row.*

**PLATE 186,** *continued:*

Fig. *b:* Top view of decorative monogrammed escutcheon.

Fig. *c:* Artist's rendition of an ostrich-plumed hat (circa 1895) with model in Gibson Girl hairstyle.

Fig. *d* and *e:* two views of double-pronged Fuschia ornament shown on Plate 17. Note the elongated "nodder" and hand-wrought details of flower. This type hat ornament is also shown on Plate 139.

Fig. *f:* Detail of hatpin shown on Plate 122, left grouping. Note multi-faceted crystal mounted atop simple but elegant leaf designed socket mounting.

Fig. *g:* refer to color Plate 115, *Bottom Row, left,* for exquisite color of gemstone. The artist's conception details chased silver mounting and thistle-shape of multi-faceted stone.

Fig. *h:* drawing amplifies elaborate chasing of claw mounting for ¾" gemstone shown on Plate 69.

**PLATE 187,** *page 136*

Photo by Dana Getman, Collection of Mrs. E. G. Getman

A. Composite arrangement of primitive-type hatpin holders. The author designates term "primitive" to any holder which is primarily *homemade* as compared to the *mass-produced factory-made* hatpin receptacles. Primitives are represented by handy-work such as glass tubes covered with ribbons, crochet, lace, beads, or hand-painted designs.

B. Assyrian gold holder. *House and Garden Magazine* (1964), advises that the mark on the bottom of the holder which reads: "Benedict" and "Assyrian Gold" on either side of a triangle, is American plated silver that was gold washed. Also, that the manufacturer was Benedict Mfg. Co., Syracuse, New York, doing business from 1890-1922. According to collector Getman, her research revealed that "Assyrian Gold" is an alloy of copper and zinc which produces a gold color. The material tends to discolor as does brass.

C. Two *Nippon* holders, hand-painted with gold accents. Floral holder marked on solid bottom: "A & O hand-painted Nippon"; scenic holder marked "China E.-OH-hand-painted".

**PLATE 188,** *pages 142 and 143*

Photo courtesy William Bergmann, Author's Collection

Hatpin holders of yesteryear with their modern-day reproductions and look-alikes. See Chapter VI for details on how to detect the differences.

**PLATE 189,** *page 137*

Photo by George Castro, Author's Collection

This *Art Nouveau* portrait hatpin in sterling silver typifies Aubrey Beardsley's influence (1872-1898) during the period known as *L'Art Nouveau.* Exquisitely chased ornament is set w/ three sapphires and is one of a pair. Its mate is identical except for stones which are green in color.

**PLATE 190,** *page 59*

Drawing by Joyce Fairchild

This is an enlarged and detailed drawing of the souvenir hatpin shown on Plate 93.

Mrs. Roger A. Pryor in *"Reminiscences of War and Peace"* which tells of life in Washington during the unhappy period of the Civil War, records a mind's eye picture for us of what it was like to "shop" at the nation's capital:

*"There were few shops. But such shops. There was Galt's, where the silver, gems and marble were less attractive than the cultivated gentleman who sold them; Gautier's the palace of sweets, with Mrs. Gautier in an armchair before her counter to tell you the precise social status of every one of her customers and, what is more, to put you in your own; Harper's, where the*

**PLATE 190,** *continued:*

*dainty, leisurely salesman treated his laces with respect, drawing up his cuffs lest they touch the etheral beauties; and the little corner shop of stern Madame Delarue, who imported as many (and no more) hats and gloves as she was willing to sell as a favour to the ladies of the diplomatic and official circles . . . one night, the boxes had arrived and I could peep at the bonnets and choose the best one for myself. Thus it was that I once bore away a 'divine creation' of point lace, crepe and shaded asters before Madame had seen it."*

**PLATE 191,** *page 8*

"Victorian Fashions and Costumes from Harper's Bazaar: 1867-1898"
Edited and with an Introduction by Stella Blum.
By permission of Dover Publications, Inc., New York

"Harper's Bazaar" Christmas cover, issue 12-25-1897, is the epitome of costume in the Victorian era. Hat, hair, and hatpins were "assembled" and made part of the important accessories to the "Paris Reception Gown" with its extravagances of lace, velvet and sable fur.

*"The hat worn with this gown is a large soft velvet toque the same shade, trimmed with two long ostrich plumes fastened with a rhinestone buckle. Just under the brim to the left side is a rosette of satin ribbon with another rhinestone buckle."* (And not a mention of hatpins!)

**PLATE 192,** *page 101*

Drawings by Joyce Fairchild From the Author's Collection

Detailed drawings illustrating the many shapes of hatpin holders with varied pin holes and other size openings to accommodate assorted gauges of wire pins and prongs.

**PLATE 193,** *page 137*

Photo by R. E. Stambook, Collection of Renee Marshall unless otherwise indicated.

Sears' *"Spring 1911"* Catalog listed the following under *Cases, Outfits, bags, and Novelties: "No. 8F1535 — Fruit Pin Cushion, Natural Finished Fruits . . . Plush Covers . . ."*

The plush pear pincushion shown on this Plate (left), is from the collection of Delma Peery. Thrust through the pear is a 9¾" pin with 4" pierced molded amber head from the collection of Sybel Heller. Ten hatpins in pincushion are of molded and pattern celluloid and imitation plastics: 5¼" steel pin w/ 4" two-mold celluloid head w/ molded facets made to represent jet; 8¼" white pin w/ 1¼" red plastic pretzel-shape ornament, mounted in chased patch-finding; 4" steel pin w/ 1½" molded and patterned French Ivory head; 4¼" steel pin w/ 4½" two-color molded Art Deco ornamental head; 8" white pin w/ 1¼" round metallic bezel mounting w/ fake cabochon malchinte head; 4¼" white pin w/ 4½" black celluloid feather-shaped ornament, mounted in 1½" overall unusual chased and filigree gilt mounting accented w/ two brilliants. (Detail of this hatpin shown on *Plate 178.*) 8" gilt pin w/ 3" twisted imitation amber head; 4¼" brass pin w/ molded patterned plastic w/ hand-painted highlights of spider in web. This insect spinning a web denotes good luck. 8" brass pin w/ 1⅝" brass bezel mounted molded plastic head w/ oriental symbols, (detail on *Plate 100.*) — Author's collection; and 4½" white pin w/ 2" Art Deco stylized scallop shell in pattern mold.

The French Ivory hatpin holder is identical to that advertised in the Sears' *"Fall 1915"* Catalog, listed under *"White French Ivory . . . No. 8D8915 . . . these pieces are of Fine Grade French Ivory (grained celluloid) . . . Hat Pin Holder, Height 5¾ in. Shipping Wt. 4 ounces."* (Holder from the collection of Joyce Roth.)

Four hatpins in above French Ivory holder: *l-r* — 5" short brass modern-day souvenir pin is the Ku Kui Pod and was purchased at a museum in Hawaii in 1974; 6" white pin w/ 2¼" pierced two-mold painted Art Deco celluloid; 4½" white pin w/ 4" unusual metallic bezel-type mounting for 3¾" grained French Ivory head; and 4½" brass pin w/ 3¾" two-mold, two-color Art Deco ornamental head.

**PLATE 194**, *page 137*

The center multi-color beaded hatpin head is on a 12″ pin. Its handmade beaded embroidery is circa 1830-1840 and is fully described on *Plate 16*. Author's collection.

Two-piece heavily beaded 12″ scalloped-edge center-piece with ½″ beaded fringe. An 8½″ pincushion w/ 2¾″ plush center for pins, sets within a velvet circle of bottom center-piece. Pincushion has ¾″ looped beaded fringe on 8-pointed star design.

Detail for triangular pin (lower left) shown on *Plate 199, fig. a. and b.* Hatpins in two-piece set from the collections of Joyce Roth and Renee Marshall.

**PLATE 195**, *page 137*

*l-r* — Overlay of glass and beautifully enameled with cloisonne inset on metal hatpin holder. (Rare). Pins and holder from the collection of Sybel Heller. (Detail drawing of filigree hatpin on Plate 199.)

*Front* — Seven hatpins from collection of Joyce Roth.

*Center* — 3¾″ tall porcelain half-doll with 5½″ arm-spread raised to 4″ ballerina pose of superb grace. Applied and painted porcelain arm-bands, necklace and earrings. Four sew-holes with base incised with numerals and word "Germany". Figural in remarkable skin-tones has a face with heavily shadowed hazel eyes typifying the carefree "flapper" of the twenties, yet with the serious undertones of the newly "free" woman of that dance-crazed era when almost "anything goes". Individually molded fingers and finely detailed, sculptured, torso, is part of this prized half-doll with its exceptional quality of both porcelain and sculptured elegance.

4¾″ tall holder w/ 3½″ solid base unglazed bisque figural holder. Incised with crown and sunburst and letter "R", and three illegible initials. Oriental seated figure in kimono with spread fan and Geisha hairstyle, is delicately tinted pale green over pink bisque. Although figure is Oriental in design, the mark is of European manufacture and is evident in the occidental shape of the hand-painted eyes and brows. (Pins from the Collection of Renee Marshall)

**PLATE 196**, *page 137*

4½″ china hatpin holder was advertised in Sears' *Fall 1915* Catalog as: *"Embossed in basket weave design, tinted ivory. Decorated with raised pink and yellow roses with green leaves."* (Marked: Made in Germany) Three hatpins from collection of Renee Marshall.

Center hatpin has an 11″ white pin w/ 2½″ wooden pear-shaped black painted head which resembles a darning spool. Collection of Joyce Roth.

*Center Pincushion:* 3½″ x 13½″ velvet lace-covered w/ beaded applique and 14 various assorted shapes and lengths of jet hatpins. Collection of Renee Marshall.

4″ tall tub w/ solid base, w/ 30 pin-size storage places. Figural pin holder of 3 crying babes. Author's collection. (Two pair of 4″ pins shown on *Plate 9*.)

**PLATE 197**, *page 137*

Chased and engraved sterling glove-ring with hand-wrought figurals of the Chamois, a goat-like antelope of the mountainous regions of Europe and Asia. The Chamois is highly prized for its skin. In this instance, it's the *teeth* of the animal which are preserved as trophies in both ring and matching hatpin. The hatpin is shown on Plate 111 with another trophy-tooth hatpin head.

**PLATE 198**, *page 105*

Contrast of size ornament and pin to human hand. (See Plate 2 for full size bird hatpin in color.)

**PLATE 199**, *page 69*

Fig. A and B, detailed drawing for Plate 194 showing bezel-mounted stone in elaborate filigree gilt mounting. (Side and top views)

Fig. C and D, detailed drawing for Plate 195, showing top and side views of faceted amethyst, bezel-set in gilt with circle of brilliants with border of fancy filigree.

**PLATE 200**, *page 64*

Fig. A and B, side and top view in detail of piercework frame set with four large stone and smaller brilliants. (See this hatpin on Color Plate 20)

**PLATE 201**, *pages 46, 47, and 48*

A track enthusiast returning from Los Alamitos Raceway in California, jokingly mentioned how his woman companion picked her bets by closing her eyes and stabbing the racing form with her pencil. Lillian Russell was accused of doing the same with her hatpin!

And Len Norris, cartoon-master for *"The Vancouver Sun"* has a "hatpin lady" who chooses her night classes with the same sort of blind luck. This popular cartoon character is never seen without her pair of long hatpins . . . even in her nightcap.

**PLATE 202**, *page 100*

"Kewpie" hatpins and holders are highly collectible items. Enlarged detail of "Kewpie" hatpin and one showing its 1″ size in comparison to hand-size. Bottom of 3/16″ "Kewpie" feet of sterling hatpin marked: "Sterling — Trade Mark — Kewpie — c." Rare figural hatpin. "Kewpie" hatpin holders are shown in color on Plate 49.

**PLATE 203**, *page 86*

Part of 15,000-18,000 hatpins once the collection of Dr. Leon A. Katzin, DDS., and the late Beatrice Katzin. Note the sign, *upper left* — "Part of the LARGEST COLLECTION of ANTIQUE HATPINS in the world".

This picture was taken at one of the many antique shows in which the Katzins exhibited throughout the country.

**PLATE 204**, *pages 56 and 57*

Pforzheim, Germany, is one of the world centers of jewelry manufacturing. From their Jewelry Museum collection of hatpins are the following unique examples:

*Top, l-r* — 7″ gilt pin w/ 1⅓″ ornament; silver w/ carnelian-cabochon, (circa 1907-8); 7″ gilt pin w/ 1½″ silver and blue enamel ornament designed by Georg Kleeman, professor *School for Arts and Crafts Pforzheim*, executed by Victor Mayer (Jewelry factory), (Circa 1904); 8¼″ gilt pin w/ 1″ silver set with Cabochon-cut Amazonite gemstone; designer and maker, Karl Johann Bauer, jeweler (Munich, 1906); 5½″ gold pin w/ 1¼″ gold floral figural of red transparent enamel accented with a pearl. This hatpin, designed and executed by F. Zerrenner, Pforzheim, was exhibited at the *Exposition Internationale*, Paris, (1900).

**PLATE 204,** *continued:*

*Bottom, l-r* — 6¾" gilt pin w/ 1¼" *Art Nouveau* design in silver, Berlin (Circa 1905); 8½" gilt pin w/ 1⅓" silver and gilt head set w/ cabochon-cut amethyst, designed and executed by Karl Johann Bauer, jeweler, (Munich, 1906); 7¼" gilt pin w/ 1¼" silver ornament set with two turquoise and four Lapis-Lazuli. Designed by Julius Muller-Salem, professor *School for Arts and Crafts Pforzheim,* (Germany, 1902), made by Theodor Fahner, (Pforzheim jewelry factory); 8¼" gilt pin w/ 2" figural beetle, silver gilt with one Chrysoprase and two red glass stone eyes; designed and executed by Levinger & Bissinger, Pforzheim jewelry factory.

**PLATE 205,** *page 138*

Photo by R. E. Stambook

Rare green satin glass perfume bottle, signed "R. Lalique — France", beautiful and typical example of *Art Nouveau* master's work. Smaller figural unsigned perfume of *Art Deco* period. (Author's collection)

Hatpins *Front, left* — (Collection of Louise Alexander) 7½" pin w/ ½" gilt *Art Nouveau* full-figural flower w/ brilliant accent; 9¼" pin w/ 1¼" gilt *repoussé* ornament with enameled flower; 7¾" pin w/ 1¼" full-figural chased and engraved gilt bird's head with stone eye accents; 7" hinged pin w/ 2" gilt head depicting Aesop's allegorical tale of "Fox and the Grapes". Wax pearl grapes with metallic leaves and tendrils. Fox has green eye accent; 8" heavy gauge pin with leaf finial, full-figural bird, shown reverse side for detail of claws which circle shank and enables ornament to slide up or down.

*Center* — Shamrock shape ornament with 11" pin, 3 bezel-set 1" amethysts outlined in brilliants. (Author's collection.)

*Right* — Three 11" pins w/ 1¾" Damescene heads depicting birds, flowers, and stylized Oriental tea house. Unidentified punch hallmark. (Collection of Joe McFarlin); One 12" pin w/ 2" Damescene head engraved with mythological dragon, (Author's collection).

*Rear, right* — One 8¼" pin w/ 3" brass Art Deco flower motif, hollow ornament with bell inside which tinkles in motion. Two tiny "sound" holes appear at upper groove and lower seam. (Collection Jo McFarlin).

**PLATE 206,** *page 138*

Photo by R. E. Stambook

Hatpins *Counter-clockwise* — 3¼" gold pin w/ 1" gold karat baroque head set w/ cabochon cut amethyst, (Collection Sherry Goldwasser); 10" (replacement pin) w/ ¾" gold Karat ball crawling with eight royal asp snakes. (Egyptian Queen Cleopatra clasped an asp to her breast in her dramatic death-wish.) (Author's collection); 5" gold pin w/ ⅞" gold *Fleur de Lis* ornament with small cartouche. (Collection Joe McFarlin); 6" 14K pin w/ ½" Vermicelli head set with genuine faceted topaz and rondelle. Seed pearl top. (This hatpin advertised in *Mermod-Jaccard-King's 1916 catalogue.* The St. Louis, Mo., fine jewelry firm was established 1829). (Author's Collection); 7½" (replacement pin) w/ ¾" baroque head with tiny round cartouche marked "14K LCT" (Tiffany). (Collection Jo McFarlin); Pair 4½" gold karat pins with faceted crystal set into Vermicelli heads. (Collection Jo McFarlin); 5¼" gold pin w/ famed enamel-work of Peter Carl Faberge with gold granules and gold beading accented by six fresh water pearls and bezel-set cabochon-cut citron gemstone. (Author's collection); 8½" hinged pin with miniature full figural stylized insect in flight. Intricate *cloisonne,* each *cloison* with varied color enamels. Detailed applied legs and feelers. Hallmarked. (Collection Jo McFarlin); 4" gold pin w/ cabochon cut bezel-set Jade in floral open-work mounting. (Collection Sherry Goldwasser); 7¼" pin w/ 1" mosaic depicting the Parthenon of Athens, set into pear-shaped goldstone with gilt cage. (Author's collection).

**PLATE 207,** *page 138*

Photo by R. E. Stambook

Victorian-era sword-shaped hatpins (circa 1896-1901), all marked

**PLATE 207,** *continued:*

"sterling" with chased and engraved baroque heads. (Collection Sherry Goldwasser). Hand-wrought full figural sweet pea atop 8" sterling pin. Shank marked: "Delamothe". (Collection Jo McFarlin).

Two tiny handmade scarf or veil pins (circa 1820-1830), exquisitely executed bee in flight on 2" hinged pin. Double-winged insect on 1½" gold pin with hand-cut grooves to prevent loss or slippage. Figural has garnet eyes, marcasite accents, and detailed feet and feelers. (Collection Ron and May Knott).

Assorted collection of six hatpins: *Upper Three* — (Collection Jo McFarlin) — 9¼" pin with 2½" full figural butterfly w/ brilliants and red stone eye accents; 10½" pin w/ 1½" chased frame with filigree and three pear-shaped coral-color stones; 9¼" pin w/ 2" baroque frame set with diamond shape topaz and 4 crystal accents.

*Lower Three* — (Collection Sherry Goldwasser) — 8" pin w/ 1¾" cage bezel-set with molded blue milkglass Scarab with applied gold accents; 6¼" pin w/ 1¾" baroque open-work; 9½" pin w/ 1¼" frame with pearl grape cluster and gilt leaves.

*Art Nouveau* Lalique perfume bottle and two hand-mirrors from Author's Collection.

**PLATE 208,** *page 156*

Photo courtesy Sally Margolis

An excellent way to display hatpins is in a long plush-covered pincushion. This is a small portion of Sally Margolis' extensive collection begun over a quarter century ago!

**PLATE 209,** *page 93*

Drawings by Joyce Fairchild

Front and side view of hatpin holder with attached trinket box and cover. Lavishly hand-painted, with decorative beading, it's a rare find in today's market-place of collectibles. (See Plate 48) (Author's collection.)

**PLATE 210,** *page 99*

Drawings by Joyce Fairchild

**PLATE 211**

Courtesy Beltmann Archives

Lily Langtree, known as "The Jersey Lily," (1852-1929)

**PLATE 212,** *page 68*

Drawings by Joyce Fairchild

*Art Nouveau* transition to Art Deco is reflected in work of little-heralded exponent, Maurice Dufrene. Drawings from an early 1900 catalogue are rendered by Joyce Fairchild from the originals exhibited by Dufrene. The metamorphosis of structural change in design from the "billowing smoke" lines to a more geometric and stylized pattern, seem evident in contrasting these renditions of designs for hatpins and hair ornament.

**PLATE 213,** *page 91*

Drawings by Joyce Fairchild

*a.* Silver-deposit-ware on green glass; *b.* sterling silver dog-head manufactured by Unger Bros., Newark; *c.* detailed drawing of engraved golf club with *cartouche* for engraving; *d.* detail of insect with stones utilized for body-shape; *e.* faceted crystal in patch and illusion-type setting; *f.* detailed butterfly with stone wings on socket mounting; *g.* gilt brass Art Deco hand; *h.* engraved brass ornament with oxidized metallic figural dragon drill-set to mounting; *i.* faceted crystal set between *rondelle* onyx with pearl. (All drawings lifesize from author's collection.)

**PLATE 214,** *page 89*

Drawings by Joyce Fairchild

*a.* cabochon-cut amethyst, bezel set on brass frame with engraved metallic grapes and leaves drill-set on frame; *b.* primitive bugle beads and sequins sewn on felt which covers pin-shank; *c.* arc-type tilted setting of bezel-cut sapphire color faceted glass, in gilt cage. Arc is mounted on tubular socket, a jewelers' *finding* for hatpins; *d. Art Nouveau* woman used as an escutcheon atop open-work hatpin; *e.* gold granules applied to gilt baroque setting, accented with rhinestones and large wax-bead pearl; *f.* open-work metallic mounting for gypsy-set amethyst color stone accented by surrounding rhinestones. (All life-size from author's collection.)

**PLATE 215,** *page 88*

Photo courtesy Tom J. Lawson, England

A Viennese enamel and silver figural hatpin with blue bodice, navy sleeves, white turban and studded with red gems. 7½″ pin of late 19th century artistry, complete in case (not shown). From the collection of Tom J. Lawson.

**PLATE 216,** *page 84*

Photo courtesy Tom J. Lawson, England

Hatpin heads made by Charles Horner Ltd., on loan from their museum to Tom J. Lawson, author of "Hatpinology", an article which appeared in "*Antique Collecting*", Dec. 1974.

*From l-r, Top* — pear shaped silver mount and backing with blue green glaze; silver sword "handle" with yellow head; spiral silver strip surrounded by frame of light green composition.

*Bottom Row* — patterned silver sphere with patented clip fastening for pin. This patent 17653 allowed the user to clip-fasten the head on to the pin point and so act as a point protector; a very fine double heart shaped head with 4 glass brilliants, flat silver pear-shaped head with patented clip fastening to pin point.

# NUMERICAL INDEX FOR PLATES WITH PAGE NUMBERS
## (Credit and/or Source)

| Plate | Credit and/or Source | Page |
|---|---|---|
| 1 | R. E. Stambook, Photographer; author's collection | 105 |
| 2 | R. E. Stambook, Photographer; author's collection | 105 |
| 3 | R. E. Stambook, Photographer; author's collection | 105 |
| 4 | R. E. Stambook, Photographer; author's collection | 105 |
| 5 | R. E. Stambook, Photographer; collections of the author, Diane Mahlmood, and Joyce Roth. | 105 |
| 6 | R. E. Stambook, Photographer; author's collection | 105 |
| 7 | R. E. Stambook, Photographer; author's collection | 106 |
| 8 | R. E. Stambook, Photographer; author's collection | 106 |
| 9 | R. E. Stambook, Photographer; collection of Renee Marshall | 106 |
| 10 | R. E. Stambook, Photographer; author's collection | 106 |
| 11 | R. E. Stambook, Photographer; author's collection | 106 |
| 12 | R. E. Stambook, Photographer; author's collection | 107 |
| 13 | R. E. Stambook, Photographer; author's collection | 107 |
| 14 | R. E. Stambook, Photographer; author's collection | 107 |
| 15 | R. E. Stambook, Photographer; author's collection | 107 |
| 16 | R. E. Stambook, Photographer; author's collection | 107 |
| 17 | R. E. Stambook, Photographer; collections of the author, Delma Peery, Wind Bells Cottage Antiques. | 107 |
| 18 | R. E. Stambook, Photographer; author's collection | 108 |
| 19 | R. E. Stambook, Photographer; author's collection | 108 |
| 20 | R. E. Stambook, Photographer; author's collection | 108 |
| 21 | R. E. Stambook, Photographer; author's collection | 108 |
| 22 | R. E. Stambook, Photographer; author's collection | 109 |
| 23 | R. E. Stambook, Photographer; author's collection | 109 |
| 24 | R. E. Stambook, Photographer; author's collection | 109 |
| 25 | R. E. Stambook, Photographer; author's collection | 110 |
| 26 | R. E. Stambook, Photographer; author's collection | 110 |
| 27 | R. E. Stambook, Photographer; author's collection | 110 |
| 28 | R. E. Stambook, Photographer; author's collection with black and white photograph insert by Charlie Ferrell | 110 / 59 |
| 29 | R. E. Stambook, Photographer; author's collection | 110 |
| 30 | R. E. Stambook, Photographer; author's collection | 111 |
| 31 | R. E. Stambook, Photographer; author's collection and Dr. F. P. Walkup. | 111 |
| 32 | R. E. Stambook, Photographer; author's collection | 111 |
| 33 | R. E. Stambook, Photographer; author's collection | 112 |
| 34 | R. E. Stambook, Photographer; author's collection | 112 |
| 35 | R. E. Stambook, Photographer; author's collection | 112 |
| 36 | R. E. Stambook, Photographer; author's collection | 112 |
| 37 | R. E. Stambook, Photographer; author's collection | 112 |
| 38 | R. E. Stambook, Photographer; author's collection | 113 |
| 39 | R. E. Stambook, Photographer; author's collection | 113 |
| 40 | R. E. Stambook, Photographer; author's collection | 113 |
| 41 | R. E. Stambook, Photographer; author's collection | 113 |
| 42 | R. E. Stambook, Photographer; collections of the author and Joyce Roth; with a black and white photo-insert courtesy William Bergmann | 113 / 153 |
| 43 | R. E. Stambook, Photographer; author's collection | 113 |
| 44 | R. E. Stambook, Photographer; author's collection | 114 |
| 45 | R. E. Stambook, Photographer; author's collection | 114 |
| 46 | R. E. Stambook, Photographer; author's collection | 114 |
| 47 | R. E. Stambook, Photographer; author's collection | 115 |
| 48 | R. E. Stambook, Photographer; collections of the author and Joyce Roth. | 115 |
| 49 | R. E. Stambook, Photographer; collections of the author, Sybel Heller, and Joyce Roth. | 115 |
| 50 | R. E. Stambook, Photographer; author's collection | 116 |
| 51 | R. E. Stambook, Photographer; author's collection | 116 |
| 52 | R. E. Stambook, Photographer; collections of the author and Renee Marshall. | 116 |
| 53 | R. E. Stambook, Photographer; collections of the author and Renee Marshall. | 116 |
| 54 | R. E. Stambook, Photographer; collections of the author and Mrs. G. W. McCurdy. | 116 |
| 55 | R. E. Stambook, Photographer; collections of the author and Joyce Roth. | 116 |
| 56 | R. E. Stambook, Photographer; collections of the author, Ginny's Antiques Et Cetera, and Renee Marshall. | 117 |
| 57 | R. E. Stambook, Photographer; author's collection | 117 |
| 58 | R. E. Stambook, Photographer; author's collection | 117 |
| 59 | R. E. Stambook, Photographer; collections of the author, Wind Bells Cottages Antiques, and Susan Hendrix. | 118 |
| 60 | R. E. Stambook, Photographer; author's collection | 118 |
| 61 | R. E. Stambook, Photographer; collections of author and Joyce Roth. | 118 |
| 62 | R. E. Stambook, Photographer; collections of author and Diane Mahlmood. | 119 |
| 63 | R. E. Stambook, Photographer; collections of the author and Sybel Heller. | 119 |
| 64 | R. E. Stambook, Photographer; collections of the author and Irene Dutko. | 119 |
| 65 | R. E. Stambook, Photographer; collections of the author and Sybel Heller. | 119 |
| 66 | R. E. Stambook, Photographer; collections of the author and Sybel Heller. | 119 |
| 67 | R. E. Stambook, Photographer; author's collection | 120 |
| 68 | R. E. Stambook, Photographer; collection of The Chimney Sweep Antiques. | 120 |
| 69 | R. E. Stambook, Photographer; collections of the | |

| Plate | Credit and/or Source | Page |
|---|---|---|
| | author, Joyce Roth, and Sybel Heller. | 120 |
| 70 | R. E. Stambook, Photographer; collection of Joyce Roth | 120 |
| 71 | R. E. Stambook, Photographer; collection of Sybel Heller | 120 |
| 72 | R. E. Stambook, Photographer; collection of Joyce Roth | 121 |
| 73 | R. E. Stambook, Photographer; collections of the author, Sybel Heller, and Joyce Roth. | 121 |
| 74 | R. E. Stambook, Photographer; collection of Ginny's Antiques Et Cetera. | 121 |
| 75 | R. E. Stambook, Photographer; collection of Joyce Roth | 121 |
| 76 | R. E. Stambook, Photographer; collections of the author, and Sybel Heller. | 121 |
| 77 | R. E. Stambook, Photographer; collection of Joyce Roth | 121 |
| 78 | R. E. Stambook, Photographer; collection of Joyce Roth | 122 |
| 79 | R. E. Stambook, Photographer; collection of Joyce Roth | 122 |
| 80 | R. E. Stambook, Photographer; collection of Joyce Roth | 122 |
| 81 | R. E. Stambook, Photographer; collection of Sybel Heller | 122 |
| 82 | R. E. Stambook, Photographer; collection of Sybel Heller | 122 |
| 83 | R. E. Stambook, Photographer; collection of Joyce Roth | 122 |
| 84 | R. E. Stambook, Photographer; collection of Joyce Roth | 123 |
| 85 | R. E. Stambook, Photographer; collection of Joyce Roth | 123 |
| 86 | R. E. Stambook, Photographer; collection of Sybel Heller | 123 |
| 87 | R. E. Stambook, Photographer; collection of Sybel Heller | 123 |
| 88 | R. E. Stambook, Photographer; collection of Joyce Roth | 123 |
| 89 | R. E. Stambook, Photographer; collection of Joyce Roth | 123 |
| 90 | R. E. Stambook, Photographer; author's collection | 124 |
| 91 | R. E. Stambook, Photographer; author's collection | 124 |
| 92 | R. E. Stambook, Photographer; author's collection | 124 |
| 93 | R. E. Stambook, Photographer; author's collection | 124 |
| 94 | R. E. Stambook, Photographer; collection of Joyce Roth | 125 |
| 95 | R. E. Stambook, Photographer; author's collection | 125 |
| 96 | R. E. Stambook, Photographer; author's collection | 125 |
| 97 | R. E. Stambook, Photographer; author's collection | 126 |
| 98 | R. E. Stambook, Photographer; author's collection | 126 |
| 99 | R. E. Stambook, Photographer; author's collection | 126 |
| 100 | R. E. Stambook, Photographer; author's collection | 126 |
| 101 | R. E. Stambook, Photographer; author's collection | 126 |
| 102 | R. E. Stambook, Photographer; author's collection | 126 |
| 103 | R. E. Stambook, Photographer; author's collection | 127 |
| 104 | R. E. Stambook, Photographer; author's collection | 127 |
| 105 | R. E. Stambook, Photographer; author's collection | 127 |
| 106 | R. E. Stambook, Photographer; author's collection | 127 |
| 107 | R. E. Stambook, Photographer; author's collection | 127 |
| 108 | R. E. Stambook, Photographer; author's collection | 128 |
| 109 | R. E. Stambook, Photographer; author's collection | 128 |
| 110 | R. E. Stambook, Photographer; author's collection | 128 |
| 111 | R. E. Stambook, Photographer; author's collection | 128 |
| 112 | R. E. Stambook, Photographer; author's collection | 128 |
| 113 | R. E. Stambook, Photographer; author's collection | 129 |
| 114 | R. E. Stambook, Photographer; author's collection | 129 |
| 115 | R. E. Stambook, Photographer; collections of the author and Renee Marshall. | 129 |
| 116 | R. E. Stambook, Photographer; author's collection | 129 |
| 117 | R. E. Stambook, Photographer; author's collection | 129 |
| 118 | R. E. Stambook, Photographer; author's collection; | 130 |
| 119 | R. E. Stambook, Photographer; author's collection; Renee Marshall, and Joyce Roth. | 130 |
| 120 | R. E. Stambook, Photographer; author's collection | 130 |
| 121 | R. E. Stambook, Photographer; author's collection | 131 |
| 122 | R. E. Stambook, Photographer; author's collection | 131 |
| 123 | R. E. Stambook, Photographer; author's collection | 131 |
| 124 | R. E. Stambook, Photographer; author's collection | 131 |
| 125 | R. E. Stambook, Photographer; author's collection | 131 |
| 126 | R. E. Stambook, Photographer; author's collection | 132 |
| 127 | R. E. Stambook, Photographer; author's collection | 132 |
| 128 | R. E. Stambook, Photographer; author's collection | 132 |
| 129 | R. E. Stambook, Photographer; author's collection | 132 |
| 130 | R. E. Stambook, Photographer; author's collection | 132 |
| 131 | R. E. Stambook, Photographer; author's collection | 132 |
| 132 | R. E. Stambook, Photographer; author's collection | 133 |
| 133 | R. E. Stambook, Photographer; author's collection | 133 |
| 134 | 1910 Ladies Home Journal, Courtesy Milly Orcutt, Women's News Editor, "Antique Motor News," Long Beach, Ca. | 24-25 |
| 135 | "The Pindustry," Courtesy The Star Pin Company, Shelton, Conn. | 2-3 |
| 136 | Drawings by Joyce Fairchild from the author's collection | 96 |
| 137 | Drawings by Joyce Fairchild from original catalogue, courtesy F. H. Noble & Co., Chicago | 95 |
| 138 | Drawings by Joyce Fairchild from original catalogue, courtesy F. H. Noble & Co., Chicago. | 98 |
| 139 | Courtesy Dover Publications, Inc., New York | 15 |
| 140 | Courtesy Dover Publications, Inc., New York | 22 |
| 141 | Courtesy Dover Publications, Inc., New York | 19 |
| 142 | Courtesy Dover Publications, Inc., New York | 13 |
| 143 | George Castro, Photographer; courtesy Dr. F. P. Walkup Archives. | 20 |
| 144 | Courtesy Dover Publications, Inc., New York | 14 |
| 145 | Courtesy Milly Orcutt Archives | viii |
| 146 | Eric Skipsey, Photographer; by arrangement, Los Angeles Civic Light Opera. | 58 |
| 147 | George Castro, Photographer; courtesy Dr. F. P. Walkup Archives. | 4 |
| 148 | Courtesy Edward Parkinson, Publicity Director for The Schubert Organization, Los Angeles. | 38 |
| 149 | Photo by Still Dept., Twentieth Century-Fox Film Corp. | 21 |
| 150 | George Castro, Photographer; courtesy Dr. F. P. Walkup Archives. | 53 |
| 151 | Photo by Still Dept., Twentieth Century-Fox Film Corp. | 21 |
| 152 | Photo courtesy Imogene Chapman. | 20 |
| 153 | Photo by Still Dept., Twentieth Century-Fox Film Corp. | 21 |
| 154 | F. Collier Lankford, Photographer; courtesy Mrs. Scherry Harrah. | 23 |
| 155 | F. Collier Lankford, Photographer; courtesy Mrs. Scherry Harrah. | 23 |
| 156 | Marilyn Zander, Photographer; courtesy Fran Tucker. | 87 |
| 157 | Marilyn Zander, Photographer; courtesy Fran Tucker. | 150 |
| 158 | Courtesy Dover Publications, Inc., New York. | 74 |
| 159 | Courtesy Dover Publications, Inc., New York. | 63 |
| 160 | George Castro, Photographer; author's collection. | 134 |
| 161 | Drawings by Joyce Fairchild from the author's collection. | 17 |
| 162 | Photo courtesy Jablonec Corp., Czech | 26 |
| 163 | George Castro, Photographer; author's collection. | 134 |
| 164 | Photo courtesy Mrs. Scherry Harrah. | 29 |
| 165 | Drawings by Joyce Fairchild from the author's collection. | 43 |
| 166 | Photo courtesy Tom J. Lawson; from his collection of hatpins. | 57 |
| 167 | Ole Woldbye, Photographer; from collection Kunstindustrimuseet, Denmark. | 62 |
| 168 | Drawings by Joyce Fairchild; The Ahmanson Museum collection | 66-67 |
| 169 | Photo courtesy Hogie's Antiques. | 75 |
| 170 | Photo courtesy William Bergmann. | 76 |
| 171 | Drawings by Joyce Fairchild from the author's collection. | 77 |
| 172 | Drawings by Joyce Fairchild from the collection of Western Costume Co. | 65 |
| 173 | Drawings by Joyce Fairchild from the author's collection. | 80 |
| 174 | Photo courtesy Robert E. Jagoda, Program Advertising Service, (IBM) International Business Machines. | 78 |
| 175 | George Castro, Photographer; courtesy Dr. F. P. Walkup Archives. | 81 |
| 176 | Photo courtesy Victoria & Albert Museum, London. | 83 |
| 177 | Drawings by Joyce Fairchild from the collection of Mr. and Mrs. S. W. Reyhill, Studio Art Metal Shop. | 82-83 |
| 178 | Drawings by Joyce Fairchild from the collection of Western Costume Co., Hollywood. | 60 |
| 179 | Photo courtesy Diane Mahlmood. | 135 |
| 180 | Dana Getman, Photographer, courtesy Mrs. E. G. Getman. | 135 |
| 181 | Courtesy Dover Publications, Inc., New York. | 84 |
| 182 | Robert V. Larsen, Photographer — from his own collection. | 102-103 |
| 183 | Drawing by Joyce Fairchild from the author's collection | 28 |
| 184 | Courtesy Dover Publications, Inc., New York. | 32 |
| 185 | Drawing by Joyce Fairchild from the author's collection. | 85 |
| 186 | Drawing by Joyce Fairchild from the author's collection. | 72-73 |
| 187 | Dana Getman, Photographer; courtesy Mrs. E. G. Getman. | 136 |
| 188 | Photo courtesy William Bergmann. | 142-143 |
| 189 | George Castro, photographer; from the author's collection. | 137 |
| 190 | Drawing by Joyce Fairchild from the author's collection. | 59 |
| 191 | Courtesy, Dover Publications, Inc., New York. | 8 |
| 192 | Drawing by Joyce Fairchild from the author's collection. | 101 |
| 193 | R. E. Stambook, Photographer; author's collection, and collections of Sybel Heller, Joyce Roth, and Delma Peery. | 137 |
| 194 | R. E. Stambook, Photographer; author's collection, and the collections of Renee Marshall and Joyce Roth. | 137 |
| 195 | R. E. Stambook, Photographer; author's collection, and the collections of Renee Marshall, Sybel Heller, and Joyce Roth. | 137 |
| 196 | R. E. Stambook, Photographer; author's collection, and the collections of Joyce Roth and Renee Marshall. | 137 |
| 197 | George Castro, Photographer; courtesy "One-of-a-Kind Shop," Disneyland | 137 |

215

| Plate | Credit and/or Source | Page |
|---|---|---|
| *198* | Photo courtesy Lester Hendrix ............................. | 105 |
| 199 | Drawing by Joyce Fairchild from the author's collection.............. | 69 |
| 200 | Drawing by Joyce Fairchild from the author's collection.............. | 64 |
| 201 | Courtesy Len Norris, *The Vancouver Sun*. ............... 46, 47, and 48 | |
| 202 | Photo Courtesy William Bergmann ........................ | 100 |
| 203 | Photo courtesy Dr. L. A. Katzin, DDS......................... | 86 |
| 204 | Photo Courtesy Dr. Fritz Falk, | |
| | Dir., SCHMUCK MUSEUM PFORZHEIM, | |
| | Germany. Photo Gunter Meyer | |
| | Foto-Webe Studio, Pforzheim. ...................... | 56-57 |
| *205* | R. E. Stambook, Photographer; author's collection, and | |
| | the collections of Joe McFarlin and Louise Alexander............. | 138 |
| *206* | R. E. Stambook, Photographer; author's collection, and | |
| | the collections of Joe McFarlin and Sherry Goldwasser............ | 138 |

| Plate | Credit and/or Source | Page |
|---|---|---|
| *207* | R. E. Stambook, Photographer; author's collection, and | |
| | the collections of Sherry Goldwasser, | |
| | Ray and May Knott, and Jo McFarlin. ....................... | 138 |
| 208 | Photo courtesy Sally Margolis........................... | 156 |
| 209 | Drawing by Joyce Fairchild from the author's collection............. | 93 |
| 210 | Drawing by Joyce Fairchild from the author's collection | 99 |
| 211 | The Betmann Archives .................................. | 99 |
| 212 | Drawings by Joyce Fairchild from the author's collection............ | 68 |
| 213 | Drawings by Joyce Fairchild from the author's collection............ | 91 |
| 214 | Drawings by Joyce Fairchild from the author's collection............ | 89 |
| 215 | Photo courtesy Tom J. Lawson ........................... | 88 |
| 216 | Photo courtesy Tom J. Lawson ........................... | 84 |

*PLATE NUMBERS IN ITALICS DENOTES COLOR.*